JEWISH EDINBURGH

Jewish Edinburgh
A History, 1880–1950

M. D. Gilfillan

McFarland & Company, Inc., Publishers
Jefferson, North Carolina

LIBRARY OF CONGRESS CATALOGUING-IN-PUBLICATION DATA

Names: Gilfillan, M. D. (Mark D.), 1986– author.
Title: Jewish Edinburgh : a history, 1880–1950 / M.D. Gilfillan.
Other titles: Jews in Edinburgh
Description: Jefferson, North Carolina : McFarland & Company, Inc., 2019 | Revision of author's thesis (doctoral)—Ulster University, 2012, titled Jews in Edinburgh : 1880–1950. | Includes bibliographical references and index.
Identifiers: LCCN 2019000139 | ISBN 9780786476688 (softcover : acid free paper) ∞
Subjects: LCSH: Jews—Scotland—Edinburgh—History—19th century. | Jews—Scotland—Edinburgh—History—20th century. | Edinburgh (Scotland)—Ethnic relations.
Classification: LCC DS135.E55 E34 2019 | DDC 941.3/4004924—dc23
LC record available at https://lccn.loc.gov/2019000139

BRITISH LIBRARY CATALOGUING DATA ARE AVAILABLE

ISBN (print) 978-0-7864-7668-8
ISBN (ebook) 978-1-4766-3565-1

© 2019 M.D. Gilfillan. All rights reserved

No part of this book may be reproduced or transmitted in any form or by any means, electronic or mechanical, including photocopying or recording, or by any information storage and retrieval system, without permission in writing from the publisher.

Front cover images © 2019 Shutterstock

Printed in the United States of America

McFarland & Company, Inc., Publishers
 Box 611, Jefferson, North Carolina 28640
 www.mcfarlandpub.com

For Alexander, Nathan,
Freya-Rose, and April

Table of Contents

Acknowledgments ix
Preface 1
Introduction 5

1. The Origins of Edinburgh Jewry 11
2. New Arrivals 22
3. Edinburgh's Jewish Quarter, 1880–1910 58
4. Battles at Home and Abroad, 1911–1918 103
5. A Community United, 1918–1932 127
6. The Fight Against Fascism, 1933–1945 158
7. Postscript, 1945–1950 194

Conclusion 201
Chapter Notes 209
Bibliography 231
Index 241

Acknowledgments

This book originated from a Ph.D. thesis that I commenced work on at the University of Ulster in 2009. During the three years of research which followed, I received a great deal of assistance from a range of organizations and individuals, and I would like to take this opportunity to thank them. The research project was first made possible by an award from the Department of Education and Learning, and I thank Stanley Black and everyone else involved in granting me the funding to pursue this area of research.

In the earliest stages of my enquiry into the history of Scottish Jewry, Harvey Kaplan at the Scottish Jewish Archives Centre was crucial in pointing me toward potentially fruitful avenues of research, and he has continued to help me in ways too numerous to list here. He performs an invaluable service for scholars in this field. I would also like to thank Ray and Jackie Taylor for their role in providing me with access to the minute books of the Edinburgh Hebrew Congregation. This access was granted at great inconvenience to them. Their patience, hospitality, and willingness to answer my questions during the earliest days of my research remains greatly appreciated.

I extend special thanks to Jenni Calder, without whom I would not have been able to locate Rabbi Salis Daiches' papers. Conversations and e-mails with Jenni about Rabbi Daiches helped me gain a more full understanding of Salis than I could have gained solely through his papers. Thanks are also due to Michael Tobias for corresponding with me regarding the early Edinburgh Jewry, and to Kenneth Collins for responding helpfully to my e-mails regarding his past works on Scottish Jewry.

Toward the end of my research, I benefited greatly from a summer fellowship on the Holocaust and Jewish Civilization at Royal Holloway, University of London. The fellowship, funded by Royal Holloway and the Holocaust Educational Foundation, helped refine and crystalize some of my thoughts and arguments, and I owe particular thanks to Rachel Century, Bob Eaglestone,

Chaim Weiner, Dan Stone, and the late David Cesarani for making my time there enjoyable and intellectually stimulating.

Thanks are also due to my supervisors, Pól Ó Dochartaigh and Robert McNamara, for their assistance throughout this project. I consider myself very fortunate to have had the benefit of their guidance. Helpful comments and suggestions also came from other members of the Ulster History Department, including Neal Garnham, and Allan Blackstock. The study was further improved thanks to helpful comments and suggestions from Tony Kushner.

There are academics, librarians and archivists who assisted me with this project and are too numerous to name here, but to all of them I extend my sincere gratitude.

Lastly, and most importantly, I would like to thank my wife Carolyn, and wider family.

Preface

Since the late 1950s interest in the history of Jews in Scotland has greatly increased, with a growing number of articles, books, undergraduate dissertations and doctoral theses shedding ever more light on a hitherto neglected subject area. This interest has, in part, arisen from a broader backlash from the "Celtic periphery" against the strongly Anglo-centric bias of existing British-Jewish historiography, as well a desire to recover and record the past of what are now rapidly dwindling provincial Jewish communities. It is surprising then that despite the amount of work that has been carried out on the history of Scottish Jewry, the experience of Jews in the Scottish capital has been largely overlooked. Since the scholarly exploration of Scottish-Jewish history, and the history of Jews in Britain more generally, will remain incomplete until due attention is paid to the oldest Jewish community in Scotland, this book is intended to go some way toward addressing this gap in our understanding.

Although the field of Scottish-Jewish history was pioneered by Salis Daiches and Abraham Levy, much of what we know today was first outlined by Kenneth Collins in a number of significant works: *Aspects of Scottish Jewry* (Glasgow: Glasgow Representative Council, 1987); *Go and Learn: The International Story of Jews and Medicine in Scotland* (Aberdeen: Aberdeen University Press, 1988); *Second City Jewry: The Jews of Glasgow in the Age of Expansion, 1790-1919* (Glasgow: Scottish Jewish Archives, 1990); and *Be Well! Jewish Immigrant Health and Welfare in Glasgow, 1860-1914* (East Linton: Tuckwell, 2001). These important forays into the history of Jews in Glasgow have since been furthered by Ben Braber in his *Jews in Glasgow, 1879-1939* (London: Vallentine Mitchell, 2007), and by scholars such as Henry Maitles, William Kenefick, Harvey Kaplan, and a growing number of undergraduate and doctoral students. However, a definite bias toward the study of Glasgow Jewry persisted, encouraged by the ready availability of Glasgow-related archival material held at that Scottish Jewish Archives Centre. This emphasis on Glasgow only received significant revision with the publication of Nathan Abrams' *Caledonian Jews: A Study of Seven Small Communities in Scotland* (Jefferson, NC: McFarland, 2009). Following the publication of Abrams' important and ambitious work, it seemed that almost every area of Jewish settlement in Scotland had received scholarly attention. However, there remained a need to comprehensively explore the history of Jews in the Scottish capital, a community that produced, among others, the first Jewish chairman of the Scottish Premier League, one of the youngest MPs ever to sit in the House of Commons, and numerous scholars including a tutor of the young Kaiser Friedrich Wilhelm.

Seeking a new perspective on Scottish history, and intrigued by both the opportunity and the challenge inherent in undertaking a project designed to address this gap, I started my research into the history of Edinburgh Jewry in early 2009. It quickly became clear that one of the reasons this community had received little scholarly attention was an apparent lack of available historical material. Detective work, coupled with the generous assistance of a small number of knowledgeable and willing individuals, gradually led to the unearthing of more primary material than I could have hoped for. This study thus came to incorporate an array of Jewish archival documents including minute books, official correspondence, event programs, Zionist society records from the 1890s, financial records, and annual reports. Other materials have been sourced from the National Archives, the National Archives of Scotland, the National Library of Scotland, the Mitchell Library, and from private individuals.

Official records used in the preparation of this book include naturalization certificates, military appeals tribunal records, declassified files from the Office of the Secretary for Scotland, Court of Session papers, and trial papers. Numerous church records have also been employed, including those of the Edinburgh Jewish Medical Society, a missionary branch of the Free Church of Scotland. The vast majority of this material has not previously been used in an academic study. This book benefits greatly from the use of Rabbi Dr. Salis Daiches' extensive collection of private papers and correspondence. Daiches was Edinburgh's Rabbi from 1918 to 1945, and was regarded as "Scotland's Rabbi." These invaluable papers cover three decades of Daiches' communication with a range of major figures in British-Jewish and Scottish history, including moderators of the Church of Scotland; Neville Laski, president of the Board of Deputies of British Jews; Leopold Greenberg, editor of the *Jewish Chronicle*, and two Chief Rabbis. This correspondence broached many topics including anti–Semitism, the conversionist activity of the Scottish missions, the status of "provincial Jewry," Jewish life in the Scottish capital, and refugees from Nazi Germany. A range of memoirs and newspapers have also been used, including the *Jewish Chronicle*, the *Jewish Echo*, the *Scotsman*, *The Edinburgh Evening Dispatch*, and *The Glasgow Herald*.

It is my hope that in conveying the rich and complex of the history of this important community, something will be added to our understanding of the history of Scottish and British Jewry. Just as importantly, however, it is hoped that this story will be seen as part of Edinburgh's and Scotland's past: the shared history of Scots and Jews.

Introduction

In May 1790, Sir John Sinclair, MP for Caithness and lay member of the General Assembly of the Church of Scotland, conveyed his plan for a parish-by-parish survey of the nation. The survey was to gather statistical information from all corners of Scotland, with the aim of establishing a complete picture of its geography, its economic life, and its people. A set of 160 questions was issued to the senior clergyman of every parish and, by 1799, the project was complete. The minister for Cluny, County of Aberdeen, recorded that:

> No large river runs through the parish, but the brooks and rivulets abound in trouts, pike and eels. And the large rivulet or burn of Cluny, breed pearls. Some years ago, a Jew employed people to fish them, and a great many were got, some of them large and of good water, which were carried to London to be disposed of.[1]

A return from Drainie, County of Elgin, noted that, in the parish, "there is no lawyer, writer, attorney, physician, apothecary, negro, Jew, gypsy, Englishman, Irishman, or foreigner of any description."[2] The clergyman for Kelso, County of Roxburgh, included among his "miscellaneous observations" that, "there are three Roman Catholics, and one Jew in the parish,"[3] and it is this statement that comprises the only Scottish Jew recorded by the First Statistical Account of Scotland. In fact, if it was not for the reference to the Jewish resident of Roxburgh one might be forgiven for assuming that there were no Jews in 18th-century Scotland. This was an assumption made by the minister for Kilmartin who argued that not only were Jews entirely absent from the country, but offered as explanation his opinion that "this not being a commercial country, money is slow in its circulation, so that there can be no inducement for a Jew to reside in it."[4]

Scotland in the 18th century was only on the cusp of industrialization, but it was home to a number of Jews. Edinburgh, its capital, had been home to a very small number Jewish individuals and families for at least 150 years.[5] The scholars, artisans, and traders who made Edinburgh their home were overlooked, for unknown reasons, by Edinburgh's clergymen. In the few records we have in relation to these settlers, there is nothing to suggest that they dressed conspicuously or were greatly different, in dress or custom, from their Gentile neighbors.[6] Of those that did come and go during this period, the majority left little evidence behind, and their story becomes all the more difficult to recover, remaining incomplete and on the verge of myth.[7] An opportunity exists, however, to take advantage of greater resources in relation to Edinburgh's more modern Jewish community, those who arrived in greater numbers than the city had ever seen toward the end of the 19th century, and who made Scotland their home.

Themes and Structure

The majority of this book focuses on the impact and experience of those Jews who departed from the Russian Empire and its environs in the latter half of the 19th century, and who made Edinburgh their home, as well as the experiences, actions and reactions of established Edinburgh Jewry. Interactions between the immigrant population and the established Edinburgh community comprise a major aspect of the study. This book charts the initial waves of immigration, and attempts to construct a socio-economic profile of the new immigrants. This is combined with a qualitative analysis of primary sources relating to welfare provision for Jewish immigrants in Edinburgh. The reaction of non–Jewish Scots is also examined.

Following analysis of the issues faced by Jewish immigrants on arrival, the study proceeds with an evaluation of Jewish life in Edinburgh. Religious life is examined. The book charts the rise and decline of Edinburgh's smaller Jewish congregations, and the concerns held by Jewish religious leaders regarding the twin dangers of secularization and conversion. The latter emanated mainly from the activities of the Edinburgh Jewish Medical Mission, and its evangelical work among recent arrivals. An assessment of this organization and its impact on Edinburgh Jewry forms another important aspect of the study. The book continues with an analysis of the education and social mobility in the community, and the development of Zionism, and political and cultural organizations.

The Great War had a considerable impact on the historical trajectory of Edinburgh Jewry. The war memorial of the Graham Street Synagogue is testament to those killed in action, and their story forms part of this history. An investigation into the presence of several Edinburgh Jews at the Lothian and Peebles Military Appeals Tribunal is also carried out. In 1921, all records pertaining to Appeal Tribunals were destroyed with the exception of those relating to the districts of Lothian and Peebles, and Mid-Staffordshire, which were retained as samples. Some of the personal testimonies contained in the appeals themselves offer insight into the lives of Edinburgh's Jews in 1916. The emergence of xenophobia and anti-German feeling during the war is also examined from a Jewish perspective.

The interwar period and the Second World War were periods of crisis for Jews around the globe, and the questions raised by these crises are a key focus. How did Edinburgh's Jewish population respond to the rise of domestic and continental Fascism? Particular attention is paid to the activities of the Edinburgh branch of the British Union of Fascists. Rabbi Dr. Salis Daiches had an ongoing exchange with anti-Semitic MP and founder of "The Right Club" Archibald Maule Ramsay, and their dueling letters to the *Scotsman* are covered. The response of Edinburgh Jewry to news of atrocities in Nazi Germany, and to the Holocaust is also analyzed.

The Second World War saw the arrival of Jewish refugees from Nazi Germany, as well as a considerable number of Jewish children evacuated during the *Kindertransport*. Of course, Jewish life went on. This period also saw the consolidation of the religious community under the Edinburgh Hebrew Congregation; and the genesis of the Salisbury Road Synagogue, which still serves the city's Jews today, is also covered in this history. The postwar years are notable for the establishment of the state of Israel, and the demographic decline of Edinburgh Jewry. It is often argued that many other provincial Jewish communities in the United Kingdom and Ireland saw the assimilation of the younger generation and this combined with onward migration to London, the United States and Israel contributed to numerical decline, and the rise in the average age of the Jewish population. It is proposed to test whether this is the case for Edinburgh. A concluding chapter briefly compares the experience of Edinburgh Jewry to that of Glasgow, and other British centers of Jewish habitation during the period in question, in order to elaborate on any unique qualities, or indeed commonalities, which may be attributed to the Edinburgh experience.

The book proceeds in a chronological format, but a strong thematic element is also apparent, broaching such topics as: Jewish economic activity, education and social mobility, religion and culture, and issues of assimilation and acculturation. The majority of the study is concerned with a period spanning some 70 years, during which time there was mass emigration from Russia, technological advancement in transport and in all walks of life, changes within Scottish society, two world wars, and genocide targeting Europe's Jews. It is necessary, therefore, to incorporate these events in a manner relevant to the study. The book uses a wide variety of source material to argue that, like its counterparts across Britain, from its genesis Edinburgh's Jewish community was engaged in a struggle both to integrate and to maintain its distinctiveness. In many respects the Edinburgh Jewish experience bears great similarities to broader trends in British Jewry, and it also becomes apparent that the story of Edinburgh's Jews is to some extent unique.

British, Scottish or Provincial?

Due to the balance of community populations, the overwhelming majority of histories of Jews and Judaism in Britain have focused exclusively on England. There has thus been a corresponding tendency for the names "England" and "Britain" to be used interchangeably and, in a development likely to vex in a post-devolution era, Scottish-Jewish history has come to be seen as part of a wider "Anglo-Jewish" historiography. Further, Todd Endelman has stated unapologetically that "the history of the Jews in Britain is overwhelming the history of Jews who lived in *English* cities," and that "since the number of Jews who lived in Scotland and Wales was never large, folding them into 'Anglo-Jewry' does not distort the overall picture."[8] The histories of provincial communities, particularly those on the "Celtic periphery," have tended to be neglected or judged negatively because of their perceived failure to "distort the overall picture," of major metropolitan Anglo-Jewry.

This reasoning assumes, however, that the broadly similar economic, religious and political profile of metropolitan Jewry was alone sufficient to produce uniformity in the Jewish experience across the nation. Implicit in this is a neglect of regional and national political, social, judicial, and cultural variations in Great Britain. Endelman states that concerns about the meanings of terms such as "Britishness" and "Englishness" are entirely modern, having emerged "at the start of the twenty-first century, with the devolution of Scotland and Wales."[9] However, as this book demonstrates, Edinburgh's Jews, from the earliest date of their settlement, were confronted with legal, political, religious and cultural challenges which had at their root some quite fundamental differences between Scotland and England, and their ability to deal with these challenges was heavily influenced by local rather than national conditions.

Moreover, there is evidence that some Jews in Edinburgh saw themselves first and foremost as Scottish Jews. For years Salis Daiches protested against the name "Zionist Federation of England," which labeled an organization with Scottish, Welsh, and Irish members. David Daiches recalled that his father argued that "he, as the Edinburgh rabbi representing a Scottish constituency, could not logically be a member of an organization whose title proclaimed itself purely English."[10] For the purposes of this study, the term "Anglo-Jewry" is used only in conjunction with organizations and communities whose mandate or borders did not extend beyond England. The term "British-Jewry" is used to describe organizations with a broader influence, and when referring to Jewish communities throughout Great Britain. It is hoped that through the clarification of these terms, the book will bestow a greater semblance of diversity upon Britain's Jewish communities and acknowledge the specific national identity that they often expressed.

This project is intended to be seen in the context of "local" British-Jewish historiography, a field that was pioneered to a large extent by Cecil Roth in the immediate postwar period. Writing in 1956, Roth complained about the mass of historiography on Anglo-Jewry which tended to look into the distant past, often with very narrow geographical scope, "almost conveying the impression that no Jews lived elsewhere in England in the period under question." If the Jewish history of provincial England can be described as "under-researched," then this description belongs even more so to that of Scotland. Dr. Roth once wrote that "we will never obtain a comprehensive or a balanced view of the achievements and vicissitudes of (the Jews of Britain) until such gaps are filled and more remote communities, with more recent generations, have received adequate treatment." This project is designed to go some way toward that goal.

It should be noted, however, that Roth's work has itself come to be seen as problematic. Todd Endelman has stated that Roth and other historians linked to the Jewish Historical Society of England "tended to approach their subject in a spirit of uncritical admiration.... Their version of Anglo-Jewish history was whiggish, apologetic, and triumphalist, emphasising the harmony between Jewishness and Englishness, while minimising the discordant aspects of the assimilation process."[11] Similarly, Tony Kushner has argued that "until the 1970s local Jewish studies in Britain mirrored those elsewhere and were designed to celebrate achievement, rootedness, and longevity of presence."[12]

A "new school" of historians thus emerged in the late 1970s and 1980s, led by Bill Williams, Tony Kushner, and David Cesarani, which sought to "overturn the cosy, sanitized view of Anglo-Jewish history associated with Roth" and to shed light on hitherto downplayed aspects of the British-Jewish experience such as poverty, communal division, and anti–Semitism.[13] However, as Todd Endelman has stated, this school of thought has tended to produce "a tale shot through with failure and discord, to which there is not always a happy ending," and some elements of this historiography, in particular those elements with an emphasis on class and social conflict, have actually risked "creating a false image of the past to the extent that it ignores the specifically Jewish dimensions of its subject."[14]

This study makes a contribution to British-Jewish historiography not merely by shedding light on the hitherto neglected history of the Jewish community of Edinburgh, but also by contributing a study which incorporates elements of both schools of thought as well as introducing new themes and subjects. As such, this study acknowledges economic advancement as well as enduring poverty, settlement as well as transience, tolerance as well as antipathy, harmony as well as divisiveness, and success as well as failure. This book re-evaluates the nature of anti–Semitism in Scotland, and addresses topics which are almost entirely absent from existing historiography, the most significant being the Jewish relationship with the Church of Scotland.

1

The Origins of Edinburgh Jewry

Records and evidence of a Jewish presence in Scotland before the 18th century are rare. As a result, "much of Scottish Jewish history is surrounded in mystery, myth, rumor, and conjecture."[1] In 1929 Rabbi Dr. Salis Daiches, then Rabbi to the Edinburgh community, offered his opinion that "Scotland remained for the Jew throughout many centuries a *terra incognita*," and that it was "doubtful whether a Jew was seen north of the Tweed before the middle of the seventeenth century."[2] Echoing the remarks of a clergyman at Kilmartin in the First Statistical Account of Scotland, Daiches argued that "Scotsmen do not seem ever to have been in need of the assistance which Jewish merchants and financiers were able to give to other nations."[3] Furthermore, he argued that "international commerce was not sufficiently developed to bring Jewish merchants to Scotland."[4]

This economic explanation is valid to an extent. Most trade in Mediaeval Europe was not conducted in urban centers, which were at that time both small in size and very few in number, but at trading fairs which would occur only occasionally. In England, these fairs were often grand events, carried out beyond the jurisdiction of autonomous corporate entities—the burghs, and "it was the policy of the kings and magnates to encourage aliens to visit England with foreign commodities and to give them a status for dealing in them."[5] However, in Scottish fairs, which were completely under burghal jurisdiction, "aliens had no status in them at all."[6] William Cunningham argued that because of Scotland's policy of enforcing burghal jurisdiction in relation to commercial trading, "the towns were successful in preventing the Jew and the Lombard from getting permanent footing in the country."[7] While these explanations from Daiches and Cunningham are similar, their difference is both clear and important. While Daiches suggested Jews were absent from Scotland because of a lack of "pull" factors, as well as the deterrent effect of the country's religious and political quarrels, and warring clans, Cunningham argued that Jews and other foreigners were deliberately excluded.

Despite speculation that some Jews may have fled northwards from the expulsion from England in 1290, and that a handful of wealthy Jews had financial interests in the country or with the Scottish crown, the complete lack of evidence would suggest that significant Jewish settlement during this period was extremely unlikely.[8] Abraham Levy argued that following the expulsion "it is natural to surmise that some of these refugees may have made their way northwards."[9] However it is equally, if not more, likely that the appeal of reconnecting with family and stable communities across the Channel outweighed the uncertainty offered by a tempestuous new land which directly bordered the nation which had exiled them.

Although Herbert Willett asserted in 1932 that in the 16th century, "there were Jews from Spain in Scotland, who came to be an integral part of the population of Edinburgh," he offered no evidence, and it appears rather that recorded Scottish-Jewish history began in the 17th century.[10] Levy stated that the first recorded Jews in Scotland were converts to Christianity, and that of these few persons "some were obscure or nameless."[11] Those who left more complete documentation included the first and third occupants of the Chair of Hebrew and Oriental Languages at the college in Edinburgh.[12] Julius Conradus Otto, a native of Vienna, was the first of these teachers, taking his position in 1641. The third occupant of the Chair, Paulus Scialitti Rabin took up his position in 1655. The town council minutes recorded his appointment: "The Council Admitts and receives Paulus Scialitti Rabin converted from the Jewish Religion to the Christian faith to professe his skill and knowledge in the orientall tongues within this Burgh."[13] Other than converted Jews teaching Hebrew at the University, there is no evidence of further Jewish settlement in Edinburgh at this time. It is not unlikely however, that following the readmission of the Jews to England in the latter half of the 17th century, a trickle of individual Jews, converted or otherwise, had begun to settle in other parts of Scotland, particularly the border towns.[14] Indeed, one entry in the Kirk Session Minute Book of the Peebles Parish Church, dated April 7, 1667, records permission for the Kirk Treasurer "to give the minister at Kirkwood three pounds Scots to give the converted Jew."[15]

Toward the end of the 17th century a number of court cases involving Jews occurred in Edinburgh, and these litigations provide an outline of both the settlement of professing Jews and the beginnings of Jewish commercial activity in the city. In January 1692, an Abraham Turing, who is likely to have been Jewish, issued court proceedings against the Magistrates of Edinburgh, claiming unfair treatment by the local authorities. Following his arrival in 1685, Turing had established himself as a manufacturer of hats in the Canongate area, outside the city walls. He had arrived in Edinburgh claiming to have fled persecution in his unspecified country of origin, and "having to take himself for refuge in this kingdom."[16] In the period immediately following his arrival he appears to have encountered little difficulty in establishing himself. Court documents state that "upon application ... he had the benefit of naturalization allowed him, and permission to become a manufacture of hatts." He brought servants with him, and "settled himself and family in the Canongate." Turing, "during the late kings Reign enjoyed all the priveleges [sic] and immunities" of a full citizen. A problem seems to have arisen when the local magistrates objected to his wish to use materials, "which he must import from foreign countries." Seeking Turing's further integration into the commercial community of the city, possibly as a means of gaining some control over his means of doing business, the magistrates ordered that Turing first become "burgess and guildbrother of the place." Turing submitted to their request, but brought his case against the magistrates when the prohibition on his use of foreign imports remained in place. Unfortunately, only one document relating to the case has survived, much of which is damaged. In what remains intact and legible, no mention is made of Turing's religion. However, Turing's legal action carried echoes of a slightly earlier incident.

In 1691, Edinburgh's council had been faced for the first time with the issue of permitting professing Jews to trade inside the city walls. One David Brown had petitioned for the right to trade within the city walls, and while at first this right was granted without tumult, the decision was later objected to by the Dean of Guild. A council debate was subsequently convened to arbitrate the issue, concluding when the council treasurer, Hugh Blair, declared that "Jewes as such are not to be considered or treated as other infidels they being the ancient people of God and the seed of Abraham of whom as considering the flesh Christ came."[17] Blair's plea for tolerance swayed the chamber, and from that point on professing Jews were permitted to trade and reside in the city.

However, the objection of the Dean of Guild prefigured later ambivalence, if not outright resistance, toward Jews and Jewish traders in Edinburgh. In 1698 an entry was made in the Burgess Roll reminiscent of the Turing case. A Moses Mosias had obtained permission to trade in Edinburgh, but admission to the right of burgess and guildbrother in this instance was withheld until he converted to Christianity.[18] Further, Jews in Scotland could find themselves marginalized in legal terms. David Vital states that in 1712 a Scottish court was urged to disallow the evidence of a Jew on the grounds that Jews were "inhabile in law, considering the root hatred they bear all Christians."[19]

As well as being motivated by Christian anti–Judaism, resistance to Jewish settlement in Edinburgh also took an opportunistic form. In 1717, one Isaac Queen was not only denied the right of burgess and guildbrother, but was also denied the right to trade in city unless he paid 100 pounds—a privilege

David Brown had been granted free of charge. Salis Daiches stated that Isaac Queen was a man of obvious wealth, and that in an "illegal and reprehensible" move, the city authorities could not resist engaging in some extortion. Daiches argued that "such procedures did not encourage Jews to come to Scotland."[20] There was certainly no steep climb in the Jewish population of the city. Between this date, and the last decade of the 18th century, the only Jew on record in Edinburgh is Joseph Hart Myers, a native of New York who graduated with a medical degree from Edinburgh University in 1779.[21]

The difficulties faced by Scotland's earliest Jewish settlers can be explained in part by the fact that even though Jews themselves were largely absent from the country, libels and prejudices associated with them had long since made their way across Hadrian's Wall. There is evidence that Scotland was capable of absorbing, via cultural osmosis, broader hostile English and Continental perceptions of Jews and Judaism. Ben Braber writes that "events in England as well as Christian doctrine could have caused and enforced anti-Jewish prejudices in Scotland."[22] During Scotland's experience of the Black Death in the mid-14th century, when it was doubtful if there was a single Jew in country, anti-Semitism was a feature in the commentary of the East Lothian chronicler Walter Bower.[23] This was concurrent with a thread of European thought which held that Jews had in some way caused the plague, the most common explanation being that Jews were "poisoners of wells, mass murderers of Christians."[24]

Anti-Jewish sentiments and tropes also found some expression in Scotland's cultural output. The Scottish Enlightenment philosopher David Hume stated in his *Essays and Treatises on Several Subjects* (1758) that:

> where any set of men, scattered over distant nations, have a close society or communication together, they acquire a similitude of manners, and have but little in common with the nations amongst whom they live. Thus the Jews in Europe, and the Armenians in the east, have a peculiar character; and the former are as much noted for fraud, as the latter for probity.[25]

Among Bishop Percy's *Reliques*, a collection of English and Scottish folk ballads, is an adaptation of the ballad "Sir High, or the Jew's Daughter," sent from Scotland in 1765. Testifying to the fecundity of certain anti-Jewish myths, as well as the ability of Scotland to absorb these myths from its closest neighbor, the ballad is a slightly altered version of the tale of "Little Hugh of Lincoln." The subject of the ballad, of which there are at least 21 versions, was a young boy alleged to have been the victim of a ritual murder in 1255, committed by the consent of "all the Jews of England."[26] Anthony Julius writes that "it is by song that members of non-literate cultures keep themselves informed both of their history and of current events. They tend to share a common repertoire of tunes; song-versions of common interest tend to emerge very quickly; these versions are modified, elaborated upon, as they circulate in the culture."[27] The Scottish adaptation is notable for the extent to which it remained true to the original legend, and for the extent to which it had been adapted to the Scottish dialect:

> Than out and cam the Jewis dochter,
> Said, Will ye cum in and dine?
> I winnae cum in, I cannae cum in,
> Without my play-feres nine.
>
> Scho powd an apple reid and white,
> To intice the young thing in:
> Scho powd an apple white and reid,
> And that the sweit bairne did win.
>
> And scho has taine out a little pen-knife,
> And low down by her gair;
> Scho has twin'd the young thing and his life,
> A word he nevir spak mair.[28]

By the end of the 18th century, patterns of Jewish settlement in Edinburgh began to change, with the presence of Jewish couples, families, and eventually a community, becoming a feature of life in the city. This development was part of a larger trend in British-Jewish demography which saw 8,000 to 10,000 Ashkenazi Jews arrive in Britain between 1750 and 1815.[29] Most of these immigrants arrived from Central Europe where legislation governing where they could live and how they could do business had become increasingly restrictive.[30] While some arrived with capital and business experience, a substantial number "lacked material resources or artisanal skills and on arrival took to low-status itinerant trades to earn a living."[31] The majority of these immigrants settled and remained in London, but this period also saw the development of small, scattered "clusters of Jewish residents" in areas increasingly remote from the great metropolis.[32] It was against this backdrop that the nucleus of a Jewish community in Edinburgh was formed.

Both Levy and Daiches recorded a Herman Lyon, dentist and chiropodist, as purchasing the first Jewish burial plot in Calton Hill, Edinburgh, in 1793. Despite council entries stating that the plot was "for the Jews," both Levy and Daiches concluded that the plot was solely for the use of himself and his family, and ruled out the possibility of the presence of other Jewish families in the city at the same time. However, while the plot may have been for the Lyon family alone, a libel case from 1790 proves that there was certainly a larger Jewish presence in the city at that time, and that a community, undoubtedly a very small and troubled one, had been formed.

In July 1790, a case was brought before the magistrates of Edinburgh in which "all parties are Jews."[33] Rose Nathan had initiated proceedings against "Francis Bevilin or Berlin alias Abraham Barnet or Burnett" following revelations that he had been spreading rumors that she was, "lying in naked bed with other men ... and that she had been seen by others lying with other men than her husband in different houses and places in and about Edinburgh Canongate and Leith."³⁴

Bevilin, in his defense, stated that Nathan was "an adulterous whore, sinner and a lewd and infamous and unchaste woman ... and that no decent or creditable person should have any dealings or keep company with her." Bevilin informed the court that he had been established in Edinburgh for "several years in the line of Teacher of Drawing in which he has met with great encouragement." The trial report stated that, "the defender is of the Jewish religion, of which there are very few in Edinburgh, and as he has been longer known here than any of the others he has felt a kind of responsibility for the general good behaviour of the few of his Israelitish brethren that reside in this place."³⁵

Other details illustrate a slowly growing Jewish community as early as the 1780s. Rose Nathan's husband, Henry Daniel, was as an engraver of glass, and following difficulties in securing employment in both London and Edinburgh, Francis Bevilin came to his assistance. Bevilin claimed that he came to feel a sense of responsibility for the well-being of his younger companion. This relationship was then said to have been disrupted by the arrival of Herman Lyon, the dentist and chiropodist mentioned by Levy and Daiches. The trial report continues:

> In the same way, a Mr. Herman Lyon, another of the Defenders brethren, a dentist and extractor of corns having come here about two years ago, but without a shilling in his pocket and the Defender though an utter stranger to him maintained and supplied him with money until he got into employment. The defendant likewise thought himself entitled to take some concern in Mr. Lyon's behaviour.³⁶

Herman Lyon, after securing employment, took up residence in the Canongate. Soon after, Rose Nathan and Henry Daniel moved into his home as lodgers. "A report or surmise afterwards arose and reached the defendants ears that an improper intimacy subsisted between Mr. Lyon and Mrs. Daniel."³⁷ Bevilin is said to have confronted Lyon about his alleged improper behavior, and the defendant claimed in court that Lyon had initially agreed to move away from Rose Nathan—only to find himself subsequently served with a summons. Among the witnesses were William Scott and James Lyon. Scott noted that the episode had been a considerable disturbance to "the Brethren here,"³⁸ suggestive of a wider circle of Jewish residents in the city. Bevilin was convicted of defaming Rose Nathan and was punished with a considerable fine.

In helping each other find employment, lodging with each other, and communicating with each other, it is undeniable that a group of Jews, albeit a small one and almost certainly without formal religious leadership, was extant prior to the 19th century.³⁹ It is also clear that the Canongate area of

Edinburgh was the site of this early Jewish community. Outside the city walls, the Canongate area was home to a variety of traders, artisans and merchants. Once the main route into Edinburgh, by 1780 the area had declined dramatically from its once great status. Its atmosphere was punctuated no longer by the homes of princes and nobles, but rather by the odors of the fleshers and bakers, and the cacophony of the wrights and blacksmiths.[40]

A contemporary, Allan Ramsay, said of the area:

> O Canongate, puir eldrick hole,
> What loss, what crosses does thou thole,
> London and death gars thee look droll
> And hang thy heid.[41]

In 1793, the same year Herman Lyon purchased his burial plot, the British government ushered through an immigration bill to coincide with the outbreak of war with France. All foreigners over the age of 14 were required to register with local authorities, where they would be added to a list of resident aliens. The slow but steady increase of the community, along with the origin of the city's new Jewish citizens, was recorded in 1794, when Herman Lyon registered along with 18 other Jews, including Moses Daniel, who may have been a relative of Henry Daniel. In total, 10 people declared their previous country of residence to be Holland.[42] Abel Phillips confirmed that the rest originated in Germany, Paris and St. Petersburg.[43]

In 1817, this small community had grown sufficiently in size and means to establish the first synagogue in Scotland in a rented room at 22 North Richmond Street, at the corner of Richmond Court.[44] The main part of the tenement was converted to a 67-seat synagogue.[45] Salis Daiches posited that by 1820 "there were about a hundred of them in the city," and that many of the new settlers originated in Hamburg and Bremen.[46] This, again, was part of broader demographic changes in British Jewry. While immigrants who arrived in Britain between 1750 and 1815 had varied from unskilled peddlers to large-scale merchants, Todd Endelman states that "those who arrived in the Victorian Age tended to be drawn from the 'respectable' ranks of German Jewry."[47] The new immigrants were attracted by Britain's increasing centers of "conspicuous consumption," and they established businesses as "purveyors of jewelry, cigars, antiques, toys, picture frames, leather goods, and other luxury items."[48] Levy and Daiches assert that Edinburgh's new Jewish immigrants were wealthy and "consisted mainly of those trading in clothing, furs and jewellery and the import of goods from the Continent."[49] This new, wealthier element worshipped alongside a working-class, artisanal Jewish population. The 1837 report of the Commissioners of Religious Instruction recorded 90 "Hebrews" in Edinburgh. Of these, one half were categorized as "poor and working class."[50] Indeed, the stipend for the minister, Moses Joel, was recorded as being so small as to necessitate his "looking to other means for his support."[51]

An unfortunate case from the 1820s casts some light on the level of wealth among the more successful Jewish immigrants in Edinburgh. The National Library of Scotland holds among its rare newspapers a clipping from around the time of this small influx of Jewish merchants. One of them bears the headline, "An account of the trial and sentence of Charles and Margaret M'Mahon accused of the murder and robbery of a Jew on the Easter road to Leith."[52] The defendants stood accused of strangling Alexander Phillips, a dealer in furs. Among the items recovered from the defendants were "a green silk shawl, a silver snuff-box, and a brown leather purse with steel clasp, three watches and forty pounds in notes, gold and silver." Moses Henry Lisenheim, who would later go on to lead the new Jewish community in Glasgow in 1823, was called as witness.[53]

At the time of the murder Lisenheim was the proprietor of a public house in Leith, but had recently moved to Edinburgh. His wife had operated the public house in his absence and in the course of doing so, had become acquainted with the defendants. Surprised by their sudden wealth, and hearing of the murder of Alexander Phillips, she informed her husband. Lisenheim subsequently met with Phillips' father where he gathered information regarding the stolen items. After attempting to purchase a number of watches from the defendants, and quickly realizing that they matched the description he had been given, Lisenheim contacted the police.

The article covering the trial laid special emphasis on the Jewishness of the victim and the witnesses, as evidenced in the headline. In fact, it is quite late in the article that "the Jew" is named, and a sense of curiosity and novelty is evident in its the inclusion of such details as the fact that Lisenheim was "sworn in the Jewish form, with his hat on his head, and hand upon the Old Testament." This is not necessarily suggestive of anti-Semitism, but it does demonstrate that the case was seen as having unique qualities because it involved Jews. The defendants were found guilty and transported for 14 years.

Daiches, Roth, and Levy concurred that the first verifiable minister of the Edinburgh community was Moses Joel. Joel was licensed as a *shochet* in 1831, and appears in various city directories from 1823 to 1834 as a clothier or "priest of the Jews."[54] Joel would be succeeded by five ministers until the arrival of the Rev. Jacob Fürst from Middlesborough in 1879 ushered in a period of hierarchical stability.[55] The slow growth of the community is indicated by the fact that the hall in Richmond Court was sufficient for the Jewish population for no less than 52 years.[56]

One leading Edinburgh Jewish family at this time were the Ashenheims. Jacob Ashenheim's name first appears in Edinburgh directories in 1829. A jeweler by trade, he also served as president of the Edinburgh congregation, and his son, Lewis, graduated in medicine from Edinburgh University in 1837. Lewis was a Hebrew scholar, and wrote passionately on the subject of the Hebrew language in the Diaspora. If his life in Edinburgh was a largely pleasant one, this was not reflected in his writings. In one of his essays he wrote that, "It is true we are in a 'strange land'; it is true we are degraded and despised; yet though still suffering under all these conditions, we have still the spirit to defend our only consolation, which is our language."[57]

Not all of Edinburgh's Jews as this time were scholars or wealthy traders, and some seem to have been sufficiently impoverished to have succumbed to the material inducements offered by local missionaries. The Edinburgh *Evangelical Magazine and Missionary Chronicle* recorded in January 1841 that one "Moses the Jew" and his three-year-old daughter were baptized at the New-street Church, Canongate.[58] Converted Jews from the Continent also began arriving in Edinburgh as evangelists. In March 1850, a converted Prussian Jew arrived in Edinburgh at the behest of the Church of Scotland, and was quickly set to work in the Cowgate area with the task of converting "vast amounts of Roman Catholics."[59]

By the 1850s a number of poor immigrants, from other parts of Britain and further afield, were beginning to settle in the city. Among them were the traveling jewelers Thomas and Abraham Jacob, and Thomas' wife Hannah. They resided at South Richmond Street, which would go on to become a center of Jewish habitation in the city toward the end of the century. Todd Endelman argues that at this time "Jewish poverty went hand in hand with crime, squalid surroundings, low-status trades, and coarse behavior."[60] During the 1810s and 1820s there had been a "skyrocketing" of Jewish convictions at the Old Bailey.[61] In keeping with these broader trends, Abraham Jacob was arrested and imprisoned for theft not long after his arrival in Edinburgh, and in 1859 Thomas and Hannah were themselves arrested and convicted for stealing a deposit receipt from an inebriated acquaintance. Perhaps indicative of a sense that the Jewish population had come to be seen by the local press as less of a novelty, in contrast to prior court cases involving Jews, and publicity surrounding them, the Jewishness of the defendants was barely noted.[62]

The middle of the 19th century was an important time for the Jews of the United Kingdom. The election of Baron Lionel de Rothschild to Parliament in 1847 sparked agitation for a "Jew Bill" which would permit him, and other Jews to sit in the legislature. Debate was widespread and often bitterly anti-Semitic. Articles carried by *Blackwood's Edinburgh Magazine*, a Tory-supporting publication, from the period 1820 to 1850 offer a glimpse into the religious anti–Semitism which then prevailed among elements of Edinburgh's upper middle class. In an 1827 article on "The Monopoly of the London Retail Orange Trade by the Jews," the publication championed the right of Irish immigrants to sell oranges on the streets of London, and denounced Jewish competition. The article stated that "the sweet voices of ten thousand Irish are eclipsed by the sonorous growl of one of these circumcised dogs, who, notwithstanding the march of mind and general spread of intelligence, have always persisted in under-selling the migratory orange-merchants of Erin."[63]

An article entitled "Judaism in the Legislature" in December 1847 emerged within days of the introduction of the "Jew Bill" to Parliament. While the article began benignly with the assertion that "the principles of Protestantism *abhor* persecution," the editorial swiftly adopted the hallmarks of religious anti–Semitism: "It is unnecessary to detail here the especial doctrines of Christianity; but the Jew rejects them all, charges them with falsehood.… Therefore we cannot expect any *assistance* from the Jew in defending our religion, or our religious rights."[64] This was part of a larger pattern of thought which held that the admission of any non-Christian to Parliament would compromise the "religious, moral, and historic foundations of the state." David Vital stressed that for some "the overriding question for Parliament to consider and to affirm was whether Christianity was or was not the true religion."[65] Within this context anti–Catholicism, Scotland's "traditional" prejudice, was effectively marginalized in the cause of combating what was felt to be a graver, anti–Christian, threat. The article concluded with the statement: "We solemnly declare, that much as we deprecate Papist influence, we think that all its hostility is not to be dreaded the hundredth part so much as political power in Jewish hands."[66]

By the summer of 1850, the anti–Jewish rhetoric of the same publication had descended into even cruder arguments, incorporating motifs associated with economic anti–Semitism. The Jew Bill was declared an "obnoxious measure" that was "most dangerous to the Empire."[67] Statements such as "we are no bigots," shared the page with assertions that "by being equally a member in all countries, he is equally an alien in all … his only country is his counting house,–his only city is the Exchange."[68] The author asked "is mere money to be the qualification for giving legislative power? What is patriotism to the Jew?"[69] It was further claimed that "the Jew is a condemned man," having rejected Christ.[70] The article stated that "Him they rejected, and the rejection has been answered by national ruin," and concluded with the admonition that "the Jew *must not* enter the Christian legislature."[71]

However, political thought in Edinburgh was not voiced exclusively by *Blackwood's Edinburgh Journal*. Polly Pinsker has argued that in contrast to Edinburgh's Tory outlets, Whig journals such as the *Edinburgh Review* "strongly supported the Jewish claims from the very first," with several impassioned pleas made by that publication on behalf of the cause of civil liberties.[72]

We have no way of knowing how Edinburgh's small Jewish community reacted to these debates and events. We do know that the community maintained its slow and steady growth. Some families moved on, having great success elsewhere. Lewis Ashenheim traveled Europe before settling in Jamaica, and a John Lazar left Edinburgh in 1836, and went on to become mayor of Adelaide, South Australia in 1855.[73] For those that remained, the city changed around them. The Richmond Court synagogue had given way to dwellings, and in 1868 a replacement was found in Ross House, Park Place.[74] It was a small building, enough to meet the needs of a small congregation, but the nature of Edinburgh Jewry would change in only a couple of decades. This change would not be brought about by local or even national events, but rather by circumstances in the distant Russian territories.

By 1881, Polish and Russian Jews were increasingly suffering the effects of a Jewish population explosion which had not been matched by an expansion of the Jewish economy.[75] As russification policies had intensified, and legislation inhibiting the economic interaction of Jews with the peasantry was implemented, a steady stream of Jewish emigrants had commenced moving westwards as early as the middle of the century.[76]

The volume of this migration greatly increased when Tsar Alexander II was assassinated on 13th March 1881. The modest program of reforms he had enacted, which among other things admitted Jews to the universities and schools, was abandoned overnight by his successor. Alexander III, in a reaction against Marxism and liberal opposition rested his sights on the Jewish population as scapegoat both for his predecessor's assassination and for the nation's turmoil. Educational quotas were imposed, Jews were banned from some professions, and even the demographic make-up of their townships was to be regulated. Traditional Russian anti–Semitism rose to the surface, resulting in sporadic violence carried out by the Tsarist Black Hundreds.[77]

The result of these cumulative causes was a mass exodus of Russian Jews, many of whom sought new opportunities and a new life, as much as they sought to flee the persecutions of the old one. They were aided by innovations in transport and communication. North America was the final destination of choice for the vast majority of these emigrants, but as they fanned out across Western Europe, many stopped in Vienna, Berlin, Paris, and London. Some stopped because they could afford to go no further, while others settled because they had found what they had sought. Such was the state of many Jewish immigrants who emerged from the docks at Leith, and made their way to Edinburgh.

2

New Arrivals

> *It may appear a harsh and selfish thing to say, that it is well the refugees only pass through Scotland. To leave them here would be to fill the streets of Edinburgh with thousands of beggars, to embarrass all the charities of the country, and to impoverish our local Jewish brethren.*—the Rev. William Paterson, 1891.[1]

By late 1881 the situation in Russia had worsened. Violence occurred sporadically across the Russian Empire, beginning just six weeks after the assassination of Alexander II. As pogroms broke out in Odessa, Minsk, Kovno and elsewhere, vast numbers of Jewish economic migrants and refugees departed the Russian territories and made their way to the West. Those migrants who found their way to Leith were disgorged in their thousands, to be met by the combined forces of a small Jewish and Christian effort to aid to them. The following chapter examines Edinburgh's Jewish and non–Jewish response to this great migration, as well as the immediate challenges faced by those migrants who decided to go no further, and make Edinburgh their home.

Anti-Semitic persecution peaked in Russia in the latter half of 1881, though it was the beginning of 1882 before news of pogroms began to circulate in Britain with significant frequency. Thus, it was only in February 1882 that the people of Edinburgh, both Jew and Gentile, began to react to an increasingly volatile situation in the East. This reaction was geared, at that time, not toward the aid of incoming refugees, but toward the sending of aid to Russia. In the early 1880s the flow of Jewish migrants through Leith, and Scotland as a whole, was minimal compared to the waves experienced toward the end of the decade. On 3 February 1882, on the same day that the Reverend Dr. Teape of St. Andrews Episcopal Church, Edinburgh, expressed sympathy with the plight of Russian Jews, the Edinburgh branch of the Anglo-Jewish Association gathered at the Park Place Synagogue. At this meeting, "resolutions were passed expressing grief and horror at the outrages upon the Jews in Russia and sympathy with the sufferers. A Committee was appointed to raise subscriptions."[2]

Less than two weeks later, this small effort to raise money for the victims of Russian persecution had moved beyond the confines of Edinburgh's small Jewish community, embracing the city as a whole, and involving key figures from the local political and clerical class. Under the presidency of the 71-year-old Lord Provost of Edinburgh, George Harrison, a mass meeting was held in Edinburgh, "at which resolutions were passed deploring the atrocities on the Jews in Russia."[3] A letter was read from future prime minister the Earl of Rosebery, whose estate lay on the banks of the Forth, sympathizing with the aims of the meeting, and conveying his regret that he could not join in this expression of the "indignation of the City of Edinburgh at the outrages perpetrated upon the Jews in Russia."[4] It was decided at this meeting that the resolutions should be forwarded to the prime minister, William Gladstone, and the foreign secretary in the hope that some influence could be exerted on Russia which could end the persecution. In addition, an "Edinburgh Fund for the Relief of the Sufferers" was established.

By 3 March 1882 the fund had raised £462, of which more than £68 came from the relatively poor Edinburgh Hebrew Congregation, and by the end of July the fund had raised a total of more than £539.[5] In April 1883 an edition of *The Edinburgh Review* carried an article on "Persecution of the Jews," which was described by the *Jewish Chronicle* as "generally favorable in tone" but showing a "remarkable want of grasp of the question as a whole."[6] This opinion on the article is indicative of a sense that while there was great dismay at the persecution directed at Jewish victims, there was very little real understanding, at least in Gentile Britain, of its causes.

In these years immediately preceding the influx of Russian-Jewish refugees, Edinburgh's native Jewish population had remained largely unchanged, in terms of numbers and composition, from its state in the middle of the century. Edinburgh Jewry was still largely descended from the hundred or so Jewish settlers who had arrived in the city during the first two decades of the 19th century.[7] Some had come from England, specifically London, and others came from further afield. Those who immigrated from continental Europe in the middle of the 19th century tended to arrive "with greater resources—a secular education, prior experience in large-scale commerce, access to capital—and a broader cultural outlook"[8] than those who would arrive at Leith toward the end of the century.[9] This English-speaking, acculturated community never ascended to a social summit comparable with the higher-ups of London Jewry, such as the Rothschilds. There were no inter-marrying high families, and they were certainly not as wealthy.[10] In many ways they were typical of Orthodox communities in other provincial centers throughout Britain, relatively autonomous, generally following guidelines from the Board of Deputies, and the *Beth Din* in London. The Reform movement, which emerged in Britain in 1840, was shunned by the Edinburgh community, as it was by the majority of British Jewry who perceived it as a perilously close step to complete assimilation.[11] The acculturated Jew in Edinburgh would have struggled, like many throughout Britain, to "find a way through which he could define his religious and ethnic identity, so that he could be accepted in the modern secular world and yet retain his specific Jewish orientation."[12]

Typical of this more established generation of Edinburgh Jewry, Jacob Michael had arrived from Herzingtorn, Posen, in 1855 at the age of 20. He quickly became established in Edinburgh's South Bridge in the manufacture and wholesale of timepieces, and also traded in Swiss and American watches. Harfield's "Commercial Directory of the Jews," published in 1894, discloses that Michael's business was established just three years after his arrival in Edinburgh.[13] Actively engaged in religious as well as commercial life, he was Edinburgh's only *Mohel* until 1879, often traveling all over Scotland to perform circumcisions for the country's minuscule and scattered Jewish communities. One of the original founding members and trustees of the Park Place Synagogue, he also served as its president and treasurer, respectively, for 12 years. Equally typical of this older generation was the fact that his children moved away from the city—his son studied to become a medical doctor before moving to London.[14]

Other leading members of Edinburgh's small Jewish congregation were engaged in very similar trades. For example, David Goldston, who served as president and treasurer of the community for several years during the 1870s and 1880s, started a wholesale retail and watch business, and also sold imported German, French and American clocks. He too operated out of Edinburgh's South Bridge, and by 1894 he had bequeathed his business to his son Ernest, who had been born in Edinburgh in 1864.[15] A slightly later example of the leading membership of Edinburgh's Jewish community at that time is Alphonse Louis Reis. Born in Liverpool in 1860, his birth certificate listed his father as a "bullion merchant."[16] He engaged early on in commerce as a jeweler, and later branched out into the selling of postcards and other "fancy goods" from his two Edinburgh shops based on the South Bridge and Leith Street.[17]

This small community, while reacting to reports of persecution abroad, was largely concerned with more local and common issues in the first half of the 1880s. By 1880, a small Hebrew school was run for the children of the community under the direction of the Rev. Jacob Fürst and a Miss Salmon.[18] Another concern of the congregation was the running of the Edinburgh Hebrew Philanthropic Society. It is noteworthy that this society had been founded in 1838 by "non–Israelite," James Douglas of Cavers. Douglas had "for some time anonymously remitted handsome sums for the relief of the Jewish poor," and his society later grew to involve both Jewish and Gentile businessmen in the city.[19] Unfortunately the records of this organization are no longer available, rendering any precise assessment of the numbers of Jewish poor in the city prior to the influx of Russian immigrants impossible.

Despite the small size of the community much effort seems to have been geared toward the maintenance of religious practice, and the prevention of secularization, conversion, and assimilation. During a sermon in September 1881, the congregation at Park Place were told to "look to our brethren of another faith in Scotland, who are proverbial for their strict Sabbath day observance, and although knowing that their first day is not heaven ordained as our seventh day, still they keep it as a strict day of rest."[20]

The community appears to have been youthful, augmented as it was by young businessmen and their families, as well as numerous Jewish medical students at Edinburgh University. Young Jewish men from all over the United Kingdom and beyond came to study medicine in the city, as well as the children of the local community. In earlier years Jews would have been attracted to Scottish Universities by their lack of religious entry requirements. Among these earlier Jewish students in the city was Aaron Hart David, born in Montreal in 1812. He commenced studying medicine in his native country before proceeding to Edinburgh in 1833 to finish his studies.[21] Later students were attracted both by precedent and by advertising directed at Jewish students in the United Kingdom. One such example was a letter written to the *Jewish Chronicle* in 1871. "Lennie" from Edinburgh wrote that

> The "Modern Athens" boasts of a University second to none in the world. The Edinburgh Schools of Medicine and Surgery are famed far and wide, and many of the most eminent men in these professions have received their training here.... There is a synagogue here, and the services are conducted in a strictly orthodox manner; and religious instruction can also be obtained. The city is very healthy, and the surrounding scenery delightful.[22]

Most students however, like Aaron Hart David, appear to have returned home or moved on after completing their course of study. The congregation was also augmented, in the early 1880s, by the occasional presence of Jewish soldiers stationed in the area. In early 1883 the Board of Deputies successfully lobbied military authorities to provide leave for Jewish soldiers during High Holy Days. Subsequently, on the first day of Passover in that year, the Park Place synagogue welcomed a Jewish private from the Third Dragoons, one of many soldiers who would attend services with the congregation in future years.[23]

Refugees

By 1884, the steady but small trickle of Russian-Jewish immigrants into the city, arriving from other parts of the United Kingdom as well as through the port at Leith, began to increase in volume. Reports reached the *Jewish Chronicle* that attendance at New Year services had exceeded the capacity of the Park Place synagogue for the first time in its history as a Jewish place of worship. By Passover 1887, the *Jewish Chronicle* noted that "the synagogue was quite unusually attended. There was no standing room to be obtained.... In addition to the synagogue, the branch synagogue, which has been in existence for the last twelve years, has also been well attended."[24]

Just as the fabric of the Park Place synagogue was beginning to groan under the weight of immigration, so too was political discourse in Britain as a whole. By May 1887, the Board of Trade issued a parliamentary paper drawing attention to the impact immigrants were having on the domestic economy, "touching in places on the part taken by Polish Jews in the movement."[25] The report was reviewed by the Jewish Board of Guardians in London, who proceeded to communicate with provincial leaders in order to get a clearer picture of immigrant economic activity in the country as a whole. Having gathered this information, the Board of Guardians published its report in the *Jewish Chronicle*. The report concluded with:

> a few quotations from provincial correspondents giving impressions as to the influx of foreign Jews into Edinburgh, Hull, Glasgow, and Birmingham, where there seems to have been some immigration of Polish Jews of recent years affecting the tailoring trade in Edinburgh, Glasgow, and Birmingham, and the glazing and cabinet-making trades in Edinburgh and Hull, though in the latter place the immigration is said to have been slow and gradual.[26]

Thus the impression was given by correspondents in Edinburgh that, in contrast to the situation in Hull, the influx of Jewish immigrants into the city since 1882 was not "slow and gradual." It was also suggested that these immigrants had an impact on several trades in the city.

By 1890, persecution in Russia peaked once again, and the Reverend Fürst was moved to refer at length to atrocities perpetrated in the East during his New Year address in September of that year. In October 1890, the Prime Minister William Gladstone addressed a crowd in Edinburgh on the subject. Gladstone had for years been dogged by accusations of anti–Semitism, stemming mostly from his opposition to the removal of Jewish disabilities in the 1840s. Having previously expressed "grave doubts about the propriety of permitting Jews to sit in Parliament" and often resorting to the public use of "rhetoric of an almost crassly profane character," Gladstone was now keen to vocalize his disdain for this new wave of persecutions.[27] To the gathered crowd at Edinburgh he said:

> I am grieved to say that the accounts we receive of the civil oppression that is now, apparently, being practised on the Jews, and the accounts we receive even of personal and corporal cruelty in some cases inflicted upon them, are in the last degree painful and repulsive. Although you have not many Jews resident in Scotland, you have yet

some of that race at the present moment who excites your warmest and kindliest sympathy.[28]

The flow of refugees had again reached such a level in July 1891 that Jewish residents in Edinburgh "raised a small fund, wherewith to supply the poor travellers with the refreshments and a substantial breakfast before their departure for Glasgow." It was noted by local aid organizers that even though the vast majority of refugees were transmigrants destined for the United States, it was becoming impossible to cope with the large number of immigrants arriving twice a week. The president of the Edinburgh Hebrew Congregation, Samuel Glasstone was forced to publish an appeal for help in the *Scotsman*, and within a week almost £200 had been raised "mostly contributed by Christians."[29]

Samuel Glasstone was also honorary secretary of the Russian Refugees Relief Society, an "umbrella organization" embracing the Jewish community and several of the Christian churches and charities. In addition to conducting an ongoing aid operation at Leith, the Society also made a point of recording individual cases in order to inform the public at large as to both the state of the refugees and the reasons behind their journey from Russia. Among these accounts were the stories of a former innkeeper from Odessa who received police orders to leave by midnight, and a widow from Nishni-Novgorod who was threatened by the police that she would be robbed if she did not leave the country. "The following night people entered her dwelling and took everything they could carry away and broke up the remainder."[30] A young watchmaker from Ufa was able to bribe officials to permit himself, his wife, and their six children to stay in the town, but once his funds ran out he too was expelled.[31]

Chair of Divinity at Edinburgh University and future Moderator of the Church of Scotland, the Rev. William Paterson, another leading member of the Russian Refugees Relief Society, recorded seeing "sorrowful bands of exiles week by week."[32] He, and others working at Leith, had been horrified in October 1891 by the arrival of 53 severely malnourished Jewish emigrants from southern Russia. Having had minimal sustenance for most of the passage to Leith, these migrants found that their arrival at the port coincided with the Day of Atonement. After a period of fasting in accordance with Orthodox teaching, some of them had to be treated at Leith Hospital. One man among them explained that he had not been expelled from Russia, but had fled to avoid the harsh terms of conscription operated by the Russian army against Jews, in particular the low rate of pay relative to his income as a corn merchant.[33]

Glasstone took the education of the wider public in Edinburgh very seriously in regard to the persecutions. In 1891, the Russo-Jewish Committee of

London had produced a pamphlet entitled "Darkest Russia" for distribution among the Gentile population of Britain and Ireland. It was aimed at addressing the British public's "want of grasp of the question as a whole." Motivating this campaign was a desire to encourage protest against the persecution, and generate sympathy with its victims. It was further hoped that this sympathy would help combat anti-alien or anti–Semitic feelings generated by the scale and speed of migration. Writing to the *Jewish Chronicle* in 1891, Glasstone hastened to add that "in the far north, in Edinburgh, we are trying to do our share of the work in the good cause." He continued:

> I ordered 200 copies (of "Darkest Russia") and sent them by post to our subscribers, and also to the Editors of the principle papers in Scotland, and to the principal clergymen, medical men, lawyers etc., in Edinburgh, and by this I may hope we may arouse public feeling on behalf of our poor down-trodden race in Russia; that the Christian public in Scotland feel for our people, we have very good proof in the past few weeks by the very generous response to our appeal for funds for the relief of the poor refugees who pass through Leith on their way to America via Glasgow.[34]

William Paterson, in a review of the Relief Society's activities from the period 15th July to 11th December 1891, stated that aid had been administered to 4,126 individuals at Leith alone. The Reverend Fürst had earlier stated that "Edinburgh Jews had, perhaps, recently done on behalf of their persecuted brethren more than any other Jewish congregation in the provinces."[35] This aid consisted of "over £336 in money and possibly twice as much in clothing."[36] Paterson added that, "it may appear a harsh and selfish thing to say, that it is well the refugees only pass through Scotland. To leave them here would be to fill the streets of Edinburgh with thousands of beggars, to embarrass all the charities of the country, and to impoverish our local Jewish brethren. "[37]

This attitude is just as likely to have been held by the Jewish members of the Relief Society. There was a conviction, held generally among assimilated British Jews and exemplified in numerous articles in the *Jewish Chronicle*, that the refugees and immigrants should be allowed into the country, but that in order to guard against anti–Semitism a dual-pronged strategy should be employed: providing poor relief to the destitute in order to minimize the burden on local authorities, and providing the means and encouragement for an onward journey to the United States or elsewhere. In addition, Kenneth Collins states that "appeals were made to Jewish leaders in Russia to encourage their communities to stay where they were and not to swell the ranks of impoverished Jews in Britain."[38]

Persecution was ongoing in mid-1892, and as a response the Free Church of Scotland issued a formal declaration on 20 May of that year stating that the Church leadership "deeply sympathize with the Jews in Russia under the cruel persecutions they are enduring."[39] This was followed a day later by a formal declaration from the Church of Scotland expressing "sympathy with the Hebrew people in their trials."[40] When the Edinburgh Russian Refugee Relief Society gathered for its first annual meeting in July 1892, the treasurer submitted a balance sheet showing that "8,334 Russian refugees had been assisted with food and clothing, and some had been assisted with a little money."[41] Refugee aid in the city was further supplemented with grants issued to the Edinburgh Jewish Board of Guardians by the Russo-Jewish Committee in 1895, 1897, and again in 1899.[42]

It is apparent, however, that there were occasional, yet significant, lulls in the volume of migration through Leith, Edinburgh, and Britain as a whole. The tide of immigration ebbed and flowed, largely in direct correlation to events in Russia. For example, the period 1881–1883 was clearly one of increased migration, and can be directly attributed to the fact that "pogroms started on the 12th April 1881 in Elisavetgrad and remained endemic and irrepressible until the middle of 1882, but even in 1883 there was a minor wave."[43] The infamous "May Laws," "attacking the basis of Jewish economic life in Russia," had been promulgated in 1882.[44] The last pogrom in the Russian interior occurred in 1884 in Nishni-Nogorod.[45] It is also became apparent that following an initial period of settlement the trend among succeeding waves of migrants was for onward migration to the United States. For example, a report on Russian and Polish Jewish immigrants in Edinburgh, compiled by the Board of Trade and covering the year 1894, stated that:

> There has been no increase of destitute aliens during the past 12 months. There are about 200 families of Russian and Polish Jews in Edinburgh and Leith, and they are all employed. During 1894 about 10 or 12 men and women passed through the city from Hamburg to the Clyde to set sail for America.[46]

It was added that these figures were similar to those seen in Leeds, Sheffield, Sunderland, and Bristol. In fact, the level of migrant Jews settling in Britain during 1894 was so low that the *Jewish Chronicle* confidently asserted that the figures "fully confirm our remarks on the monthly returns to the effect that the tide of immigration is slackening."[47] A year later the *Jewish Chronicle* asserted that, "it has been shown how small our immigration really is ... the whole movement for restricting immigration was a sham based on unreality."[48] When the Trades Union Congress met in Edinburgh in September 1896, the gathering was marked by its lack of discussion of alien immigration, a topic which had fuelled debate in trades unions and government circles in previous years.

A delicate balance between sympathy for the refugee and antagonism toward the immigrant is demonstrated succinctly by the changing attitudes of the Earl of Rosebery to restrictive legislation. Having expressed "indignation" at persecution in 1882, in 1894 Rosebery asserted that if the immigration of foreign Jews was left unchecked, Britain would "become the dunghill of the world with regard to the waste population shot upon our shores."[49] Distrust of the figures gathered by the Board of Trade was also rife among "restrictionists" such as Arnold White, a London-based journalist convinced that the figures were gathered and manipulated by "an unchecked and irresponsible body of Jews."[50] There were, however, many who openly opposed the tactics and attitudes of White and his cohorts. The Rev. William Paterson, of the Russian Refugee Relief Society in Edinburgh, wrote to the *Jewish Chronicle* in September 1891 stating that:

> Mr. Arnold White may endeavour to tone down Russian asperity as he pleases; but those who witness the sorrowful bands of exiles week by week, and see the brutality of Russian administration focussed before their eyes, must accept the circumstances as they exist, in all their naked horrors.[51]

The efforts of the *Jewish Chronicle* in highlighting the various reports and figures published by the Board of Trade can be said to have been part of an overall policy in regard to the immigration of foreign Jews. Certainly, the leading figures of British Jewry fully sympathized with their persecuted co-religionists, and keenly supported the principles of asylum and charity. However, as Bernard Gainer states, they were also acutely aware that "while as refugees from Tsarist persecution they were welcomed, as sweaters of labour they were denounced, and as participants in an in fact illusory competition for jobs with British workmen, they were the object of exclusive alien legislation."[52]

Thus, in order to effectively combat the charges of restrictionists, the focus of British Jewry on a national level was on bringing accurate statistics to bear on the exaggerated claims of those opposed to immigration. On a more local level, ensuring that as many migrants moved on as possible was another major concern. For those who could not, or would not, move on, the focus then shifted toward the provision of charity and employment, and the prevention of the Jewish poor from becoming reliant on relief from the Poor Rates. To this end, the role of local Jewish charities was one of crucial importance.

The Jewish Charitable Effort in Edinburgh

Edinburgh's established Jewish community faced challenges in meeting the needs of both transmigrants and those who decided to settle permanently in the city. From the earliest phases of the great migration, these challenges necessitated the involvement of existing charitable networks within the community, as well the creation of new charitable and philanthropic endeavors.

In addition to the Edinburgh Hebrew Philanthropic Society, which dated from 1838, the small community was already operating in 1875 a "Lying-In

Society" which gave help to new mothers.[53] By 1892, it had been renamed the "Jewish Ladies' Benevolent Maternity Society."[54] In 1891 Phillip Eprile and Joseph Still, members of the council of the Edinburgh Hebrew Congregation, founded the Hebrew Benevolent Loan Society. Phillip Eprile was heavily involved in the charitable efforts undertaken by the congregation, and had been since his arrival from Russia in 1876. He moved for a time to Glasgow, where he established the Glasgow Benevolent Loan Society, before returning to Edinburgh. He also sat on the Edinburgh Board of Guardians.[55]

The Hebrew Benevolent Loan Society operated on a minimum subscription of one penny per week, collected by Mr. Eprile and Mr. Still from those who had subscribed to the charity. Loans were then granted, following application to a Committee, to "the industrious poor Jewish inhabitants in Edinburgh," who would then, presumably, use that money either for subsistence or to get started in small-scale business.[56] The loans would then be repaid in small amounts over an extended period of time, collected by Eprile and Still during their weekly collection of subscriptions. During the second annual general meeting of subscribers to the society in June 1893, an examination of the balance sheet showed that loans totaling just over £100 had been given during the financial year. Individual loans had varied in sums from £1 to £5.[57] By May 1896, total annual distribution of loans had exceeded £328, administered in varying sums to 75 applicants. It was noted to the great pleasure of those present that as total income for the society during the financial year had been over £390, the society was now operating on a surplus.[58]

Demand for the services of the Hebrew Benevolent Loan Society continued relatively unabated for the remainder of the decade. Loans were granted to 69 applicants in the financial year 1897–1898, totaling just over £312, and the following year it was recorded that £352 had been loaned to 77 applicants. If the figure of 200 Russian and Polish Jewish families given by the Board of Trade in 1894 remained roughly constant in the years immediately following the report, then one could surmise that approximately one third of these immigrant families were in some way reliant upon assistance from this society. The treasurer noted in 1899 that "great discretion was used by the Committee in granting the loans, and it was with gratification they learnt that they were productive of great good to the recipients."[59]

In addition to the Hebrew Benevolent Loan Society, Jews struggling with poverty could resort to the auspices of the Edinburgh Jewish Board of Guardians. The Board of Guardians, unlike the Benevolent Loan Society, does not appear to have been a permanent fixture within the community. Before 1902, it was frequently disbanded and reconstituted, probably as the need arose. During the period of mass immigration, it was first reconstituted in 1892, as a report in the *Jewish Chronicle* notes that in March 1895 the Edinburgh Board of Guardians held its third annual concert and dance. Christians were often heavily involved in contributing to and organizing fund-raising events for the Board—the third annual concert was attended by "upwards of 400 people, mostly Christians."⁶⁰ It is also clear that the Edinburgh Board of Guardians was subsidized frequently by the Russo-Jewish Committee in London, owing to the fact that Edinburgh representatives took on much of the responsibility for Jewish immigrants arriving at Leith. However, during his Passover sermon in 1897, the Reverend Fürst "urged on his congregation the necessity of resuscitating the local Jewish Board of Guardians."⁶¹

By 1902, the Board of Guardians had been re-established on what would become a permanent basis, but its leaders were forced to appeal for assistance to the funds "which were in a very low state, as the demands of the society had very considerably increased."⁶² The financial year had seen the Board help "one hundred and twenty-nine casuals and twenty-nine local families."⁶³ Despite the difficulties facing the Board, it seems to have been largely effective in its goal of keeping new immigrants and resident Jews from coming under the auspices of the Poor Rates. Board of Trade figures showed that Edinburgh saw only "small increases" in the number of destitute immigrants during 1902, a situation it shared with Glasgow, Newcastle, Bradford, and Birmingham.⁶⁴

An article appeared in the *Jewish Chronicle* in September 1906, arguing the case for Benevolent Loan Societies as opposed to grants being made by the Board of Guardians. The article explained that "there is a loan department attached to nearly all of the Boards of Guardians in the larger, provincial towns."⁶⁵ The *Jewish Chronicle* argued that the figures "point to the remarkable conclusion that in the provinces about one family in ten are constantly 'hard up,' and have recourse annually to this kind of relief." In an echo of Victorian attitudes to poverty, it was stressed that this method of poor relief was preferred as "it has the two-fold advantage of being exceedingly economical in administration, and of not pauperising the recipient."⁶⁶

The ebb and flow of migration patterns may go some way to explaining the inconsistent manner in which the Board of Guardians functioned. The years 1894 and 1895 would have appeared, as it did to those authoring editorials at the *Jewish Chronicle*, to have signaled the "slackening off" of immigration to, and migration through, Britain. It is likely that, as the heaviest flow of immigration seemed to be over, the leadership of the Edinburgh Jewish community felt efforts should shift from charitable to philanthropic efforts. To this end, it was logical that new immigrants who wanted to make a life for themselves in Edinburgh should be weaned off the charity of the Board of Guardians, and onto the kind of "productive" economic path offered by the Benevolent Loan Society. This would certainly go some way toward explaining the erratic utilization of the former, and the consistent and successful status of the latter. It should also be considered that the functioning of a charitable system based on loans was conditional upon the permanent or at least semi-permanent residency of the recipient. A loan borrowed in Edinburgh was unlikely to be repaid from New York. Thus, this focus on loan distribution rather than grants would suggest that focus had shifted from those "passing through" to those now residing permanently in provincial Britain.

What became apparent, however, was that the years 1894 and 1895 did not mark the end of Britain's role as a hub of transmigration or the destination of choice for many immigrants. These years were a deceiving anomaly, and when this period of relative calm came to a dramatic close, it took many in the country by surprise, and made subsequent years appear all the more uncertain. In January 1899, the increasing number of Jewish poor in Edinburgh necessitated the calling of a special meeting, at which it was decided that a concert and ball should be held in order to raise an emergency fund.[67]

The communal charitable effort in aid of Jewish refugees in Edinburgh and Leith was further augmented by acts of individual altruism. Philip Dresner, a native of Galicia, had arrived in Scotland in 1871.[68] He became a member of the Park Place synagogue, and established a business as a jeweler and clothier in Leith. He was elected to the Parochial Board of Leith Town Council in February 1892. It represented the "first local honour conferred upon a Jew in Leith or Edinburgh."[69] Dresner and his wife made a regular habit of entertaining and aiding migrants who had decamped at Leith. In April 1892 he visited the inmates of the South Leith poor-house, providing entertainment. Following this, his wife "distributed among the inmates a plentiful supply of sugar, tea, and tobacco."[70]

Another example is the philanthropy of Maurice Isaacs, who had become president of the Edinburgh Hebrew Congregation in 1891. Isaacs had been born in Edinburgh in 1840, and engaged in business as a clothier.[71] As well as assisting those within the Jewish community, he was also elected chairman of the Simon Street Soup Kitchen in 1902—a facility which aided all of Edinburgh's poor regardless of religious or ethnic background.[72]

Philanthropic activity was expected from the wealthier members of the Edinburgh Hebrew Congregation. It was viewed as an obligation of those more fortunate, as well as a more "civilized" means of supporting the community's poorer members. This is perhaps best illustrated by a meeting of the Edinburgh Board of Guardians held in January 1902, which discussed at length the growing perception that some of these wealthier members were not meeting this obligation. Harry Michael, treasurer of the Edinburgh Hebrew Congregation, "pointed out that the door-to-door collection was a relic of the Ghetto days, which every enterprising Jewish community was doing its best to eradicate from the ennobling realms of charity." He added that the Board had been "left to their own devices" by "members of the community from whom support might reasonably be expected."[73]

Criticism of the wealthier members of Edinburgh's Jewish community also came from Christian quarters. The end of 1904 saw a debate erupt in the pages of *The Scotsman*, between the Edinburgh Jewish Board of Guardians and one R. Scott Moncrieff, a member of the Christian-operated Society for Relief of Foreigners in Distress. While not explicitly linked to the Aliens Bill, the debate concerned provisions for destitute immigrants. The charge that the Board of Guardians was withholding funds and failing in its duty to provide for recent immigrants was met with fierce condemnation by that organization. Under the heading, "Jewish Refugees in Edinburgh," Moncrieff outlined what he perceived to be grave neglect by the Board.[74] He charged that the Edinburgh Board only offered recent immigrants enough money to help them move to another city, and argued that Jewish refugees had told him that the Board offers only, "eighteen pence and a ticket for a journey further…. Others declare that the Board here has not helped them even with eighteen pence."[75]

The Edinburgh Jewish Board of Guardians had earlier responded to criticism by stating that, "we also have a home where the Society which we represent provide board and lodgings for a period of two days and two nights for any of our casual poor, and that wholly at the expense of the Board." The representative of the Christian organization undertook to investigate these premises and subsequently reported his findings. He claimed that he found the home for refugees to consist of two small houses, one in the tenement area of Richmond Street, and the other in Dalrymple Street. Richmond Street had by this time become something approaching a Jewish ghetto, and was home to an increasing number of Jewish jewelers and traveling salesmen.[76] In one house, which consisted of three rooms, Moncrieff found only one room occupied, and the person occupying that room was "in charge of the place."[77] In the other house, which had only one room, he found "a Jewish family (man, wife, and children) evidently very, very poor." Moncrieff then went on to make a statement with obvious reference to the impending Aliens Bill, as well as to the general feeling that immigrant Jews were a social and economic burden. He stressed that,

> My object in raising this enquiry is to ascertain what the Board and the Jewish community in this city are doing for the relief of the destitute refugees of their own race amongst us—an inquiry which we have every right to make, as it is forced upon us by the apparently increasing immigration of such aliens into our country, giving cause for no small anxiety on the part of thoughtful men, in view of the vast number of unemployed people throughout the country, very many of whom have been brought to sore destitution.[78]

After making further allegations that the Board was withholding funds when faced with those who needed them, Moncrieff continued with a reiteration of the charge that immigrant Jews represented unfair competition for jobs. He argued that,

For many, many years the Jews have dwelt among us in absolute security under our government, and wholly free from molestation, as Jews on the part of our people, though these have seen them prospering in many ways of labour which, but for their presence here, would have afforded means of support for many men and women of our own race.[79]

He concluded by stressing that, "I do not see, in justice to our own people, the present immigration of Jews can be allowed to continue unrestricted, as there is every prospect of its steadily increasing in volume for many months to come."[80] The minute books of the Edinburgh Jewish Medical Mission reveal that its members looked upon this episode with some sense of satisfaction, linked to their belief that Christian organizations were proving more effective at combating Jewish poverty than the Board of Guardians. An entry for 19 January 1905 reported that "a number of the wealthier Jews in Edinburgh had been showed up by Mr. Scott-Moncrieff's letter to *The Scotsman* to raise funds for relief of destitute refugees."[81]

Another source of aid to Edinburgh's refugee and immigrant community came from Lord and Lady Rosebery. Lady Rosebery was born Hannah Rothschild, only child and heiress of Baron Meyer de Rothschild. She "remained a steadfast Jewess, notwithstanding her marriage."[82] Although frequently spending time in London, where she attended the Central synagogue, Lady Rosebery and her husband also spent a great deal of time at the estate in Dalmeny, on the banks of the Forth. From this location, it appears that they had a keen interest in the well-being of Edinburgh's Jewish community.

In 1885, Lady Rosebery invited the children of the Jewish Bible class to picnic at Dalmeny, and in 1887 Lord and Lady Rosebery invited 100 pupils from the Edinburgh Hebrew School to celebrate Queen Victoria's Jubilee.[83] Lady Rosebery frequently requested the attendance of the Reverend Fürst, where she discussed "subjects relative to the local congregation and other religious matters."[84] In October 1888, Lady Rosebery visited the Hebrew School in Park Place, "distributing buns and sweets among the children," as well as supplying the school with "writing-desks, work boxes, and other useful articles."[85]

Tragedy struck this family of benefactors in November 1890 when, following contamination of the water-supply at Dalmeny, Lady Rosebery died of typhoid. It was noted that "during her illness she frequently sought Jewish ministrations." After her death,

> Lord Rosebery, in accordance with the express wishes of the deceased, sent for the Rev, J. Fürst, minister of the Edinburgh Hebrew Congregation, with a request that all the last rites should be carried out according to the prescriptions of the Jewish religion.[86]

The Reverend Fürst then proceeded to Dalmeny with six ladies from the Edinburgh Hebrew Congregation "where they performed their sad functions."

The *Jewish Chronicle* stated in her obituary that "she was a liberal supporter of the Edinburgh Jewish charities, and made it evident by many touching incidents how warmly her heart still beat for her people."[87]

The death of Lady Rosebery did not mark the end of that family's involvement with Edinburgh's Jewish community. Almost two years exactly following the death of his wife, and during his time as foreign secretary, Lord Rosebery donated £20 to the Jewish Ladies' Benevolent Maternity Society. Then, in 1897, two years following his resignation as prime minister, he donated £50 toward a new synagogue for the community. By 1898, Lord Rosebery was continuing to invite Jewish children to Dalmeny.[88]

Lord Rosebery's involvement with Edinburgh's Jewish community is important not just on a local level, but also takes on national significance when one considers that the issue of alien immigration contributed in part to his downfall as prime minister after only 15 months in government. His early opposition to alien immigration was used by his Unionist rival Lord Salisbury, who introduced an Aliens Bill in 1894 "in order to embarrass Rosebery."[89] During the first reading of the Bill, Rosebery declared that he was "not prepared to offer much objection" to the principles of excluding destitute immigrants.[90] However, only one week after the reading, Rosebery radically changed his mind, stating that there was no need for such harsh restrictions. Bernard Gainer stated that "the reasons for this abrupt change remain unclear for he never rationalized it."[91] The issue is often overlooked in historical surveys of Liberal politics, and even by some of the most eminent Rosebery biographers.[92] While Gainer conceded that the fact that "he married a Rothschild might well have weighed with Rosebery, or his Liberal conscience," it would appear that Rosebery's close involvement with, and patronage of, Edinburgh's immigrant Jewish community has not previously been considered.[93] There were other factors involved; for example, immigration figures for the period suggested that the flow into Britain had peaked, and some in Rosebery's own cabinet weighed in against restriction.[94] However, it is not unlikely that Rosebery's links with the immigrant Jewish community in Edinburgh may also have had some impact in the way in which he viewed such communities throughout the country, and contributed in some manner toward his decision to reject alien legislation.

That the Jewish charitable effort in Edinburgh was largely effective in keeping immigrant Jews from becoming reliant on local Poor Rates is suggested by reports compiled by the Board of Guardians and the Board of Trade. According to a report published by the *Jewish Chronicle* in May 1894, "in Edinburgh only two Russian or Polish families were reported to be destitute."[95] The report continued that, in total, 35 Jews in Glasgow, Edinburgh, and Leith "received relief from the Poor Rates, whilst in all Irish towns only 3 Jews were so relieved."[96] It should be conceded that these figures were compiled during a year of comparative calm at Scotland's ports, and the method involved in compiling them was not expounded upon. However, the availability of Jewish charity in the city certainly seems to have been sufficient in helping a significant number of migrants become fit and able for an onward journey, and also seems to have provided Jewish settlers in the city with the means to subsistence and economic betterment. Figures taken in 1908 demonstrated that even at peak population, Edinburgh's immigrant Jewish community had only 10 families reliant on Poor Law relief.[97]

Another hallmark of the success of Edinburgh's charitable efforts was the low level of crime among the Jewish immigrant population.[98] In 1894, council-member J.H. Waterston delivered an address at the Park Place Synagogue, during which he explained that one of his duties was that of periodically visiting the police cells in the different district stations. He told the audience at Park Place that "during all the time he had done so he had not once found a Jew among the prisoners."[99] Kenneth Collins points out that "Rev. Fürst conducted services on both days of Rosh Hashanah, the New Year, in the Calton Jail in September 1900,"[100] but it would appear that such instances were rare. In May 1906, the *Jewish Chronicle* published a return showing "the declared religious creeds and denominations of the prisoners in each of His Majesty's Prisons." This publication was quite possibly in response to anti-alien agitation which often focused on immigrant criminality, and given that this period witnessed the peak of Jewish populations in Scotland, its findings are noteworthy. The figures showed that "in Scottish prisons, there was one Jew in an Edinburgh gaol; three in Glasgow; and one at Peterhead."[101]

What little crime did occur seems mainly to have been directed at other Jews. For example, in 1893 a spate of robberies targeted synagogues in Edinburgh and Glasgow, and knowledge of the whereabouts of the items concerned strongly suggested Jewish perpetrators.[102] Similarly, when a robbery took place at the Graham Street Synagogue in July 1903, it was again apparent that the culprit must have attended services there and had some knowledge of where certain keys and items were held. Reports in Edinburgh's press often treated such events with a degree of mockery. For example, following the 1903 robbery the *Edinburgh Evening Dispatch* stated that the details of the theft were uncovered "after a long and tedious process of dumb show and dancing dervish work, caused through the inability of our informants to speak English."[103]

The achievements of the Edinburgh Hebrew Congregation in terms of immigrant relief are noteworthy due to the fact that the community was, in the main, a poor one. This communal poverty was most visible during the early 1890s, as the condition of the synagogue in Park Place came to symbolize the community's economic strain. One visitor from London was so shocked at the state of affairs he witnessed in Edinburgh that he wrote to the *Jewish Chronicle* immediately upon his return. Finding the synagogue "stowed away in a remote corner behind the University and the Students Union," he stated that the building was "tiny, poverty-stricken, decayed, and severe to ugliness!"[104] In addition, "the humble inhabitants" of Edinburgh's West End had set up another branch in the Dalry district, which was "in meaner quarters still: a gaunt, iron building" with "*Judisch* notices" on the walls.[105] Of those who had seceded from the Edinburgh Hebrew Congregation, the correspondent stated that they located "themselves in one of the poorest and least eligible districts of the city, where the presence of a Jewish meeting-house can only tend to excite the hostility of its rowdy inhabitants."[106]

Maurice Isaacs was moved to reply. He conceded that "our community, unfortunately, is a poor one, and so little can be raised among ourselves, that up to now we have scarcely had the strength to 'cry for help.'" He added that it was his "ardent wish" that one day the community should have "a synagogue worthy of this city, and large enough for our requirements."[107]

Assistance in charitable endeavors often came from Christian quarters, however, it must be stated that Jewish figures in Edinburgh occasionally found themselves working against Christian charitable efforts in the city. It became clear in the years immediately following the immigrant influx, that there was a Christian element within the city of Edinburgh who saw, in the impoverished and vulnerable state of these Jewish newcomers, an opportunity for a significant proselytizing effort, a mission to the Jews.

The Missions and the Migrants

Although Scotland arrived comparatively late to missionary activity directed against Jews, the missions of the 19th century were rooted in the fact that "a concern for the Jewish people was present in Scotland right from the time of the Reformation."[108] Allan Harman argues that:

> desire for the conversion of the Jews was maintained in Scotland by evangelical ministers down into the nineteenth-century. However, the concern for Israel seems to have been heightened by the arrival in Scotland of quite a number of Jewish people in the early part of that century.[109]

As the 19th century progressed, a number of missions were sent by the Church of Scotland and the Free Church of Scotland to various European nations, as well as to Palestine, Egypt and Turkey. There was some dissent. In June 1862, a John MacFarlane wrote to the *Jewish Chronicle* expressing sympathy with Jews suffering persecution in Eastern Europe, and added, "I have been strongly opposed to our Free Church of Scotland employing missionaries for the conversion of the Jews." He added that he had raised the issue at two consecutive General Assemblies in 1860 and 1861.[110] Since missionary activity continued unabated, we must assume that such dissenting voices were in the minority.

The arrival of huge numbers of destitute Jewish migrants in Scotland at the end of the century provided many churches and societies with an opportunity to evangelize within their own locality. The resources employed by these organizations, and the zeal with which they attempted to convert Jewish migrants, resulted in Scotland, and Edinburgh in particular, playing host to some of the most remarkable and controversial missionary endeavors in Britain.

That Scotland was at the forefront of the mission to convert Jews to Christianity was made clear by the Chief Rabbi, the Rev. Dr. Hermann Adler, during his visit to Edinburgh in late May 1886. While noting that there was some antipathy to the missions in Scotland, highlighting *The Scotsman*'s "trenchant satire," he asked, "was it right to go forth into other lands in order to seek and convert the Jew, whilst at home there was that mass of vice and immorality seething in the great cities and villages of Scotland?"[111]

Within a few months of the Chief Rabbi's speech, it became apparent that missionaries were no longer solely at work in "other lands" but were active on the streets of Edinburgh. In August 1886, the Reverend Fürst of the Park Place synagogue wrote at length on evangelical tactics in an article titled "The Conversionists in Edinburgh."[112] He described a "disgraceful affair" involving a "very intelligent and respectable young man of the Jewish persuasion" who had recently arrived in Edinburgh. The young man had arrived with letters of recommendation from his previous employer, a Scottish merchant who had hired him in Alexandria. He proceeded to a number of potential employers, ultimately finding himself "in the hands of an expert missionary who told him that the Jew has no right whatever to obtain employment unless he be converted." The young man was apparently in such distress that he agreed to this proposition. He was then immediately taken to a Church, where plans were made to formally convert him the following Sunday. No mention of employment was made. As Sunday came and went, the missionary "was very much disappointed to hear of the non-arrival of the neophyte." The young man had "enquired for Jews" and was eventually taken to the Reverend Fürst, who kept him at his home for a few days before making plans to help the young man leave Edinburgh to find employment in London.

The Reverend Fürst expressed shock at the scheme employed by this particular missionary, but he also seems to have been greatly disturbed by the fact that the wider congregation of the Church involved "greatly rejoiced" at the prospect of converting this vulnerable young man and others like him. Incidents like this would have introduced some caution into the level of cooperation between Jew and Christian in the city, especially since Christian charity toward Jews in the period was so often accompanied by a Christian message. A report even reached the *Jewish Chronicle* in January 1903 that missionaries in Edinburgh were attempting to "allure the innocent Jewish children, by means of amusements and juvenile luxuries to attend their meetings."[113]

Public meetings on the subject of persecuted Jews in the 1890s were regularly attended by both proselytizing Christians and local Jewish leaders. In the early 1890s the two sides appear to have avoided discussion of the issues which divided them, focusing instead on the issue of ongoing persecution and its causes,[114] but silence on the subject was not permanently maintained. On the first day of Pentecost in 1895, the Reverend Fürst preached to a large audience which included a number of Christian clergymen. In an address geared as much to the Gentile as the Jew, he stated:

> Let other nations rejoice with their "Jewish Mission Report," let them boast of all their thousands they have spent during the past year for the sake of persuading a worthless adult and a homeless man and helpless child of the seed of Abraham to change their God and their religion for one which is not theirs, and who, for the sake of money and position, and most from sinful wickedness withdraw their allegiance from the God of their Fathers, and sever their union with Israel's race.[115]

Jewish Edinburgh was, however, not without its defenders among the Christians of the city. Local businessman Mr. Munro Hogg wrote an open letter "To the Jewish Missions" in November 1898 stating that it was "great unkindness and even cruelty to try and turn them away from their holy religion."[116] In 1902, Hogg wrote directly to one Dr. Cunningham, a leading member of Edinburgh's Jewish Mission, "pointing out the futility of mission work amongst Jews, particularly when such work was conducted by persons totally ignorant of Jewish ideals and customs."[117]

By 1902, it was clear that a great many eastern Jews would not merely "pass through," and the missions turned their attention to gathering statistics on Edinburgh's resident Jewish community. A report compiled by the United Free Church's Medical Mission to the Jews in that year put the number of Jewish individuals "resident" in Edinburgh at 2,500 "but it is known that besides these there are very many Jews who live here temporarily."[118] The same report stated that "the great majority of these Jews have been refugees from oppression in Russia, but more especially, of late years, in Roumania [sic], and a very large number of them are found living in a ceaseless struggle with direst poverty."[119] The *Jewish Year Book* (1901–1902) listed Edinburgh as having the 10th largest Jewish community in Britain and Ireland, just behind Dublin, Hull and Newcastle, and this was using a conservative estimate of the Jewish population of the city.

That the Jewish population of the city increased greatly at the turn of the century is illustrated by figures from the Edinburgh Jewish Medical Mission. In 1895, 80 patients went to the dispensary, and 170 prescriptions were issued. By 1905 the number of Jewish visitors to the dispensary was 1308, and 800 prescriptions were issued.[120]

As early as 1902 the Jewish Medical Mission, operated by the United Free Church, were offering Hebrew and English classes to recent immigrants.[121] The Mission had been created on 7 June 1900, following the amalgamation of the Edinburgh Jewish Dispensary and the Jewish Mission, two separate committees which had been in operation since 1896.[122] A charity claim filed with the Inland Revenue in 1909 stated that any income received by the Mission is applied to "medical purposes and evangelical teaching to Jews." It also requested that the property at 24 Nicolson Street, which served as the Mission headquarters, be exempt from property tax.[123] Later in the claim, the Mission stated their objectives as "to supply medical aid and evangelical teaching to Jews in Edinburgh and it is supported by voluntary subscriptions and bequests. A considerable amount is expended on charity to the poor."[124]

In its early years of operation, the Mission was aided by a converted Jew named David Sandler. The Mission's report for 1902 states that Sandler had been a medical student at Edinburgh University for several years, "with the object of qualifying himself for employment as a Medical Missionary to Jews."[125] Commencing in October 1901, Sandler devoted much of his time, on a voluntary basis, to the running of the dispensary as well as evangelical work. In December 1901 he made a suggestion to the Mission directors that they should provide "two or three Jewish periodicals such as the *Jewish Chronicle* as … the Jew will appreciate very much our paying attention even to his want of newspaper reading."[126] Sandler made such an impression with the directors that he was appointed Chief Missionary in March 1902.[127] A year later Dr. Sandler moved to Constantinople as a United Free Church Missionary to the Jews.[128]

Dr. Sandler was later replaced by a Yiddish-speaking, converted Jew from Palestine named Leon Levison, who would go on to receive a place in posterity for his services to messianic Judaism, in addition to a knighthood for "services to Russian Jewish relief."[129] On the activities of this group, one young "Hebrew Christian" reported that "I have valuable help from Mr Levison, and while teaching them we do not neglect the opportunity to tell of Jesus, the Son of David, who is the Christ."[130]

Levison ran language classes at the Mission's premises at 46 Lauriston Place for Jewish immigrants on Mondays and Thursdays from 7 p.m. to 9:30 p.m. "which are well attended, a goodly number coming regularly." He also performed "from thirty-five to forty visits a month to those who cannot come to the Mission, owing to illness and various other causes." Of these visits he adds that "I have been received with open arms, and sometimes I cannot get away from houses. The Jews do like discussions on religious subjects."[131]

Levison would have been attuned to the value of language classes as a conduit for Christian teaching. According to his brother Nahum, Leon had wanted to learn English as a boy, and the only English teaching available was that offered by the School of the Free Church of Scotland Mission. Nahum stated that "English lessons continued, and the discussions also included the claims of Jesus as Messiah."[132]

In addition to "doorstep" missionary activity and language classes, the Mission also operated a hospital. In 1905 alone the hospital treated over 1,000 destitute Jewish immigrants in need of medical assistance.[133] The vast majority were poor Russians who required their medical advice in Yiddish. One condition for treatment was imposed: "that the Jews listened to the Word of God while they were awaiting attendance at the dispensary. That Word was given in Yiddish by Leon."[134]

It is quite clear that the Jewish Medical Mission was targeting recent immigrants for conversion, as opposed to the more acculturated element of Edinburgh Jewry. This transparency is illustrated if only by the geographical location of the Mission over time, as it moved closer to the areas of Jewish ghettoization near the Graham Street synagogue in 1906, and then into Nicolson Street after the Great War.[135] The annual report for 1907 reveals that there was some anxiety among Mission members about the move. It is unclear whether this anxiety was due to a realization that the move was highly inflammatory, or whether being close to the Synagogue would do more harm than good in terms of conversions. In his annual address, Levison stated that:

> a year ago there had been doubts in the minds of some as to whether our proximity to the Synagogue might not be an obstacle, but these doubts are now happily dispelled, more Jews having been attracted to the Mission on account of its position than had ever come to the old quarters in Spittal Street.[136]

The attitudes displayed by some of the Missionaries are quite remarkable, and during the annual meeting in 1907, some statements were made which bore the hallmarks of religious anti–Semitism. An anecdote was relayed to the members present regarding a Jewish man who, during a Bible class run by the Mission, disputed the fact that Jesus was the Messiah. The man was referred to as a "bigoted Jew."[137] Furthermore, the treasurer and secretary, John Lusk, told the audience that, "Jewish obstinacy and intolerance have been powerful since Israel became a nation."[138]

At the annual meeting in 1908, Lusk linked persecution to opportunity, stating that "continued persecutions in recent years have caused many to think, and in our city, and wherever Jews are to be found, a growing spirit of enquiry is found."[139] Other dubious comments included those of the Rev. James E. Houston who told the assembly that "it could hardly be said that usually the Jews were in themselves a loveable people. But an interesting people they certainly were, even on account of their nationality." Mr. John Gavin saw the levels of mass migration as a culmination in the story of the "Wandering Jew," arguing that "the Jews are today a living evidence of the truth of Scripture and of the Messiah whom they themselves deny." The Rev. Robert Law, said that while Edinburgh's Jews "formed an important element in the general population of the city," they should consider their work as a foreign mission since "though sojourning in their midst, the Jews were, and would remain, a separate people."[140]

Despite these suspect statements and dubious tactics, the Mission does seem to have been successful in attracting young women and mothers to its language classes and Sunday schools. That conversions took place is undoubted, although numbers seem to have been very modest.[141] It should also be added that ministers showed restraint and patience when contacted by Jews seeking conversion. In contrast to the rapid path to baptism that perturbed the Reverend Fürst, the Edinburgh Medical Mission in one case took seven months to follow through on a baptism request from one young Jew, and the average seems to have been around six months.[142] Weekly attendance at a Hebrew Christian Sunday service in Edinburgh averaged about 27, and an annual picnic organized by the Church attracted no less than 150 individuals in 1907.[143] This small success could be attributed, at least in part, to the material aid offered to Jewish immigrants. Mrs. McIntyre, leader of the Women's Meetings, wrote in her annual report for 1907 that, "many of the women brought babies and young children."[144] As the infants "were a rather disturbing element to the peace of the meeting," a crèche was established in an upstairs room. It was added that "a cradle has been given as a gift, and also toys and games, and a kind young lady, Miss Roberts, comes to amuse the young Israelites during the hour the address is given."[145]

Considerable comment was made on the women themselves. McIntyre stated that "not only is the diversity of nationality among our Jewesses considerable, but their educational attainments are also varied." Thus, some of the women were described as "remarkably intelligent," while for others it was found "beneficial to provide, from time to time, a little elementary instruction."[146] It was also stated that the women exhibited "sobriety, industry, and affectionate response to kind treatment." In 1907, the Women's Meeting established a small sewing circle, which provided some employment, "the remuneration for which has helped them a little in their struggle for subsistence." Poverty among the women was often apparent. McIntyre noted that "the poverty has been so great that many of the girls who come to my classes are nearly bare-footed, and I have had to get a subscription from the funds to provide them with boots, to prevent them getting ill this terribly damp and wet winter."[147] In his address to the Mission's annual meeting in 1908, Leon Levison referred at length to the poverty of Edinburgh's Jews. Levison informed the gathering that "it is in visiting that our greatest difficulties lie, owing to the heart-rending poverty and distress. Our hearts and souls are stabbed to the core by the sights we behold."[148]

It could be argued that the missionaries were quick to read too much importance into the behavior of Edinburgh's Jewish population. For example, the abandonment of dietary law by assimilating, secular, or indeed starving Jews was portrayed in the following terms in the Mission's annual report for 1907:

> The old wall of exclusiveness is fast being broken down; the scrupulosity regarding "meats" and "drinks" etc, is far less rigidly observed among the Jews; very many are quite ready to sit at a Gentile table, and partake of food with us, without regard to the minutiae of "kosher" (clean) and "treifa" (unclean). Many former hindrances, therefore, to social intercourse, are being removed.[149]

This naivety on the part of the missionaries often led to public embarrassment. The *Edinburgh Evening Dispatch* carried an article in July 1902 in which it was argued that:

> £1,100 has been spent on the "conversion" of three Jews in Edinburgh, and not one of these has been faithful to the new creed. We are accustomed to hearing a great deal about the conversion of these Jews, over whom ministers in Assemblies almost shed tears of thankfulness, but we never hear from the same conveners of these scamps when they have bolted or kicked over their traces.[150]

The article continued to argue that this is "unfair" to the public, who contributed funds to the Missions. It also stated that the methods employed by the Missions showed "them to be but agencies for the development of rogues and loafers." It concluded with the assertion that "there is no question of the sincerity and exalted ideal of the missionaries, but their sincerity and zeal are blind."[151] The topic remained a point of discussion for over a month, with an article in August 1902 commenting on the fact that "another Jew who was converted in Edinburgh and handsomely assisted monetarily has quietly slipped to London and gone among his Jews friends there without mentioning his conversion."[152]

The apathy of the press toward conversion was often tainted with derogatory expressions regarding the Jews involved. They were "rogues and loafers," untrustworthy, and not worthy of the money and effort expended on them. This antagonism was just a small part of the wider expression of anti-alien feeling which swept Britain in the first decade of the 20th century, and which culminated in the Aliens Acts of 1905 and 1911.

A Hostile Reception

In June 1894, an adolescent by the name of Gilhooly found himself at the Police Court in Edinburgh. His crime was that he and his gang had organized the persistent and ongoing harassment of a Jew named Joseph Fineberg at his home in North Richmond Street. The bailie made it clear that he felt the motivation behind this harassment was anti–Semitic and xenophobic, adding that he had no doubt "these people were very much annoyed by these boys."[153] The targeting of Jewish families by groups of Edinburgh youths was ongoing in 1898. At a meeting of the Hebrew Social and Literary Association at the Graham Street Synagogue, W.T. Munro Hogg stated:

> One would think they would draw the line at boys and girls at school; not at all, children are singled out for special attack also, and to such a degree that parents have, again and again, reluctantly to interfere to prevent their children being abused and persecuted at our schools.... Many do not know of this shocking persecution to which many of you are subjected to in Edinburgh and will scarcely believe me when I tell them about it.[154]

Expressions of negativity toward Edinburgh's immigrant Jewish community were not limited to delinquent youths. In 1899, during a debate held in Edinburgh Town Council on whether music should be permitted in West Princes Street Gardens on Sundays, a petition in favor of the move was produced, with many of the signatures coming from areas of predominantly Jewish habitation. The dean of guild, William Ormiston, was reported to have asked, "What fool of a Gentile wandered into the Jewish quarter for the purpose of getting these Ishmaels of mankind to sign?"[155] He continued with the assertion that the Council should not allow itself "to be dragged at the heels of a Godless mob of Jews and infidels, but would rise like a wall of fire about their much-loved isle."[156] This reference to defending the "isle" strongly suggests that Ormiston was against the immigration of foreign Jews, as well as their participation in what he viewed as an attempt to desecrate the Christian Sabbath.

Edinburgh's Jewish leaders were disturbed by Ormiston's outburst. Within the week, three letters appeared in the local press condemning the language used. The Reverend Fürst referred to Ormiston's remarks in his sermon the following Saturday, and wrote to the town clerk "asking him to call on the Dean of Guild to withdraw the remarks he made."[157] Ormiston's response was coolly received, not surprising perhaps given the far from unequivocal apology he extended to Edinburgh's Jewish community. While conceding that he "may have used strong language on the subject," he stressed that it was "unwise that any Jews should have interfered with the manner of spending the Christian Sabbath."[158]

In July 1901, W.T. Munro Hogg again moved to defend the city's Jews. In a letter to the chief of police he stated that

> In the course of my visits, I find that many of them are much annoyed and ill-used by boys and girls who, when they discover the people to be Jews then proceed to annoy them by throwing rubbish into their shops, annoying and vexing their children, and in other ways showing their hatred and dislike and all upon the ground that they happen to be Jews.[159]

The first report by *The Scotsman*, which operated under a Tory-Unionist political outlook, reflecting fears about increased immigration came in June 1902. During the period in question, articles in *The Scotsman* were heavily imbued with opinion, with the result that there were few reports concerning the immigration debate which were not expressive in some way of a Tory-Unionist political agenda. Under the headline, "Undesirable Foreigners in Edinburgh," the article of June 1902 made it clear that the "foreigners" in question were Jews.[160]

On 16 January 1903, *The Scotsman* waded further into the immigration debate under the headline, "Alien Immigration in the Provinces."[161] In an article notable not just for its strong condemnation of foreign immigration, but also for its particular focus on the Jewish community, frustration was expressed at an alleged omission of the "provinces" in government and media treatments of the "Aliens Question." It began emphatically with the assertion that, "public attention here has been almost exclusively directed to the foreign immigration question as it affects the East End of London; and there is, perhaps, some little risk of our many provincial ghettos escaping notice altogether." The article went on to alert the reader to, "the formation and gradual spread of a perfect series of Jewries in the great trading and industrial centres of the kingdom." These "Jewries" were then described as being characterized by the "dirt and nastiness, the squalor and crime, superstition and vice, which are the salient features of the Hebraic settlements that one finds in the Russian and Polish frontier districts."

The Jews of the provinces were singled out as being particularly undesirable, being "lower, if that is conceivable, in intelligence and resource than those entering by way of the Thames." Admiration was shown for the highly selective and restrictive immigration policy of the United States, and Glasgow and Edinburgh were said to be enduring "swelling congregations." Yiddish was mockingly imitated at one point, followed by the statement that, "everywhere one hears the strange jargon that marks the foreign Jew." Jews were alleged to live in, "wretched and dirty little holes, foul-smelling and untidy." They were said to be inassimilable, since "in no city of the United Kingdom are the foreign comers so exclusive, so pertinacious in their caste proclivities, and so difficult to approach." Another contemporary source, referring to all immigrant communities in Scotland, noted that although "the second generation is bilingual ... inter-marriages with the Scotch are rare."[162]

The author of the article partook of the notion, common in the East

End of London, that the entire country was being "swamped" by dirty, foreign Jews, with a predilection for criminal behavior. The writer argued that, "the alien question has come to the front as a matter pressing for solution," since "the aliens have poured in for the last few years in hordes, small in themselves, but aggregating largely." Glasgow was singled out as being "positively inundated by foreign Jews in recent years." The article ended with an appeal to the anti–Semitic image of the Jewish octopus, and the admonition that, "there are very few centres of trade and industry where the alien settler has not fixed his tentacles and paved the way for his 'landsman's' coming."

The proportionately vast increase in the Jewish population of Scotland should be placed in the context of Edinburgh's growth during the period. Between 1881 and 1901, the population of Edinburgh grew almost 29 percent from 320,549 to 413,008.[163] The third statistical account of Scotland states that between 1881 and 1901, 24,000 migrants came to live in the city.[164] If the figure of roughly 2,000 is taken as the Jewish population of Edinburgh in 1901, then it can be said that Jews accounted for only 8 percent of Edinburgh's migrants. Italians, Highlanders and Islanders, and the Irish had arrived in hundreds and thousands, seeking work in the city's industrial districts as well as laboring jobs in the port at Leith. To illustrate just how cosmopolitan the city was becoming, one census excerpt showed that a "tenement block in Commercial Street in Leith housed three Germans, two Swedes, one Norwegian, a Dane and an Italian."[165]

While Jews represented only one part of a wider picture of immigration to Scotland, and Britain in general, it must be stated that that in terms of the political climate of the period, the term "immigrant" came to be synonymous with eastern Jews. One article in *The Scotsman* in 1911 maintained that "the largest foreign community in the city consists of Jews.... They are principally Russian Jews; probably not more than a score of German Jews."[166]

In May 1903, the *Edinburgh Evening Dispatch* printed an article titled "A Crusade against the Jews," in which it was stated, on the authority of a local estate agent that "the average Jew is an undesirable tenant."[167] Significantly, several letters were subsequently received by the editor from both Christians and Jews, defending the city's Jewish community. By the end of the month the paper was forced to issue the following statement, which is worth quoting in full:

> The Jewish people are proud of their record and their race, and it is perhaps a wholesome sign that so many of them should have jumped so eagerly into the breach to defend their compatriots from the aspersions of certain house-factors. In doing this our correspondents, rather ungenerously, as we think, fall foul of ourselves for publishing the opinions of these factors. This we did without in any degree professing to affirm or question their accuracy. There are, of course, Jews and Jews, just as there are Christians and Christians, and this may be said of the Jews in Edinburgh, as has been repeatedly

asserted before the Alien Commission in London, that they are singularly law-abiding and industrious in the sense of being orderly and desirous of living in harmony with their neighbours. They are seldom—if we except some degraded exceptions who live on the misery of their female victims—brought up for the offences which swell the statistics of crime, and the reason for this seems to lie in their sobriety, in which respect they set an example to their Christian neighbours.[168]

As 1903 progressed, and the "Aliens Question" became a national debate, *The Scotsman* continued to give disproportionate attention to the arguments made in favor of restricting foreign immigration. In February 1903, the newspaper carried a report on the meeting of the Glasgow Municipal Commission on the Housing of the Poor.[169] Despite the fact that the meeting was intended to discuss "pauperism" in general, the article devoted particular attention to the witness statement of one Professor Smart, who deviated from the preceding themes under discussion. In response to a question relating to the number of unskilled laborers living in poverty, Professor Smart took the opportunity to rail against alien immigrants, who "were a menace to the industrial life of the community, and besides reducing native employment and wages, contributed largely by their habits to overcrowding and supervision by the local authority."[170]

By the early summer of 1903, a Royal Commission on Alien Immigration had been set up with the express purpose of determining the impact foreign immigrants were having on the nation. *The Scotsman* carried regular reports on the matters under discussion by the Commission, which was headed by Major Evans Gordon, MP for Stepney and one of the most vocal advocates for restricting alien immigration in Britain. This regular reportage on the progress of the Commission suggests that there was indeed "provincial" interest in the immigration debate, and that it was not solely of importance to London.

In May 1903, *The Scotsman* reported on a sitting of the Commission, during which the subject of "Aliens in Scotland" was under discussion.[171] During the sitting, Mr. J. Pinto, a Jewish immigrant living in Glasgow, was questioned by Major Evans Gordon. Pinto began by stating, "the total Jewish population of the place was about 6000, and although the majority of them were foreigners, very few had come there direct from the Continent, whilst a large percentage were natives and children who had been born in the country and were therefore British subjects." In contrast to the statement given by Professor Smart less than three months earlier, Mr. Pinto argued that, "overcrowding amongst the foreign Jews did not exist in Glasgow" and that "during the past five years not more than six prosecutions ... for overcrowding had taken place against the Jews." He finished by stating that "rents had not been affected either," that "many of the sons of foreign Jews had joined the local Volunteer Corps," and that "there was a marked absence of serious crime among the Jews." The final say, however, was given to Major Evans Gordon, who put it to Mr. Pinto that "the foreign element in Scotland was leading to a decrease in the standard of wages, and that Scottish miners had complained about competition from foreigners."[172]

The subject of aliens in Scotland remained a preoccupation of the Royal Commission for the remainder of May 1903. Only 10 days after Mr. Pinto's appearance before the Commission, the subject of alien workers in Scottish mines emerged again. The events of this sitting appeared in *The Scotsman* under the heading, "Employment of Foreigners in Scottish Mines."[173] The witness statement was given on this occasion by a Mr. Ronaldson, "His Majesty's Inspector of Mines for the Western Division of Scotland." He had been called before the Commission to give an insight into "the life and characteristics of alien workers employed in Scottish mines." In his opening remarks, Mr. Ronaldson stated that the immigrant workers, "mostly came from Poland," and that "very little exception could be taken to them." The report continued that, "he had for many years examined the records to see whether they were responsible for any accidents in the mines, and he had not found one incident." This was in response to allegations, common at the time, to the effect that foreign workers caused accidents due to poor communication and language skills, and inferior foreign training, if in fact they had any training. Ronaldson continued to praise the immigrant workers for their "sobriety and industrious habits."[174]

This seems to have raised the chagrin of Major Evans Gordon, who proceeded to cross-examine Mr. Ronaldson, putting it to him that the foreign workers were undercutting wages, and were taking advantage of openings created by striking Scotsmen. In response to Mr. Ronaldson's claim that the immigrant workers didn't break rules, Evans Gordon responded asking, "Their numbers are increasing are they not?" and followed this by asking Ronaldson if he was suggesting that, "work in the mines would be diminished were it not for the foreigners." When asked how he accounted for the opposition to alien immigration from the Scottish Miners' Union, Ronaldson replied, "Well, I suppose it is Scotland for the Scottish. I cannot tell the exact reason."

Having secured the desired answer, Major Evans Gordon is reported to have read out a section from the *Labour Leader*, a publication of the Miners' Union. In this extract, an account is given of a dispute in the district of Tannochside "owing to certain foreign workmen being willing to work for a rate of wage which was lower than that current in the district." The article concluded with the closing statement, not of the witness, but of Major Evans Gordon, who stated that, "at a time when there is an over-surplus of labour, these foreigners are employed in places that could be occupied by British workmen."[175]

In February 1904, the *Daily Mail*, argued that:

> the East End of London is not the only place infested by the superfluous alien. In the south of Scotland it appears there are 4,000 Polish Jews working in the coal mines, and the stringent regulations to prevent explosions must be so much greek to the majority of the them.¹⁷⁶

The home secretary, Mr. Akers-Douglas, was forced to issue a statement explaining that mines inspections had shown that the foreign miners were no cause of danger, and that 1,600 foreigners were employed in Scotland's mines. It was clear, however, that the vast majority of these foreigners were not Jews but Gentile Poles, Germans, Scandinavians and Lithuanians. As the Reverend Fürst stated, in response to the *Daily Mail*,

> It may be observed that Mr. Akers-Douglas does not state that all, or any, of the aliens referred to are Jews, and there is no reason to think that they are. During the twenty-five years I have been in Edinburgh, thousands of poor Jewish aliens have passed through my hands, and only two or three had at some time or another been employed in a mine.¹⁷⁷

By May 1904, opinion on the immigration debate within the pages of *The Scotsman* mellowed somewhat. It is likely that this mellowing occurred because statistics on immigration were coming to light following several reports by the Royal Commission, the Board of Trade and also through published summaries of transmigration. In the main, these reports suggested that the "swamping" rumors proffered by agitators were not founded on fact, and that the majority of foreigners were transmigrants whose ultimate destination was the United States. Yet, while reactions to the "Alien Question" were perhaps not as full of alarm, alien immigration remained a concern.

Following the publication of figures by the Board of Trade in May 1904, *The Scotsman* warned that "the outflow of native and the inflow of alien population in these islands are movements that deserve to be carefully watched."¹⁷⁸ The article continued by arguing that, "by their combined effect they are slowly bringing about important changes in the economic condition and in the very constituents of the population, especially in large towns." Using the figures from the Board of Trade, the report stated that, "149,000 were taken from the native population and 14,000 were added to the alien population of the United Kingdom." Yet although stressing that Jews, "in some respects form an undesirable element of the population," the report concluded with the assertion that in London, "they contribute only 0.74 per cent of the pauperism." Thus, it would appear that the emergence of firm statistics led to more considered reporting on the immigration debate in Scotland.

The outflow of the native population and the influx of foreigners was a particular concern in Scotland. As early as 1899, leading Labour politician Keir Hardie gave evidence to the House of Commons Select Committee on emigration and immigration. Having been informed that more people left Scotland than entered it, he replied that, "it would be much better for Scotland if those 1,500 were compelled to remain there and let the foreigners be kept out.... Dr Johnson said God made Scotland for Scotchmen, and I would keep it so."[179]

December 1904, when the passing of the Aliens Act seemed increasingly likely, saw the increased profile of its most public advocate, Major Evans Gordon. In that month Gordon wrote an article on the "Aliens Question" which later appeared in *The Scotsman*.[180] Dismissing the figures published by the Board of Trade as inaccurate and misleading, Gordon proceeded to reiterate the charges of the anti-immigration lobbyists in a manner reminiscent of dystopian fiction. He argued that while other nations may benefit from immigration, "our aliens are struggle-for-lifers at the very bottom of the human scale."

> They intensify the overcrowding in the congested districts; they press into the glutted market for unskilled labour; and drag down the standard of living in the callings in which they engage to a level that is almost below anything that can be called human.

Evans Gordon continued with the allegation that, "the percentage of aliens tried in court had risen from seven per cent in 1892 to 22 per cent in 1902, and to 25 per cent in the first session of 1903." He concluded by pandering to anti-alien sentiment in Scotland:

> At Leeds this year Mr. Smilie of the Scottish Miners' Federation, moved a resolution urging the Government to take such steps as should prevent the influx of foreign unskilled labour into the mines of Scotland. He said that 200 unskilled foreigners were employed in Lanarkshire, and not 200 could speak half a dozen words of the English language. They were a source of constant danger to their fellow workers.

On 1 January 1906, the Aliens Act came into force, and "although not the first legislation controlling aliens, it was the first attempt to establish a system of immigration control upon entry."[181] Highly contentious, the legislation was for anti-immigration lobbyists not restrictive enough, and for those opposed to its implementation it was too restrictive. On 2 January, *The Scotsman* reported on its first day as law. Under the headline, "The Aliens Act in Force," the article covered events at Leith, Dover, Grimsby, Hull, and South Shields. On Leith, the report commented that officials "have had no occasion to enforce its provisions, as their have arrived from foreign ports only two steamers, none of which brought immigrants." Grimsby, where some immigrants were selected for deportation, received most attention. There, "no less than twenty-two of them failed to satisfy the requirements of the new Act. They were mostly Russians, Polish Jews, and Finns. Tailors and labourers by trade, all were practically destitute dirty, and clothed in rags." The inclusion of the immigrants' professions had significance in that most competition in terms of jobs was believed to emanate from artisans and those in the unskilled professions. The implication was that the Act, in its first day, was already "protecting" jobs.

A sense of disappointment was evident when *The Scotsman* reported on the operations of the Act in its second day.[182] In marked contrast to the energy expended in agitating for the Act, the Act itself represented an anti-climax to restrictionists in that it allowed for only a very small minority of immigrants to be classed as "undesirable." On Leith the article stated that "the only passenger who could be regarded as an immigrant had ample qualification to put him outwith the official category of undesirable alien." While the reporter awaited the first rejection at Leith, London was reported as rejecting "a number of passengers.... They were principally Russian refugees and Polish Jews." The Act was portrayed as working against the criminal alien, in one section titled, "An Undesirable Alien." A Solomon Markovitz, described as a German Jew, was reported as having been charged under the Act after being convicted of "loitering with intent to steal." He was to be "sent out of the country as an undesirable alien" after spending three months in prison.

Arguably, *The Scotsman* found the Act most admirable and effective as a means of removing the "criminal alien." In its first few months of operation, the newspaper published regular reports of foreign criminals charged under the Act. In February 1906, under the headline, "The Aliens Act and the Criminal Class," the newspaper covered the cases of "two aliens, Isidore Steiner and George Fraser" as well as another "seven alien criminals" for "offences including stealing jewellery and warehouse breaking."[183]

However, the view that the Aliens Act should be harsher became more prevalent as the year progressed, and deportations from Scotland failed to materialize. Also, it was becoming rapidly apparent that the Act "permitted the overwhelming majority of aliens to continue to land."[184] Frustration at loopholes in the Act was expressed in an article titled, "Another Band of Gypsies from Germany."[185] Over 50 German gypsies were said to have entered Scotland, arriving separately in order not to contravene Section 1 of the Aliens Act which rendered the Act only applicable "to vessels carrying more than 20 alien steerage passengers." The article was printed in April of 1906, and it was indeed quite possible that a great many immigrants were becoming versed with the more vulnerable facets of the Act, and adjusting their means and point of entry accordingly. This vulnerability was portrayed with frustration by *The Scotsman*, which pointed out that these most recent arrivals were the "same tribe as the others," referring to a wider group of around 100 gypsies in Scotland. The article stated that the gypsies "apparently desire to join forces." The "swarthy travellers" were said to have been "kept on the move by Edinburgh police," and much was made of the fact that "none of them could, or would, speak intelligible English."[186]

A substantial section of the article was devoted to the loopholes in the current Act, and speculation as to whether or not pressure should be brought upon the home secretary to close them. The tone was one of exasperation that this group, which was sure to "join forces" with the others, was able to enter the country. That they were undesirable, and probably criminal, was suggested in one section at the conclusion of the article. The gypsies were to be taken to Glasgow, "escorted across country by police, with the idea of preventing them deciding to encamp." The author felt compelled to add that, "no attempts were made by the wanderers to beg or steal."[187]

The notion that the Aliens Act should be directed mainly at Jews and gypsies is apparent when one compares the manner in which *The Scotsman* treated its impact on other groups. For example, Scotland, and in particular Edinburgh had a sizeable Italian community. In May 1906, just a matter of weeks after berating the influx of "swarthy travellers," *The Scotsman* turned its attention to "Italian Ice-Cream vendors and the Aliens Act."[188] Gone were the allusions to filth, crime, and economic competition. Indeed, this particular instance saw a number of Italian immigrants whose desire was "to go to Glasgow to fill situations there in connection with the ice-cream business," and *The Scotsman* felt that since these men "had the means of obtaining employment so as to support themselves, the men should not be prevented from landing." The uneven application of the Aliens Act is indicative of the fact that, "underlying the explicit political goals of immigration control, the aim to keep out undesirable aliens answered, anti-alien, and at times anti–Semitic, demands which particularly focused on the exclusion of Eastern European Jews."[189]

During these years, Jews were also marked out for special discussion, and presented in a negative light, during enquiries into Sunday trading. During a discussion by the Commission on Sunday Trading in May 1906, Mr. Thomas Hunter, town clerk of Edinburgh, felt moved to declare that about 45 Jewish-owned businesses were operating on Sundays in the city—a figure which seemed less impressive following his concession that the total number of businesses operating on Sundays in the city was "about 1,300."[190]

By 1908, the peak flow of migration to, or through, Scotland had passed. The immigration that continued consisted of the occasional movement associated with chain-migration—once the pioneer succeeded in becoming economically secure, he was in a position to invite his family to join him. A couple of events at ports in Britain are sufficient to demonstrate this. In March 1908, Itzig Woffenberg was detained at Grimsby along with his wife, daughter and son. Woffenberg was 60 years old, and a butcher by trade. He provided more than sufficient evidence that he was not destitute, that he fulfilled the financial requirements laid out under the Aliens Act, and he explained to immigration officials that he wished to travel with his family to join his daughter and son-in-law in Edinburgh. The officials stated that Woffenberg's daughter, aged 15, was more than welcome to join her sister, but the rest were denied entry on the grounds that Woffenberg was too old, couldn't speak English, and "the conditions of trade were against his being able to support his family in this country."[191] In September 1908, Nochim Davidson was also detained at Grimsby. He was allowed to enter the country only when one of his three brothers living in Edinburgh traveled to give testimony on his behalf, and guaranteed that he would be set up in employment as a traveling salesman.[192]

More than two years after the passing of the Aliens Bill, *The Scotsman* was still portraying immigrant Jews in a negative manner. In April 1908, in the middle of a report covering the importance of the Jewish vote in local elections in England, the writer dwelled on the perils of chain-migration and the supposed disloyalty of Jewish immigrants,

> The newly naturalized Jew ... has his eyes fixed on his relatives or parents in the lands which he has left, and judges political matters not from the standpoint of an English citizen but from that of a member of a persecuted race.[193]

Frustration at the lack of expulsions under the Act peaked again in July 1908, with the publication of official figures for 1907. The headline was quite telling—"The Expulsion of Criminal Aliens, Laxity in Scotland."[194] The article quoted figures showing that, "only one recommendation came from Scotland against 289 from England." It continued:

> This shows one out of every nine aliens sent to prison in England was recommended for expulsion, and only one out of 241 in Scotland, or otherwise that if the proportion had been the same in Scotland as in England there would have been 27 recommendations in Scotland instead of one.

The writer suggested that there was "an extraordinary shyness or indisposition on the part of the Criminal Courts in Scotland in the administration of the Act." Moreover, the reporter stressed that "the matter has not escaped the notice of the Home Secretary who refers to the paucity of recommendations from Scotland as 'remarkable.'"[195]

Breaking down the figures in terms of nationality, and noting the significant leniency shown in England toward Americans as opposed to Poles and Jews, the report asserted that, "the Courts are less disposed to recommend Americans for expulsion than aliens whose racial affinity is more remote." Reflecting on the figures overall, the writer concurred with the Home Office that, "this piece of Unionist legislation has proved successful." The report concluded with the following, and it is worth quoting at length,

> The alien question in Scotland has several phases. There are two classes of aliens who have greatly multiplied in recent years, and who are not especially welcome. It goes against the grain with most people to find an alien population from Eastern Europe speaking a language, unfamiliar even to the learned, founding communities in our

western mining villages. Another class … has developed in every town and village a trade which it has been found necessary to place under special police supervision.[196]

The allusions here were to economic competition, in the form of Catholic Lithuanian coal miners, and Jewish immigrants linked with crime, especially prostitution. The writer called for a further restriction of immigration, since it was then impossible "to restrict the influx of either class if they are not destitute on arrival." The report finished with the assertion that, "there seems to be no good reason why harbour should be given in this country to aliens who have shown by breach of our criminal law that they were unlikely to be honest and reputable members of the community," and that every foreign criminal should be "sent back to the care of his own people."[197]

Early the following year, *The Scotsman* reflected on the expulsion figures for the last quarter of 1908. Since a national breakdown was not provided by the Home Office at that date, *The Scotsman* was left to comment on figures for the United Kingdom as a whole. The figures showed that "ninety undesirable aliens were expelled from the country" during the quarter, and that "the total number expelled during the whole of last year was 356, compared with 317 in 1907."[198] The tone became negative as the report discussed the fact that of 699,288 alien passengers landing in the United Kingdom, only 61,680 could be classed as transmigrants. The article also noted that, "the number of aliens refused leave to land during the year was only 604 compared with 798 in the previous year." Referring to 21,777 alien steerage passengers admitted to the country, the report concluded with the assertion that "no information is available as to their intentions or movements."[199]

As the decade drew to a close, *The Scotsman* moved away from economic opposition to alien immigration, and instead focused its attention on supporting the Act as a bulwark against foreign criminals. July 1910 saw the publication of more figures for immigration and expulsion. In a brief article titled, "Working of Aliens Act, Effect on Alien Crime," the writer reported that "the expulsion provisions of the Act are having a very decided effect upon the amount of alien crime in the kingdom." Yet the attitude persisted that controls should be even more stringent. This was evident in the statement that "it is doubted whether the influence of the provisions is made as potent as it should be."

In September 1910, *The Scotsman* reported on the trial of "An Undesirable Alien" at the High Court in Edinburgh.[200] An Austrian, living under the improbable name of James Stewart, faced charges of theft and housebreaking. The prosecution called for his alien status to be taken into account, along with the fact that "Stewart" had "previously been deported and had returned to this country." The judge, having sentenced the prisoner to three years penal servitude and deportation, expressed concern "not merely with the crime, but with the statutory provision for the expulsion of undesirable aliens." Thus it appears that while members of the Scottish judiciary were attracting criticism from the media for failing to deport enough foreigners, some judges were themselves dissatisfied with the provisions for carrying out such expulsions.

At the close of the decade, *The Scotsman* had one final comment on the "Aliens Question."[201] In the week before Christmas 1910, shots were exchanged following a failed robbery in Houndsditch, London, between police and a gang of Latvian Jews. Three police officers were mortally wounded. Only a few days after the deaths, and with the identity of the suspects still unknown,[202] *The Scotsman* argued that they "were evidently experienced Continental burglars." Furthermore, the article expressed the opinion that the Houndsditch murders "do not stand alone as evidence of the risks that both police and people run from these desperate characters, recruited from the dregs of Continental crime that find harbourage in the East End of London and in other crowded centres." The writer argued that these murders were mere symptoms of "the fact that there are, living among us, a large class of criminals of alien nationality and customs, familiar with, and prone to use, the knife." This new criminal, who was "not of home growth," was "less amenable to our home methods and weapons of control." The reporter raged that "it is plain beyond cavil that the murders were the work of adepts and past masters in desperate crime, foreign importations and trained and exercised in a foreign school." It continued to speculate that the perpetrators were likely to be "a band of Polish or Lithuanian Jews." The writer declared these Eastern European immigrants to be "a mass of incendiary and revolutionary men, criminal in instincts and habits." The article concluded with the warning that this type of crime "might possibly prove infectious—unless precautions are taken to prevent this hideous danger spreading."[203]

The Houndsditch murders would go on to create a new wave of anti-alien agitation in 1911, one that would provoke the harsher regulations so consistently called for in *The Scotsman*. This time the Bill in question made specific reference to "alien criminality," and was titled "The Aliens (Prevention of Crime) Bill."

The reception of Jewish refugees and immigrants in Edinburgh, by both Jew and Gentile, bore a resemblance to that witnessed in many parts of Britain. Early responses to persecution in Russia were admirable in their strength of conviction, and notable in their generosity. The period was highlighted by the close cooperation of Edinburgh's Jewish and Christian communities, and the actions of Scottish churches in contributing substantial aid toward those who lost their homes during the expulsions. The early period of persecution witnessed the combined effort of Edinburgh's clerical and municipal authorities, and the numerous funds and public awareness projects that this effort supported.

Yet Edinburgh's response to Jewish immigration was both multi-faceted and continually evolving. Edinburgh's Jewish community struggled with its own poverty in order to provide for those who came to augment it. Its leaders engaged in philanthropy, and encouraged others within the community to do all in their power to help those less fortunate. When this was not forthcoming, it often led to acrimony and was a source of discontent. Edinburgh's Jewish charitable effort was able to survive and succeed through innovation and cooperation with external bodies, as witnessed in the creation of the self-sustaining Benevolent Loan Society, and the numerous grants awarded by Jewish organizations in London. By such means, Edinburgh's Jewish charitable effort was successful in its goal of keeping the vast majority of its immigrants off the Poor Rates, and provided enough support to prevent its newest members from resorting to crime in order to survive.

Edinburgh's Jewish leaders were forced to confront the challenge of Christian missionaries, whose tactics often preyed on the poverty and destitution which marred the lives of many Jewish immigrants. The attitudes of the missionaries changed over time, from optimism at the outset of their endeavors in the city, to pessimism and frustration bordering on anti-Semitism in later years. The missionaries saw little real success during their time among the city's immigrant Jews, and the receipt of material aid was often naively misinterpreted as a sign of "an emerging spirit of enquiry."

Perhaps the most interesting evolution in Edinburgh's reaction to Jewish immigrants was the move from sympathy to antipathy. The early protests at Tsarist persecution and the admirable cooperation of Jew and Gentile steadily dissolved as the Jewish victim abroad became the Jewish neighbor at home. As such, Edinburgh and Scotland were not immune from the anti-alien sentiment which swept the nation in the first decade of the 20th century. Contemporaries struggled to imagine how this new community could possibly integrate, and often resorted to the kind of slanders and bigoted attitudes which they so loudly denounced when uttered in the East. Much of it, of course, was rooted in confusion and ignorance of Jewish life and religious practice. It is to the economic, social, and religious life of these early immigrants that this study now turns its attention.

3

Edinburgh's Jewish Quarter, 1880–1910

Several streets to the east of Nicolson Street, taking in the Richmond Streets, the Pleasance, and its immediate environs, was for many years inhabited almost exclusively by Jews.[1]

The development of Edinburgh's Jewish community prior to the Great War should be understood in the context of the period, which was one of mass migration involving many different immigrant groups. It is equally important that any assessment of Jewish communal life in Edinburgh should be seen against the backdrop of the city as a whole. Although Edinburgh's immigrant Jewish community was in some respects insular, particularly though perhaps unsurprisingly in relation to religious and cultural practices, this community was subject to economic and social influences beyond its confines and control. This chapter seeks, in one respect, to connect the story of the Edinburgh's Jewish immigrants with that of their environment. Jewish immigrants could choose to settle in Edinburgh, but the harsh realities of tenement life in the slums would have been a far cry from the benevolent metropolis they may have envisaged before their journey from the East, or indeed from the marvelous Georgian facade which first greeted them on their arrival. This chapter examines the conditions in which Edinburgh's Jewish community began to develop following the years of migration, up to the introduction of the Aliens Bill of 1911, before going on to explore the various facets which comprised Jewish communal life in the period.

Scottish society at the turn of the century was coming to terms with changes in its population. Between 1861 and 1901, the population had increased by almost one and a half million.[2] Immigrants in Scotland, from outside Britain and Ireland, accounted for only 47,000, with the result that while some elements of the English press were bemoaning a rapidly increasing population as well as the "swamping" of the nation by foreign hordes, Scottish society was forced to contend with the fact that during the 19th century the country had "lost more of her citizens by emigration than she gained by the influx of others."[3] In fact, Scotland lost a higher proportion of her natural increase through emigration between 1881 and 1930 than any other Western European country except Norway and Ireland.[4] One contemporary declared that the scale of the Scottish Diaspora meant "the Scot is as international as the Jew."[5]

The roots of this emigration lay to some extent in the decline of the crofting class and changes in the Scottish economy, which offered opportunities for some more than others. Those whose skill, expertise, and way of life lay in the glens saw little of attraction in Scotland's burgeoning industrial centers. Ian Adams stated that, "during the nineteenth century Scotland experienced what has been called the 'urban transition'—the change from an overwhelmingly rural society to a predominantly urban one."[6] In the 1860s and 1870s the Scots were renowned for marine engineering, and by the 1880s "iron was giving way to steel, sail to steam" and it was the Scots who took the lead in the rebuilding of the merchant fleet.[7] In addition to heavy engineering and iron and steel production, Scotland also took the lead through its coal mining. A full quarter of the Scottish labor force was employed in either coal mining, ship-building, or mechanical engineering.[8]

Mining towns grew, and the cities swelled. By 1911, "Scotland was the second most urbanized country in the world" after England, and "30% of Scotland's population in 1911 lived in Glasgow, Edinburgh, Dundee, and Aberdeen."[9] A sizeable number of this new population of city-dwellers originated outside Scotland, most notably in the case of the Irish, who had arrived in their thousands throughout the 19th century. Immigrants, unlike the crofters and other emigrant classes, perceived opportunity in these changes. Henry Maitles stated that "of the 3,300,000 Polish Jews in 1920, 76 per cent were urban ... the Jews traditionally had been restricted to and attracted to certain trades and commerce which tended to be urban."[10] When they emigrated, Jews overwhelmingly "gravitated towards the cities."[11]

Resentment toward this new foreign population often combined with anxiety at the continuing emigration of native Scots. An 1851 *Report on the Census of the City of Glasgow and Suburbs* concluded that:

> Within the last ten years the children born here of Irish parents have been very numerous; but these of course are all put under the heading of Scotch. While, therefore, there appears to be an increase of 2.07 percent in the present enumeration above that which the Irish bore to the population of 1841, the real number of inhabitants who are imbued with Irish characteristics, habits, feelings and religious sentiments is infinitely greater.[12]

Thus it is apparent that in some quarters there was a perception of Scottish identity based on religion, "characteristics," "habits," and "feelings" which was not only exclusive but which was also rendered the culture and way of life of some outsiders to be fundamentally "incompatible with being 'Scotch.'"[13]

The latter half of the 19th century confronted the officials of Scotland's chief cities with an unprecedented housing problem. Demand, arising from a rapidly increasing urban population, far outstripped supply, resulting in a property boom in the 1870s. The rush to make money "gave rise to a great deal of jerry-building."[14] Conditions in these unsafe buildings were made worse by the desire of landlords to profit from occupational density. A 19th century report on Edinburgh's housing situation stated that one tenement had 59 rooms, and contained "fifty-six families and two hundred and forty-eight people, without a water supply of any kind."[15] By 1861, a third of Scotland's population was living in one-roomed dwellings, and of these 8,000 lacked windows.[16]

This manner of housing the growing urban population carried other risks—a one-roomed dwelling "had double the infant mortality rate of that of four rooms. It had three times the death rate from tuberculosis."[17] Sir John Gorst's 1907 survey of child health in Great Britain and Ireland, found that 75 percent of Edinburgh's children were "ailing in one way or another, principally from disease of the nose, throat and ears."[18] In fact, at the beginning of the 20th century, Scotland's economic and industrial progress was not matched by progressive social care, and as a country it "lagged behind the improving standards of the developed nations."[19] It was in this dynamic, changing, and uncertain Scotland that Edinburgh's Jewish immigrants found themselves in the years 1880–1910, and it is to the Jewish district of the city that this study now turns its attention.

Housing

Between 1880 and 1900, an area of Edinburgh, primarily comprising the Pleasance, Nicolson Street, North Richmond Street, South Richmond Street, and Roxburgh Place became the center of Jewish habitation in the city. It was to this collection of streets that the Dean of Guild, William Ormiston, referred to as the "the Jewish Quarter" during a heated debate on Sunday trading in 1899.[20] Of the 76 Jewish businesses in Edinburgh recorded in Eugene Harfield's 1894 *Commercial Directory of the Jews*, 49 were located within this network of streets.

The extent to which this residential clustering was deliberate remains unclear. Kenneth Collins seems to suggest it was a deliberate occurrence, stressing the "familiarity" of the ghetto atmosphere, and the sense of security and tradition that came with a district not only heavily populated by Jews, but also offering Jewish bakeries, butcher shops, guest houses and even a kosher dairy.[21] Henry Maitles concurred, arguing that, "it was natural for non-English speakers to congregate initially, a welcome in an unwelcoming atmosphere."[22] David Daiches argued that for Edinburgh's Jews, the continuity offered by bringing elements of life in the *Shtetl* to their new lives in Edinburgh was a crucial means of ensuring the preservation of a Jewish identity. In both religious matters and the manner in which they led their day to day lives, "for Jews continuity was bound up with identity, and to break with tradition meant to risk existence as Jews."[23] Linda Fleming stressed an urge to recreate a Jewish home in a foreign land, arguing that, "for newly arrived Jews on the social scale, it did represent a semblance of home, a *Shtetl* in urban Scotland, which provided many of the features of a Jewish communal infrastructure. Not quite the golden land, but good enough it seems."[24]

Similarly, Irena Kudenko and Deborah Phillips argued that Jewish geographical concentration in Leeds was "central to the preservation of a distinctive religious identity and a traditional interpretation that discourages social mixing with outsiders."[25] Alternatively, they offered the explanation that "clustering supports a sense of communality based on socio-cultural differences, arising from a shared past."[26] That many of the eastern European Jews in Edinburgh had a shared past is not unlikely, with many possibly originating in the same village. Max Mendick recalled that his father first arrived in Leeds from Lithuania. Facing a lack of opportunities there, he acted on the fact that "he'd heard that there were a lot o' folk from our village in Edinburgh."[27]

However, there are also arguments that this recreation of the ghetto was not purely the result of deliberate clustering. Gorbals resident Ralph Glasser recalled that attempts were made to inhabit the city of Glasgow more sporadically, in the belief that "a mixed building was less likely to attract the impulsive anti-Semitic attack."[28] However, it is not only evident that residential clustering did occur in Edinburgh and Glasgow, but also that identifiable Jewish districts emerged in Stepney (London), Leylands (Leeds), and Strangeways (Manchester), as well the countless streets and squares inhabited mainly by Jews in hundreds of towns scattered throughout the "provinces."

One explanation is that in every city there tends to be a district where accommodation is cheapest. This could be said of the densely populated tenements of what would become the Edinburgh Jewish quarter, as well as the Gorbals and the other areas mentioned previously. The majority of immigrants would not have had the money for accommodation other than the one-roomed "houses" in the tenement blocks. The disparate settlement of Edinburgh's older, wealthier community suggests that while religious and cultural bonds were strong, for them this did not necessitate living in close quarters with one another. David Daiches states that Edinburgh's Scottish-born Jews were adamant that practicing their religion did not compel the duplication of "the life their fathers had led in the East European ghetto."[29] If "Jewishness" was one of the reasons behind residential clustering, it was a type of "Jewishness" at odds with that pursued and practiced by the established community in Edinburgh.

Another, though related, explanation for residential clustering was the practice of sub-letting by resident Jews. Linda Fleming explains that, in Scottish cities,

> Private landlords owned either entire buildings or single flats, and properties were let to tenants through the medium of "housing factors." These middle men had the responsibility of leasing and maintaining the building. Thereafter, sub-letting by tenants themselves was commonplace, and lodgers taking one room, or more often the share of a room, was a usual domestic arrangement.[30]

That some Jews in Edinburgh were sub-letting to newly-arrived Jewish individuals and families is beyond doubt. During a litigation case in 1901, an Albert Isadore Bernstein sued S. Epstein, a tenant who had fallen behind in rent payments for his home in Merchant Street, a few blocks north-west from the "Jewish Quarter." Epstein counter-claimed, arguing that Bernstein had failed to pay him for goods he had produced in his profession as a tailor.[31]

Discrimination in housing may also have played some role in the ghettoization of Edinburgh's new immigrants. One contemporary stated that "before the First World War it was very, very hard for a Jew to get a house. One landlord after another: "No Jews!" If your name was Finkleberg then he'd say "No." So you'd just change it to Faulkner or something and if you didn't have a Semitic nose then you might get it."[32]

Landlords and "housing factors" in Edinburgh may also have partaken of the view, popularized by restrictionists in Britain at the time, that Jews were bad and undesirable tenants. A report in the *Scotsman* in February 1903 argued that Jewish immigrants "contributed largely by their habits to overcrowding and supervision by the local authority."[33] It is evident from the newspaper articles discussed in the previous chapter that some elements of public opinion at the turn of the century held Jews responsible for overcrowding in the slums, as well as associating areas of Jewish predominance as rife with filth, disease, and crime.

It is likely that residential clustering in Edinburgh and elsewhere occurred because of a combination of these factors. A shared religious, cultural, and even local history would have encouraged recent immigrants to live side by side. This would have fostered a sense of security, and aided the preservation of social, religious, and cultural traditions. The economic situation of these immigrants would have demanded that they live in the least expensive accommodation in the city. Of these areas, the rubber workers sought cheap accommodation in the Dalry district in the west of the city, while the majority of new immigrants found their home in the tenements not far from the Royal Mile. Jewish residential clustering would have been further encouraged by the practice of Jewish individuals sub-letting to new immigrants, and prolonged by the unwillingness of some landlords and house factors to let properties to Jews in more "respectable" areas.

Clues as to how Edinburgh's Jewish immigrants adapted to life in the slums can be gleaned from memoirs, newspaper articles, and reports on how Jewish immigrants lived in similar areas. Popular prejudice about squalor and filth in Jewish and Irish homes is often contradicted by some contemporary accounts. In Sir John Gorst's survey of the health of the nation's children, he noted that, in terms of parental responsibility, this "is already well performed by some of the poorest workers of this country, by the Jews settled in our great cities, whose poverty has caused them to be regarded as 'undesirable aliens.'"[34]

The study continued with an analysis of child nutrition in the slums of Leeds, which showed "the superior height and weight of Jewish boys and girls as compared with Gentiles," despite the fact that "the parents of the two sets of children were equally poor and their homes equally dirty and overcrowded."[35] As some means of explanation, Gorst quoted a Dr. Eichholz as saying that both Jews and Irish "make a great point of caring for their young children—it is in fact a matter of religious obligation with both—with the result that these two types very usually stand apart in the poorer neighbourhoods from the general degeneracy."[36]

Infant mortality in Jewish and Irish families was reported to be lower than the average for residents of slum districts, due in part to their alleged "better views as to the duty of a mother to her new-born child."[37] Cormac Ó Gráda noted that infant mortality rates among urban Jewish populations were lower across Ireland, as well as among Jewish immigrants to London and the United States. Definitive conclusions as to why this occurred are difficult to arrive at, though a consensus has been reached that diet, community support systems, sanitary laws and "the long experience of Jewish communities with urban living," contributed to the trend.[38] In the case of Edinburgh, its Jewish district may even have been marginally better than similar areas of Jewish immigrant habitation elsewhere in Great Britain. For example, Edinburgh was one of the few areas of the country in which a tuberculosis dispensary was operated, and this was pointed out by Jewish activists in 1910, who demanded a similar measure be introduced in Stepney.[39]

It also appears that the 1885 Housing of the Working Classes Act had been enforced more rigidly in Edinburgh than elsewhere. The Act gave local officials the power to condemn dangerous and unhealthy dwellings and often enforced quotas on the number of tenants who could inhabit a building. In Edinburgh, enforcement of the Act often came under the responsibility of the Sanitary Inspector. In November 1903, the Edinburgh Jewish Medical

Mission found that their rented premises at 15 Spittal Street, which housed Jewish converts and employees as well as acting as headquarters for the organization, had been condemned as unfit to be occupied as a dwelling place. When repairs carried out by the landlord proved unsatisfactory, the organization was forced to relocate.[40] During a meeting of the North London Jewish Literary and Social Union on 6 March 1902, the subject of housing and congested living conditions was raised. It was discussed how the Housing of the Working Classes Act might be better enforced in the area. It was noted that:

> By that means the number of occupants of a room either for working or sleeping purposes would be strictly limited. In Edinburgh the Act had been put into effect with considerable success. Sub-letting would thereby be done away with to a considerable extent, and if they were successful in breaking up the congestion they would confer great benefits on London Jewry.[41]

Also, in the area of disease, a report by the *Lancet* in 1888, recounted that "so far as the danger of infection is concerned, Edinburgh is better protected than many other towns, for here the compulsory notification of infectious diseases is enforced."[42]

Residential clustering did, however, have implications for the ability of Edinburgh's Jewish immigrants to interact with their non–Jewish neighbors. In a sense, the re-creation of the ghetto was so complete as to preclude the need for goods and services outside the community. Relationships and interactions with Gentile citizens are not quantifiable, but some conclusions can be derived from anecdotal evidence and the manner in which the ghetto was structured. For example, Evelyn Cowan, referring to the Jewish ghetto in Glasgow argued that for many immigrant Jews, "in our ghetto-like existence, the City of Glasgow seemed far away, the world even more remote."[43] On the infrastructure of the community she states that like Edinburgh, "very few of us lived outside that district. We had our own meeting places, dance halls, and especially our own type of food-shops. Congregating exclusively with our own kind, we hardly knew any Christian people."[44]

David Daiches stated that the vast majority of poor Jewish immigrants in Edinburgh "lived a life of self-contained Jewish orthodoxy."[45] While this study shows that participation in the commercial, professional and cultural life of Edinburgh was quite common among the upper strata of Edinburgh Jewish society, such interaction was rare among the first generation of the poorer immigrants resident in the Old Town tenements, or in the streets of Dalry. In order to gain a more complete understanding of how Edinburgh's Jewish community interacted with their Gentile neighbors and with one another, it is thus important to consider not only where they lived, but also the economic, religious, political, cultural and structural make-up of the community as a whole.

Religious Organization and Community Division in Jewish Edinburgh

That the Scots were themselves a people scattered throughout the globe is evidenced by the many newspapers in Canada, the United States, Australia and New Zealand, which carried a section devoted to "Notes from Scotland." Even in these broad surveys of events "back home," the growth and development of Scotland's Jewish community did not go unnoticed. Of these, perhaps the *Otago Witness*, published in New Zealand, is most notable. Having carried sporadic reports on Scotland's Jewish communities from at least the early 1890s, in July 1907 the newspaper informed its readers that "Mr. J.O. Kemp, advocate, in supporting an application by a Jewish grocer for a license to sell liquors, said that 20 years ago the Jewish community in Edinburgh consisted of only four families. Now the city had four Jewish churches, with four ministers, presided over by a Rabbi."[46]

While the figure of four families is a gross understatement of Edinburgh's Jewish population in 1887, the fact remains that Edinburgh's Jewish population, small by comparison with other cities of its size, was divided into as many as four congregations.[47] Aside from the established Edinburgh Hebrew Congregation, and in keeping with national trends, Edinburgh saw the rise and fall of a number of small immigrant religious societies, known as *chevroth*, during the period under examination.

Bill Williams has argued that in addition to divisions between established and immigrant Jews in Britain, there were significant factors influencing division *within* Jewish immigrant populations. As the result of differences in national origin, religious style, and conflict over "ways of being Jewish,"[48] as well as the influence of local personalities, the earliest period of immigration saw the creation of several *chevroth* in Edinburgh which, like those in Manchester and elsewhere, "were often no more than two back-yards covered with metal sheeting, a back room or an attic."[49] As time went on, and the socio-economic position of these immigrants improved, attempts were made to expand the individual *chevra* and "to convert it into a place of worship which would reflect its size and the improving status of its memberships."[50] This often involved a move to better premises, the appointment of a qualified rabbi, and the seeking of legitimacy by placing the congregation under the authority of the Chief Rabbi in London.[51]

The Park Place synagogue, home to the Edinburgh Hebrew Congregation, lay within the shadow of Edinburgh University. It was consecrated in 1868, and by 1880 still mainly served those assimilated, middle-class Jews whose families had settled in the city decades earlier. When a group of Jewish workers, comprising no more than 35 families, arrived from Manchester in 1879, seeking work at the Caledonian Rubber Company, they established a synagogue in Caledonian Crescent which lay in the western Dalry district of Edinburgh. By 1890 the premises used by these Dalry workers was known as "the *blecheneh Shul* because of its tin roof."[52] The congregation at Dalry had grown to such a size in 1890 that its premises were enlarged and redecorated. The Rev. Jacob Fürst was invited to carry out the consecration of the new premises, and presided over a congregation of members and "a number of Christian friends." In his address, Fürst acknowledged that separate religious arrangements were in some way necessary given the distance between the homes and workplace of the Dalry workers, but nonetheless urged "the members to keep closely united with their brethren of the old synagogue in Edinburgh, and to join in all their efforts to live in brotherhood and peace."[53]

The synagogue at Dalry continued to flourish at least in terms of numbers, and in 1892 yet another synagogue was consecrated in the district. On this occasion the ceremony was carried out by the Chief Rabbi.[54] A correspondent for the *Jewish Chronicle* in 1893, described the circumstances of the community, pointing out that "the humble inhabitants of the Dalry extremity of the city—a suburb in the West End of Edinburgh—have in consequence of the distance they live from Park Place, been constrained to establish a small branch of the present synagogue, worshipping in meaner quarters still: a gaunt, iron building."[55]

Links with the rubber works remained strong. When the Dalry synagogue found itself in debt in 1899, the Jewish manager of the Caledonian Rubber Works advanced it £70.[56] The manager of the Caledonian Rubber Works at that time was a D. Levenson, who lived in Gardner's Crescent, just outside the Dalry slum.[57] This assistance from Levenson was not sufficient to end the financial woes of Dalry's religious Jews. By March 1899, the "furnishings and effects" of the *Chevra* synagogue in Caledonian Crescent were "sequestered for rent." A Sheriff's warrant was subsequently obtained, permitting the sale of these goods by an auctioneer. The *Jewish Chronicle* explained that "the synagogue was in bad repair, with the result that the congregation gradually deserted it."[58] Other facilities in the area were used for a short time, though financial difficulties remained chronic. In 1908, a bazaar was held in aid of the congregation, during which the Reverend Fürst delivered a speech stating that "the congregation had had a long and hard struggle for many years to support the synagogue and school, and deserved encouragement from within and without."[59]

A number of smaller congregations were also formed during these years. A group arrived from Leeds seeking employment in a slipper factory in Guthrie Street, just outside the main Edinburgh ghetto. It was said that a small room in the factory was "fitted out as a synagogue."[60] In 1902, a small group of Hasidic tailors left London to take advantage of a strike among Edinburgh's tailors, and later "formed the nucleus of what was to become the Edinburgh Independent Hebrew Congregation."[61]

By far the most significant rival congregation to the Park Place synagogue was the congregation which had its synagogue first in Roxburgh Place, and later in North Richmond Street in the heart of Jewish Edinburgh. The precise date of the founding of this synagogue remains unclear. Collins cites the *Jewish Chronicle* of 22 January 1895 as recording the founding of the congregation in Richmond Street.[62] However, reference is made to the Edinburgh New Hebrew Congregation as early as 1890, and there is further reference to a meeting of the Edinburgh New Hebrew Congregation at the synagogue in North Richmond Street in 1893.[63]

Divisions within Edinburgh's Jewish community were noted by the Rev. Dr. Hermann Adler, Orthodox Chief Rabbi of the British Empire, during his visit to the city in July 1892. While speaking positively of the impressive achievements of the community, in terms of improving its infrastructure and maintaining religious observance, he informed the congregation at Park Place that, "it had filled him with grief and concern to think that there should be some ill-feeling, some lack of concord and brotherly fellowship between them and the professors of the same creed in that city."[64]

The roots of this "lack of concord" lay to a great extent in the social and economic gap between the wealthier members of the Edinburgh Hebrew Congregation and those who came to join it during the late 1880s. A series of letters to the *Jewish Chronicle* in November 1893 shed light on the origins of this discord, and the differing viewpoints held by the Edinburgh Hebrew Congregation at Park Place, and the Edinburgh New Hebrew Congregation now based in North Richmond Street. Maurice Isaacs, president of the Edinburgh Hebrew Congregation explained, in a letter dated 10 November, that:

> There is no doubt that those who have considered themselves justified in separating from us … have largely done so by reason of the scanty comfort we could offer them, and it is my ardent wish that, should the time come when we can be in a position to build a synagogue worthy of this city, and large enough for our requirements, that we will unitedly worship under one roof.[65]

Soon thereafter, a response was received from Bernard Turiansky, president of the Edinburgh New Hebrew Congregation. Expressing disagreement with Isaacs' assertion that the split came about due to "scanty room and comfort," Turiansky argued that the split came about due to "certain grievances and harsh treatment by the officials of the congregation."[66] These grievances concerned the alleged marginalization of recent immigrants in the decision-making process, and a sense that a condescending attitude was displayed toward recently arrived Jews by the established community.

The aforementioned Maurice Isaacs certainly had little in common with the newly arrived immigrants, at least on an economic and social level. Born in Edinburgh in December 1840, he ran a successful business as tailor and clothier. In 1890 he was elected to the Edinburgh Chamber of Commerce,[67] and by 1893 he had been chosen to chair the annual dinner of the Edinburgh Merchants Association, and was a Master of the Rifle Lodge of Freemasons, "the first Jew that has filled the Chair in any Lodge in Edinburgh."[68] In November 1904, Isaacs was added to the Commission of the Peace for Edinburgh—the first Jew to become Justice of the Peace in the city. He was joined two years later by Alphonse Louis Reis—another wealthy, British-born member of the Edinburgh Hebrew Congregation.[69] By contrast, Bernard Turiansky had arrived from Russia in the early 1880s, and ran a business which sold wholesale jewelry pieces to traveling salesmen, as well as furniture, from his premises one block south of the Old Town ghetto. He was naturalized in 1886.[70] Although neither man was entirely representative of his respective congregation, their backgrounds did, to a notable extent, reflect the make-up of their membership.

Of course, such splits along class and religious lines were not peculiar to Edinburgh. Nor were they peculiar to Jewish communities. However, in the early years of the 20th century, it is clear that such divisions were nonetheless a cause of concern and anxiety among British Jews. These concerns were not rooted solely in the belief that division was bad in itself, but also that division was a barrier to the Anglicization of the new immigrants. The last decade of the 19th century witnessed several attempts at the creation of larger synagogues in London which would bring newcomers under the same roof as British-born Jews, in a move described by David Cesarani as "an Anglicizing device and a death sentence on the *chevrahs*."[71]

Louis Hyman, in his study of Jews in Ireland, argued that splits were inevitable given the stresses endured by both newcomers and established communities. It was common for a large number of recent immigrants to break away from the parent congregation to re-create something closer to the religious practice they would have been more familiar with and felt more comfortable with. This pattern can be clearly seen in Edinburgh. Often the necessity for separate religious institutions arose because of reasons of geography, the poorer members requiring facilities closer to their area of residence. Subtly different religious traditions also played a role. Hyman states that in Ireland, "the newcomer was neither intellectually nor spiritually prepared to enter at once into liturgical fellowship with his Irish-born brethren in faith."[72] In addition, "differences of language, character, and temperament kept them apart."[73] Cormac Ó Gráda writes that Dublin's "'English' Jewish community was mainly middle class and English speaking, its workplaces and residences well dispersed across the city. It was inconspicuous and bent on integration."[74] Furthermore, the established community of Dublin tended to regard the newcomers as "rather ignorant and uncouth, and overzealous in religious orthodoxy."[75]

Despite having some wealthy members, the Edinburgh Hebrew Congregation was nonetheless poor by comparison with larger communities throughout Britain. In late 1894, the Corporation of Edinburgh moved to evict the congregation from the premises at Park Place under a special Act of Parliament for city improvement. In December 1895, the Edinburgh Hebrew Congregation filed legal proceedings challenging the takeover of the property, and seeking arbitration of the matter through the Court of Session. During the course of proceedings, representatives of the Edinburgh Hebrew Congregation stated that they would accept £4,000 for the property at Park Place. The Corporation agreed to meet the asking price as well as the costs incurred in bringing the case to the Court of Session.[76]

On Sunday, 26 August 1896, after serving Edinburgh's Jewish community for 28 years, the Park Place synagogue was draped in white for a closing ceremony. During a service of "an unusually impressive nature," the Reverend Fürst chose communal unity as the central theme to his address. He urged on those present:

> The requisites essential in order that the peace of any community could be preserved, and useless contention could be avoided, and asked them to unite hand and heart, course and action, so that nothing but brotherly union and a peace founded on the fear of God may reside within them.[77]

It was remarked that at the conclusion of the sermon, "a very pathetic prayer was offered up, which moved the entire congregation to tears."[78]

By July 1896, the leadership of the Park Place synagogue had settled on a former church in Graham Street as sufficient for their requirements. Correspondence negotiating the sale reveals that the final fee for the property in Graham Street was just over £2,412.[79] The relatively weak financial capabilities of Edinburgh's Jewish community are illustrated by the fact that in 1879 the Glasgow Hebrew Congregation moved to the Garnethill synagogue, which had been built at a cost of £14,000.[80] By December 1896, Maurice Isaacs was forced to make a public appeal in the *Jewish Chronicle* for the funds necessary to alter the church and make it suitable for use as a synagogue. Maurice Isaacs himself donated £100, though he added in his appeal that "according to estimates, a sum of £4000 is needed."[81] By February 1897, donations had been received from the Chief Rabbi, N.M. Rothschild and Sons, and also from the Lord Mayor of London, Sir George Faudel-Phillips, a Jewish philanthropist who made charitable work the central theme of his time in office.[82] In June, Lord Rosebery donated a further £50 to the renovation fund.[83] Alterations to the property were ongoing in October 1897, but work was finished in February 1898, by which time "internally, the building has been entirely overhauled and redecorated, and an electric light installed."[84] The Chief Rabbi consecrated the new synagogue in January 1898.[85]

When the Chief Rabbi visited Edinburgh again in May 1907, the subject of community division in the city was again the focus of his address. Urging Edinburgh's Jews to eschew their "morbid tendency to quarrel," he called upon the members of the four synagogues to unite.[86]

In religious terms (that is, the issue of Judaism rather than "Jewishness,") there was ostensibly little cause for division among Edinburgh's Jewish community. Although some services may have differed from others in terms of the language they were delivered in, Orthodox Judaism was very much common to all those with an affiliation to any synagogue in Edinburgh. In fact, despite the different premises and management committees of the various branches, for some time they shared in the services of the Reverend Jacob Fürst as minister. In January 1904, having completed 25 years of service to Edinburgh's Jews, the Reverend Fürst explained that "when he came to Edinburgh the Jews formed one congregation with two places of worship, and now they had three places of worship with one congregation. He purposefully said one congregation, because he rendered services, and ministered to the whole community without any distinction whatsoever."[87]

By 1893, however, the smaller congregations began moving away from this arrangement. Rabbi Salis Daiches later wrote that the newcomers began the "appointment of Rabbinic functionaries who came from abroad with the new settlers and were able to satisfy their religious needs."[88] During Yom Kippur in 1893, services were delivered at Park Place by the Reverend Fürst, at Dalry by a Rev. M. Cohen, and at Richmond Street by the Rev. Isaac Levine.[89] The Edinburgh New Hebrew Congregation was later headed by Rabbi Jacob Rabinowitz, who arrived in Edinburgh in 1899, though the Reverend Levine remained for a time to assist him. In 1904, during a meeting of Jewish leaders in Edinburgh, Rabbi Rabinowitz drew attention to "the poverty of many Jewish resident families" in his congregation, and was instrumental in the creation of a Bread, Meat and Coal Society.[90]

That the Edinburgh New Hebrew Congregation was at this time still a largely Yiddish-speaking group, under "irregular" religious leadership, is suggested by the performance of Rabbi Rabinowitz as witness during a criminal trial in Liverpool in 1904. It was noted that he "was unable to understand or make himself understood in English, so the learned judge addressed him in German." In keeping with trends among recently established immigrant religious societies, Rabinowitz, then about 35 years of age, stated that his congregation did not recognize the Chief Rabbi. He stated that he had "obtained the degree of Rav" from his father in Poland and that he recognized no formal religious hierarchy. When pressed, he stated that the only degree of difference among *Rabbonim* was "that one Rav is cleverer than another."[91] The case, and in particular the performance of Rabinowitz, was highlighted by the *Jewish Chronicle* as an example of "Jews who had been some time in England, remaining a foreign element."[92] Frustration was expressed at the persistence of informal religious frameworks, and the refusal of new congregations to observe the structure and hierarchy of established British Jewry. The view that this refusal was a major obstacle to communal unity, and thus to Anglicization, was key to the stance of the *Jewish Chronicle*. Despite these divisions, in Edinburgh there remained a degree of inter-congregational cooperation in matters concerning the representation of Jewish Edinburgh in national organizations. In 1892 the Edinburgh Hebrew Congregation, the Dalry branch synagogue, and the Edinburgh New Hebrew Congregation joined in expressing their frustration that "when the congregation consisted of only fifteen members it sent a representative to the Board of Deputies, whereas now with three synagogues, the important community of Jews in Edinburgh are not represented on that body."[93] Also, when a branch of the Anglo-Jewish Association was re-established in Edinburgh in 1894, Maurice Isaacs occupied the position of president, with Bernard Turiansky taking that of treasurer.[94] Another cause which went some way to uniting Edinburgh's Jews was that of Zionism.

Early Zionist Movements in Jewish Edinburgh

Not all Jews in Edinburgh were strictly religious, and for those who sought to express a Jewish identity outside the synagogue, Jewish communities often had a range of political and cultural organizations which provided such an outlet. Kenneth Collins states that that in Glasgow, for those Jews who did not maintain membership of the synagogues, friendly societies provided a means to communal involvement outside organized religious structures.[95] Of these societies, Zionist organizations were among the most popular and the most enduring. In August 1890, Scotland's first Zionist group was founded in Edinburgh. The group was a branch of *Chovevei Zion*, or Lovers of Zion.[96]

Chovevei Zion had its roots in the East and had in large part been exported to the West along with the flow of Russian refugees. Western Jewry, having benefited from decades or even centuries of emancipation, had gradually minimized the position of Zion in Jewish identity. In some cases, it was "even being exorcized by reformers and secularists."[97] By contrast, Russian Jewry, laboring under the oppressive laws of the Tsars, remained more attached to the memory of the Holy Land. For many, "the recollection of its loss was a visceral wound."[98] This cultural memory was imbued with more importance following renewed oppression in Russia. Zionism was subsequently born from this renewed persecution, along with the persistence of anti-Semitism elsewhere in Europe. The resulting need for security, and the trend toward nationalism which swept Europe toward the end of the 19th century, also played major roles in the founding of early Zionist organizations.

The first branches of *Chovevei Zion* were scattered among the towns and cities of the Russian Pale, founded upon the belief that "there is no salvation for the People of Israel until they establish a government of their own in the land of Israel."[99] How exactly this was to be achieved was something never fully clarified by the movement, though it tended toward the raising of funds for small farm colonies, such as Rehevot and Chadera, and support of the Jewish farmers and artisans who inhabited them. In 1884 a conference of Russian branches of the movement had reached a consensus "on the financing of Jewish settlement in Palestine as their first priority," and by the end of the decade the organization had been established in Britain under the direction of leading Sephardic Jews, Colonel Albert Goldsmid and Eli d'Avigdor.[100]

In April 1891, an Edinburgh branch, or "tent," was convened to elect its officials. A Mr. M. Schapira was elected as the tent's "commandant," with the Reverend Fürst of Park Place and the Reverend Levine of Richmond Street taking positions as secretaries.[101] Support for Edinburgh's new Zionist society was forthcoming from Christian quarters, although motivations were often tainted by the influence of Christian theology and references to prophecies in the Book of Revelation. In December 1891, the Rev. William Paterson, Chair of Divinity at Edinburgh University and future moderator of the Church of Scotland wrote to the *Jewish Chronicle* on the subject of Zionism. At that time, he had been heavily involved in the aid of Russian refugees, having founded the Russian Refugees Relief Society in July. During the course of his letter, he argued that after the aid of refugees,

> The next thing which occupies the attention of many in Scotland is to help Israel to occupy the land of their fathers ... in no country are the prophecies of the Bible more revered than in Scotland.... The colonisation of Palestine, which may be a problem of the future, must be accomplished wisely and systematically.[102]

Edinburgh's Zionist leaders were enthusiastic in seeking support for the movement from non-Jewish sources. Marcus Levy, a picture-frame manufacturer in the city, and at that time honorary secretary of the Edinburgh Tent, wrote to "Chief Commander" Joseph Prag in July 1891, stating that the Reverend Paterson "wishes to establish an honorary Chovevei Zion Society in Scotland, entirely submissive under your rules and management he hopes to get hundreds or perhaps thousands of members."[103] Paterson's ambitions were again outlined in a letter he wrote personally to Dr. Hirsch, secretary of the London headquarters, in August 1891. Paterson professed to have "special means of telling all Scotland about your work, and I desire to do so soon, for the Scottish nation is interested in the Jews." Paterson thought of himself as the leader of "Gentile Zionism" in Scotland, and presumed a great deal about the willingness of Scots to support the cause. At the conclusion of his letter he implored Hirsch "if you have any other idea of any way in which the Scottish people can help you, will you please let me know soon, on how we could in any way advance your interests."[104]

Paterson was well-received in Edinburgh, and his efforts to aid Jews on several fronts were appreciated by community leaders. Marcus Levy wrote to Hirsch in August 1891, praising Paterson's "high position in life and his warm heart towards our Jewish people." He added that he wished "to have many more such friends as he is."[105] However, Paterson's ambitions were treated with some skepticism by the London Tent, and this skepticism was communicated to representatives in Edinburgh some months later. On the morning of 30 December 1891, the Reverend Paterson summoned the leaders of the Edinburgh Tent, where "with tears in his eyes," he conveyed the "letter of discouragement" which he had received from Dr. Hirsch. It is unclear whether or not Hirsch did not sympathize with the principle behind the drive to "recruit" an honorary Gentile Tent, or whether he simply doubted its chances of success. The letter only conveyed the reluctance of Hirsch to send London "promoters" to the first meeting of the Honorary Edinburgh Tent, which was scheduled to take place on 11 January 1892.[106]

Plans for the meeting did go ahead, and during a meeting at *Chovevei Zion* headquarters in London in January 1892, it was remarked by the leader of the meeting that a "zealous friend" in Edinburgh, highly likely to have been Paterson, had "enlisted the sympathy of the Lord Provost, the Dukes of Abercorn and Argyll, and several other influential gentlemen in Scotland, and a great demonstration will be held in the Scotch capital on 11th January." It was added by the speaker that "it was hoped that some good work will follow, and England will imitate the example of Scotland."[107]

The "great demonstration" was a large meeting held in the Free Assembly Hall. Of the "several hundred" in attendance, the majority were Jews, though most of the speakers were Christian, "one of whom ... appeared desirous to utilize the movement for proselytizing purposes."[108] The array of notables and aristocrats expected by Paterson failed to attend. The Rev. Dr. MacGregor, of St. Cuthberts Church, Edinburgh, and a moderator of the Church of Scotland introduced a motion intended to embrace large numbers of non-Jews in the Zionist cause. It was seconded by the Rev. William Paterson. The wording of the motion is worth stating in full:

> That a Scottish auxiliary be established, embracing Christians of all denominations, entitled "The Scottish Society for the Restoration of Jews in Palestine." That the objects of the society will be to aid the *Chovevei Zion* Association in their work in every way in its power, morally, financially, and politically; and to help deserving Jews to obtain land in Palestine for colonisation by loans of money on easy terms.[109]

The *Otago Witness* recorded in its coverage of the event that the Rev. William Paterson, influenced by his experience in aiding Jewish transmigrants and immigrants, had argued that helping Jews relocate to Palestine would act as a form of "self-defence, since many hundreds of the refugees had been denied entrance into New York, and many of them were returning to this country."[110] It is obvious therefore, that Christian motivations for the support of Zionism in Edinburgh could be complex, and that even if Paterson did not personally subscribe to an anti-alien outlook, he was aware of its potency.

A series of letters from Paterson to Hirsch during the course of the next year conveyed Paterson's growing dismay at the failure of the Honorary Tent, and his realization that the vast majority of Scots were not as interested, or as sympathetic, to the cause as he had believed them to be. In April 1892 he wrote that, "I cannot say we have achieved very much in getting subscriptions." By January 1893 he had conceded that his efforts had been in vain. He wrote to Hirsch that

> I cannot report much progress here in interesting Scotch Christians in the scheme of colonization. There is first the general apathy to overcome and the difficulty of starting a new project. Over and above there is a very decided hostility to the scheme in some quarters of the "secular" press. Some even of our religious papers have shown great suspicion if not antagonism…. I fondly hoped that our Scotch auxiliary would by this time be able to send you some hundreds of pounds; but I am sorry our revenue has not been much and we have only a very few to remit. Our membership never swelled as I expected it would.[111]

The Honorary Tent was formally dissolved in April 1893, with Paterson remarking on the "surprising" level of apathy shown by Scots toward the scheme of colonization.[112]

The relocation of Jews to Palestine was never achieved with any significance by *Chovevei Zion*. Howard Sachar argues that while "attracting numerous followers, the organization remained quite ineffective as an agency of immigration,"[113] and Walter Laqueur states that "organizationally and politically the Hoveve Zion (sic) was a failure."[114] This failure had its roots in the vague and largely disorganized manner in which the organization sought its goals. It is likely that appeals to Edinburgh's Jews to migrate to Israel were very rarely made, and even more rarely acted upon, though a dedicated core of the city's Jewish community responded well to the cause of Zionism and supported it fervently through volunteer work as well as monetary contributions.

Very often, meetings of *Chovevei Zion* in the West were focused mainly on fund-raising, and the support of those small-scale farmers and artisans who were then resident in the Jewish farm-colonies of Palestine. During a meeting held at the Oddfellows Hall, in Edinburgh in March 1892, the Rev. Isadore Myers discussed the "aims and objects" of the association, and encouraged donations by giving "an account of what he had seen during a visit to the colonies in Palestine."[115] Contemporaries were aware, however, of the organization's shortcomings. Veteran Zionist and Honorary Vice-President of the Zionist Federation the Rev. J.K. Goldbloom wrote of British tents that "the influence of the *Chovevei Zion* on the man in the street was very small."[116]

In September 1893 the Edinburgh tent was visited by Colonel Albert Goldsmid. During his address he informed the gathering that, "it was also a pleasure to have a tent in Scotland, seeing that there was no nation on the earth nearer akin to the Jewish nation than the Scottish, both in their love of the Bible, and in their sympathy with all that is best in Judaism."[117] Goldsmid went on to show an awareness of the tendency of the movement to fundraise rather than actively support the colonies by other means. He stressed that, "the *Chovevei Zion* is not a charitable institution, the main object is to foster the national idea in Israel."[118]

In April 1894 Edinburgh's tent lost its "commandant," Mr. M. Schapira, not to Palestine but to Canada.[119] He was replaced by the Reverend Fürst, who himself resigned from the post just over a year later. The Reverend Fürst explained that the level of work demanded by both the position of leader of the tent, and the level of work in aiding refugees, "instead of decreasing, was greatly increasing, as the position of Jews in Russia and elsewhere was as critical as ever."[120]

By 1894, Zionism was itself undergoing significant change. Western Jews were coming to terms with increasingly difficult situation in Russia. Then, in November 1894, Alfred Dreyfus was arrested in France for high treason. The trial of Dreyfus shook western Jewry and at the height of the furor over his guilt or innocence in September 1899, the Reverend Fürst argued to his congregation that:

> Instead of justice, vile intrigues and machinations have prevailed, and when we see that justice has been neglected, an innocent man's rights violated, and that the plague of strife and hatred has not yet quenched its fury, ought we not to raise our supplications of the Father of all creatures.[121]

At the conclusion of the sermon, the Graham Street congregation joined in a prayer on behalf of Dreyfus, his wife, and children.

Theodor Herzl, then a writer in Paris and a recent convert to the Zionist cause, was "moved by the Dreyfus affair," and it is likely that the case played some role in his production of "The Jewish State," published in 1896.[122] The publication of "The Jewish State," in contrast with the pedestrian progress of the *Chovevei Zion*, "aroused an immediate reaction among the Jewish masses."[123] This reaction often manifested itself through the display of a photograph of Herzl in the windows of many Jewish homes, following its publication in the *Jewish Express*.

Herzl was also influenced greatly, perhaps more so than the Dreyfus affair, by the rise of anti-Semitic politician Karl Lueger in Vienna.[124] As a result, Herzl's writings began to increasingly reflect pessimism about the future of Jews in Europe, urging instead the movement of all Jews to a safe homeland in Palestine. The method of achieving such a goal was outlined at the first Zionist Congress in Basle in 1897, where it was explicitly stated as "the attainment of such Government consent as is necessary in order to achieve the aim of Zionism."[125]

Controversy and debate surrounded Herzl's writings, particularly in Western Europe. The *Jewish Chronicle* published an article authored by Herzl on 17 January 1896, entitled, "A Solution of the Jewish Question," during which he outlined the agenda which would later appear in more detail in "The Jewish State." Reaction from British Jews was mixed. Some felt his scheme unrealistic, while other saw Egypt or Argentina as holding better prospects for Jewish settlement. A week after Herzl's article, Benjamin Freeman, a Jewish resident of Edinburgh who had previously written to the newspaper supporting a move to Palestine, stated that, "Dr Herzl is not to be sneered at." Freeman agreed with Herzl that anti-Semitism or *Judenhetze* remained a major problem, and that "the Jews are scarcely liked anywhere." However, the achievement of government consent for the establishment of a Jewish state was viewed with great pessimism. Freeman argued:

> That the scheme is a good one there can be no two opinions, and were it practicable, I believe it would meet with the approval of a large number of coreligionists all the world over. But it is not practicable. For the formation of a Jewish State we would neither get the consent of the European governments nor would the leading Jews of Europe plead for it.[126]

Opinion in Edinburgh on Herzl's scheme varied greatly, foreshadowing a later split among the city's Zionist activists. Some felt that the acquisition of territory for a Jewish state was imperative, but were more flexible than others in terms of where that territory should be. Spiro Spero, of Edinburgh, wrote in August 1897 that "all Jews need not live in Jerusalem any more than all Scotsmen need live in Edinburgh, but by procuring a state of our own, prestige and dignity would be the lot of Jews elsewhere."[127]

In addition, a great number of Edinburgh's Jews became increasingly apathetic toward the cause, possibly because the early support given to *Chovevei Zion* failed to provide sufficient results. Freeman wrote to Dr. Hirsch in July 1896 complaining that having called a meeting of the Tent, he "could not get sufficient people to hold it. There is such a lack of interest that for the last couple of years things have been in much the same state."[128]

Support for, and belief in, Herzl's goal of gaining government permission for a Jewish state began to grow following the Basle conference in 1897. By December of that year, Marcus Levy wrote to Dr. Hirsch, stating that the

Basle conference had been a boost for Zionism, but that supporters were increasingly aware of the failings of *Chovevei Zion* as a means of achieving Zionist aspirations. Levy wrote that:

> since the Basle Conference, the Edinburgh branch has revived. The collections are very liberal and everybody is willing to help if only they can be assured that their subscriptions will bring better fruit.... I feel that the opinion of the majority is to send their money to Odessa unless they can be satisfied that they English headquarters, instead of the old promises, will do something.[129]

Relations between the Edinburgh Tent and headquarters in London deteriorated steadily as frustrations increased. Disillusionment gave way to hostility in 1898, when Marcus Levy again wrote to Dr. Hirsch informing him that:

> At our last general meeting the question of our duty to Headquarters was discussed and it has been unanimously agreed to not assist you any more financially until we see you do more practical work in Palestine. It is, I am sorry to say, the general opinion of our members that you have wasted much capital, and much more energy, enthusiasm and hope of those that have entrusted themselves to be led by you.[130]

In 1899 a separate "Edinburgh Zionist Association" was established in the city, following the founding of the English Zionist Federation in February 1899.[131] During the course of the meeting more than 250 shares were subscribed to the Jewish Colonial Trust, which had its origins at the Basle conference and represented the central financial instrument of the Zionist Organization.[132] The Trust sold individual shares in the colonies for £1.

Subscriptions to the fund also came from Edinburgh's *Chovevei Zion*. In response to an appeal from the English Zionist Federation in March 1900, the Edinburgh tent heard an address in Yiddish from Rabbi Rabinowitz. Ninety new shares were applied for, and the balance was paid on many shares which had already been applied for. The Edinburgh Zionist Association also responded to the appeal, raising money for 50 new subscriptions.[133]

The meetings of these organizations had until that time taken place in a number of small halls in the city. By summer 1900, a number of rooms at 46 Nicholson Street had been converted into a small hall, named New Zionist Hall. It had been carried out under the auspices of the Edinburgh Zionist Association, and in July 1900 the Association unveiled "the Zionist Reading Room," which according to Rabbi Rabinowitz was intended to aid the "study of our national history and literature."[134] This development reflected a larger move begun at the Second and Third Zionist Congresses, which became known as the *Kulturkampf*. Throughout Britain, societies and small independent libraries were created by Zionists dedicated to a social and educational revival of Jewish history, Hebrew, and Jewish culture.[135]

The dedication of Edinburgh's Jewish leaders to the preservation of the

Hebrew language and the Jewish religion did precede the *Kulturkampf*. Hebrew, unlike Yiddish, remained in the embrace of Anglo-Jewry. It was seen as respectable for religious and cultural reasons. It was the language of the Torah, and was studied by Jews and non-Jews alike. Hebrew education was a crucial element to most integrated communities in Britain, often representing, along with religion, the last vestiges of "transmissible distinctiveness." As a result, it was taken very seriously by the heads of Anglo-Jewry.

The Reverend Fürst and a Miss Salmon were operating a small but successful Hebrew school at the Park Place synagogue in 1880. By the middle of the decade, increased demand due to an increased Jewish population led to the search for an additional teacher of Hebrew. In the advertisement for the position in the *Jewish Chronicle*, the terms offered were an annual salary of £70, "with free home and perquisites."[136]

With the fracturing of Edinburgh Jewry in the early years of the 1890s, the break-away Edinburgh New Hebrew Congregation founded a *Talmud Torah* school in North Richmond Street, "for the purpose of giving Hebrew and religious instruction to the young."[137] Most often, in the case of the *Talmud Torah*, the "young" referred only to young males.

Educated by a Mr. Isaac Reiness and a Mr. I. Laub, the pupils "entered the school entirely ignorant even of the Hebrew Alphabet, but … they are now capable of reading and translating."[138] In the creation of a *Talmud Torah*, the Edinburgh New Hebrew Congregation was following a global trend, pervasive in the last two decades of the 19th century. Glasgow had founded its first *Talmud Torah* in April 1895—within months of the founding of the North Richmond Street school.[139] Daniel Elazar states that as well as being directly linked to the Zionist cause,

> a principal feature of the *Talmud Torah* was its existence as an independent educational institution, headed and staffed by professional educators and dedicated to modern methods of pedagogy.… The *Talmud Torah* provided intensive supplementary education, often ten hours a week, on Sunday morning plus Monday through Thursday in the afternoon or evening.[140]

In September 1899, the Edinburgh Hebrew Congregation at Graham Street attempted to follow suit. A decision was made by leaders of the congregation to found a *Talmud Torah* which would be a "free school" in the sense that the school and its curriculum would be free from the control of the synagogue, an essential feature of *Talmud Torah* schools. Funds were to be raised by voluntary contributions and a grant from the congregation. Since the establishment of a Graham Street *Talmud Torah* did not take place, one could surmise that the congregation lacked the numbers and financial support required for the establishment of such a school.[141]

In May 1900, the Rev. E.P. Phillips of Glasgow visited Edinburgh, where he delivered a sermon entitled "A Comparison of the Houses of Abraham and Eli." The sermon "showed the different results accruing from a rigid and religious, and a loose and careless training by parents of the young."[142] By 1904, a Jewish Young Ladies' Hebrew Speaking Society had been established, the object of which was "to learn Hebrew and to support Hebrew literature as far as possible."[143]

Hebrew education for Jewish women and girls in Edinburgh was certainly available, though evidence suggests that it was taken up more rarely than among their male counterparts. During a visit from the Chief Rabbi in 1907, the Hebrew school at Graham Street, then headed by the Reverend Fürst and H. Levenberg, was highly praised. Results at the school were excellent, but the Chief Rabbi noticed an absence of girls among the students, and made a point of stating that "the Gemara said that women were as important in life as men, and it was a mistake on the part of parents not to have their girls instructed in their duty to God, especially as the girls were the mothers of the next generation."[144]

In August 1900, a large number of Edinburgh's Zionists crowded into the confines of the New Zionist Hall to hear the report of Edinburgh's representatives to the Zionist Congress, of whom Rabbi Rabinowitz was the senior delegate. Rabinowitz delivered a "stirring address, in which he embodied the principles of Zionism to great advantage, and exemplified the importance of the Congress." He finished with another appeal for the audience to support the Jewish Colonial Trust "which would eventually finance the development of our future home in Palestine."[145]

During the annual general meeting of the Edinburgh Zionist Association in November 1900, the enthusiasm and great support for Zionism in the city is evidenced by the fund-raising total for the year. In all, £300 in cash had been remitted to the Jewish Colonial Trust, 152 *Shekalim* had been sold, and £21 had been collected in weekly subscriptions. The fund-raising activism of Edinburgh's Zionists and their enthusiasm for the Colonial Trust resulted in the founding of the Edinburgh Colonial Share Club in 1901. By March 1902, the club had 120 members and had raised funds sufficient for the purchase of 234 shares.[146] These figures compare reasonably with the Dublin *Chovevei Zion*, which was counted as "one of the strongest and most active in the British Isles," with a membership of 175, out of a Jewish community approximating that of Edinburgh's in terms of population size.[147] The figures compare well with the Sunderland community, which had a Zionist Association that peaked at 80 members.[148] In a Scottish context, these figures should also be compared with the nine shares purchased by Dundee, the six shares purchased by Aberdeen, the five shares purchased by Ayr, and the one share purchased by Falkirk.[149]

The meeting was held against a backdrop of crisis in Palestine. Until 1900, Jewish colonies in the country were largely under Rothschild paternalism.

While this paternalism was in many ways necessary for the colonies to survive, direct involvement from de Rothschild's agents caused consternation and led to many colonists "losing all initiative."[150] In 1900, moves were taken by the Jewish Colonisation Association of London to begin the purchase of land from Edmond de Rothschild. The new administrators of the colonies rapidly set about improving the lot of the colonists and issued an appeal for financial assistance in winter 1900. During the annual general meeting of the Edinburgh Zionist Association, it was voted that £15 be sent immediately to "the suffering colonists in Palestine."[151]

One week later, a large gathering formed at New Zionist Hall for an address by Mr. L.J. Greenberg, sessional chairman for the English Zionist Federation. At the conclusion of the address, speeches were made by W.T. Munro Hogg, and a Mr. William Grant. Grant was the editor of *Glad Tidings*, a local monthly magazine "which is very friendly to the Jewish people."[152] Hogg informed the audience that "although a Christian he attended the Synagogue regularly every Sabbath. Both gentlemen expressed their belief in the Zionist principles, and urged that they should be better supported by all Jews everywhere."[153]

Grant became a key figure in Edinburgh's Zionist Association, often lecturing on the benefits of Herzl's vision as well as the limitations of the *Chovevei Zion*. During a meeting in January 1901, he informed those gathered that:

> The *Chovevei Zion* movement, much though its promoters and adherents are to be commended, is totally inadequate at this great crisis in the condition of the Jewish race. The Zionist scheme has the appearance of more adequateness, if not for the full deliverance, at any rate for the amelioration of the millions of your brethren who are being overwhelmed by this sweeping wave of anti-Semitism. Meantime it seems to be the only remedy.[154]

The changing landscape of Zionism in Britain ultimately led to the disappearance of *Chovevei Zion* in its original form, with some of its tenets, and many of its members, being absorbed into the increasingly popular Zionist Associations which combined to form the English Zionist Federation. By 1901 *Chovevei Zion* seems to have ceased to function in Edinburgh.

However, enthusiasm for Herzl Zionism saturated elements of Edinburgh Jewry to the extent that by summer 1901 a separate "Edinburgh Ladies' Zionist Association" had been established, and by February 1902 an "Edinburgh Junior Zionist Literary Club" had been formed. The activities of the former appear to have involved organizing trips for local Jewish women and children. In this they were greatly aided in organizational and financial terms by W.T. Munro Hogg. In July 1901, he contributed heavily to an outing to Dalmeny Grounds for 215 women and children from Edinburgh's Jewish community. Forty representatives from the Ladies' Zionist Association attended the trip.[155] The following year, the joint efforts of Hogg and the Ladies' Zionist Association provided for an outing to the seaside village of Cramond for 300 Jewish men, women and children from Edinburgh.[156] The Ladies' Zionist Association also devoted themselves to providing "suitable attire for poor Jewish children" and teaching them "religion and history, besides giving them occasional treats."[157]

The founding of the Junior Zionist Literary Club was a project of Solomon Stungo, a 30-year-old shopkeeper from Russia. Stungo was a committee member of the Edinburgh Hebrew Congregation as well as the corresponding secretary of the Edinburgh Jewish Colonial Share Trust. Solomon's wife Helena acted as treasurer for the Ladies' Zionist Association. During its first meeting in February 1902, 30 members were enlisted, and it "was resolved that each member should subscribe 4d monthly, and be a shekel payer."[158] A week after the founding of the club, Solomon Stungo addressed a gathering of its members at Zionist Hall in Richmond Street, explaining Zionism "in a simple and interesting manner."[159] Within a few months, Solomon Stungo had been elected honorary president of the club. Solomon's younger brother Symon was elected secretary of the club. The young members also resolved that they should bring in the necessary instructors to commence Hebrew and Jewish history classes.[160]

Enthusiasm continued to grow in the community, and in March 1902 "an overflowing mass of Jews, one of the largest ever held in Edinburgh" gathered at Livingstone Hall to hear an address on Zionism by Mr. Jacob de Haas, secretary to the First Zionist Congress, and editor of the *Jewish World*.[161] Jacob de Haas, who also served as secretary to the Federation of American Zionists, was a staunch opponent of inter-marriage and many aspects of Jewish assimilation, as well as a major proponent of Zionism. In 1901 he published *Zionism: Jewish Needs and Jewish Ideals*, which displayed great concerns about the tendency toward assimilation among many of Britain's Jews. He argued that "the assimilating school" had attempted to:

> reduce as far as possible, the distinguishing marks of Judaism; in the practices of daily life the abandon whatever is demonstrably Jewish, and ... there have not been wanting men who have gone to the logical conclusion and advocated the ending of Jewish trouble by the destruction of the Jewish race.[162]

In December 1902, de Haas caused a near-riot in New York, by espousing his strong views on Jewish life and the Zionist goal of a national home in Palestine.[163] In Edinburgh he told the Jews of the city that "great attention should be given to the teaching of children in Jewish history and Hebrew as a living language."[164]

Support for political Zionism was expressed in a letter from Symon Stungo to the *Jewish Chronicle* in 1903. Challenging the arguments of British anti-Zionists, and echoing the sentiments of Herzl and de Haas, Stungo argued that:

> Every nation, however small, possesses a piece of territory, and that of the Jews is in Palestine. Therefore in Palestine the Jews—as a nation—would be respected and esteemed, whereas in any other country we should be told to "go home" like a bad dog, who poked his nose wherever he was not wanted! It seems the Jewish people have no desire to end their tragedy. Wander, wander, wander, from the door of one country to another, always claiming, with pride and cocksureness, the "hospitality" of our scorners![165]

There was never a separate "Scottish Zionist Federation," and interaction between the Zionist clubs of Edinburgh and Glasgow was quite minimal beyond their mutual participation in the English Zionist Federation. Despite its name, the English Zionist Federation embraced Scottish, Irish and Welsh Zionists as well as their English counterparts. In December 1903, Percy Baker of Glasgow delivered an address to the members of the Edinburgh Literary Zionist Society. Baker was later instrumental in the founding of a Zionist Association in Ayr in 1904.[166] Although the *Jewish Chronicle* interpreted this as a strengthening of "the Zionistic union between Edinburgh and Glasgow," such speeches were given on a regular by representatives of a range of regional Zionist societies, and there is little evidence that there was particularly close cooperation between Scottish Zionists at this time.

By 1904 Zionism was in the midst of crisis. Joseph Chamberlain, colonial secretary, had offered Herzl an "East African Scheme," which was essentially the promise of land in Uganda for Jewish settlement. Herzl, like the majority of European Jews, was split on the measure, acknowledging at the start of the Sixth Zionist Congress that, "Uganda was not, and could never become Zion," but also that the scheme could suffice as an emergency measure to protect persecuted Jews.[167] In January 1904 a meeting of the Edinburgh Zionist Association was addressed by Mr. P. Weitzman of Glasgow, who expressed sympathy for Herzl's support of the East Africa Scheme. The opinion of Edinburgh's Zionists on the subject is indicated by a resolution introduced by Solomon Stungo and carried by those present, including Rabbi Rabinowitz: "This meeting of Edinburgh Jews thanks Mr. Weitzman for his excellent address, and pledges itself to do its utmost to promote the Zionist cause under the able leadership of Dr Herzl."

Theodor Herzl's death on 3 July 1904, seemed to worsen divisions on the East Africa Scheme. Symon Stungo wrote to the *Jewish Chronicle* in September 1904, stating that, "the death of Dr Herzl, far from re-opening the old sores, ought to have healed them up."[168] Stungo appears to have favored the dropping of the scheme, if only to aid a Zionist reconciliation. He argued that, "the quicker it is dropped, the less dangerous it will become."[169] The World Zionist Organization at the Seventh Zionist Conference, in the summer of 1905 finally rejected the scheme.[170]

The goal of achieving territory for Jewish colonization outside Palestine was not abandoned by all Zionists. In the aftermath of the "Uganda Congress" a group, led by Israel Zangwill, seceded under the banner of the "Jewish Territorial Organization (ITO)." Known as the "territorialists," they remained committed to the Uganda Scheme, and remained deeply skeptical of the likelihood of securing a charter for the settlement of Palestine.[171] During a meeting of Edinburgh Zionists in November 1905, a branch of the Jewish Territorial Organization was founded in the city, and a resolution was unanimously carried "expressing confidence in Mr. Israel Zangwill."[172]

The Edinburgh Zionist Association remained extant, and there are indications that relations between the EZA and the Edinburgh branch of the Jewish Territorial Organization were very good. During a meeting of the General Council of the English Zionist Federation, held in Glasgow in January 1906, representatives of the Edinburgh Zionist Association introduced a motion which would allow territorialists to be represented at the Zionist Congress. The motion was emphatically defeated.[173]

A meeting of Edinburgh Zionists in March 1906 reaffirmed a commitment to the cause of seeking territory outside Palestine. A resolution was carried pledging support for the Jewish Territorial Organization "morally and financially," and declaring the "fullest confidence in the Executive Committee of the ITO, together with its President Mr. Israel Zangwill." The meeting concluded with the enrolment of new members.[174]

In September 1906, the Edinburgh Zionist Association continued in its effort to bring about a mutual understanding between the English Zionist Federation and the Jewish Territorial Organization. Edinburgh's representatives introduced a motion to this effect at the biennial meeting of the central committee of the English Zionist Federation in London. The unique position of Edinburgh's sympathy with the ITO is indicated by the fact that the motion, "was not moved, and fell to the ground."[175]

Zionism would remain an important part of Jewish life in Edinburgh, and this was partly due to the fact that it was so heavily embraced by the young. In February 1910 the "Young Men's Zionist Culture Association," was created with the aim of spreading "Zionism among the younger generation."[176]

The Economic Life of Edinburgh Jewry

Prior to the influx of new immigrants into the city, Edinburgh's established, assimilated Jewish community consisted of a relatively small number of families engaged in "merchanting, tailoring, the jewellery trade, the manufacture of fancy goods and a range of other business activities."[177] Prime examples of this established merchant class can be found among the entries in Eugene Harfield's 1894 *Commercial Directory of the Jews in the United Kingdom*, such as the Goldston's and the Michael's, who had been established in the city since at least the middle of the 19th century. They formed a small but successful element of the commercial life of the city, providing an eclectic range of items and goods such as imported clocks, watches, and decorative pieces. They were able to take advantage of the fact that Edinburgh's "prime demand out of its comfortable professional incomes was for food and drink, clothing or housing.... Beyond basic needs, incomes went on conspicuous consumption. This meant handmade goods produced by skilled craftsmanship of high quality."[178]

With the arrival of large numbers of impoverished immigrants, the economic profile of Edinburgh Jewry changed dramatically. Many new immigrants arrived in Scotland with no skills at all, and relied upon unskilled, low-capital trading to provide for themselves and their families. In and around Edinburgh, this often involved the door-to-door selling of inexpensive jewelry and watches.[179] The practice of this kind of selling in Scotland was by no means peculiar to the Jewish immigrant community. In fact, Jews had been preceded in this trade not only by the Scots themselves, but also by many Italian immigrants who arrived in the country in the middle of the 19th century.[180] Many had experience of engaging in this form of trade in their country of origin, and it had the added attraction of requiring little English.

Harvey Kaplan's analysis of the 1901 Scottish census reveals that of a sample of 491 working Jews resident in Edinburgh, 130 were engaged in peddling, comprising 27 percent of the sample and forming the largest group of economically active Jews. Of these, only three were women. This figure of 27 percent compares with 16 percent in Glasgow.[181] Often peddlers would describe themselves simply as jewelers, watchmakers, or picture dealers. If one accounts for this, then the total number of peddlers in Edinburgh in 1901 can be assumed to be significantly higher. Henry Maitles estimated that 10 percent of Glasgow's Jews were involved in peddling in 1906, but that in Edinburgh the figure remained "an even higher percentage."[182] This would suggest either than Edinburgh's Jewish immigrants tended to have fewer skills than their Glasgow counterparts, or that the city offered fewer opportunities for alternative employment than the area around the Clyde.

Henry Maitles speculated that the reasons why Jews were largely absent from employment in the shipyards and engineering factories of Glasgow lay in contradictory perceptions, held by employers and union leaders, which rendered Jews to be "at one and the same time, scabs and militants, lazy and industrious."[183] Other reasons include the suggestion that Jews had a different "tradition of skills."[184] In any event, these reasons apply little to the economic profile of Edinburgh, which had forfeited industrial growth to Glasgow in most sectors but brewing and printing, and remained a city of service industries, bankers, and lawyers. Suzanne Audrey has suggested that even though Jews, like Italian immigrants, refrained from entering into competition with native Scots in the industrial sphere, "in establishing businesses and providing services, they were vulnerable to the accusation of profiting at the expense of the local population."[185]

In the early years of the 20th century, commercial travelers did form an established part of the local economy, and newspapers regularly carried advertisements from wholesalers actively seeking peddlers. For example, Stubs. Ltd., based on Princes Street in Edinburgh placed an advertisement in the *Jewish Chronicle* in 1903, seeking "a traveller for retail jewellery, drapery, and house furnishing trade; references and security required; good opening for an energetic man."[186] Harfield's directory records no Jewish businesses on Princes Street, and it is very likely that Stubs Ltd. was in fact a gentile-owned business, which acknowledged that Jewish immigrants provided an experienced and willing labor force at a low wage. The presence of Jewish peddlers in the city was therefore, for some, a welcome one.

It is likely that some new immigrants persisted in this type of trade out of choice. Nathan Abrams states that, "many of the first arrivals in the late nineteenth and early twentieth centuries were commercial travellers—poor peddlers and hawkers—looking for new business opportunities throughout Scotland."[187] It is also likely, however, that many Jews would have sought to branch out into professions they had previously been prohibited from entering; after all, Scotland was a new country, with more to offer than simply new ground in which to ply an old trade. Hawking was also a notoriously difficult way of making a living. Max Mendick wrote of his father,

> My father was one o' the Jews who didnae make a great success there. He sold cheap jewellery to the farmers. He had this jewellery box, and he used to gather up most o' his jewels in a lodging-house in Galashiels, and he'd travel to farms and sell watches to farmers. Most Jews did that kind o' thing, some would sell jewellery, some would sell slippers, some would sell drapery, some would sell pictures. He didnae do very well anyway.[188]

Under the Pedlars Act 1871, anyone who "travels and trades on foot and goes from town to town or to other men's houses, carrying to sell or exposing for sale any goods," was compelled to apply for a Pedlars Certificate. This certificate was obtainable from the chief officer of police in the relevant district. The applicant must have been resident in the area for at least one month, and the officer had to be satisfied that "the applicant is above seventeen years of age, is a person of good character, and in good faith intends to carry on the trade of a pedlar." After 1881 the certificate was obtainable without an application fee.[189]

Peddling required little in the way of capital, and was a fast way to engage in commerce. Goods could be acquired through credit and the supply of references, or a small amount of capital could be advanced from relatives, or through organizations such as the Benevolent Loan Society, the *chevroth*, or other congregational aid societies.

Edinburgh's peddlers would base themselves in their tenements, setting out each day to sell their wares in the streets of the city, or traveling further in the hope that the villages surrounding the city could provide the custom they required to make a profit. From the fact that contemporary reports reflect persistent poverty among Edinburgh's Jewish immigrants, one could conclude that Max Mendick's father was not alone in his difficulties.

The growing number of peddlers did however ensure a boom period for the Jewish wholesalers of jewelry pieces and watch parts in the city. In what was almost a Jewish "micro-economy," hawkers would purchase quantities of jeweler and watch components from wholesalers in the city, before producing a finished article and selling it. If they were successful, and plied this trade long enough, it was not impossible for an enterprising peddler to become the proprietor of a successful business of his own. Success could also mean the chance to arrange for more family members to be brought to the country, in the kind of chain-migration witnessed in the Italian, and later Pakistani and Chinese communities. Louis Hyman writes of Dublin's peddlers that, "soon the enterprising ones learned the sources of their wares and supplied the next contingent of settlers with stock-in-trade, and in the course of time many of them became wholesale merchants and manufacturers."[190]

For those unskilled Jewish immigrants who did wish to advance themselves economically by other means, the city would have offered few prospects. Language and a lack of education would have formed a formidable barrier to many. Ben Braber states that they "usually lacked the skills and contacts to take up positions in heavy industry."[191] Furthermore, some sectors of the city economy were hostile toward the employment of Jews. An annual report by the Edinburgh Jewish Medical Mission in 1913 stated that,

> even in this Christian city of Edinburgh there is a certain amount of ill-feeling against Jews, hence there is great difficulty in finding employment for even the most skilful.... Accordingly the majority have to betake themselves to hawking in hardware, jewellery, and lace, or selling fruit in the streets.[192]

Interestingly, when Leon Levison arrived in Edinburgh at the turn of the century, he found no opportunities despite his tailoring skills. Forced to find manual labor among Gentiles, he was subsequently "bullied and ridiculed," because he was "a foreigner and a Jew."[193] His son would later speculate that Levison found it difficult to find employment as a tailor in Edinburgh as "it was a trade largely in the hands of the Jews and it may be that doors were closed by his unwillingness to hide his Christian faith."[194] Suzanne Audrey argues that in Scotland, "religious affiliation influenced the employment opportunities of both Jews and Catholics as some firms openly promoted a Protestant ethos."[195]

After peddling and hawking, the manufacture of clothing was the trade most Edinburgh Jews engaged in during the years 1880–1910. Census returns are available showing the occupational distribution of Polish-born males in Scotland from 1881 to 1921. While it must be stated that not all Poles in Scotland during this period were Jewish, it can be stated with confidence that the majority were. Census returns are only as reliable as the responses given on them, and as a result they can offer only a guide to the researcher who comes to rely on them.

In 1881, the majority of Polish males in Scotland were employed in tailoring and peddling, with a sizable number also involved in the manufacture of furniture. The number of independent wholesalers and retailers was very low. Figure 1, based on details contained in Eugene Harfield's 1894 commercial directory, is valuable as a general guide to the trades engaged in by the city's Jewish population. It demonstrates that by 1894 there were 20 Jewish wholesalers in the city. Most of those listed as jewelers actually sold their wares as commercial travelers, and were likely to be customers of the wholesalers. Only a few of those listed were engaged in the tobacco trade, though about 18 percent of Glasgow's Jews were employed in tobacco-related occupations.[196] Few were employed by gentiles, although some, based on census returns, often employed Gentile servants in their homes.[197] This was at a time when it was relatively inexpensive to hire maids and servants, and those who did do not seem to have been particularly wealthy.

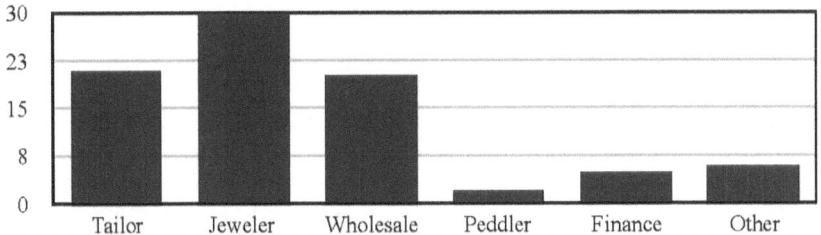

Edinburgh's Jewish clothing manufacturers produced a diverse range of garments. Henry Solomon had operated a traditional tailor's workshop in Bristo Street since 1856. By 1894, more than 20 Jewish businessmen had established workshops making waterproof garments, shoes, boots and slippers. Most of these businesses also sold their products wholesale. In addition, many wholesalers, such as Phillip Dresner in Leith, did not limit their production to clothing, selling jewelry and drapes from the same premises.

The majority, if not all, of these businesses, employed mainly Jews, leading T.M. Devine to conclude that, "the Jewish immigrant economy was remarkably self-contained. The majority ran or worked in Jewish-owned businesses."[198] This system, which embraced several trades, worked in favor of both employer and immigrant. The employer would have a low-wage employee, and the immigrant could find a source of employment which could otherwise have been lacking, in the form of general labor or apprenticeships. The tendency toward Jewish cooperation and patronage would also have contributed to the maintenance of some semblance of community cohesion. Max Mendick recalled that within the first few months of his family's arrival in the city, "my sister became a tailoress workin' for another Jewish woman who kept a tailor's shop. She took me to Weinstock Cabinet Makers in Balcarres Street where I got a job as an apprentice cabinet maker for 18 months."[199]

One negative aspect to this type of "closed" economic system was that the formation of exclusively Jewish working relationships certainly did little to combat the ghettoization of Edinburgh Jews. David Feldman argued that the trend also contributed to an increasingly negative perception of immigrant Jewish workers. He stressed that Jews came to be seen as "economic individualists whose loyalties were to other Jews rather than to members of the same class."[200] Nowhere was this sentiment more prominent than during strikes.

In early 1902, non–Jewish Glasgow tailors won an increase of half a shilling an hour following a period of strikes. By 1903, Edinburgh's employers were coming under similar demands. In response, Edinburgh employers persuaded their Glasgow counterparts to withdraw their concession, and "join them in an attack upon the craft regulations of the Scottish National Operative Tailors." In doing so, their goal was to remove certain restrictions and pave to way for the employment of "outworkers, non-unionists, day-wage men, and apprentices."[201]

Since the contemporary political climate was thick with the fog of anti-alien agitation, the prospect of usurpation by foreign workers would have been a formidable concern to those on strike. Henry Maitles points out that tailoring "was first noted as a Jewish trade in Glasgow in the early 1870s. The Scottish Tailors Union complained of wage undercutting in 1875 and beyond."[202] However, rhetoric during the strikes focused almost exclusively on the demand for an increase in wage and protection for workers, rather than focusing on alien competition.

The Edinburgh Tailor's Strike of 1903 did bring to the surface underlying issues surrounding Jewish involvement in the tailoring trade throughout the country, and certainly goes some way to demonstrating what David Feldman described as a perception of Jewish "economic individualism." In July 1903, a conference was called by Jewish trade union leaders in London to discuss "means of preventing the strike work from being done by Jewish tailors. The delegates decided to organize a mass meeting at one of the largest halls and to call upon those engaged upon such work to abstain from doing it."[203] Kenneth Collins informed us that at least one sizable group of Hassidic Jews left London to take advantage of the strike, and settled in Edinburgh.[204]

It is thus clear that Jewish leaders were aware that the presence of Jewish workers during such a major strike would only serve to reinforce perceptions that Jews were lacking in class allegiance. It is also apparent that there were a minority of Jews who were perfectly willing to cross the picket line if such an opportunity arose. A week after the conference, a resolution was produced by leaders of the meeting at Whitechapel Road which stated:

> It is desired to place on record its sympathy with the Edinburgh strikers and to appeal to tailors generally to refuse Scottish work. At the same time it was intended to defend the Jewish worker against the unfounded charges of blacklegging laid at the door of all Jews, although it was the action of only a few of them.[205]

T.M. Devine has argued that Jews did not compete directly with Scots in the labor market.[206] While this was most definitely the case in terms of employment in heavy industry and mining, there is sufficient evidence to suggest that in commercial life, particularly in trades such as tailoring, this was not the case. There is also evidence that this competition was the cause of a great deal of tension in the city, and a growing antipathy toward Jewish immigrants. Tailoring, boot-making, shoe-making, and cabinet-making were the "sweated trades," and it was argued by contemporaries in London that in these trades "the native artisan was being undercut and displaced by immigrant competitors."[207] Sweating was the practice of employing a large number of workers at extremely low wages. Writing of sweated workers in Scotland, Henry Maitles states that these employees would then work "long hours in terrible conditions and by doing so undercut the rate paid to fully skilled workers for the job."[208] During an interview carried out by the House of Lords Select Committee on Sweating in 1899, John McLaughlin, a tailors' trade union leader stated that "the wholesale sweaters in Glasgow are chiefly Jews and the number is said to be increasing, though on this point evidence is somewhat scanty."[209]

The New York–based journal, *The Outlook*, carried an article in 1903, in which it quoted a Dr. Smith as stating that "the Jews are now so numerous that their competition appreciably affects the rate of wages in certain industries ... the Jews in Scotland have very nearly monopolized the manufacture of ready-made clothing."[210]

Sweating was not a uniquely Jewish phenomenon, though it combined with fears of "swamping" in London to generate an image of a criminal foreigner who was also an economic threat. In Scotland, the sweating system was seen largely as a tool of employers, who utilized it in an effort to break the unions. Even when immigration levels raised concerns about large numbers of immigrants willing to work for a low wage, the gaze of Scots was perhaps more likely to fall on the Irish than the Jews, particularly in Glasgow. In fact, the 1936 *Report on the State of the Irish Poor in Great Britain*, contained witness statements which reflected that many Scots still held views that as well as being idle and lazy, the Irish were at the same time "undermining attempts to strengthen employment rights by their willingness to work hard for low wages," and that "wages were lowered by Irish workers."[211] There was a strikingly similar logic behind many of the accusations of sweating leveled against Jews during this period.

The fact that sweating did occur in some Jewish workshops weighed heavily on Jewish leaders who were aware of its potential to fuel anti-Jewish sentiment. The Chief Rabbi made the issue of sweating a key point for discussion during his 1907 tour of the country, and in Edinburgh he urged all congregations that they "should taboo the "sweater," a villain who he hoped was not to be found among the Jews of that district."[212]

There is some evidence that sweating was a problem in Edinburgh, though it does not seem to have featured in discussions associated with the Edinburgh Tailor's Strike in 1903. In June 1888, *The Lancet* carried a report of the Special Sanitary Commission on the Sweating System in Edinburgh.[213] The report began with the assertion that although Edinburgh was an important national center for "the higher branches of the tailoring trade," sweating was not a major problem in the city. Nonetheless, the vast majority of the article concerned itself with an evaluation of the Jewish sweating which was taking place in the city. The article began by arguing that the first major influx of Jewish immigrants to Edinburgh occurred in the aftermath of the 1873 tailors strike. The agents of Master Tailors were said to have been "sent to London and elsewhere, and a number of Jews, both German and Russian, were brought to Edinburgh. Some were single and others came with their families." The article continued by stating that these Master Tailors offered their new Jewish employees lodgings, security for the payment of rent, and work which could be undertaken in the Jews' own homes.

Jews were represented as providing a particularly malevolent form of foreign competition for the native Edinburgh worker. The article stated that the Danes who had been imported following the 1866 tailors strike worked in workshops rather than at home, "fraternized with the Scotch tailors, joined their union, and thus ceased to compete against the native labour." The report asserts that the chief result of the 1873 strike was to "firmly implant Jew tailors in Edinburgh … greatly extending the home-work system."[214]

The sweating of non-Jews was acknowledged by the report. It was stated that many tailors in the city "often suffered from total want of sanitary convenience," and lack of ventilation and working space seems to have been commonplace in many of the worst workshops. However, the focus of the majority of the article rested on Jewish tailors in Edinburgh. One Jewish sweater was said to provide "a good many uniforms for the police," and another operated in premises where "the front door could hardly be shut, and the bottom was eaten away by rats.... This sweater has sometimes obtained sub-contracts for making uniforms for the municipality." A process was outlined whereby a master tailor obtained a contract from a local authority requiring uniforms. This tailor then delegated the work first to Jewish cutters, who would then pass on the work of finishing the garments to the workers of a Jewish sweater, before the items finally returned to the original contractor. A contractor standing atop a pyramid of cheap Jewish labor was likely to undercut his rivals when bidding for contracts, illustrating that the economic impact of Jewish sweating could be felt at the top level of the trade, as well as at the bottom.

Another interesting aspect of the article was its reference to Jewish-Gentile relations in the slums of Edinburgh. That the two populations remained to a great extent segregated was strongly implied, and the natives of the city were reported to have been "greatly disturbed by their Jew neighbours, who worked through all Sunday and made much noise." Jews were also accused of being dirty and bad tenants, though the author of the report states that the Jews interviewed were not "slow in finding fault with the Scotch." It was thus suggested that there was a degree of ill-feeling between native and foreign inhabitants of Edinburgh's slums during the period of immigration.

Despite the bias of the *Lancet* in maintaining such a focus on Jewish sweating in Edinburgh, and the fact that workers in tailoring represented the second largest economic group in Edinburgh Jewry, numbers would still have been small enough to preclude any direct impingement upon the livelihood of Edinburgh's native workers, who numbered at least 600 master tailors during the strike.[215] Such comparatively small numbers, together with the predominance of the home-based pattern of work, ensured that no Jewish workers union formed in the city. One must also take into account the high level of self-employment among Edinburgh's Jews, and the subsequent lack of a numerically significant, stable class of employed workers.

It is also clear that there were Jewish efforts on a national scale to minimize competition between the foreign and native worker. In an effort to reduce the pressure of Jewish immigrant competition on local economies, the *Jewish Chronicle* began publishing district reports and economic profiles toward the end of the 1890s. These reports were intended to help prevent the overconcentration of Jewish workers in the provinces. One such report from January 1898 urged Jewish workers to avoid settling in Edinburgh as, "employment with the tailors and shoemakers is bad."[216]

Ben Braber has highlighted a connection between the ready-made clothing industry and peddling in Glasgow. The process would start with "small, often family-based workshops," which would produce clothing parts. These parts would then be assembled in large warehouses by major manufacturers. Jewish tailors and their families were able to form such small workshops because the venture required "little capital and the part-work, which in general required few skills, could be carried out at home by family members and lodgers."[217] Once assembled, "the hawkers formed an important outlet for this industry."[218] In cases where the wholesaler was Jewish, and Edinburgh certainly had a number of Jewish wholesalers, the production and sale of ready-made clothing and small items of furniture could be an exclusively Jewish affair.

Edinburgh's Jews, like its other residents, were equally prone to the fluctuations of the economy, and demand for their goods. In hard times, those who did manage to accrue enough capital to move up the economic ladder could have these gains snatched away. It was an unreliable path to economic advancement. Ben Braber stated that for many Jews, "hawking was an occupation to which many resorted after becoming unemployed or in slack times." Evelyn Cowan recalled that during her father's lifetime, "he opened and closed, albeit rather hastily, at least a dozen men's outfitters' shops in various parts of the country."[219]

When even peddling failed to generate sufficient income, often all that remained was the kind of crippling poverty which marked the pages of the *Jewish Chronicle* and the mission reports. This kind of uncertainty, and the daily challenges of living and working in a new country certainly took its toll. Evelyn Cowan recalled that, "the men worked long hard hours in their shops. Their wives became prematurely old from constant childbirth and continuous, monotonous domestic work."[220] For this group of first-generation migrants, social and economic advancement was rare and hard-won.

However, it is apparent that some of the immigrants, regardless of their cultural background, arrived in Edinburgh with a determination to assimilate, or at least thoroughly integrate, and a desire for their children to take advantage of new opportunities. It was to the children of this first-generation of Jewish immigrants that the opportunities of a new life were bequeathed, and it was against a background of destitution and the harsher realities of immigrant life that some of the most remarkable instances of social and economic advancement took place. For example, Professor Sir Abraham Goldberg, born in Edinburgh in 1923 to a Lithuanian father and an illiterate Ukrainian mother, went on to become one of the world's leading experts on enzyme deficiency. His father was a traveling salesman.[221] The children of recent immigrants would have gone to ordinary schools as Edinburgh, unlike Glasgow and other provincial Jewish centers, lacked a facility for education of Jewish children in any form other than the Hebrew lessons at Sciennes Place. While there, their education was the same as any other child in the city, with the only difference of note being that they were excused from taking part in the singing of hymns. One Jewish child later recalled, "my father did not speak a word of English, but he went to school at night to learn English.... It did not happen overnight. It took some time. The children of immigrants integrated immediately. We went to ordinary schools."[222] It is to the secular education of Jewish children in Edinburgh that this book now turns its attention.

Jewish Children and Education in Edinburgh, 1880–1910

Edinburgh University has a long history of offering educational opportunities to Jewish youths. Kenneth Collins has charted the history of Jews and the study of medicine in Scotland, and it should suffice to state here that Jewish students from around the globe have for over 200 years been attracted to Scotland's Universities because of their lack of religious entry requirements.[223] Edinburgh University had also welcomed a number of Jewish students from the city's early Jewish community. Many subsequently left the city and scattered throughout the globe. One such example was Abraham Harris, born in Edinburgh in 1836, and educated at Edinburgh and London. At the age of 23 he left for Jamaica, and then moved to Charleston in South Carolina. He returned to Europe to take up a position as English tutor for the German Royal Family, where the future Kaiser Friedrich Wilhelm was one of his pupils. He again returned to the United States where he spent the rest of his life ministering to the Jewish congregation of Richmond, Virginia.[224]

Edinburgh's Jewish population at the end of the 19th century was a youthful one. Even in 1881, prior to the great waves of immigration, approximately 45 percent of the city's Jews were under 16 years of age. Only 3 percent were over the age of 60.[225] Harvey Kaplan's sample of 1,318 individuals from the 1901 census, revealed that 46 percent of those listed were aged 14 or under and a further 46 percent were aged 15 to 44. Kaplan states that, "only ten men and seven women were aged sixty-five or over."[226] In addition, 55 percent of the individuals listed were born in Britain and Ireland, "compared to 39% in the Gorbals and 48% in Leeds," and 39 percent had been born in Edinburgh or Leith.[227]

Other than a higher number of native-born individuals, Edinburgh's Jewish community in 1901 was very much similar in its make-up, particularly in its youth, to other Jewish communities throughout Britain and Ireland. The migrants from Russia tended to be in their early twenties, and often resided in several towns in Britain and Ireland before they settled in Edinburgh. Census data suggests that a number of them had children shortly after their arrival, and census entries for "place of birth" of the children of these immigrants often reveal a brief stay in Ireland, or a prolonged residence in England. Using data from Harvey Kaplan's census analysis, it is evident that children born during these interim residences prior to settlement in Edinburgh formed 16 percent of Edinburgh's population in 1901.[228]

The children of migrant Jewish communities, and the high percentage born in Britain, were a source of concern for Jewish leaders eager to preserve religious and cultural traditions. Recent research in the field of cross-cultural psychology has stressed the importance of age at migration, illustrating that over time the acculturation gap between parents and children increases. Immigrant children, even if not born in Scotland, were more "capable of quickly picking up the new language and learning cultural behaviours and traditions."[229] As Abel Phillips states, parents, often illiterate and lacking any command of the English language, had to contend with the fact that their "sons and daughters [were being] brought up in this new environment, becoming conversant with the English language through English books and newspapers."[230] Of course, the main way in which Jewish children were introduced to this "new world," was through the school system.

Anecdotal evidence suggests that a small number of parents in Edinburgh resisted sending their children to school, and it is highly likely that the reason behind this action was the fear that the schools could be instrumental in the destruction of Jewish orthodoxy among the youth of the community. Before Max Mendick arrived in the city, he recalled that "an old Jew" had returned to Lithuania having resided for some time in Edinburgh. He explained to other villagers that he was "appalled" at regulations in the city, and that one of the main reasons for his return was that, "if you don't send your kids to school, the police will come and take them away from you."[231]

Such cases seem, however, to have been in the minority. Todd Endelman has argued that it was not uncommon for new immigrants to take "advantage of their new surroundings to shed or dilute their Jewishness."[232] For parents of this mindset, sending their children to Edinburgh's schools would have been viewed positively, both for the opportunities that education would bring and the assimilation that such an education contributed toward. In addition, they would have prevented their children from attending the Hebrew classes and other Jewish educational facilities offered by the synagogues, and concern among community leaders about the frequency of such parental choices is evident.[233]

For those parents who did wish to preserve the "transmissible distinctiveness" of their Jewish heritage, a balance was sought in which the benefits of secular education could be reaped without harming the preservation of religious and cultural traditions.[234] When discussion occurred about the possibility of creating a Jewish school in Glasgow in the first decade of the 20th century, the search for such a balance was at the forefront. Kenneth Collins states that while most parents wanted to preserve their traditions, "many parents were worried about the idea of a Jewish school because, as immigrants, they still felt the need to be regarded as part of the wider community and did not wish to see their children segregated within the school system."[235]

Thus, while the re-creation of ghetto life in Britain, and the segregation which accompanied it, was chosen for reasons including security and convenience; it is clear that a great many immigrants desired that their children should move beyond this segregation, maintaining their religious customs, but integrating with their gentile neighbors in a manner more akin to that pursued by established British Jewry than to the social exclusivity of Edinburgh's "Jewish Quarter."

Whether they desired it or not, Edinburgh's Jewish community lacked the size and resources to construct and administer a school providing education on non-religious subjects. Edinburgh's Jewish children therefore filtered through a number of the city's primary and secondary schools, many of them centers of academic excellence. From a large number of articles in the *Jewish Chronicle*, it is clear that the majority of Edinburgh's Jewish school children attended one of three schools.

James Gillespie's School had been founded in 1803, funded by the legacy of wealthy tobacconist James Gillespie. Control and responsibility for the school was later assumed by the Edinburgh Merchant Company, which by 1879 had formed large day schools, with fee-paying on a modest scale and also offering charitable free places.[236] In 1908 it was then handed over to the Edinburgh School Board. The school was originally based in Bruntsfield Place, moving to Gillespie Crescent in 1908, before moving again to Bruntsfield Links in 1914.[237] It was responsible for the education of around 1,000 boys and girls in the first decade of the 20th century, and was operating a primary and secondary department. Based at Gillespie Crescent, the school was approximately one mile from both the Dalry community and the main area of Jewish habitation in the city. The *Jewish Chronicle* printed many reports on Jewish success at the school. For example, in July 1889 it was reported that one child received a silver medal and first prize in French, two children won bursary's entitling them to free education for set periods of time, and several other Jewish children also won minor prizes.[238] The Reverend Fürst's daughter Emily attended the school, as did Louis and Maurice Turiansky, sons of Bernard Turiansky, head of the Edinburgh New Hebrew Congregation.[239] Relations between the school and Jewish community leaders were healthy, and in May 1889, Her Majesty's Inspector of Schools communicated to the Reverend Fürst that "all Jewish children attending the Merchant Company, James Gillespie's Schools, will have their final examination by Her Majesty's Inspector on Tuesday 4th June, instead of Wednesday and Thursday as previously arranged, on account of the Feast of Pentecost."[240]

Jewish pupils also attended George Watson's College in significant numbers. George Watson's College had been founded in 1870, following the conversion of a hospital into a day school by the Edinburgh Merchant Company. It had a roll of 1,000 pupils (it educated only males) by the end of 1871, and was at that time based at Archibald Place.[241] The school's first headmaster was Dr. George Ogilvie. Ogilvie apparently had a good relationship with the Edinburgh Hebrew Congregation, as he attended the consecration of the Graham Street Synagogue in 1898.[242]

Among those attending George Watson's College in 1888 were George and Henry Goldston, sons of David Goldston, then president of the Edinburgh Hebrew Congregation. Both boys were admitted in 1881, aged eight (George) and five (Henry).[243] Their older brother Ernest had been admitted in 1871 aged eight, and was followed in 1877 by Michael aged ten, then by Saul, who was admitted in 1878 aged seven.[244]

It is clear, however, that this kind of education did not always lead to a break with tradition in occupational terms. David Goldston had been born in the Russian Empire in 1839. The Edinburgh and Leith Post Office directory for 1873–1874 lists him as living then at 108 Nicholson Street, and his occupation was listed as "carver and guilder."[245] By 1877, the family had moved to 29 Buccleuch Place, and were still there at the time of the 1901 census. Ernest, Michael, George, and Henry were still at the home in Buccleuch Place. Ernest and Michael had gone into watch-making and George and Henry both went into the manufacture of hosiery. A younger son, Benjamin, was however listed as a dentist's apprentice.

Perhaps the most successful Jewish pupil at the school was Isaac Lipetz, who obtained numerous prizes at the school, and was "awarded no fewer than six scholarships during his attendance thereat."[246] Like many Jewish youths, Isaac went on to study medicine at Edinburgh University, where he graduated in the winter of 1909.[247]

The acquisition of bursaries, grants, and cash prizes would have been of great importance to poorer families with ambitions to send their children to such an institution. Fees per quarter for George Watson's College in 1886 ranged from twelve shillings and sixpence for Elementary Pupils, to one pound, seven shillings and sixpence for Junior Pupils and two pounds and two shillings per quarter for Senior Pupils.[248] Reduced fees were granted only to sons of Church of Scotland ministers, particularly the sons of missionaries, and also for the sons of members of the Merchant Company of Edinburgh.[249] In addition, bursaries were available to approximately 60 pupils per year, and were based solely on academic performance.[250] The meritocratic nature of the bursaries and funds such as Heriot's Trust was a catalyst for working class advancement in the city. Michael Fry notes that "altogether, upwardly mobile members of the working class felt the trust was there for them and did a great job of meeting their needs."[251]

Despite these opportunities, the age at which some Jewish pupils entered the rolls of Edinburgh's premier schools suggests that most Jewish parents could not afford the modest level of fees until after their child had acquired a bursary. It is also clear that some pupils would change school on the basis of acquiring a bursary. Maurice Turiansky, having attended James Gillespie's for some years, left for George Watson's in 1902 after being awarded a Burgh Committee Bursary, tenable for four years at that institution.[252]

Another Merchant Company school, Daniel Stewart's Institution, provided places for Jewish students, as did the Royal High School, one of Europe's oldest schools. Again, the acquisition of bursaries was crucial and Michael Brown, a Jewish pupil was notable in 1895 for securing a four-year scholarship at Daniel Stewart's.[253]

The early years of the 20th century saw a number of young Edinburgh Jews, many the children of immigrants, graduate in various medical disciplines at Edinburgh University. Louis Turiansky obviously excelled in his field, leaving James Gillespie's School at the age of 16 to enter the University of Edinburgh. He was "the first Jewish student to benefit by the Carnegie Grant in Scotland," and passed his final examination at the age of 21.[254] Three years earlier, Louis' brother Benjamin had also graduated in medicine from Edinburgh University.[255]

The number of local and international Jewish students at the University was sufficient for discussions to be held in January 1909 regarding the possible "formation of a Jewish Students' Society."[256] Although that first meeting of Jewish undergraduates concluded that it was "inadvisable to found a separate organization," such an organization was established in March of that year.[257] The link between the city's Jewish community and the student body is evidenced by the chairmanship of these meetings by Mr. Symon Stungo—vice-president of both the Edinburgh Jewish Board of Guardians and the Edinburgh Zionist Association. Also, earlier in the decade, the Edinburgh Hebrew Congregation had welcomed a number of colonial students studying at the university.

The range of subjects studied and professions engaged in by the city's Jewish students was diverse. In October 1907, 17-year-old Sydney Rosenbloom was elected as the youngest ever sub-professor at the Royal Academy of Music. Sydney had been born and educated in Edinburgh. He was the son of a Polish immigrant father and a mother of "German-English parentage."[258] The Reverend Levenberg, who had ministered to the Dalry congregation between 1904 and 1908, had studied music at Heriot Watt College, and left for Portsmouth shortly after his graduation.[259] William Wedeclefsky graduated with an MA in 1908, following a period of study in Mathematics and Hebrew, where he gained first prize in "the Arts section of Senior Hebrew."[260] The Reverend Fürst's son Isaac had taken a course in law and in 1900 he became the first Jew to be admitted to the Scots Law Society.[261]

The range of professions engaged in by this often British-born generation would have taken them into environments quite different from the enclosed nature of Edinburgh's Jewish community. As some means of achieving a workable balance between these two worlds, the period 1880–1910 saw the founding and development of a large number of cultural and religious organizations geared toward the preservation of Jewish religion and identity in the next generation, as well as forming a bridge to further relations with society outside the ghetto. Foremost among these organizations was the Young Men's Social and Literary Association, founded after a meeting of 40 young men at the Park Place synagogue in March 1889.[262] It was later renamed the Jewish Young Men's Literary Society, and then the Edinburgh Jewish Literary Society. It is still in existence, "the oldest surviving society of its kind in Great Britain."[263] The society was originally intended to be a gathering of young men, and even married young men were prohibited from joining until a resolution was passed in 1895.[264] According to Abel Phillips, it was founded in order "to maintain the traditions of that form of Jewish life which they found in their homes, without losing contact with the intellectual life of their new milieu."[265]

The group first met in the schoolroom of the Park Place synagogue, which was illuminated only by the "dim light of gas jet burners," and among those first members we find Michael Goldston and Isaac Fürst.[266] Suggestive perhaps of the frustration young Edinburgh Jews felt about divisiveness in the community, one of the first rules of the society was a ban on discussions of religious or theological matters.[267] It also ensured that room would be left for the discussion of a range of issues beyond the scope of a religious sermon. The formation of the society represented a move toward creating cohesiveness in the community outside the religious sphere. Ruth Adler states that:

> They raised money to buy a piano and formed an orchestra. People whose English wasn't good enough to understand the lectures could still enjoy the meetings.... People came from all sections of the community, from those who laboured in the rubber works ... to all kinds of professionals and academics.[268]

Lectures and debates became central features of the society, which met on a fortnightly basis during the early years of its operation. Abel Phillips points out that "in the 1880s there was of course no lack of themes to stimulate the Jewish mind." Migration waves, the Zionist movement, and the rise of modern anti-Semitism in France, Germany and Russia formed the basis for many debates and discussions.[269] The Reverend Fürst occupied a central role within the organization, and seems to have been important in the maintenance of Jewish themes on the society's agenda. In November 1889 he gave an address on "The Hebrew Language," in which he "expressed the hope that the members would continue to study their original tongue, so as to deserve the name of Hebrew young men."[270] The activity of Edinburgh's missionaries provided enough material for a debate to be held on the subject in March 1896. The speaker concluded that, "a Jew who knew and studied the history of his race could never become a convert."[271]

The role of clergy in literary societies, and the extent to which these societies should be affiliated to synagogues and focus on "Jewish" topics was a topic of debate among Britain's Jews. At the first "Conference of Literary Societies" held at Queen Square House, London, in June 1902, a total of 24 literary societies, of which "more than half are domiciled in the provinces" were represented, among whom was the Rev. J.A. Gouldstein of Edinburgh.[272] A Mr. S. Rosenbaum delivered a paper titled, "The Programmes of Literary Societies," advocating that literary and social groups should discuss "scientific, political, and other lectures of general interest," as well as "those of a purely Jewish character."[273] It was added by Mr. Israel Abrahams that this range of topics should be particularly pursued by the literary societies of smaller communities where "the local Jewish Literary Society was likely to be the only local institution of its kind to which a mind would be likely to belong."[274] Abrahams did however add that it should be the goal of Jewish Literary Societies to focus as much on Jewish issues as possible, since evidence had shown that it actually formed a very minor part of the lecture programs of many societies. A delegate from the East London Communal League provided information which suggested that as little as 10 percent of lectures organized by Jewish Literary Societies concerned Jewish history or culture, and that Jewish lecturers comprised only 10 percent of those invited to speak.

These figures seem representative of Edinburgh's Literary Society during this period. Despite the occasional lecture on Hebrew and Jewish history, the Society was notably outward looking in its lecture program. Some of the more mentionable lectures of the period were Alphonse Louis Reis' lecture on "Government Policy in Ireland," Saul Goldston's address on "The Jacobite Rebellion of 1745," and Mr. S. Benjamin's discussion of "Labour and Capital."[275] The "Irish Question" seems to have been of particular interest to the members as the "Irish Home Rule Question" was the subject of a lengthy and well-attended debate in 1896.[276] This is possibly because some parallels were drawn with Zionist aspirations.

Christians were always made welcome, and a great many reports of these lectures report large attendances. W.T. Munro Hogg was a frequent speaker, and Christian professors and professionals were also regularly invited to speak. In February 1906, Councillor Leishman from the Edinburgh School Board was invited to discuss "Education."[277] Links with the Edinburgh School Board would have been strengthened further by the fact that the Reverend Fürst's daughter Emily had been employed by the Edinburgh School Board since 1898.[278]

As much as Edinburgh's lecture program varied greatly, and was often lacking in a "Jewish" dimension to its discussions, it is clear that it was closely affiliated to the Edinburgh Hebrew Congregation. This link between synagogue and literary society was the subject of debate as much as the content of its program. During the first Conference of Literary Societies in 1902, it was argued by some representatives that "too close a bond between the Society and the Synagogue was not desirable."[279] The reasoning behind this was that it was felt that "discussion should be open and free, and this could not be done if there were too close a connection with the synagogue."[280] It was felt by the majority of representatives that the synagogue should support the society, but that as it attracted "Jews of every class," it should be left to develop on its own. Implicit in this discussion may have been the feeling that under the direction of the Edinburgh Hebrew Congregation, the literary society could become something of an assimilationist device, designed to bring the children of the immigrant class into line with the aspirations of established Jewry. The Edinburgh New Hebrew Congregation established their own "Edinburgh Hebrew and English Young Men's Literary Institute," under the chairmanship of Reuben Eprile, a watch salesman, in February 1890.[281] Its first lecture was on "Machinery versus Manual Labour."[282]

A glimpse into the political leanings of the Edinburgh Hebrew Congregation's young Jewish men was revealed by the outcome of a mock parliamentary debate, held in January 1910. The case for Labour was supported by Symon Stungo, with the Reverend Fürst's son Simon advocating for the Liberals. A Mr. Lucas Levy put forth a case for supporting the Conservatives. Eschewing a tendency toward support for socialism, common among immigrant Jewish populations at this time, the youth of the Edinburgh Hebrew Congregation voted in favor of the Liberals "by a large majority."[283]

The Edinburgh Literary Society flourished and attracted many members and a great deal of enthusiasm. By its third annual meeting the society's finances were in a "most prosperous condition," reflective of the health of the society as a whole. It went on to organize "social habits, annual dances, and summer picnics," and in 1909 it spawned the Jewish Amateur Dramatic Society.[284] The Dramatic Society quickly devoted itself to charitable activity, starting in January 1909 when it gave a performance in aid of a poor local Jewish family.[285]

Furthermore, the success of the Literary Society provided a worthy example for a range of cultural organizations which sprang up to engage Edinburgh's Jewish youth. In 1901 a Jewish Amateur Orchestral Society was formed.[286] Although conducted and headed by the Rev. Isaac Levine, of the Richmond Street congregation, the orchestra embraced a wide cross-section of the community, and performed not just in the city's synagogues, but also at lodging houses and music venues throughout Edinburgh, often donating the proceeds to Jewish charitable causes.[287]

In November 1905, a branch of the Jewish Lads' Brigade was founded in Edinburgh just over 10 years after Colonel Goldsmid established the first brigade in London's East End.[288] Based on the Church Lads' Brigade, which was itself an imitation of the Boys' Brigade, a central aim of the Jewish Lads' Brigade was "to facilitate the racial integration—if not the assimilation—of Jewish immigrant boys living in East End ghettoes into the 'host' English community."[289] Similarly, in July 1910, an Edinburgh Jewish Lads' Athletic Club was established, which brought Jewish youths from various backgrounds into contact with non-Jewish youths on a regular basis. A contemporary report stated that, "a number of athletic clubs in Edinburgh have intimated their desire to meet the Jewish Lads' Club in friendly contest."[290]

John Springhall argued that the emergence of such youth movements among Jewish communities not only suggested willingness for Jewish immigrant youths to integrate with their non-Jewish peers, but also betrayed the influence of the "public-school ethic," and the "British tradition" of the young sportsman who was heir to the Empire. Springhall quoted one Jewish figure as arguing in favor of such movements which would develop and improve "the narrow chested, round-shouldered, slouching son of the Ghetto, who it was promised would become converted with extraordinary rapidity into an erect and self-respecting man, a living negation of the stigma which has long disfigured our race."[291]

The Literary Society in Edinburgh and the city's other youth organizations flourished during these early years. They thrived upon the youth of the community, and the popular and able leadership of the Reverend Fürst who was satisfied to see these organizations as some means of promoting Judaism and Jewish history and culture among the young. These societies also acted as a conduit between the culture of Edinburgh's Jewish community and the political, economic, and cultural milieu beyond the ghetto. They were, to an extent, unifying organizations, which served to attract all classes, and brought together the pious and the religiously apathetic. The Jewish youth organizations of the "migrant era," were the domain and, in some ways the producer, of that new educated youth who would go on to forge in earnest the links between two worlds, the Old Town ghetto and the Scotland beyond it.

This examination of Jewish communal life, in the era of immigration and reaction, reveals the many strands which came together to form Edinburgh's Jewish community. Differences in nationality, religious practice, language, occupation, economic and social status, political affiliation and even age should encourage one to abandon any notion of the Jews of Edinburgh being a homogenous unit. The era under examination witnessed the ghettoization of most of Edinburgh's immigrant Jews, and the development of an insular commercial economy, built largely upon the peddler and the craftsman. Zionism helped bring together some of the fraying strands of Edinburgh's

Jewish population, and aided the preservation of vital aspects of Jewish identity and tradition during a period of great change.

Common to the majority of Jews in the city was a desire for the preservation of Judaism and Jewish culture in the next generation, though there were varying interpretations as to what this meant. It was in this generation of Jewish children, mainly born in the British Isles, that the bridge between the world of the immigrant and the world outside the ghetto was truly formed. Raised as Jews, in Jewish homes, in Jewish districts, they also embraced the city in which they lived. They attended the same schools as their non-Jewish counterparts, and in some cases excelled and moved away from the occupational profile of their parents. They were what Rabbi Salis Daiches later referred to as, "the future of Scottish Jewry."

4

Battles at Home and Abroad, 1911–1918

> *The Edinburgh community is a comparatively small one, but it is, to quote Kipling, a terror for its size. No community in the United Kingdom has been rent by such internecine strife, nor has any city resounded with so brazen a clash of communal arms.*[1]

During the period commencing with the introduction of the Aliens Bills of 1911, and ending with the cessation of the Great War in 1918, Edinburgh's immigrant Jewish community was confronted with a worsening of the problems which had plagued it during its formative years. The community during this period remained largely segregated from Gentile Scots, and the center of Jewish settlement in the city remained the area around North Richmond Street described by one contemporary as "one of Auld Reekie's auldest and reekiest parts."[2] Edinburgh's Jewish charities and philanthropic schemes continued to battle with chronic poverty, a task which became harder when the Great War began to affect trades which had previously been the sole source of subsistence to Jewish workers. Communal division intensified, and new tactics employed by Edinburgh's evangelical Christian missions placed the city's Jews under national scrutiny. The outbreak of war saw Edinburgh become a "prohibited city," and with this measure came the internment or deportation of many of the city's non-naturalized Jews, and the formation of an Edinburgh Jewish Representative Council to defend Jewish interests. The war brought challenges to those Edinburgh Jews who served with Scotland's regiments, as well as those who resisted conscription and found themselves before the Military Appeals Tribunals. It is the aim of this chapter to examine the response of Edinburgh's Jews to these challenges, and to assess the ongoing life of the community in spite of them.

Segregation and Community Division

A few years prior to the Great War, Howard Denton was born Hyman Zoltie. Denton's father had been a tobacconist from Bialystok in Russian Poland, and after migrating to Edinburgh, his father began a career as a traveling salesman. When his parents married in 1902, the "house" they moved into was a single rented room. Denton recalls that in order to provide for his growing family, his father moved from selling "nothing but slippers made by my grandfather" to selling "anything people might need."[3] Denton's memoirs, *The Happy Land*, provide an invaluable glimpse into the manner in which one young Jew, born in Edinburgh, perceived others within and without the city's Jewish community during the period in question.

According to Howard Denton, interaction between immigrant Jewish families and Gentile Scots in the 1910s remained at much the same level as during the preceding three decades. He stated that although Edinburgh was notable for the "way it readily welcomed and assimilated the Jewish people," and although "we did not feel threatened by being in a strange place," the "Jewish Quarter" remained "like a little island of foreignness in the centre of Scotland's ancient capital."[4]

Perhaps foremost among the reasons for this continued social segregation was the belief of many immigrant Jews that such segregation was essential to the preservation of orthodox tradition. Denton recalled that his father "never faltered from the strict faith of his upbringing."[5] He further explained that, "all around us were the Scots but our parents regarded them as goys, outsiders we were not encouraged to mix with. My father wanted to keep us well within the orthodox tradition and, dutifully, I would refrain from mixing with the Scottish children."[6] The rapid increase in Jewish youth organizations in these years coincided not only with an increase in the number of Scottish-born children, but also with the fact that many were now of an age where interaction with Gentiles was increasingly unavoidable. Correspondingly, the years preceding the outbreak of the Great War witnessed a rapid expansion in the number of Jewish social outlets for the community's youth, as the community's elders, and some committed younger Jews, sought to minimize potentially harmful interactions with Gentile culture.

In addition to pre-existing institutions such as the Jewish Literary Society, the Young Men's Zionist Association and the Edinburgh Jewish Lads' Athletic Club, the period January 1911 to February 1914 saw the inauguration of no fewer than nine Jewish youth organizations, a remarkable number given the size of the community. In January 1911, a meeting was held to form a "Daughters of Zion" organization, which would act as the female counterpart to the Young Men's Zionist Association. Meetings were thereafter held conjointly, along with social events and dances.[7] By the end of the month, a

Jewish Historical Society had been formed, and in May 1911, young Jewish males were encouraged to participate in the Edinburgh Jewish Cricket Club.[8] In March 1912, a club was established to provide young Jewish men in the city with the facilities to engage in boxing, wrestling, weight-lifting, and gymnastics.[9] Within a year, a separate Edinburgh Jewish Young Men's Association had been formed, shortly followed by an Edinburgh Jewish Rambling Club, an Edinburgh Jewish Debating Club, a Hebrew School at Sciennes Place, and in February 1914 a Jewish Girls Social Club had been inaugurated.[10]

A number of letters written from concerned Edinburgh Jews to the editor of the *Jewish Chronicle* during these years revealed that the creation of many, if not all, of these organizations was directly related to community anxieties about the dangers of cultural assimilation. In June 1911, Mr. L. Ockrent, joint honorary secretary of the Young Men's Zionist Association explained that his organization intended to open a Jewish library because, "in Edinburgh, at the present time, there is no opportunity given to the Jewish youth of reading literature on Judaism and Jewish matters."[11] In a speech to the Young Men's Zionist Association and the Daughters of Zion less than two weeks later, veteran Zionist Joseph Cowen informed his audience that assimilation was not to be achieved

> by obliterating the differences of individual nations. There were people who had their certain specific duties to carry out, and the brotherhood of man was to be gained rather by recognising these differences than by cutting out and destroying them. They strove for Jewish ideals, Jewish culture, they were not forgetful of the Jewish past, and they hoped for the Jewish future.[12]

Similar sentiments were expressed in January 1912 by Lewis Rifkind, a senior figure in both the Young Men's Zionist Association and the Edinburgh University Jewish Students Society. Rifkind had been born in Lithuania, and had moved to Edinburgh with his family in 1902 at the age of 10.[13] Rifkind argued that there was a "cold indifference and complete apathy" prevailing among "the young Jewish generation." Although the situation was "deplorable," Rifkind argued that Jewish youths were not to be blamed, since they had been "brought up in a non-Jewish environment and imbibing Christian culture," and that it was therefore "natural" for them "to lose all interest in their nation and become indifferent to its woes and joys." Rifkind had been instrumental in establishing a Hebrew department at the Young Men's Zionist Association, with the aim of "encouraging the use of Hebrew as a language among the members of the society,"[14] though he felt the surest way to combat the malaise of young Jews was to increase the availability of Jewish literature in English.[15]

A Literary Society syllabus for the year 1912–1913 reveals that in December 1912, a joint discussion was held between the Edinburgh Jewish Literary Society, and its Glasgow counterpart. The topic of the discussion was: "That there is a decline in the interest of the Jewish youth in the Jewish religion."[16]

In February 1913, Lewis Rifkind was again instrumental in the creation of the Edinburgh Jewish Young Men's Society, which had been established to "promote social intercourse among Jewish young men in the city, great numbers of whom have drifted into Christian clubs and societies, and have gradually become estranged from the Jewish community."[17]

Rifkind's solution to the perceived apathy of young Jews, and the dangers posed by "Christian culture," was not universally supported. A letter from an anonymous Edinburgh Jew, under the name "G," in January 1913 argued in favor of a traditional Jewish education based around the learning of Hebrew, rather than simply increasing the amount of Jewish education in English. The letter stressed that the state of Hebrew education in Edinburgh had deteriorated to a level that should arouse "shame and sorrow" in all sectors of the city's Jewish population. "G" states that "the existing synagogues are empty on Sabbaths. Our communal workers fail to note our chief need—the religious teaching of children. I am convinced that there are many young men who never enter a synagogue even on High Festivals, because they are ashamed at not being able to read their prayers."[18] The letter goes on to argue that the city's synagogues fail to provide Sabbath and Holiday services for children, and that this had been the case since the size of the community increased due to immigration. Another important aspect of the letter was that the writer pointed out that "the poor children of non-members (with the exception of a very few) get no Hebrew teaching at all."

While one must account for some exaggeration in a letter so obviously borne out of anxiety, particularly in relation to the claim that all the city's synagogues lay empty on Sabbaths, the statements about a "disconnected" Jewish youth, a lack of Hebrew education, and an apparent class divide in Edinburgh are corroborated to some extent by other sources. Shortly following, and possibly in response to, the publication of the letter, Jewish representatives approached the Edinburgh School Board seeking permission to use a school at Sciennes Place for the purpose of evening classes in Hebrew for the city's Jewish children and young adults. The Edinburgh School Board granted the request and, in addition provided books "free of charge, and the fee paid for tuition is returned to those who attend regularly." It was proudly noted by the organizers that this was "the only class of its kind in the United Kingdom." A further coup for the organizers of the Hebrew School was the recruitment of Mr. Solomon Hennenson, an "Orientalist and Rabbinical Scholar" who was also a teacher of Hebrew at Edinburgh University. Mr. Hennenson provided his services to the Hebrew School at Sciennes Place free of charge.[19]

Interestingly, those Jews who, during this period, became successful enough to move beyond the "Jewish Quarter" often continued to frequent the area. Howard Denton described how his family continued to do their "shopping and socializing" almost exclusively within the Richmond Street area. He added that, "our Happy Land must have seemed like a self-imposed ghetto to local Scots people."[20] Despite this self-segregation, relations between Scot and Jew in Edinburgh were by now largely benign. A report by the *Jewish Chronicle* in 1911 concluded that "there are no social obstacles placed in the way of Jewish professional men in Edinburgh. There is nothing to prevent them from climbing to the top of their various ladders, for the relations between the general population of Edinburgh and the Jewish community are quite cordial."[21] The attitude of the Scottish press also seems to have mellowed toward its "alien population." In January 1911 an article appeared in *The Scotsman* stating that although Edinburgh had "a fair proportion of foreigners from the Continent of Europe," the city was also "free from the undesirable alien." Edinburgh's Jews, described as "the largest foreign community in the city," are said to be "hard working and law-abiding people." Italians were similarly described as "peaceful and thrifty."[22] When a pogrom broke out against Jews in the Welsh town of Tredegar, and the villages around it, the *Edinburgh Evening News* condemned the actions as something akin to "the work of a drunken Russian mob." The article further expressed the sentiment that, "judging by the conduct and behaviour of the Jews in Edinburgh they are honest, industrious, law-abiding citizens, who in their independence and sobriety are an example to the rest of the community. They look after their own poor and are quiet and inoffensive."[23] It is clear therefore that Gentile Scots felt that the self-segregation of the city's Jews in no way inhibited their role as good citizens. In fact, by being "independent," "looking after their own poor," and remaining "quiet and inoffensive," Edinburgh's Jews were held up by the local press and prominent politicians as a paragon of good citizenship.

The isolation and seclusion offered by this preponderance of social and educational venues and activities offered only a superficial solution to the deeper questions posed by the immersion of Jewish youth in a Gentile world. Howard Denton explained that while he felt "isolated by being the only Jewish boy in my class,"[24] and embarrassed at arriving at school late every day in order to "miss the Christian prayers and hymns,"[25] he was also aware that times were changing for his own generation. Describing how he once made his way to a café on Yom Kippur, he was stunned to find the establishment "full of Jews."[26] He was later told by the owner of the café that "she always had lots of Jewish customers on fast days. It gave us a good laugh but also it was a fair indication of how the old ways were dying out as we all began to live more like the Scots around us."[27] Even though his father, "never faltered from the strict faith of his upbringing," Denton explains that, like an increasing number of Jewish youths in Edinburgh, neither he nor his siblings "grew up to share his orthodox beliefs."[28] Of course, the leading figures of Edinburgh

Jewry continued to move in the city's influential circles. By this time, Maurice Isaacs had become a member of the Merchants Association and a Justice of the Peace. The Reverend Fürst had even become a Probation Officer, ministering to local youths who had committed petty crimes, as well as assisting the local Prison Commissioner.[29] The participation of Edinburgh's Jewish leaders was frequently sought by the city's administrative leaders. In February 1911, Maurice Isaacs and Mr. H. Michael represented the Jewish community at Edinburgh's Conference of Public Morals, an event linked with the National Social Purity Crusade.[30] The Saturday following the conference, The Reverend Fürst delivered a special sermon expressing his agreement with the movement. The sermon was attended by "the Lord Provost and his wife and many members of the Town Council."[31] When the Lord Provost, Sir William Slater Brown, formed a Council on Child Welfare in 1911, he appointed both The Reverend Fürst and Isaac Fürst to the Council for Edinburgh and Leith, and also appointed Isaac to the Edinburgh Executive Committee, an example of the high esteem in which Edinburgh's Jewish leaders were held by their non-Jewish counterparts.[32]

If it can be said that by the 1910s the barriers between Gentile and Jewish Edinburgh were beginning to crumble at the edges, the same cannot be said about some of the barriers which existed within the Jewish community. Issues of class, and divergent backgrounds and traditions helped maintain the serious divisions between the older, established Jewish community and the new, largely impoverished immigrant Jewish community.

Howard Denton's family was affiliated with the South Clerk Street–based Central Hebrew Congregation, which had evolved from a *chevra* and was thriving by 1910, no doubt benefitting from its central position within the "Jewish Quarter," and a large membership drawn from the poor immigrant classes. An advertisement in the *Jewish Chronicle* in January 1910, requesting applications for the position of Minister to the congregation, reveals a great deal about the congregation, and it's desire to further its own integration. The stipulations that "some knowledge of English is indispensable" and that applicants must "undertake to preach in English within one year" suggest that members were becoming both more proficient in English, and were open to their religious services being conducted in that language. Nonetheless, applicants were also expected to "know the Hebrew language thoroughly" and be "able to conduct Hebrew classes on strictly modern pedagogic lines."[33]

Denton recalls that his family and other congregants at the Central Hebrew Congregation felt that "the Jews who went [to the Edinburgh Hebrew Congregation] were the ones who spoke most English and had become more assimilated into Scottish life. They tended to be better off financially than the families who worshipped at our Central Shul."[34] Social divisions were often starkly visible within the "Jewish Quarter." Destitute recent arrivals walked the streets attempting to sell "a sack of sponges or some cheap wares," passing "westernized Jews, urbane and blasé in their adopted tweeds." Still further up the social scale were those "successful Jews who made a point of parading their wealth in elegant silks and expensive worsted cloths."[35]

The wealthy were in the minority. A reporter from the *Jewish Chronicle* visited the city in July 1911, and recalled that, "in Edinburgh a great deal of sadness is caused by poverty, which in some parts of the ghetto is exceptionally acute." The "ghetto" was described as "merely Whitechapel on a small scale ... it effervesces with the same bustling hand-to-mouth life, and is populated by the same Rembrandtesque types, so heterogeneous and yet so similar. One meets the same bent and hoary Jew hobbling along with his basket, and the same "young bloods," covered with smiles and cheap jewellery."[36]

The majority of these poor Jewish families worshipped at the Edinburgh New Hebrew Congregation at North Richmond Street, or at the Central congregation. The Central congregation was at this time rapidly increasing in size, a fact that likely played a role in the decision, in late September 1911, of the Rev. Jacob Teitelman, to take up a position as Minister to the Central congregation. Teitelman has previously been minister to the Edinburgh New Hebrew Congregation for nine years.[37] By November 1912, approximately 450 worshippers were attending the Central Hebrew Congregation during the High Festivals, a number which necessitated plans for the purchase of a building for the purposes of converting it to a synagogue.[38]

The publication of a letter in the *Jewish Chronicle* outlining these plans brought to the surface deep-seated class grievances between the Central congregation and the officials of the Edinburgh Hebrew Congregation. A degree of ill-feeling between the congregations had been brewing since the visit, in late June 1912, of Rabbi Dr. Moses Hyamson, a candidate for the position of Chief Rabbi. Hyamson was later defeated by Rabbi Dr. Joseph Hertz. In early July, Mr. J.H. Fred, honorary secretary of the Central Hebrew Congregation wrote to the *Jewish Chronicle* stating that Hyamson had recently visited the Edinburgh Hebrew Congregation, and had dined with the president and treasurer of that organization without informing any of the other congregations of his intentions to visit the city. Mr. Fred alleged in his letter that the reason behind this "unpardonable slight" was that Hyamson was merely lavishing attention upon those congregations which held a vote in Rabbinate elections, the Edinburgh Hebrew Congregation being the only congregation with such a vote in Edinburgh.

A rejection of these allegations from the Edinburgh Hebrew Congregation was made a week later by Isaac Fürst, son of the Rev. Jacob Fürst, and now a senior lawyer and secretary to the Edinburgh Hebrew Congregation. Fürst argued that the visit to Edinburgh had been decided upon at very short notice, following a trip by Hyamson to Glasgow. This explanation failed to satisfy officials at the Central Hebrew Congregation, and a letter was subsequently sent to the editor of the *Jewish Chronicle* by president of the congregation, Mr. Louis Liverman. In his correspondence, Liverman stated that there existed a serious gulf between the congregations, and that he had not personally met with Isaac Fürst for over eight months, and that in the twenty-eight years he had been living with Edinburgh, there were some officials at the Edinburgh Hebrew Congregation that he had neither met nor had dealings with.[39]

These rifts deepened in July 1914, following an official visit by Rabbi Hertz during which Hertz heavily criticized the state of Jewish education in the city, despite the establishment of the Hebrew school at Sciennes Place. It could be inferred that the problem lay more in non-attendance rather than a lack of provision. A letter from "D.O." shortly following the visit revealed that Rabbi Hertz had called together a meeting of the city's congregations, though "the only congregation which refused was the premier and oldest so-called English congregation."[40] The author concluded by expressing the belief that if the wealthy and influential members of the Edinburgh Hebrew Congregation persisted with their "lack of support," the future of "the rising generation" would be one in which poorer Jewish children would be in no need to of Jewish schools due to their estrangement from all things Jewish. In later correspondence, D.O. accused the leadership of the Edinburgh Hebrew Congregation of being disconnected from the situation of poor Jews in the city, and that they were "either ignorant of the state of education which exists in Edinburgh, or that they are blind to the duties which have been entrusted to them."[41]

Poverty and Class Consciousness in Jewish Edinburgh

Reports from the Edinburgh Jewish Board of Guardians and the city's Hebrew Benevolent Loan Society reveal that demand for financial assistance from the Jewish poor increased rather than decreased with time. During the peak immigration period between the years 1897 and 1906, the Hebrew Benevolent Loan Society aided an average of 70 families annually at an average overall total of approximately £330.[42] The financial year 1910–1911 saw the same organization provide aid to 98 families at a cost of £531. Of this sum, it was concluded by the administrators of the organization that £61 was very unlikely to be repaid, due in part to the extreme poverty of some of those in receipt of aid.[43] During the same financial year, Edinburgh's Board of Guardians received £153 in donations, but the president, Mr. H. Michael appealed to the community stressing that a sum of at least £300 was required, "in order to deal in a proper manner with all the genuine cases of distress which were brought to them."[44]

These figures suggest that the social and economic mobility experienced by some elements of the community was not all-pervasive. The figures also suggest that the majority of those who arrived in the city as destitute aliens remained as such over the ensuing years, and that peddling and hawking was inadequate as the sole means of providing economic independence. Evidence of enduring hardship among first generation immigrants is available from other sources. The Edinburgh Jewish Medical Mission report for 1913 stated that "Edinburgh has a non-resident floating Hebrew population which is constantly fluctuating."[45] In the same year the mission distributed over 240 allotments of clothing, cash, and coal among the Jewish poor, and provided over 700 medical assessments and treatments.[46] It is likely that although immigration from Europe had declined greatly from its height during the early years of the 20th century, there was still a significant amount of population movement within Scotland and Britain as a whole, as immigrants struggled to find a location in which they could settle permanently.

In response to this persistent poverty, and the situation of those still in transit, Edinburgh's Jewish community mobilized on many fronts. In February 1911, a "Sister of Mercy," charity was founded by a Mrs. H. Frankel. Members were requested to contribute one half penny per week, with the aim of helping "the poor at marriage, and on occasions of death."[47] Just one month later the Jewish Amateur Dramatic Society decided unanimously that "all the proceeds of entertainments will be distributed among deserving poor Jewish families."[48] By 1915, Edinburgh's various friendly societies had joined forces and were jointly operating out of Achei Brith Hall in Potter Row.[49]

It would be too simplistic, and in fact erroneous, to state that there were two classes in Edinburgh. There was a wealthy minority, comprising figures such as Alphonse Louis Reis, and Maurice Isaacs, who had risen from relatively humble beginnings in the middle of the 19th century to own the clothing giant, B.Hyam & Co, with its branches in London, Edinburgh, Belfast and Dublin.[50] Beneath this upper strata were the wholesalers, and a small number of young, university-educated Jews who had not moved on from the city, such as Isaac Fürst. Beneath this "managerial" or "professional" class were small-scale shopkeepers, skilled tailors, bakers and butchers. At the bottom were the hawkers, peddlers, and the sweated, semi-skilled labor of the clothing sweatshops.

Henry Maitles stressed in his 1991 article, "Jewish Trade Unionists in Glasgow," that recent research on Jewish communities in Glasgow, London, Leeds and Manchester had contradicted "a major strand of argument pre-1914" which held that "Jewish workers were less class conscious and militant than other workers."[51] Evidence suggests that poor Jews in Edinburgh were aware of class differences in the community and in the country as a whole.

Evidence of such concerns emanates not only from the nature of communal division in the city, but also from instances of labor organization and political activity. Howard Denton recalled that one of the main difficulties poor Jews faced in Edinburgh was not discrimination, but exploitation, often by other Jews higher up the economic ladder. He recalled that, "I may not have been discriminated against, but the place I worked in was an absolute sweatshop. The address was impressive as it was in Hanover Street, just off Princes Street. However, we occupied the crowded top floor. Many of the men still worked in the old-fashioned position, sitting cross-legged on top of a table." He added that, "there were a great many little tailoring concerns scattered all over our part of Edinburgh, very often run by Jews and employing Jews."[52]

In July 1914 there was Jewish involvement in a local union of clothing workers. In a dispute involving "some seventy or eighty Jewish tailors and tailoresses in Edinburgh," a young female worker in a Jewish workroom "was asked by her employer to leave." The *Jewish Chronicle* reported that an unspecified "local union" became involved, and after some negotiations a stalemate was reached. The report concluded that, "although the Jewish master tailors are in the midst of their very busy season they state that the quarrel is a very petty one and they are determined to stand firm."[53] The article in question did not elaborate on whether this union was a Jewish union, or a local, non-Jewish organization. Given the small size of the community, it is unlikely that there were sufficient Jewish workers in the tailoring trade in the city to form a viable trade union of their own. The alternative, of course, raises the possibility of Jewish and Gentile cooperation in trade matters. In either case, it is clear that some Jewish workers in Edinburgh were aware of the benefits of union membership, and were prepared to defend their class interests through industrial action.

Class consciousness in Edinburgh was also in evidence in the political activity of the city's Jews, and this class consciousness was in some cases expressed in conjunction with Zionism. In 1912, at the age of 20, Lewis Rifkind, founder of the Young Men's Zionist Culture Association, and key figure in the Edinburgh University Jewish Students Society, joined Poale Zion, a socialist Zionist political movement. Poale Zion had its origins in Russia at the turn of the century, and had arrived in Britain in 1906.[54] The organization sought the creation of a Jewish nation along socialist lines, though contemporary opinion suggested that "the Poale Zion consider the class struggle to be the paramount issue."[55] The socialist aims of the movement led to three applications for acceptance to the Second International, in 1907, 1908, and 1911. All three applications failed due to the fact that nationalism was a crucial part of the movement's hybrid nature. Paul Keleman states that "Lenin, Luxemburg, Kautsky and Otto Bauer, despite their divergences on the national question, all agreed that it was not desirable for Jews to develop either a sovereign or an autonomous national existence."⁵⁶ As a result, the movement was anomalous to both Zionism and Socialism, and certainly during the 1910s it remained on the fringes of Jewish political life.

The existence of an Edinburgh branch of Poale Zion predated Lewis Rifkind's involvement. In 1911 the organization had convened a national meeting at Zion Hall in Lothian Street, where delegates from London, Leeds and Glasgow joined like-minded Jewish workers in Edinburgh.⁵⁷ Evidently Poale Zion was largely unsuccessful in popularizing its aims—we are given no indication as to attendance at the conference, but the secretary of the Central Committee, a Mr. Miller from Leeds, stated at its conclusion that he "deplored the lack of energy in the movement."⁵⁸ It is possible that Rifkind attended this conference, and that it inspired him to join the movement some time later.⁵⁹ After joining, Rifkind found himself as "almost the only English-speaking member," of the movement in Britain at the time, and "his adherence to its ranks was hailed as an event in the annals of the party."⁶⁰ Within two years, Lewis Rifkind was head of Poale Zion in Edinburgh, and represented the Edinburgh branch at the eighth annual conference in Glasgow in 1914.⁶¹ By 1916, the Edinburgh branch had styled itself the Jewish Socialist Labour Party.⁶² Socialism failed to find a significant following in Edinburgh during this period, within our without the Jewish community. Michael Fry states that, in Edinburgh, those "few young converts to the exotic creed of socialism found their efforts ... confined to the 'propagandist and educative.'"⁶³

During the period 1890–1920, the majority of Edinburgh's Jews resided in an area which comprised the parliamentary constituency Edinburgh Central.⁶⁴ From the period 1885 to 1918, the electorate for Edinburgh Central comprised approximately 7,500 persons. The impact of Jewish votes on the constituency would have been minimal given the small size of the community, along with the fact that non-naturalized Jews couldn't have voted. However, the interest of Edinburgh's Jews in local and national politics is indicated by the invitation of the Jewish Literary Society to Charles Price, MP for Edinburgh Central, in 1912.⁶⁵ Price, a Liberal had held the seat since 1906, and continued to hold it until 1918. From the creation of the constituency in 1885, Edinburgh Central had been a Liberal stronghold, until Labour took the seat in 1918. It was a Labour constituency thereafter until a defeat by the Conservatives in 1931.⁶⁶

Edinburgh Jewry and the Great War

Edinburgh Jewry was impacted by the Great War almost immediately following the commencement of hostilities. The growth of anti-German and generally xenophobic sentiments led to the outbreak of what could arguably be described as Scotland's first pogrom. The incident occurred not in Edinburgh, but in the seaside town of Leven in Fife, where the *Edinburgh Evening News* reported that a "German Jew" had derided the British Navy and had "his shop wrecked" by an "angry crowd." The newspaper had stated that "Leven has no love for Germans," and that "the premises of a German Jew, carrying on a fishmongers business under the name of Simon Harris, were completely wrecked." Locals accused Harris of "making no attempt to conceal his regard for the Germans, and hoping that the British Navy would meet with a speedy defeat." Harris, who was then aged 18, was even accused of displaying a German flag in his shop window. The *Edinburgh Evening News* stated that a crowd had gathered upon hearing that Harris had displayed the German flag, and that the crowd began hissing and then throwing stones, breaking all the windows of the shop. Local police were unable to stop the mob, due to its size, which was estimated as being between 4,000 and 5,000. After a number of constables sustained injuries, extra police assistance was sought from nearby Methil, though by that time Harris had been forced to seek refuge in the back of the premises behind a locked door. The premises and stock were completely destroyed, and most of the stock was strewn about the street. The police eventually restored calm, but it was felt necessary to have Harris lodge in police cells for the evening for his own safety.[67]

As the closest major Jewish center, Edinburgh's Jewish leaders became both concerned and heavily involved in the aftermath. Isaac Fürst, on first hearing of the incident, traveled to the police station at Leven to meet with Simon Harris, and make enquiries about the background to the incident. His discoveries were deeply at odds with the circumstances reported by the local press. Fürst wrote to the *Edinburgh Evening News* in the days immediately following the incident, stating that Harris was clearly a natural-born British subject. Fürst went on to state that the accusations that Harris had uttered derogatory remarks about the British Navy, and that he had displayed the German flag, were false, and that in fact, Harris sympathized fully with Britain, the land of his birth. Fürst concluded that:

> He is a Jew, but the ignorant assumption that every Jew is necessarily a German and hence made the object of hatred as an enemy of this country, is appalling. It should be born in mind that Jews of all classes have, along with their fellow-citizens, manifested their unswerving loyalty to this country in every conceivable direction in the righteous cause for which it has drawn the sword.[68]

Though Isaac Fürst's report led to the issuance of a full apology from the *Edinburgh Evening News* to Simon Harris, the editor of the *Jewish Chronicle* noted in his own account of the episode that it was an unfortunate fact that, "there are countless incidences where the same sort of thing occurs."[69]

David Cesarani has pointed out that, "physical violence against Jews occurred in several towns and cities in 1914 and 1915; Jewish shopkeepers around the country were so afraid that they took to displaying in their shop windows their naturalisation papers or old photographs of themselves in the Russian army."[70] Stefan Manz argued that, "during the First World War, Germanophobia swept through Scottish society just as it did through English," and that, "xenophobia ... was located right in the midst of Scottish society."[71] While many immigrant Jews in Edinburgh may well have felt under increased pressure to undergo the naturalization process, the cost remained prohibitive. As a result, Home Office naturalization records reveal no great increase in applications during the period 1914–1918. During the period, only 26 Jews resident in Edinburgh applied for naturalization, among them Solomon Hennenson, teacher of Hebrew at Edinburgh University and the Sciennes Place School.[72]

Louis Saipe, in his study of the Leeds Jewish Welfare Board, comments that the war had a profound effect on the economic life of Leeds Jewry, dramatically increasing unemployment in the community.[73] The outbreak of war seems to have had a similarly devastating effect on Edinburgh's poorest Jewish workers, particularly those in tailoring and cabinet making.[74] By September 1914, the Jewish Young Men's Association convened a special meeting to devise "ways and means to alleviate the distress among the Jewish poor caused by the present crisis."[75] In addition, peddlers began to find it impossible to sell their goods due to the introduction of the Aliens Restriction Order, which operated along the east coast of Britain and a distance of 50 miles inland, in addition to declaring certain areas, towns and cities "prohibited" to undocumented foreign citizens. Since many of Edinburgh's Jewish peddlers sold their wares in the coastal towns of Fife, a vital source of income was cut off. A report from Glasgow's Jewish Executive Council in September 1914 stated that it was aware of "the great difficulty experienced by Jewish travellers and others under the Aliens Restriction Order ... in gaining admission to certain small towns in Scotland through their having no documentary evidence to prove their Russian nationality, and that in certain towns Jews were not being permitted to reside permanently or temporarily."[76] Two months later, the Board of Guardians created a Young Ladies' Aid Society, "for the purpose of making special collections for a fund for necessitous cases and to meet applications for the relief of those who have suffered in trade on account of the war."[77] The Board of Guardians and the Young Ladies' Aid Society also had to contend with a new problem. The city of Edinburgh itself had been declared a prohibited area, resulting in the internment and expulsion of dozens of Jewish families.[78]

By the beginning of 1915, a lack of coordination between the Board of Guardians and numerous other aid societies led to calls for the establishment of an Edinburgh Jewish Representative Council, along the lines of the recently established Glasgow Jewish Representative Council. A Mr. R. Cohen, resident in Edinburgh, wrote to the *Jewish Chronicle* in February stating that while "there are several institutions in Edinburgh, each in its own way doing good" it would be better "if a council were formed of representatives of all these existing institutions."[79]

The internment of 25 Glaswegian Jews and eight Jews from Edinburgh, under the Aliens Internment and Repatriation Order, at Wakefield internment camp in May 1915 provided the impetus for the establishment of the Jewish Representative Council, with Isaac Fürst serving as president. Kenneth Collins states that the primary concern for Council members was establishing contact with relevant government bodies on behalf of those "Edinburgh Jews who had been interned as aliens."[80] The internment camp at Wakefield was a converted amusement park on the outskirts of Leeds, and began taking its first inmates shortly before the sinking of the *Lusitania* in May 1915. After the sinking of the luxury liner by a German U-boat, the government adopted a harsher stance toward German-born and undocumented foreign subjects, and the number of internees as Wakefield increased dramatically. In addition, the sinking of the *Lusitania* provoked a series of anti-alien riots across Scotland, including a violent demonstration against German butchers in Edinburgh.[81]

A synthesis of this growing Germanophobia and anti–Semitism was in evidence during a mass meeting in Glasgow in April 1916. The meeting was devoted to discussing the "enemy alien question," and during proceedings one speaker stated that, "the German Jew in this country is the worst type of Hun." A letter appeared in the *Edinburgh Evening News* shortly thereafter claiming that, "the entire country is in the grip of the German octopus.... Many of our leading politicians are but the pawns of wealthy German Jews."[82]

By the end of May 1915, Wakefield detention camp held 1,322 individuals from across Britain, many of whom were wealthy businessmen. Charles Walker writes that the camp was, "regarded by the authorities as a privileged one for a 'superior class' of people, with many of the internees being able to pay for better food and accommodation."[83] The camp also had entertainment facilities, including eight tennis courts, a three-acre field, and a gymnasium. Although barbed wire surrounded the camp, it was felt that since the majority of internees at Wakefield had only a loose affiliation with Germany, they were not a "threat to the safety of the realm."[84]

By the end of July 1915, the combined efforts of the Glasgow and Edinburgh Representative Councils in lobbying the Scottish Office resulted in the release of all Scottish Jewish internees. However, by that date a new threat had emerged—deportation. By mid-July 140 Scottish Jews, both men and women, had been scheduled for repatriation.[85] Isaac Fürst's subsequent appearance before the Scottish Office Advisory Committee prevented the impending deportation of all but one individual, a Jewish lady married to a

German "in a good position," who had only been in Edinburgh to visit family.[86] Fürst had argued that the deportation of blameless Jews would represent a grave injustice, and stated that many had already endured hardship having already been "compelled to leave Edinburgh some time after the outbreak of war, and practically all took up their residence—a temporary one—in Glasgow."[87]

In response, the Scottish Office introduced new provisions whereby Jewish Representative Councils would be authorized to "deal with the Jewish cases and to communicate applications direct to London instead of through the local police officials."[88] Guarantees of good behavior would also now be accepted from the Councils rather than British subjects, as had recently been the case, and bloc exemptions were granted to those cases submitted by the Councils.

A month later, the Reverend Fürst was contacted regarding the welfare of another type of internee—prisoners of war. Fürst received a letter in early August from the Commandant at Stobs Detention Camp, near Hawick, that plans were being drawn up to "set apart a portion of the general burial ground for Jewish purposes."[89] Stobs, by that time, held both interned "alien enemies," and prisoners of war. On 15 June 1915, the camp held 1,098 civilians and 1,278 POWs. By 13 April 1916, numbers had increased to 2,269 civilians and 2,323 POWs.[90] Fürst, accompanied by Mr. H. Michael, president of the Edinburgh Hebrew Congregation, visited the camp shortly after receipt of the letter, and ascertained that it housed 55 German-Jewish POWs. It was arranged that the Reverend Fürst would be permitted to provide services for these Jewish soldiers during High Holy days, and also that he would be able to consecrate a portion of ground for burial purposes.

Standards of hygiene at the camp were low, and the high concentration of prisoners in very basic accommodation was conducive to illness and disease. In the 18 months up to April 1916, 12 prisoners died.[91] It is not improbable that the letter to the Reverend Fürst was prompted by the death of at least one German-Jewish prisoner of war.

Enlistment

Edinburgh Jews had a history of military service before the war began, often serving in some of Scotland's most illustrious regiments. The outskirts of the city also played host to military bases, where Jewish soldiers were often resident. In 1900, the Graham Street congregation held a memorial service for Major-General A.G. Wauchope, Commander of the 2nd Black Watch for the reason that he had championed the religious liberty of those Jewish soldiers under his command. Wauchope had written to the Reverend Fürst in

1895 requesting details about service times in order that he could make arrangements for the attendance of the Jewish soldiers under his command.[92]

There is evidence that some of these soldiers experienced a level of bigotry and common prejudice. In 1902, a South African newspaper reported that a volunteer for Tullibardine's Scottish Horse was a young Jewish man from Dunfermline keen to participate in the Boer War. The report, employing an anti–Semitic and anti–Scottish stereotype, stated that the young man "was a thickset youth with such excessive nasal development as to indicate that all he had in common with Scotland was an aptitude for acquiring wealth." A Captain Bruce is said to have asked the young man if he was Scottish. Upon receiving an affirmative reply, Bruce persevered enquiring, "Where from, Palestine?" When the volunteer replied that he was from Dunfermline, Bruce then said, "And I suppose your name's M'Tavish?" The report continues:

> The Scotchman with the big nose let not a muscle on his face move. "Na," he said, "ma name's Solomon. Ah'm a Jewish Scotsman." This was unanswerable, and Solomon was ordered into the ranks of the applicants who had passed the first step. "That's just the man they want over there," commented one of the officers afterwards, "if De Wet can outwit a Scotch Jew he will have to be very smart."[93]

Just six months after Solomon's enlistment, Harold Reis, son of Alphonse Louis Reis, was promoted to orderly to Colonel Ivison Macadam, as part of his service in the 5th Queen's Rifle Volunteer Battalion of the Royal Scots. As part of his duties, Reis accompanied Colonel Macadam in his role as Brigade Major of the Scottish Volunteers during the coronation of Edward VII.[94]

Within months of the outbreak of hostilities in the summer of 1914, young Jewish men from Edinburgh volunteered for service. By September, the community had suffered its first wounded. Victor Freedman, aged 32, and ordinarily resident at Albion Road in Edinburgh sustained a bullet wound to the right arm between Cambrai and Le Cateau. He had been serving as Gunner with the 52nd Battery Royal Field Artillery.[95] Records show that a Private Joe Cowan and Private Leopold Szapiro were both serving in France with the Royal Scots Edinburgh Battalion as early as October 1914. In addition, Sapper Jack Alexander was stated as enlisting in the Officers Training Corps at Edinburgh University in November 1914.[96]

Jewish sacrifice amidst the carnage of war helped erode some of the prejudices of earlier years and generations. One report from the trenches stated that in response to allegations from an English soldier that Jews were "doing nothing" for the war effort, a Highlander from the Black Watch responded that Jews were, "doing their duty. We had three with us, and bonnier lads and braver I don't wish to see. They fought just splendid." Another commented that, "we had ten in our company, all good fighters, and six won't be seen again. So don't say a word against the Jews."[97]

A meeting was held by the Jewish Young Men's Club in mid September

1914 for the purpose of forming a company of 100 men "to drill for Home Defence." The meeting was addressed by the General Staff of the Scottish Command.[98] By November, Jewish wounded were arriving in increasing numbers at Craigleith Military Hospital in Edinburgh. Members of the local community scanned the pages of the *Jewish Chronicle* for information on Jewish wounded at the hospital, and often paid them visits, providing them with copies of the *Jewish Chronicle* and cigarettes.[99]

In August 1915, a Lance Corporal A.L. Nathan from Edinburgh was wounded and taken to the 16th General Hospital in France. It was reported by the *Jewish Chronicle* that Lance Corporal Nathan first served with the Seaforth Highlanders, then with the 4th Royal Scots (Queen's Edinburgh Rifles) and then with the London Scottish. One of his brothers served with the Royal Garrison Artillery, and another was a Lieutenant in the 17th Royal Scots. Nathan also had 12 cousins serving, and was the third of his family to be wounded.[100] Stories of patriotic Jewish families such as the Nathan's were widely publicized in the Jewish press, and by Jewish leaders eager to combat accusations, based on prejudice, that Jews were not "doing their bit." In October 1915, Symon Stungo wrote to the *Edinburgh Evening Dispatch* "dealing exhaustively with the part the Jews are playing in the war." Stungo stated that almost 100 Edinburgh Jews were serving in various branches of the armed forces, "an excellent record for a Jewish community of some 500 families."[101] The final total of serving Edinburgh Jews was 153, with 20 killed in action.[102]

The war appears to have engendered reconciliation among feuding factions within Edinburgh Jewry. Against the backdrop of recruitment drives, drills for Home Defense, and visits to Jewish wounded, a joint Board of Shechita was established in Edinburgh to administrate the provision of kosher food. Negotiations had been starting and stopping for many years, and the achievement was hailed as a turning point, and as the sole result of "the good feeling which now exists among the congregations."[103]

The beginning of 1916 saw the commencement of another trial for Edinburgh's Jewish community, in the form of the resurgence of the Edinburgh Missions. In late 1915, Leon Levison established an organization called "The Edinburgh Russian Relief Fund." Ostensibly, "The Fund" was a war charity, organizing collections and Flag Days across Britain in the aim of raising money in aid of Russian Jews displaced by the war. In early 1916, Levison approached the London Jewish Committee seeking endorsement and financial assistance for his new enterprise. During a subsequent meeting with Leopold de Rothschild and Claude Montefiore in London, Levison presented himself as a professing Jew. Within days of becoming patrons of the fund, both gentlemen were informed that Levison was in fact a missionary to Jews in Edinburgh, and a supporter of missionary activity abroad. They revoked their patronage and a national scandal erupted as Jewish congregations around the country rushed to sever contact with the missionary-tainted organization.[104]

By February 1916, a spotlight had fallen on Edinburgh's Jewish community, the last community to have links with Levison's fund. Particularly vexing was the fact that two members of the Edinburgh Jewish Representative Council sat on the Executive Council of the Edinburgh Fund.[105] Leopold Greenberg, the editor of the *Jewish Chronicle*, made a point of addressing Jewish leaders in Edinburgh directly in his editorial from 4 February. He stated:

> It is obvious that a very grave issue is involved—an issue affecting the honour of the community and its security.... We put it to the Edinburgh Jewish Representative Council whether, in the new circumstances which have arisen, they do not think it advisable to put an end without delay (if they have not done already done so) to their co-operation with an organization in whose composition the missionary element is strikingly predominant, and from which the leaders of British Jews have now completely and without qualification dissociated themselves.[106]

By 11 February, Greenberg was calling on leading London Jewish leaders to venture to Edinburgh and force action from officials there. Edinburgh's leaders were, he argued, participating in a "communal scandal," and it was claimed that Isaac Fürst was a personal friend of Levison. In retaliation, Fürst accused Greenberg of carrying on an unjustified campaign against the Edinburgh Fund, and actively "suppressing the truth."[107]

The intervention of London's Jewish leaders was never required. The information contained in the first of Greenberg's articles had trickled through to the Jewish citizens of Edinburgh, who evidently had never previously been informed as to the complete nature of the Edinburgh Fund and its organizers. A community meeting was called by the Edinburgh Hebrew Congregation, during which a Mr. Liverman, possibly president of the Central Hebrew Congregation, resigned from his position on the Edinburgh Fund. Isaac Fürst subsequently claimed that his own involvement with the Fund was in a personal capacity rather than as a member of the Edinburgh Jewish Representative Council. Resolutions expressing extreme opposition to the Fund were issued by the Edinburgh Jewish Young Men's Association and Poale Zion. Shortly after its commencement, the meeting was forced to adjourn amidst turbulent scenes.[108]

In the weeks following, Isaac Fürst was placed under local and national pressure to sever his links with Levison's Edinburgh Fund. His only high-profile supporter was Israel Zangwill.[109] During a meeting of the Edinburgh Jewish Representative Council one week after the aborted communal gathering, representatives voted "by an overwhelming majority" to sever their connection to the Fund. A resolution was passed stating that no Council member could sit on the Fund, and faced with a question as to where his loyalties lay, Isaac Fürst left the meeting.[110]

Fürst's resignation from the Representative Council did not mark the end of the Fund controversy. In early 1917, Leopold Greenberg issued legal proceedings against the Edinburgh Fund under the War Charities Act, 1916, Chapter 43.[111] The case was eventually brought before the secretary for Scotland, Robert Munro. Greenberg's case was based on the claim that the Fund was not being used for "the relief of the Jewish victims of the war in Russia: but is used for propagandist purposes."[112] In a memorandum, the secretary for Scotland outlined the fact that:

> Mr. Greenberg has a very thin case. He admits that the funds of the charity are spent on the relief of distressed Jews, which is confirmed by other enquiries. All but £1000 or so was distributed in Russia by the same organization that acts for the London Relief Fund. His objections then are simply: 1) That the organizers of the Edinburgh Fund are propagandists with ulterior motives, 2) That it is wasteful to have two funds for the relief of distress among Jews. As to 1), no doubt his objection is sound from the point of view of the Jewish community, if his allegations are justified: the son of the Edinburgh Rabbi Fürst, recently President of the Edinburgh Jewish Representative Council, apparently thinks differently, as he is a member of the executive. But anyhow, it is ridiculous to ask the Secretary for Scotland to take action to prevent the proselytizing of Jews; as to 2) the Act does not cover this point at all.[113]

New government initiatives, introduced in 1916, brought new challenges and difficulties for Edinburgh's Jewish community, particularly those men of fighting age who had not volunteered, and had no wish to volunteer. As early as 1915 the government was aware that the scale of the conflict would require greater manpower than was currently available under a purely voluntary scheme of recruitment. In July 1915, a National Registration Bill had authorized the registration of all persons between the ages of 15 and 65. Harold Shukman stated that the aim of the Bill was to "regulate manpower for military and industrial use. As the Local Government Boards received completed registration forms, men of military age and those in essential work were separately listed."[114] Eliminating those in essential work, friendly aliens, and those unfit to serve, it became clear that there remained just under two million British men capable of serving in the armed forces.[115] As a compromise the Derby Scheme called on men to "attest" that though they had not volunteered, they agreed that they would be obligated to be called up if and when the government required them. Harold Shukman stated that by that time it was clear that life expectancy in the trenches was appalling, and as a result, over one million men "simply refused to attest."[116]

By January 1916, as a Bill for compulsory service looked increasingly likely to be passed, Jewish leaders began to call on "our young coreligionists who have not yet rallied to the cause" to volunteer before enduring the "dishonor" of having to be conscripted. In a lengthy editorial on conscription and military service, Leopold Greenberg argued that "if they do not attest voluntarily they will very soon be compelled to do so."[117]

Impending conscription and increasingly miserable conditions on the Home Front seem to have provoked a rush to enlist. Benjamin Eppel was born in Edinburgh in 1895, and had been educated at Heriot Watt and James Gillespie's School, before becoming a printer in 1914. Shortly after the outbreak of war he joined the Royal Scots, and he was serving in Alexandria when he wrote home to his brother Bertie in early April 1916. Bertie must have given him news that a large number of Edinburgh Jews had rushed to sign up, as Benjamin wrote that he was "glad to hear all the boys have listed and not before time too.... I met a lot of Edinburgh lads here and they say that the town is very miserable just now so I don't wonder at them listing."[118]

On the evening of 2 April 1916, an unprepared Edinburgh lay prone as two German airships approached the Firth of Forth. No blackout was in force, and as navy ships defended their position in the port of Rosyth, the airships turned their attention to the city of Edinburgh. In the attack, 37 bombs were dropped killing 10 people, among them 3 children. A further 11 people were injured.[119] Benjamin Eppel, then serving in France, wrote to his mother shortly thereafter stating that, "the boys coming back from leave tell me it is very miserable there. I suppose the Zeppelin's gave them a fright."[120] Optimism that victory was in sight was apparent in Benjamin's letters from July. He wrote to his mother that, "we are on the advance now and have got the German's on the run. Our guns are simply playing hell with them, and I don't think they can stand out very long." By December he was writing that "Fritz is fairly beaten now, and it is only a matter of days." Three months later Benjamin was wounded in his right hand and arm when a shell exploded beside him in Maillet-Mailly. He later recalled: "I was blown up and struck temporarily dumb."[121] Benjamin Eppel's war was over.

By July 1916, those individuals who resisted conscription or who had failed to attest were brought before Military Appeals Tribunals. The Tribunals were established for local districts, and Edinburgh's Jews came under the Military Appeals Tribunal for Lothian and Peebles. Records pertaining to these Tribunals were destroyed in 1921, following a decision by the Ministry of Health. However, the records of the Middlesex Tribunal and the Lothian and Peebles Tribunal were kept as samples. More than 1,000 appeals were made to the Lothian and Peebles Tribunal, and of these, 35 men can be identified as being Jewish, of whom 21 had failed to attest.[122] Of the 35 cases, 27 appeals were made on the grounds that enlisting would force serious hardship upon the families of the enlisted men. These objections often came from those who ran small shops, or were commercial travelers. Hyman Phillips, a 40-year-old draper protested that he was a naturalized subject, resident in Edinburgh for 12 years, and that, "my whole capital is sunk in the business and I am dependent on it for a livelihood."[123] The majority of objections based on serious hardship also claimed that those objecting were the sole source of support for elderly parents and younger siblings.[124] Five objections were made on the grounds of conscientious objection, one on grounds of occupation, and two on grounds of ill health. Only one appeal was granted.[125] The occupations of those who appeared at the Lothian and Peebles Tribunal ranged from tailors and commercial travelers, to medical students and furniture dealers. The age of the appellants ranged from 18 to 40.

Simon Harris, the fishmonger from Leven, was among those objecting to military service, and his lengthy statement provided an insight into events at Leven, and his life since the incident. Recalling the riot, he stated that,

> Until Aug 15th 1914 I carried on a business at Leven, Fife. But owing to certain statements that I was a German and held pro-German views my business was wrecked by a crowd of 4,000 people and I almost lost my life owing to the hooliganism of the riot. My father had a business at Methel and he also was forced to leave the place and close down his business. We came to Edinburgh and I started a business for my father but owing to the persistent rumours that he was a German he had to leave again and he has been unable to get a livelihood since.[126]

Harris objected to military service on the grounds that he had to support seven brothers and sisters ranging in age from three to seventeen, and that as he could not find a replacement to run his business, conscription, like the riot, would mean "my business will be ruined again." He also argued that, "my parents and myself have been persecuted and slandered since the riot at Leven took place, and extreme hardship, financially and domestically, will ensue unless I am exempted." The statement highlighted anti-German sentiment during the period, and also showed the manner in which some Jewish families faced a struggle to remove the stigma of being declared "German Jews," regardless of the fact that such accusations were baseless. The tribunal ruled that the participation of Simon Harris in the war would bring no serious hardship to his family and dismissed his appeal.[127]

By 1916, Edinburgh had three kosher butchers—Mr. Brown based in St. Leonard's Street, Mr. Hoffenberg based in South Richmond Street, and Mrs. Pass, also based in South Richmond Street. Mr. Brown and Mrs. Pass were the two largest providers of kosher meat in Edinburgh, and both had sons who appeared before the tribunals. Harry Brown and George Pass both based their appeals on the argument that they were essential to the operation of their parent's business, and that their absence would bring serious hardship to their parents and the community. Harry Brown's father argued that, "it being a shop to supply the Jewish community, a Jewish man is necessary to prepare the meat according to the Jewish rites." Their appeals were dismissed.[128]

Among those appealing on the grounds of conscientious objection was Lewis Rifkind, who appealed on the grounds that, "believing as I do that the most sacred thing I possess is human life, I cannot under any circumstances and under the threat of any penalty take life or help others to take life."[129] The other four conscientious objections were based roughly on the same theme.[130] In January 1916, Jewish religious leaders had addressed the issue of war, and obligations regarding unclean food and keeping of the Sabbath. The *Jewish Chronicle* argued that "there can be little doubt that the conscientious objection by Jews refers to the quite understandable reluctance to violate the Sabbath day and the dietary laws—a necessity which army service would instantly impose."[131] David Cesarani noted that cases of Jewish objection on the grounds that Judaism enjoined pacifism were the subject of "disparaging observations" in the general press, and that Jewish leaders and the Jewish press, while displaying a certain objectivity toward those who appeared before the tribunals on these grounds, made it clear that "In our belief no Jew ought or can claim exemption *qua* Jew."[132]

Evidence from the Lothian and Peebles Tribunal suggests that explicit reference to Judaism was not a factor in the vast majority of cases of Jewish conscientious objection. Insights into the specific views of Edinburgh's Jewish conscientious objectors are readily available, and the appellants often included lengthy statements with their appeals forms. Abel Bernard Freeman asserted in a lengthy statement that he was "prepared to be shot for my principles which I will not allow to be violated," but like Lewis Rifkind, this conscientious objection was based on his belief that, "since the military machine involves the wholesale slaughter of my fellow man I cannot assist its functions in any way."[133] The only case of conscientious objection based on a reluctance to violate dietary laws and the Sabbath came in the form of a powerful and emotive statement from Jacob Napthali Wedeclefsky, an 18-year-old medical student from Moncrieff Terrace who had not attested under the Derby Scheme. Wedeclefsky stated:

> As an orthodox Jew, I cannot break the observance of the Sabbath and the Jewish Dietary Laws relating to *treifa*. These laws are broken in the army; therefore as a strictly orthodox Jew who has always adhered, and shall always adhere, to our religious observances, it is impossible for me to serve in the army.... The present case is not the first time that our religious observances have been put to the test. We have sacrificed, for many years continuously all material wealth and financial advantages for the sake of our orthodoxy.... All our life has been a consistent and continuous sacrifice for religion. Our beliefs are not sudden or temporary, or due to the war.[134]

Wedeclefsky argued that he and his family had "endured ... years of physical and domestic hardship in the most extreme degree, when we could have assured of a comfortable and easy life by neglecting our orthodox religion." He went on to state that, "each one of our family has had opportunities of earning a substantial income, but this always involved the breaking of the Sabbath and we therefore refused the opportunities. For the same reason, bursaries, both at school and at the University, were not competed for." It is notable that Wedeclefsky makes no mention of social obstacles or prejudice standing in the way of Jewish progress in the city. In fact, he stressed that there were ample opportunities for Jews to make a good living—as long as they were willing to compromise on some of their religious tenets. He concluded his statement by arguing that, "military service is incompatible with the true conception of the orthodox Judaism that we must maintain." The Tribunal was brief in its decision:

> In this case, the applicant, who is 18 years of age, states that he is an orthodox Jew, and unable on that account, to join the Army, as military service would involve infraction of his tenets.... After consideration, the Local Tribunal were of the opinion that there would be no serious hardship in the event of the applicant joining the Army, and further, they were not satisfied that he had a conscientious objection to combatant service.[135]

This decision was not unusual. Those acting as officials at the Tribunals tended to be "elderly and militant."[136] Of the 16,000 conscientious objections registered nationally, only 300 were granted absolute exemption.[137] Some with serious objections, noting the odds against them at the Tribunals, forged exemption certificates in an attempt to avoid service. In early 1917, Joseph Levinson, a peddler residing with local auctioneer Samuel Braverman, went on trial in Edinburgh, having been discovered in possession of a forged classification certificate. The judge sentenced Levinson to a prison term, having been satisfied that Levinson was using the forged certificate "as evidence that you were excepted from military service—all contrary to the Defence of the Realm Consolidation Act 1914, Section 1."[138]

By mid-1917, government attention turned toward utilizing the fighting potential of "friendly aliens" resident in Britain, specifically Russians. In an agreement known at "The Convention," the British and Russian governments "caught these friendly aliens in a web of obligation," to fight for the British Army or return home and fight for the Russian forces.[139] Max Mendick, born in Lithuania and resident in Edinburgh in 1917, recalled that after the introduction of conscription, all Russian Jews in city, who had failed to become naturalized, were required to register with the local police. They were later given the option of enlisting in the British army or returning to Russia to fight with the Tsar. Mendick, like many other Russian-born Edinburgh Jews, was reluctant to take either option. In the event, he was declared medically unfit.[140] Harold Shukman argues that "the resistance shown by recent Russian-Jewish refugees to the idea of military service to a large extent reflected the norms of their previous existence."[141] This "previous existence" was dominated by the threat of conscription into the Russian Army, with its notoriously harsh conditions. Mendick's own father had fled Lithuania in 1903 following rumors of a war with Japan.[142] Such concerns permeated immigrant Jewish communities. Shukman stresses that, "immigrants to not change their social attitudes and behaviour overnight, even when they are strongly motivated to integrate into their newly adopted society."[143] Of the 30,000 Russian Jews eligible for service, half "slipped through the bureaucratic net ... about 4,000 joined the British Army, a similar number were excused on medical grounds, others because they were doing war work."[144] A small minority made the return journey to Russia.

In total, 20 Edinburgh Jews were killed in action during the course of the war. The casualties ranged in age from 17-year-old Jack Cohen to 42-year-old Louis Rapp.[145] Among the casualties were Manuel Berman and Samuel Goldstein, who had both appeared before the Military Appeals Tribunal on grounds of ill health. Manuel Berman had appealed on the basis that he was unfit to serve due to "neuralgia in the head," in addition to the fact that he was the only son, and sole source of support to his parents. He had also informed the Tribunal that he suffered from a painful deformity of his right foot. Berman was recruited to the Royal Scots shortly after his failed appeal in May 1916, and was killed in action in Germany on 29 March 1917 aged 24.[146] Samuel Goldstein, an accountant's secretary who had appealed on the grounds that he suffered from inflammation of back and knee joints, was killed in France, aged 25, while serving as a Private with the Royal Scots 9th Battalion.[147]

The war brought challenges at home and abroad for Edinburgh's Jews. It had forced some to confront pressures to assimilate, and sacrifices had to be made in the preservation of tradition and religious orthodoxy. Some were evicted from the city, and a sizable number were interned. Many that remained were forced to make a living in an increasingly restrictive environment, one in which foreigners of any type could be looked upon with deep suspicion. The war had come at a time when issues such as poverty, class and communal division were increasing in importance and potency rather than receding with time. However, in the crucible of these pressures, and against the backdrop of sacrifice in France, a community began to emerge, which was, perhaps, more united than at any time since the arrival of the first wave of Russian immigrants more than three decades earlier. The pressures placed on the community aided cooperation in the form of representative councils and communal structures, which in turn placed communication and mutual representation before the interests of individual congregations. By 1915, a joint Board of Shechita had been established for the first time in the city, and this new spirit of cooperation reached its pinnacle on 13 January 1918. At a gathering of officials from both the Central Hebrew Congregation and the Edinburgh Hebrew Congregation, a resolution was passed amalgamating the two into one united organization.[148]

5

A Community United, 1918–1932

> *Tragic and depressing as the aftermath of the last war was for a time, I personally received considerable encouragement and inspiration from your friendly, engaging personality and your scholarly sermons. I know too how indebted the Edinburgh Jewish community are to you for bringing together all sections of the community into one united body.... It was no mean achievement when one recalls the strong factional feelings which existed in those days.*—Asher Levinson to Rabbi Dr. Salis Daiches, 1943.[1]

Following the amalgamation of the Edinburgh Hebrew Congregation and the Central Hebrew Congregation, the Edinburgh Hebrew Congregation selected a team of delegates to travel to London and throughout "the provinces" in an effort to find a suitable replacement for the late Reverend Fürst. On 21 October 1918, having interviewed "many gentlemen" the council of the Edinburgh Hebrew Congregation decided to issue "a call" to Rabbi Dr. Salis Daiches.[2]

Daiches had been born in Vilnius, Lithuania in 1880, and had spent his early childhood in the Lithuanian village of Kudirkos Naumiestis, then known as Neustadt-Schirwindt. His father was the notable Rabbi Israel Daiches, later spiritual head of Leeds' orthodox Jewish community, and "part of a family line of Rabbis which remained unbroken for 500 years."[3] After attending school at a *Gymnasium* in Königsberg, Germany, Salis went on to study philosophy at Berlin University, as well as attending the Hildesheimer seminary. He subsequently graduated with a Ph.D. in Leipzig, following research "into the relation of David Hume's philosophy to history,"[4] before settling in England in 1907.[5]

After brief periods spent at Hull and Hammersmith, both Salis and his older brother Samuel occupied the pulpit of the Sunderland Hebrew Congregation for a combined total of fourteen years, ten and a half of those owing to Salis.⁶ Salis Daiches was notable not just for his secular educational attainments, which were unusual among the immigrant Jewish clerical class at that time, but also for the fact that he "held a full rabbinic diploma which allowed him to perform all religious functions and to legislate on Jewish law and ritual."⁷ These qualifications convinced the delegates of the Edinburgh Hebrew Congregation that "Dr Daiches was the most suitable Minister, indeed, the one who came most nearly to fulfilling the requirements in Edinburgh."⁸

By late 1918, Daiches had received separate approaches from both the Edinburgh Hebrew Congregation, and the leaders of the Central Hebrew Congregation. The fact that the two congregations, although united on paper, where separately seeking a minister, is indicative of the precarious nature of the amalgamation.⁹ It is clear from sources that those at the Central Congregation were mainly foreign-born, were adamant that they required a preacher to minister to them in Yiddish, and were possibly unhappy with the manner in which services were led at Graham Street.¹⁰ After some consultation with representatives from both synagogues, Daiches made it clear that any move to Edinburgh would be dependent on full unity of the congregations, and that the "call" must be made unanimously.¹¹

Daiches gave serious thought as to whether or not he should leave Sunderland, even going so far as to seek the advice of the Chief Rabbi, Joseph Hertz. Hertz wrote to Daiches on 12 December 1918, stating that,

> There is a sphere in Edinburgh much more commensurate with your abilities than could be found in Sunderland.... Moreover, Edinburgh is a great Metropolis and you will be surrounded with cultured people among whom your representation of Judaism will, I am sure, be of the utmost value to us, while the University will, also I think, provide ultimately a scope for you.¹²

After receiving confirmation of a unanimous call, Daiches wrote to the Council of the Sunderland Hebrew Congregation on 15 December 1918 stating that he wished to resign. He explained that he "had been influenced by the desire to secure a larger scope for his activities."¹³ He was formally inducted as spiritual head of the Edinburgh Hebrew Congregation on 9 February 1919, and he moved to the city with his family in March of that year.¹⁴

Daiches came to Edinburgh with certain fixed goals. In an interview with the *Jewish Chronicle* in July 1922, he explained that his "first object in Edinburgh was to unite the different sections of the community, and to do away with the distinction between foreign and English which prevails in practically every community in this country."¹⁵ He later added that another of his aims was to influence Scottish public opinion against attempts made by the Jewish Mission Committees of the three Churches of Scotland to convert Jews in Scotland and abroad.¹⁶ To these professed goals can be added Daiches' desire to advocate publicly for Judaism and Jewish communities in Scotland, to challenge anti-Semitism, to realize his own ambition to become the *de jure* head of Scottish Jewry, and to improve the organizational structure of Edinburgh Jewry, and Scottish Jewry in general.[17] David Daiches recalled that another ambition of his father's was to "build a splendid new synagogue in a pleasant part of the city, a synagogue which could easily accommodate all the Jews of Edinburgh and would in addition have an attached *Beth Hamedrash* where the older and more traditional members could pray three times daily and conduct their Talmudic study circle."[18] It is the aim of this chapter to assess the extent to which Rabbi Daiches achieved these goals, and the resulting impact on Edinburgh's Jewish community.

Communal Unity

On his arrival, Rabbi Daiches assumed the leadership of a community riven by long-standing grievances, and one with a national reputation for being particularly prone to inter-communal disputes. Edinburgh resident Michael Marcus had written to the Jewish Chronicle as late as 1917 complaining that, "the situation is painfully ridiculous.... Competition supersedes co-operation. Unity is as foreign to English [sic] Jews as an iceberg would be in the tropics."[19] In order to bring about the unity of Edinburgh Jewry, Rabbi Daiches had first to reconcile the foreign-born members of the Central *Shul* to the largely Scottish-born Edinburgh Hebrew Congregation. However, despite the "unanimous" call, throughout the first five years of his role as Rabbi, Daiches found himself ministering to these two groups separately. David Daiches recalled that his father "would worship and preach on Saturdays at the Graham Street *Shul*, though he would visit the other at regular intervals and preach there in Yiddish."[20] This situation persisted until January 1924, when Central worshippers were forced to abandon the premises at Roxburgh Place due to the state of disrepair into which the synagogue had fallen.[21] Until this time, Rabbi Daiches seems to have been content with this arrangement, and to have been largely sympathetic to the needs of the worshippers at Roxburgh Place. Court documents from 1924 recounting the early years of Daiches' leadership state that, "the Roxburgh Place Synagogue was retained ... on account of its being situated in a neighbourhood thickly populated with Jews, and for the benefit of the members of the Congregation who did not find themselves at home in a Synagogue where the sermon was preached in English."[22]

David Daiches states that his father would change his behavior for foreign-born Jews, eschewing "the reasonable tone of twentieth-century inquiry" and adopting "the sing-song tones of Talmudic exposition."[23] He would respond to requests for guidance "scrupulously and conscientiously."[24] Daiches, in his training and education, was perfectly suited to fill the role of "old-fashioned administrator of rabbinical law" as well as the articulate voice of modern, Scottish-born Jewry. These personal qualities contributed considerably to the welding of the two congregations.

Of more pressing concern to Rabbi Daiches was the existence of the Edinburgh New Hebrew Congregation, still based at North Richmond Street. Unlike the Central Hebrew Congregation, the Edinburgh New Hebrew Congregation was not linked in any significant way with the congregation at Graham Street, and was still clinging to its independence despite dwindling numbers. Within months of his arrival in Edinburgh, Daiches had been requested to minister to worshippers at the North Richmond Street premises, and used this position to encourage a dialogue between the two groups. This was part of his ongoing effort to "consolidate and complete" the union between the different sections of the Jewish community in Edinburgh.[25]

On 6 March 1920, a conference was held in the Graham Street synagogue. It had been organized by Rabbi Daiches following months of dialogue, and there were representatives from all three Edinburgh congregations present. During the course of the meeting, Daiches conveyed his wish to see the community united under one body, and that this body be subject to one constitution. He is said to have "pointed out the mutual advantages to each congregation" this arrangement would provide, and to have done so in "strong and convincing terms."[26] The personal qualities of Rabbi Daiches, his determination, ambition, and his personal appeal, seem to have contributed significantly to the increased communication between the congregations. During the course of his speech, Daiches found himself "frequently interrupted by rousing cheers signifying approbation, causing on each occasion a break of a few minutes in the address."[27] The meeting ended with a resolution to unite the synagogues and delegates were appointed to arrange the details of the amalgamation.[28]

The meeting was an important first step in the process of unification, which concluded with the "signing of a legal agreement" binding the North Richmond Street congregation with the Edinburgh Hebrew Congregation on 28 March 1920.[29] Abel Phillips, treasurer and honorary secretary of the Edinburgh Hebrew Congregation wrote to Rabbi Daiches on 29 March stating that,

> at a Special General Meeting of Members of our Congregation held yesterday the Resolution embodying the terms of amalgamation with the Richmond Street Congregation was submitted and approved unanimously. It was further unanimously resolved to express to you the cordial thanks of the Congregation for your excellent work which has been so largely instrumental in bringing about the success of the negotiation.[30]

However, despite the unanimous decision of congregation delegates, shortly following the amalgamation of the synagogues a small group of highly orthodox worshippers decided to secede from this united body. These Hasidic worshippers, all from the former Edinburgh New Hebrew Congregation, styled themselves "The Edinburgh Independent Hebrew Congregation," and were led by one Isaac Hyman.

Letters from Hyman to the Chief Rabbi, written in March 1922, revealed the reasons why this group seceded. Social issues and the Hebrew education of the young, the prime catalysts of community division in the past, featured prominently. The first reason stated was that the group "desire and require an efficient Hebrew School." Hyman alleged that the teaching of "sound Judaism" was "impossible ... under the present administration," and that "the present teachers are more concerned with their private pupils than with education of the school children. We are convinced that the children whose parents cannot afford private tuition are neglected."[31]

The issue of Hebrew education for poor children in the city had been ongoing for some time. In May 1917 a public meeting had been held "to consider the state of Jewish education in Edinburgh." The unanimously carried resolution included the statement that those present, "deplore the existing state of Jewish education and proposes to take the necessary steps for the formation of a Hebrew public school, at which the history, language, and religion of our nation should be adequately taught."[32] The move had been led by Michael Marcus, Rabbi Rabinowitz, and Lewis Rifkind.

The second, related, grievance was that the group disapproved of "the paid officials of the Congregation giving private lessons." The third was that the group considered "that the Council is unjustified in entailing such heavy expenses on the community as a great many are not in a position to pay such high [seat] rents. We think our pressing need is for thorough, equipped, efficient teachers, and clergy that have a regard for all the community."[33] Hyman concluded by arguing that "a large percentage of the community have come to the conclusion that the amalgamation was a mistake, and are convinced that the ultra-orthodox will never be able to work amicably under the present regime." The letter also contained some subtle personal barbs aimed at Rabbi Daiches. The group worshipped in a small rented room at 48 Lothian Street, and David Daiches states that the congregation was known among other Edinburgh Jews as "the Bolshie *shul*."[34] He further alleged that the group was behind, "continual attempts to undermine my father's position, to discredit him in the eyes of Jew and Christian alike."[35]

Not everyone held such strong views on the dissenters. During correspondence with the Office of the Chief Rabbi, Rabbi Rabinowitz, formerly minister to the Edinburgh New Hebrew Congregation, stated that the majority of members of the IEHC were "respectable people." He further argued that "since the amalgamation of the foreign section with the English, the needs of the foreign element are not really quite satisfied, more especially in regard to the question of teaching the children."[36]

The Office of the Chief Rabbi was sufficiently alarmed by these allegations to enquire with Rabbi Daiches about the state of Hebrew education in Edinburgh. Daiches explained that "our classes are held at present in one of the finest schools in the city," and that these facilities, at Sciennes Road, had been provided by the Edinburgh Education Committee. He added that the distance of this school from the Jewish district was approximately 10 to 15 minutes on foot. Daiches explained that he initially attempted to gain the use of a school in Davy Street, which would have been closer to the "Jewish district," but that the Education Committee had refused to grant permission for those premises. Daiches also commented that "the parents of many children, probably the majority, object to the classes being held in the slums and would not send their children there."[37]

The 1923 Report on Jewish Education, written following the visit of Henry M. Adler to the Edinburgh Congregation, largely corroborated Daiches' account. Adler was an inspector of Jewish schools, and was respected for his rigorous assessments. His 1923 report on Jewish education in Edinburgh stated that, "the classrooms are amongst the best that I have seen in the Kingdom ... the accommodation has been obtained from the efforts of Rabbi Daiches. This evidence of co-operation and good will on the part of the local authority is a matter for real gratification."[38] Adler also noted that there were 76 children on the roll, and that although there were over 200 Jewish children in Edinburgh "a good deal of private teaching is done. There are not many children who are going without religious education."[39] Whatever the motivations of the members of the Edinburgh Independent Hebrew Congregation, it is clear that the group had taken issue with attempts to bring it into line with a congregation which was at odds with their traditional form of worship. It is also clear that class and the provision of education remained decisive factors in influencing the level of community cohesion. The group was convinced that many children were being overlooked by teachers who only had a concern for teaching those pupils whose parents could afford private lessons, and that the administration of the amalgamated congregation was, in essence, elitist and disregarding of their needs.

This new fissure in Edinburgh Jewry was made worse by the decision of the IEHC to appoint as their Rabbi one Alexander Levison. Levison had arrived in Edinburgh in May 1922 from London, having previously spent time in South Africa and Cork, and immediately commenced in his duties as minister to the Lothian Street congregation, subsequently forming a children's Hebrew class. However, Alexander Levison had not disclosed the fact that he was brother to Sir Leon Levison and to the Rev. Nahum Levison, United Free Church Minister in Johnshaven, Aberdeenshire. Some weeks following his appointment, Levison's family ties to these notorious missionaries became known, causing, "considerable alarm" among Edinburgh's Jews.[40] The *Jewish Chronicle* subsequently printed an article under the heading "Another

Levison," in which was expressed the opinion that Alexander Levison required "very careful watching, so that any disposition on his part may be noted in time to shield the children who form his class and the adults who constitute his Independent Hebrew Congregation from the consequences."[41] Alarm was also expressed at the fact that IEHC Hebrew classes were being held two minutes from Leon Levison's missionary base. However, IEHC officials seem to have been content that this particular member of the family had not adopted, and was not likely to adopt, Christianity. Levison's spiritual leadership of the Edinburgh Independent Hebrew Congregation continued untroubled until late 1923. From April until September 1923, Rabbi Daiches had undertaken to investigate the credentials and qualifications which Levison claimed to have earned. Chief among these claims was that he had derived his rabbinical authority from Rabbi Kook, the late Chief Rabbi of Palestine.[42] When Rabbi Daiches challenged Levison to produce this documentation he refused, and Daiches subsequently began to correspond with Leopold Greenberg, editor of the *Jewish Chronicle*. In a letter written to Daiches in May 1923, Greenberg stated that he shared doubts regarding Levison's claims and that his own investigations had shown that, "Dr Hertz has never given him *Kabalah* to practice *Schechita* in Edinburgh. Nor has he submitted himself for any examination as *Shochet*.... You will not now be surprised that the man has refused to show you his credentials as Rabbi."[43] Increasing animosity between Daiches and Levison spilled over into other spheres. Early in his role as leader of the Edinburgh Independent Hebrew Congregation, it was suggested that Levison should be welcomed into Lodge Solomon, Edinburgh's most predominantly Jewish Masonic Lodge. Daiches, who was already a member of the Lodge, strongly recommended against the move, and shortly afterwards it was discovered that Levison had joined St. Leonard's Lodge, which had as its Master his brother, Sir Leon Levison.[44]

In August, the Chief Rabbi, Dr. Hertz, wrote to Rabbi Daiches refuting Levison's claim that "I had paid an official visit during my tour in South Africa."[45] Further enquiries with Levison's former employers at the Mafeking Hebrew Congregation revealed that, "Levison was most unpopular ... and did many things which annoyed the Congregation and the Congregation were very pleased to see the last of him.... He was the *Schochet*, that is a killer of the meat under Jewish Rites.... It was found out that he did not perform these Rites though he pretended he did so when he killed. He was of a low character."[46] The Cork congregation reported that he was with them for only three months, explaining that, "we found he had not the qualities which he represented to us to have; and also owing to being hasty to the children he was teaching."[47]

Shortly thereafter Levison was publicly challenged, by both Daiches and Greenberg, to produce his credentials. Levison was able to produce only one certificate, a vague document signed by Chief Rabbi Dr. Hertz, claiming that the rest "went missing from the room he was renting in Edinburgh."[48] The document signed by Hertz was subsequently revealed to have been obtained through deception. Greenberg, having discussed the matter with the Chief Rabbi, reported to Daiches that,

> Levison first applied to the Chief Rabbi for a certificate ostensibly for the purpose of obtaining a passport to America on the assurance that he had a call to a Congregation in Wisconsin. Upon that, Dr Hertz let him have that clearly unwise certificate. Levison then appears to have made up his mind to go to Edinburgh, but did not say anything to Dr Hertz about it until about a month after, when he informed him with a cock-and-bull story that he had been called by the Edinburgh Congregation to the office of *Schochet*, Teacher, and *Mohel*.[49]

Daiches subsequently wrote a number of letters to the *Jewish Chronicle* "pointing out that [Levison] was no Rabbi and warning British Jews against him."[50] In response, Levison commenced legal proceedings against both Rabbi Daiches and the *Jewish Chronicle*, claiming £1,000 in damages from each defendant, and drawing national attention to communal disunity in Edinburgh once more. Although certain of the fact that Levison was an imposter, David Daiches recalled that his father was shocked and un-nerved by the prospect of a legal battle, and that he knew that proving that Levison was a fraud would be difficult in a court of law.[51] Greenberg was also unsettled by the prospect of a legal battle, and believed that the Scottish courts would find against them. He wrote to Rabbi Daiches in January 1924, arguing that their biggest obstacle was "the difficulty of getting justice in Scotland with their bias so strongly in favor of Conversionist activity among Jews."[52]

During the early stages of the trial, Levison produced a large number of documents purporting to prove that that he was a highly esteemed Rabbi, and was so confident of victory that at one stage he offered, via his solicitor, to drop the case if he was issued a public apology from Rabbi Daiches and paid £40 in compensation.[53] Daiches, however, requested time to carefully examine the documents, a request which was granted by the court. Upon examining the Rabbinical document from Rabbi Kook of Palestine, Daiches noted that the signature differed radically from that on his own correspondence with Rabbi Kook. Other documents which were offered as proof of rabbinical status were subsequently revealed to be from "a town in Poland which [Rabbi Daiches] was sure did not exist," "a continental *Yeshivah* that he had never heard of" and "one was supposed to be from a rabbi in some small town in the interior of Australia."[54]

Levison's confidence drained from him during this period. The Edinburgh Independent Hebrew Congregation severed all contact with him, and he quickly requested that the documents be returned to him as soon as possible as they were required for an application he was making to become head of a congregation in Wales. When Levison returned the documents a week later, it was discovered that every forgery had been removed, leaving only a small number of vague testimonials to his good character.⁵⁵ With the key documents missing, Levison's case collapsed, amidst weak protests from Levison that his landlady had accidentally destroyed all of the key evidence. The case was abruptly concluded in November 1924 with the judgment in favor of Rabbi Daiches and the *Jewish Chronicle*. Costs were also awarded to the defendants, but Levison quickly left the country without paying a penny. He most likely made his way to the United States. Rabbi Daiches' financial burden was relieved by Leopold Greenberg, who ensured the *Jewish Chronicle* covered all of his legal expenses, in recognition of the key role played by the Rabbi in dismantling Levison's case.⁵⁶

The Levison case played an important role in the history of Edinburgh Jewry, not just because of the press attention it received, but also because it so emphatically discredited the last vestiges of organized dissent within the community. The Edinburgh Independent Hebrew Congregation, in their selection of Alexander Levison as Rabbi attracted damaging blows to the legitimacy of their stance, and the congregation dissolved as a formal entity. Kenneth Collins states that the majority of members were later "reconciled to Daiches, and he to them."⁵⁷ Sharon Gewirtz argues that one of the main obstacles to the "Anglicization" of immigrant Jewish communities was "the retention of autonomous immigrant religious culture distinct from the anglicized orthodoxy of the communal elite and centred on the *chevroth*."⁵⁸ Arguably therefore, by dismantling the Independent Hebrew Congregation, the last such autonomous immigrant religious organization in Edinburgh, Daiches was also aiding, consciously or otherwise, the further integration of Edinburgh Jewry.

The case also marked the removal of perhaps the greatest threat to the position of Rabbi Daiches himself. David Daiches argues that in challenging Levison, his father had staked his reputation, career, and life's ambitions on victory in the courts.⁵⁹ Had Daiches lost the case, it could have cost Edinburgh Jewry a capable leader, whose personal qualities had already been put to use in improving the lot of the community. With victory however, Daiches' grip on the spiritual leadership of Edinburgh Jewry was stronger than at any time previously. With complete communal unity achieved, Daiches was free to pursue his other chief goals. Foremost among these was his desire to mount a major challenge to the activity of Scottish missionaries in Scotland and abroad.

Challenging the Missionaries

Sir Leon Levison's Medical Mission had been greatly disrupted by the war. The challenge mounted in 1916 by Leopold Greenberg against the Russian

Jewish Relief Fund had failed, and despite the ostracism of anyone publicly associated with the Medical Mission, Sir Leon Levison had made appearances at some of the military appeals tribunals, advocating for Jews of military age.[60] However, despite the enduring poverty of Edinburgh's Jewish community, it is clear that the ability of the Medical Mission to distribute aid to the impoverished Jews of Edinburgh had declined significantly from its peak at the turn of the century. During the war, the Mission was forced to suspend its work for prolonged periods. Total spending on the relief of Edinburgh's Jewish poor in 1916 amounted to £36 in cash, and just over £12 in medicines.[61] By way of contrast, the Edinburgh Hebrew Benevolent Loan Society was allocating an average of £380 per annum during the period 1916–1918.[62] When the war ended, the Mission reopened its headquarters in Chalmers Street though, according to a report in the *Jewish World*, it never "regained its vigour."[63]

Nonetheless, Levison's Medical Mission remained a thorn in the side of Edinburgh's Jewish leaders who, though probably acknowledging the paucity of conversions it engendered, still viewed the very existence of the organization as offensive. Feelings had been heightened again in 1919 when Levison unveiled his "Palestine Relief Fund," which the *Jewish Chronicle* subsequently described as "tarred by the Conversionist taint."[64]

Rabbi Daiches would have been aware of missionary activity in Edinburgh prior to his appointment. He had visited the city many times, mostly in order to encourage support for various Zionist enterprises, and would have read the many reports in the press on missionary activity in the city.[65] Probably as a result of these often-sensationalized accounts, it is clear that Daiches himself came to over-estimate the threat posed by Levison's organization, particularly in the early days of his leadership. Frederick Levison, son of Sir Leon, argues that, "Dr Daiches, on coming to Edinburgh early in 1919, had resented the Mission with a bitterness unknown to his predecessors, who seem to have regarded it simply as the occupational hazard of living in a Christian country."[66] It is debatable whether this attitude was in evidence in relation to the Reverend Fürst, who was often quite vocal in his opposition to the Mission, but it is apparent that Daiches did oppose missionary activity in a manner more visible and vocal than any of his predecessors and contemporaries.[67]

Shortly following his appointment, Daiches worked with the Edinburgh Jewish Board of Guardians to establish a "Jewish Medical Mission." The project, which commenced operation in March 1920, was soon abandoned because it was found, "after four months of waiting that no sick Jews were to be treated."[68] The founding of the Edinburgh Hebrew Congregation's Medical Mission coincided with the closing of Levison's Mission at Chalmers Street. Local Jewish leaders, as well as reporters at the *Jewish Chronicle*, then prematurely claimed that missionary activity in the city was finished. Under an article titled, "Exit Levison's Medical Mission," the *Jewish Chronicle* reported that the opening of the rival Medical Mission under the "indefatigable" Rabbi Daiches had been one of the main causes of the closing of the Christian Mission. Edinburgh's Jewish community was congratulated on "this happy deliverance by a new form of "ordeal"—ordeal by competition."[69]

However, within two months it became clear that the closure had merely been due to the relocation of the Christian Mission to Nicolson Street, an area with one of the highest levels of Jewish inhabitants in Edinburgh. In a letter to *The Scotsman* dated 19 November 1920, Daiches described the Mission as a "challenge to the Jewish community of this city."[70] He continued that:

> the efforts of the mission are entirely wasted, as our Hebrew Board of Guardians is both able and willing to provide for all such cases, and even employs a medical man for the purpose of visiting the sick poor in our community. Fortunately, our doctor has very little working to do, and the number of poor Jewish patients in this city that require medical attention is at present confined to two![71]

The position of the new Mission in Nicolson Street, "in close proximity to what is regarded as the Jewish quarter, and within a stone's throw of one of our synagogues," was a major source of Daiches' antagonism. He described the move as indicative of a "spirit of aggressiveness and provocativeness."[72] Daiches also questioned the necessity of a Medical Mission in the city, given the services offered by the Royal Infirmary of Edinburgh, which he argued was "distinguished by a spirit of broad-mindedness, religious tolerance, and human sympathies."[73] Daiches concluded by stating that the Mission had created "suspicion and mistrust" between Jew and Christian in the city, and calling upon its supporters to cease making donations.[74]

It is likely that the opening of the Hebrew Congregation Medical Mission did cause some problems for Levison's operation. A Jewish medical facility would have been a more appealing alternative for those Jews who only opportunistically attended the Christian Mission. Jewish charitable institutions in the city remained strong, with the Board of Guardians, Hebrew Benevolent Loan Society, and the Sisters of Mercy all still in existence, and all distributing significant amounts of aid to the Jewish poor on a regular basis.

However, given that the Mission had been suspended several times since at least 1916, other causes of disruption must be considered. The casual hostility which continued to be expressed in Scottish newspapers toward missionary activity could have eroded some of the support for the movement, although there is no evidence of any significant reduction in donations to Scotland's Conversionist funds. Rabbi Daiches seems to have been aware of the importance of the media in influencing public opinion on the matter, and he wrote frequently on the subject, and encouraged publications such as *The Scotsman* to take a negative stance on the matter.[75]

Another important factor to consider is the fact that Rabbi Daiches was scathing of both the Missions and those "bad Jews, who are ready to sell their birthright for a mess of pottage."[76] Daiches once stated that "few Jews become Christians and those that do are of the basest character."[77] The threat of social ostracism of those Jews who had pragmatically attended without intent to convert to Christianity could have been sufficient to deprive the Mission of a significant number of attendees. Rabbi Daiches made it clear in his many statements on the issue that what had perhaps been tacitly conceded under the leadership of the Reverend Fürst, would now not be condoned under any circumstances. It was alleged in a United Free Church Mission report in 1924 that "the Synagogue sets its spies and tries to intimidate those who seek to hear the Christian message."[78]

Another point worth considering is the possibility that the Mission's most opportune time had passed. Edinburgh in the first two decades of the 20th century witnessed large numbers of transmigrants passing through the city. These transmigrants could conceivably have availed of the services of a missionary organization without concern for the potential stigma which may have become attached to them, had they done so in a more stable, settled community. The Jewish population of Edinburgh was, by 1920, smaller, as the fluctuating population of transmigrants ceased to be a feature of the community. In addition, it was more settled, marginally better off financially, and was considerably improved in terms of its infrastructure and organization than it had been at the turn of the century. There were fewer sick Jews in the city than at any time previously, and those that were in the city could avail of a variety of options not linked to missionaries. There was still a significant level of poverty, but overall the community was even less vulnerable to the practices of missionary organizations than it had been previously. Faced with such a state of affairs, it is likely that Edinburgh's Christian Missionaries increasingly advocated for a more "aggressive" approach, resulting in the move to Nicolson Street. The move was short-lived and unsuccessful, and the Edinburgh Jewish Medical Mission ceased operations again in May 1921.[79]

The closure of the Edinburgh Medical Mission was little more than a partial victory for Salis Daiches. The Edinburgh Medical Mission had been just one arm of the United Free Church of Scotland's Jewish Committee, and the Committee continued to raise large amounts of funding for its many Conversionist Missions throughout Europe and the Middle East.[80] Daiches subsequently focused his energies on challenging the proselytizing policies of the Scottish Churches in their entirety, and confronted a number of senior Scottish clergy via the press. As a result, the period 1918–1930 was marked by an increasingly strained relationship between Scottish Church leaders and the man who came to be seen as "Scotland's Rabbi." Rabbi Daiches' challenge to the missionaries provoked a series of responses from Church leaders, eager to present their work in a better light. In June 1921, John Hall, Convener of the United Free Church Jewish Mission Committee, took issue with Daiches' claim that the missions lacked any sense of "real brotherly love." Stating that "the Rabbi must really be a little more careful," Hall pointed to numerous relief efforts unrelated to missionary work, and the fact that the Assembly of the United Free Church had frequently "expressed its abhorrence of oppression, and dissociated itself entirely from anti-Semitism in every form."[81]

Daiches, however, was motivated to contact the press again in December 1923, following his discovery that leaflets were being distributed in the city by the Jewish Mission Committee. The leaflets bore the heading: "Why should we support Jewish Missions?" and claimed, among other things, that 40,000 Hungarian Jews had been converted in the previous five years, and that Glasgow was as viable a target for concerted evangelical activity as Budapest, Tiberius, Galilee and Constantinople.[82]

The sensitivity surrounding the issue of missionaries, and its capacity to cause discord not only between Jew and Christian in Scotland, but also among Jews themselves was revealed in the aftermath of the leafleting campaign. In his letter to the *Jewish Chronicle* on the campaign, Daiches claimed that Anglo-Jewry and the leadership of Glasgow Jewry in particular, were failing to deal with the "threat" of the missionaries, and were pursuing an "ostrich policy."[83] Daiches was subsequently accused of over-reacting by Maurice Bloch of Glasgow, who argued that "Edinburgh is the very centre of the Jewish mission activities, and some damage has been done there in the past. Perhaps this has caused Dr Daiches undue fears."[84] Daiches retaliated, claiming that open-air meetings for Hebrew Christians had attracted as many as 350 people in Glasgow, and that although Edinburgh was the base of the Jewish mission, the influence of the organization was widespread. Daiches also added that "the position in Edinburgh is causing the conversionists less satisfaction than the position in other towns."[85]

This dispute was waged against the backdrop of a resurgence of the local Jewish missions. As early as June 1923, the General Assembly of the Church of Scotland had made moves to redouble its efforts to convert Jews within Scotland. the Rev. J.A.C. Mackellor had submitted a report of the Jewish Mission Committee, which asked:

> Why should they seek out the Jews at the ends of the earth and neglect those at their own door? Generally the Jews were good neighbours and law-abiding citizens. There was no complaint against them on that score. But their religion was a challenge to the Christian Churches, for, unlike heathenism, it was a conscious and deliberate antagonism to Christ.[86]

Under the heading "The Perversion Danger," the *Jewish Chronicle* ran an article in January 1924 warning that "although since the advent of Rabbi Daiches there has been an altogether lesser state of affairs ... still the menace and danger remain, and there are constant evidences of them."[87]

In February 1924, Sir Leon Levison re-opened his Edinburgh Medical Mission. A report from *The Scotsman* quoted Levison as saying that "the Mission is getting more and more in touch with the Jewish population of the city.... I have never seen so many people calling upon me, nor have I ever seen the work so prosperous."[88] The *Jewish Chronicle* responded to the news with resignation, stating that, "this is but the mere truth, as can be shown on any Sabbath afternoon by the large crowd of Jews, poor in pocket but absolutely bankrupt in spirit, who cluster round this Medical Mission." It was further remarked that "apparently nothing is being done, and very little can be done."[89] In June 1928, Daiches wrote with exasperation to *The Scotsman* asking how public opinion would respond "if Edinburgh Catholics were to establish in the city a medical mission to Edinburgh Protestants."[90]

The battle between Rabbi Daiches and Edinburgh's Jewish Mission Committee did have one lasting and important legacy. During a meeting of the *B'nai B'rith* in London in July 1928, Rabbi Daiches proposed that the organization should institute "something like a campaign against the Missionaries."[91] The resolution was unanimously adopted, and by March 1929, *B'nai B'rith* declared itself ready to "enter upon a campaign to fight perversionist activity."[92] It was remarked by the *Jewish Chronicle* that the new policy toward missionary activity was "largely to the credit of Dr Daiches, who has so persistently urged such measures."[93]

The issue of missionary activity hindered cordial relations between Jewish and Presbyterian religious leaders in Scotland, but it was by no means the only cause for discord. Dubious comments had been uttered at several Christian gatherings in the past, and the persistence of such attitudes in the 1920s was a source of anxiety for Rabbi Daiches. In June 1921, Daiches described as "unjustified and uncalled for" a statement by the Rev. Dr. L. MacLean Watt at a recent General Assembly, in which he depicted Jews as "standing in the way of the progress of every nation and every religion of the wide world."[94]

At the General Assembly of the United Free Church of Scotland in June 1922, Jews had been described as "the lone Esau of the nations ... wandering down the centuries with the mark of Cain upon their brow for the bloodshed of the Elder Brother."[95] In April 1923, Rabbi Daiches protested publicly at a statement written in *The Scotsman* by Dr. Norman McLean, Moderator of the Church of Scotland, in which he spoke disparagingly of the appearance of Jews in Jerusalem and commented that, "those curled Semites would enact to-day the tragedy of nineteen centuries ago."[96] An unrepentant McLean went on to accuse Zionists of doing "what they could to prevent crosses being placed on the graves of British soldiers who laid down their lives for the deliverance of Palestine," an accusation that was subsequently revealed to be baseless.[97] In fact, reports from several General Assemblies during the 1920s contained thinly veiled attacks on the Jewish religion, the "aloofness" and cultural separatism of Jews in Scotland, and Zionism was often treated with deep suspicion.[98]

Barnett Samuel, a resident of Cardiff, wrote to the *Jewish Chronicle* in August 1925 complaining about some of the statements made by Scottish delegates to the Pan-Presbyterian Conference, recently held in Wales. In particular, Samuel singled out one Professor Macdonald Webster of Edinburgh, secretary of the United Free Church Jewish Mission Committee, who presented a paper on, "The Problem of the Jew." Webster, during the course of his address, attacked "the position of the Jews in the world. He attacked the wielding of power of the Jews which he claimed was out of proportion to their numbers, and which was a challenge to the Christian Church."[99]

Professor Macdonald Webster and Rabbi Daiches seem to have developed a mutual loathing. Webster publicly complained that, "more and more it is being said that no one in Scotland today can say 'Jew,' but Rabbi Daiches must needs rush into print." He also alleged that Daiches' campaign against the missions was "the old, old story over again of the Rabbinical antagonism to Jesus Christ."[100]

Tension between Jew and Christian was further inflamed in December 1926, when Daiches protested against the distribution of Christian leaflets among the city's schoolchildren by the Edinburgh Education Authority. The leaflets advised pupils to "join the Christian Church" on reaching the age of 14 and to become "Soldiers of Christ." These pamphlets were not specifically distributed among Jewish children, but they inevitably made their way to Jewish pupils. Daiches protested at the wording of the leaflet, and publicly challenged the Education Authority, who subsequently referred the case to the Committee on Moral and Religious Education. After a prolonged period of correspondence, the wording of the pamphlet was changed in July 1927.[101]

Jewish relations with other Christian denominations in Edinburgh at this time differed somewhat from that seen with the Presbyterian missionaries. In December 1921, Dr. Henry G. Graham, Bishop Auxiliary of the Roman Catholic archdiocese of St. Andrew's and Edinburgh had put some strain on the relationship between the city's Jews and Catholics when he stated, during a denunciation of improper female dress, that "Atheistic, Masonic, and Jewish agents were working to promote immodest fashions to overthrow Catholic morals and the reign of Christ."[102] However, such comments seem to have been rare in emanating from Edinburgh's Catholic churches. In September 1923 the *Edinburgh Dispatch* printed Rabbi Daiches' tribute to the late Monsignor Stuart, chief Catholic priest and Protonotary

Apostolic in Edinburgh. Daiches stated that Monsignor Stuart "was a sincere friend of the Jews." The newspaper also reported that, "on several occasions [Monsignor Stuart] expressed his full agreement with the Rabbi's view in regard to Christian missionary activity among the poor Jews of the city."[103]

An opportunity for Jewish cooperation with smaller Christian denominations arose in 1920, when Daiches was responsible for bringing to national attention a curious anomaly in Scottish law. The law required any couples, who were not both resident in Scotland, to have their names called "on three successive Sundays in the Parish Church of the Established Churches of England and Scotland in the districts in which the parties to the marriage reside."[104] Although complaints were forthcoming from Catholics and other Nonconformists, Rabbi Daiches appealed continuously for action from the Board of Deputies over a number of years, arguing that that the law was "a real grievance" to Scottish Jews. After a fruitless 10 years of agitating for Jewish action on the question, Daiches turned to the heads of Scotland's Nonconformist Christian Churches. In May 1930, representatives of various religious denominations, including the Episcopal Church, the Congregational Society of Friends, and the Rev. Dr. Albert Brown of the Pleasance Chapel, gathered at the North British Station Hotel in Edinburgh to "consider any steps which could be taken to amend the current Scottish marriage laws." It was subsequently decided to form a committee to be entrusted with the task of "taking the most effective steps toward amending the law; and taking any action that may appear necessary to bring about the desired reforms."[105]

The Scottish Office responded by establishing a Scottish Marriage Laws Enquiry Committee in 1936, and Daiches made a "dignified and convincing presentation" during his own appearance before the Committee in March of that year.[106] Although Scotland's marriage laws were not amended until 1939, the cooperation between Jewish and Christian leaders contributed to the further integration of the community into the political, social, and cultural life of Edinburgh, and Scotland in general.

Advocating for Jews and Judaism in Scotland

One way in which Daiches sought to aid the integration of Scottish Jewry into Scottish society was to advocate publicly for Jews and the Jewish religion, with the intention that this would improve the standing of the community, and increase awareness and tolerance of Judaism. Implicit also was the hope that this would lead to a change in the position of Scottish Jewry from that of immigrant minority to a settled and integrated community which could participate in Scottish life on terms equal to that enjoyed by the native population. David Daiches recalls that his father firmly believed than one of his most crucial functions as a modern Orthodox Jewish rabbi was to "speak up for his people with dignity and equality before his fellow citizens."[107]

Daiches advocated for Jews and Judaism in Scotland in a number of ways. One was his defense of the Jewish method of slaughtering animals. In early September 1924 a conference of the Sanitary Inspectors' Association, held in Northumberland, had heavily criticized the Jewish method and urged the introduction of measures of prohibit it. Rabbi Daiches subsequently gave an interview to the *Edinburgh Evening News* on 10 September, in which he argued that agitation against Jewish methods of slaughter had been "imported into this country from Germany," and further alleged that it "owes its origin mainly to a desire on the part of anti-Semites on the Continent to make it difficult for Jews to live in accordance with their religious teachings and traditions."[108] This assertion, though perhaps ungenerous to what may have been innocent motivations on the part of the Sanitary Inspectors' Association, was employed by many senior figures in British Jewry, and was largely effective as a means of countering attacks on kosher butchery.[109] In 1922, the Ministry of Health introduced a policy whereby it would refuse to sanction any byelaws relating to animal slaughter that did not exempt the Jewish method, and by 1927 such an exemption was already in place in Edinburgh.[110] When the Slaughtering of Animals Bill (Scotland) passed through Committee on 26 July 1927, it contained a clause stating that, "the provisions of this Act shall not apply where an animal is slaughtered for the food of the Jews by a Jew duly licensed for the purpose by the Chief Rabbi if such slaughtering is carried out according to the Jewish method of slaughtering, and no unnecessary suffering is inflicted." The Act marked not only the official protection of the Jewish method of slaughter in Scotland, but was also notable for being the first British legislation to cite the power and position of the Chief Rabbi.[111]

In March 1930, Edinburgh's kosher facilities were inspected by Rabbi Levita from the *Beth Din*. This inspection of Edinburgh's butchering practices was actually the result of the Slaughtering of Animals Act (Scotland), which officially brought Scotland's *shochetim* under the legal jurisdiction of the Chief Rabbi. A report sent to the Congregation in April 1930 concluded that the *Beth Din* was "pleased to note that things are satisfactory." The *Beth Din* did however feel moved to comment on the preparation of chicken in the community, complaining that, "the present system of plucking appears to be unsatisfactory and ought to be stopped as soon as possible. This practice is not only contrary to the *Din*, but it is likely to cause serious trouble with the R.S.P.C.A."[112]

David Daiches stated that his father's "letters to *The Scotsman*, putting the Jewish position whenever it required to be put and always assuming the closest natural sympathy between Scottish Presbyterians and Jews, had been a feature of that newspaper since 1919.... They did an immense amount to create a pro–Jewish public opinion in the country."[113] A further opportunity to advocate for Scotland's Jewish communities came in 1929, with the introduction of the Local Government Bill (Scotland). The Bill, which abolished the Scottish Poor Law system, also dissolved city education authorities, and passed their powers to county councils. Funding for non-denominational schools, a contentious issue in Scotland particularly in regard to the funding of Catholic schools, had been provided by the Education (Scotland) Act 1918, and these and other measures from the 1918 legislation were protected under the 1929 Bill. Nonetheless, the abolition of city education authorities and the creation of county education committees caused concern among Jewish leaders in Edinburgh and Glasgow, who sought representation on the committees, and with it, a say in the religious instruction of Jewish pupils in public schools. In a letter to *The Scotsman* on the subject, Rabbi Daiches argued that because the Bill only guaranteed representation to those denominations who already ran day schools, the legislation was, "narrow and unsatisfactory." Daiches stated that, "I see no reason why the Jewish citizens of this country should be denied such a right," and further argued that small minorities such as the Jewish community were "even more in need of representation on the education committee than the Churches that have their own schools and have complete control over the religious education of their children." Daiches also made it clear that he opposed the idea that Catholics and non-conformists required "the establishment of their own denominational schools," arguing that by these means "their children would become segregated from the rest of the children in the country, and a spirit of isolation would be artificially fostered."[114] Following a period of lobbying by Scotland's Jewish leaders, an amendment to the Bill was subsequently approved, which broadened the provisions of the Act sufficiently to enable Jewish participation in the new education committees.[115]

Another aspect of Rabbi Daiches public defense of Judaism was his promotion and advocacy of Zionism. In November 1921, Daiches wrote a letter to the editor of the *Glasgow Herald*, complaining about an article that had appeared in that paper "which breathed the fullest hostility to Zionism."[116] The offending article had referred to "the blunders committed by Zionists in Palestine," and Edinburgh's Rabbi responded by stating that the only blunder committed by Zionists was "believing that the declaration made by Mr. Balfour in the name of the British Government, that Palestine was to be made the Jewish national home, meant what it said." The letter came at a time when British Jews were becoming increasingly disillusioned following the early enthusiasm which had accompanied the Balfour Declaration. In July 1921, one B. Levinson from Edinburgh complained to the *Jewish Chronicle* that due to Arab attacks and British inertia, "that which promised to open up a new era, the reviving episode in the annals of Jewish history, threatens to close as abruptly as it opened."¹¹⁷ Rabbi Daiches also sought the involvement of local politicians, and lobbied for the support of British politicians for the Zionist cause. In December 1922, an invitation was extended to William Graham, then MP for Central Edinburgh, to preside over a meeting on "The Present Position of Zionism" to be held at the Livingstone Hall. The meeting, which was attended by Christians as well as Jews, concluded with Graham stating that, "the realisation of the Zionist aims would be a great blessing to the world, and that opposition to the Zionist Movement on the part of Arabs and others was based on ignorance and malevolence." Graham further pledged himself to "support Zionism in Parliament."

On 23 February 1930, a delegation of the Edinburgh Zionist Association waited in the lobby of the Imperial Hotel in Leith Street in order to gain a meeting with Dr. Drummond Shiels, Labour MP for Edinburgh East and Parliamentary Under-Secretary of State for the Colonies.¹¹⁸ After Shiels agreed to meet with the delegates, Rabbi Daiches proceeded to "lay before him the views of the Association and other Jews on the present position in Palestine." Daiches urged Shiels to work for a "clearer and more definite pronouncement by the Government as to its intentions with regard to the future of Palestine, and as to the methods it was going to employ in carrying out the terms of the Mandate in respect of the establishment of the Jewish National Home."¹¹⁹ The delegates also made a case for "a larger immigration of Jews, more sympathetic officials, a recognized and reinforced police force, and the allotment of state and waste land to Jewish settlers."¹²⁰ On 27 February, Shiels wrote to Rabbi Daiches, "expressing his great pleasure at the opportunity he had of exchanging views with the members of the deputation, who, as Edinburgh citizens, had a greater claim than other people on his time and attention."¹²¹

An increased focus on gaining the support of Gentile Scots and politicians coincided with flagging support for Zionism among Edinburgh's Jews, declining Zionist funds, and the death of Lord Balfour. In May 1930, the Edinburgh Zionist Association sent out over 200 circulars advertising a meeting, which resulted only in "a very small attendance."¹²² During 1930, the Edinburgh Zionist Association followed up the meeting with Drummond Shiels by requesting a meeting with Sir Samuel Chapman, Scottish Unionist MP for South Edinburgh. A deputation, consisting of Rabbi Daiches, a Mr. Rosenbloom, and a Reverend Rosenberg, was "cordially received" by Chapman, and following a two-hour meeting, the delegates recorded that "Sir Samuel promised us his sympathy and support in Parliament, and would endeavour to influence his friends in favor of our cause."

The death of Lord Balfour in March 1930 was keenly felt by Edinburgh's Zionists, who described him as "the greatest Scotsman of our time."¹²³ Rabbi Daiches, and other Zionist leaders in Edinburgh, struggled to replace the vacuum left by Balfour's death, and in May 1930 the council of the EZA discussed the possibility of an effort "to approach the Earl of Linlithgow, Chancellor of the University, to step into the place held by the Earl of Balfour as a sponsor of Zionism."[124] In October 1930 leaders of the Edinburgh Zionist Association even discussed the possibility of undertaking a "pilgrimage to the grave of Lord Balfour," though later decided that this was "inadvisable."[125] In October 1930 it was decided to draft a resolution stating that:

> It is due to the greatest Scotsman of our time, the late Lord Balfour, that the Scottish people should make its voice heard in regard to the fulfillment of the British promise to the Jewish people, and we appeal to Scottish leaders of thought and more especially to Scottish members of Parliament to intervene with the Government.[126]

Rabbi Daiches also advanced the cause of Zionism by conducting several lectures throughout Scotland on the subject. For example, in February 1924 he addressed Edinburgh's Young People's Guild on "The Jewish Claim to Palestine," and in March 1930 he lectured before the St. Paul's Church League of Nations Association on "Palestine and the British Mandate."[127] Another manner in which Rabbi Daiches advocated for Jews and Judaism in Scotland by vigorously challenging actions or incidents which could be seen as anti-Semitic or slanderous. One example occurred in December 1921 when Daiches discovered that Chaucer's "The Prioress' Tale of the Boy Martyr" was being used as a text in Scotland's secondary schools. Arguing that he was challenging "the defamation of Jews," Daiches urged the Joint Press Committee of the Board of Deputies to lobby for its removal from circulation. The text, in which a young Christian boy is murdered by Jews, was, Daiches argued, little more than a "blood libel story" which threatened Jewish children in public schools with "cruel humiliation" in which they would be taunted as "throat cutters." The Rabbi further stressed his opinion that by educating Scottish children with such material, future generations would be prejudiced against Jews: "It may not be very noticeable today, but the seed is bound to yield its harvest."[128] On this occasion, however, support for Daiches was lacking both within the Jewish community and outside it. Professor Macdonald Webster, in his journal *The Jewish Register*, asserted that "English literature cannot be expurgated to suit Jewish palates any more than it can be edited to eliminate offence to any other nationality. We owe a debt to Israel, but it cannot be paid by re-writing English literature."[129] The Joint Press Committee responded largely with silence, though one Rev. Gerald Friedlander defended their stance, arguing that by acceding to the request of Rabbi Daiches and acting against the "well told story," the Board of Deputies would make itself "the laughing stock of the world."[130] Some figures in the Anglo-Jewish Association briefly debated urging the removal of the story from new editions of Chaucer's works, but the motion was abandoned in February 1922 on the urging of one H.S.Q. Henriques, who argued that "they could not suppress the freedom of literature."[131]

However, while in some instances Rabbi Daiches may have appeared hasty in his desire to protect the reputation of Jews and Judaism, his actions were not always necessarily in keeping with Macdonald Webster's remark that "no one in Scotland today can say "Jew" but Rabbi Daiches must needs rush into print."[132] In fact, there are two notable instances involving accusations of anti-Semitism in which Rabbi Daiches was reluctant to get involved. In 1918, one Henry Rothfield, a Jewish money-lender, was denied permission to stay at the North British Station Hotel in Edinburgh.[133] In a court case lasting two years, Rothfield was adamant that he was the victim of anti-Semitism. During the course of proceedings, it was revealed that Rothfield frequently traveled around the country conducting his business, living mostly in hotels. Having resided at the North British Station Hotel many times previously, Rothfield was surprised at being denied access to a room in late 1918. During a hearing in early 1919, the proprietors of the hotel gave as their justifying cause of exclusion the fact that "the pursuer is a German Jew and a money-lender." Rothfield subsequently admitted that he was Jewish and that he was a money-lender, but denied that he was German, stating that he was the son of Polish parents from Cracow, and that they had resided in Britain since 1878, first in Newcastle and afterwards in Dundee. Rothfield himself had been born in Britain in 1884.

The judge, Lord Anderson, even at this early stage, noted that "this is an important and interesting case," and it remains one of the key cases which set the precedent for current principles of hospitality law.[134] In legal terms, the case was interesting because it dealt with the question of whether a traveler could be denied a room, and if so, on what grounds. In historical terms, the case is interesting because of the role played by anti-Semitism in the case. It certainly had echoes of the Simon Harris case in Leven.

It was clear from the statement of the proprietors that they denied Rothfield entry on the grounds that he was in their opinion "a German Jew and a money-lender." Since Rothfield had been born in Britain, and presumably had no foreign accent, such inferences must have been made from his name and possibly his appearance. The prejudice exhibited was thus more of a general, xenophobic, possibly even anti-Semitic character rather than a more typical example of war-time Germanophobia. In this respect, the allusion to Jewish money-lending is perhaps more telling than the accusation that Rothfield was German. Rothfield's lawyers argued that the description of him as being "German" was applied "recklessly for prejudice." The case was decided in favor of Rothfield in 1919, with the award of £155. In summing up, Lord Anderson asserted that "the company is not entitled to exclude Rothfield as a Jew, and the position would have been the same if he had been a German Jew, which he is not."[135] While the *Jewish Chronicle* followed the case, Rabbi Daiches and other leading Edinburgh Jews remained silent.

In a similar instance, Edinburgh's Jewish leaders displayed a reluctance to get involved in the case of Oscar Slater, a Jewish immigrant who had been convicted of murdering an elderly woman in Glasgow in 1909. Kenneth Collins states that the case was hampered in its early stages by anti-Jewish prejudice, and that the manner in which Slater was treated during his trial carried overtones of anti-Semitism.[136] When Slater's appeal was examined in October 1927, Rabbi Daiches urged at a meeting of the Grand Lodge of *B'nai B'rith* in London that, "it would not be in the interests of Slater or of justice to push the matter as Jews."[137]

How do we account for this reluctance on the part of Daiches and other Jewish leaders in Scotland to advocate for Jews in matters relating to crime? It could be argued that the extent of anti-Semitism in both cases was never clear-cut, and that Daiches was reluctant to get involved in cases in which the "Jewish element" was ambiguous. However, Ben Braber argues that in fact such cases also highlighted "a Jewish concern about respectability and security" which had been heightened during the Aliens Act period, and that reluctance to intercede on behalf of Jews accused of crimes stemmed from anxiety that such intercessions would "justify claims of Jewish 'clannishness.'"[138] David Cesarani notes that Leopold Greenberg, editor of the *Jewish Chronicle*, often "oscillated between a blazing defiance of anti-Jewish prejudice and the belief that Jewish behaviour determined the extent of anti-Jewish feeling."[139] Thus it is clear that while Jewish figures in Scotland such as Rabbi Daiches were prepared to combat anti-Semitism and push for Jewish representation in public life, there are reasons to believe that the legacy of the Aliens Act and the accompanying xenophobic sentiment was still being felt in the 1920s. The question remains, however, to what extent this legacy influenced relations between Scots and Jews during the period under examination.

Integration and Inter-Communal Relations

In contrast to the era of the Aliens Act, the interwar period saw declining population figures across Scotland, as the result of increased emigration and decreased immigration. Michael Fry states that emigration could be linked to the "ruin of the Victorian heavy industries," and by 1931 the numbers of those leaving the country "reduced the population for the first time in the modern era."[140] Edinburgh was one of the few areas in Scotland to avoid a decline in its population, which between 1921 and 1931 rose by four percent. This anomaly has been attributed to the fact that "the city had never known an industrial revolution."[141] Nonetheless, the rate of population growth in the city had slowed dramatically. Between 1851 and 1901, the population of Edinburgh had increased by 98 percent to 413,008, but the period 1901 to 1951 saw the population increase by just 13 percent, to 466,761.[142]

In February 1924, the *Jewish Chronicle* published an article discussing "Fewer Aliens in Scotland," in which it argued that as a result of the increased adoption of British nationality, transmigration, and reduced immigration, the 1921 census revealed that the alien population of Scotland had fallen by 4,458 during the period 1911 and 1921, with the largest decrease seen in the numbers of Russian and Polish citizens in Scotland—a decrease of 3,249.[143] Russian and Polish citizens totaled 5,309 nationally in 1921, with Italians numbering 5,144. The foreign-born, non-naturalized population of Edinburgh in 1921 was just 1,725 males and 1,246 females. Of these, there were 586 Russians and 126 Poles, with Jews likely to be highly represented in these groups.[144] Thus, the "Alien Question," as it existed in the last decade of the 19th century, was one no longer worth posing, and as a cause of antagonism between Jew and Gentile, it was largely nullified.

Graham Walker argues that demographic changes in Scotland in the interwar period, particularly emigration, and the decimation of the population as a result of the Great War, did provoke Scots to seek a scapegoat. However, in this instance, it was not the country's Jewish community which was singled out for particular attention, but the large population of Irish Catholics which was viewed by Protestant churches to be "unassimilable."[145] Anti-immigrant agitation, tinged with religious prejudice was, to some extent, directed away from Jews and Italians. The groups which evolved from this atmosphere, such as Alexander Ratcliffe's Scottish Protestant League, founded in 1920, carried out a campaign "laced with violence" against Edinburgh's Catholics, who then comprised less than 10 percent of the population.[146] Another, less extremist, Protestant organization was Protestant Action, founded in 1933 by ex-soldier John Cormack, which included among its members a very small number of Jews, who joined "for opportunistic reasons."[147]

While the majority of anti-immigrant activity in Scotland was aimed against Irish Catholics, there remained a minority of vocal groups who persisted in agitating against Jews during the 1920s. The Glasgow-based *Jewish Echo* noted in 1928 that while anti-Semitism was not a prominent facet of Scottish culture, "here and there queer fuddle-headed people go about chock-full of Russian progromist ideas, religiously believing in the truth of the Protocols of the Elders of Zion. And there are small groups of British Fascisti who are almost as sure of the superiority of the Nordic race as are some Americans."[148]

The reference to American racist organizations is itself interesting, since it was clear at the time from organizations such as the Ku Klux Klan that anti-Catholicism and anti-Semitism were not necessarily mutually exclusive. The Klan had constructed a Protestant Nativist platform in which Communism, Blacks, Jews, and Catholics were deemed "incompatible with Americanism."[149] It was known at the time that both Alexander Ratcliffe and John Cormack admired the Ku Klux Klan, and Cormack later founded a cadre of Protestant Action known as "Kormack's Kaledonian Klan."[150] Assertions from William Kenefick and Aubrey Newman to the effect that "there was more tolerance of Jews in Scotland because the Catholics and Protestants hated each other so much that they had no hatred left," are perhaps, in this light, too simplistic.[151] It is unlikely that Jews felt secure in the knowledge that Scotland had another prejudice, and another scapegoat. It is not unlikely that Jews during the 1920s watched the treatment of Catholics with quiet concern.

Concerns about lingering anti-alien prejudice seem to have weighed on Rabbi Daiches. In 1924 he wrote for the *Edinburgh Evening Dispatch* under the headline "The Poor Jew: Edinburgh Rabbi's Defence of His Race." During the course of his article, Daiches referred to "agitation against aliens which had resumed in this country," and argued against accusations that Jews were slum dwellers and crooks, stating that:

> The slums that were to be found in the great cities had not been created by Jews. The Jew had found them and had been compelled by dire poverty to settle in the dirt and squalor prevailing there. They had rendered these slums much safer places for people to walk in, for women to live in, for children to be reared in, than they would otherwise have been.[152]

Daiches further stated that though the Jewish immigrant may arrive "short of bread to eat and raiment to put on, he inevitably brought with him a stock of ideas and a breadth of vision and a wealth of ambition." He concluded that it was "mere calumny to assert that the alien Jew was lowering the moral level of the native population."[153]

It is also clear that there were a number of individual anti–Semites in Edinburgh. For example, in January 1920, an invitation had been extended by the Edinburgh Jewish Literary Society to Professor Charles Saroléa, a Belgian academic employed by Edinburgh University. During the course of a lecture on "The Future of the Jewish Race," Saroléa stated that Jews were "a Freemasonry pledged to support each other," and that "the Jew had been the greatest revolutionary force of the 19th century." Rather than the traditional vote of thanks afforded to a guest speaker, Rabbi Daiches "expressed his disappointment at many of the observations made by Professor Saroléa regarding the power swayed by Jews in Germany, Austria, and Russia."[154] The views of Professor Saroléa were particularly worrying because he wrote occasionally for *The Scotsman*. In November 1922 Saroléa had written an article stating that Polish and Lithuanian Jews were "indescribably filthy and afflicted with skin disease," and that Zionism was the sole cause of Polish anti–Semitism.[155]

In October 1923, Rabbi Daiches was forced to respond publicly to remarks made in one of Saroléa's articles, in which he referred to "Communist Jews in Moscow," and "Jewish Bolshevist officials at the Kremlin."[156]

However, relations between Scots and Jews in the interwar period seem to have been largely cordial. During an interview in 1922, Rabbi Daiches stated that the attitude of the Scottish people toward Jews was "most friendly," and commented that "there is scarcely any Jew hatred, and the Jews in the larger centres, as well as in the smaller communities, live on the best terms with their Christian neighbours."[157] Daiches argued that, particularly in Edinburgh, Freemasonry had done "a lot of good in the matter of cementing the good relations between Jew and non-Jew," and that earlier in the year a Masonic service had been held in the Graham Street synagogue, attracting Christian masons from "all over the metropolis and surrounding districts."[158] During the same interview, it was also remarked that there was significant support for Zionism among Scottish Christians and Daiches added that "if it depended on the Scottish people, the Palestine Mandate would have long since become a reality."[159]

Writing five years later on "Scotsmen and Jews," Rabbi Daiches was unwavering in his belief that Scots and Jews enjoyed a cordial and special relationship. Daiches stated that after nine years "in constant touch with the Scottish Government, civic, educational, and legal authorities" it seemed to him that no nation "in the world … treats the Jew with such fairness, and shows him so much tolerance and goodwill, as the Scottish people." Rabbi Daiches, in eulogizing the Scottish-Jewish experience, often consciously or otherwise made claims not borne out by the historical record. For example, Daiches claimed that epithets like "Sheeny" were "unknown in Scotland," and that "no prejudice is shown here towards Jewish business firms, tradesmen, artisans, shopkeepers, or travellers."[160] In 1942 Daiches stated his belief that this level of tolerance and goodwill was in part "animated by a sense of reverence for the "People of the Book," and that aspects of Scottish culture were permeated with an age-old interest in Jews and Judaism.[161] Daiches notably omitted mention of the negative aspects of the Church of Scotland's "interest" in Jews. Daiches was possibly more accurate in attributing the level of esteem enjoyed by Edinburgh's Jewish community to the benevolence and good-will shown by the local press. On its jubilee, Rabbi Daiches paid tribute to the *Edinburgh Evening News*, highlighting its "liberal and broadminded outlook" and its "just and generous attitude towards racial and religious minorities."[162]

Edinburgh's Jews also benefited from the celebration of their contribution to the war effort, the relatively low level of crime in the community, and instances where local Jews had distinguished themselves in acting for the public good. In August 1919, three young Jewish men, all commercial travelers from the Pleasance area, drowned while rescuing other boats in distress on the Firth of Forth. At the funeral of Joseph Berger, whose body was the only to be recovered, "a large assembly representing all sections of the community," congregated to pay their respects to the deceased and those who perished with him. Rabbi Daiches informed those present that the conduct of the young men, all of them aged 19, "reflected honour, not only upon the brave lads who met their fate with such sublime courage, but upon the whole Jewish community."[163]

During a Jewish War Memorial event held at Livingstone Hall in February 1921, the Lord Provost, Sir Thomas Hutchison, expressed his pleasure at addressing the city's Jews, "as it gave him the opportunity to tell them how pleased he was to testify to the law-abiding character of the Jews resident in the city."[164] In December 1921 the Edinburgh Hebrew Congregation hosted a bazaar in aid of the Edinburgh Royal Infirmary and the Jewish Board of Guardians. The bazaar, which was the first of its kind in the city, brought Jew and Christian together, and at its opening the Lord Provost remarked that "he appreciated very much the efforts of the Jewish community in supporting their own poor," and that relations between the Jewish and non-Jewish communities in Edinburgh were "cordial and very creditable." He further added that "Edinburgh had good reason to be proud of its record in the late war, but no section of the community could be prouder than the Jewish on account of its excellent record in the number of soldiers it gave to H.M. Forces."[165] In March the following year the Provost's son, Captain Hutchison, in unveiling the war memorial tablet at the Graham Street synagogue, expressed his respect for the manner in which Edinburgh's Jews had "assisted the country of their birth or adoption throughout the war." He stated that "the proportion of voluntary enlistments of local Jews had been greater than that of any other section of the population, while the decorations awarded for gallant conduct in the field included the award of the Victoria Cross to Sergeant Wales, of the Manchester Regiment, a native of Edinburgh."[166] In November 1927, Alexander Stevenson, then Lord Provost of Edinburgh, appeared before the Jewish Literary Society and told those present that "he held the Jewish citizens of Edinburgh in very high esteem. As the civic head of the city he was glad to testify to the law-abiding character of the Jewish population, who record in regard to loyalty to the country and city was second to none."[167]

This acceptance by Scots was matched by increased integration by immigrant Jews, now fewer in number, and their descendants. Muriel Spark recalled that her father, typical of second generation Scottish Jews, "spoke with a strong Edinburgh accent, and although he was a Jew, having been born and educated in Edinburgh ... he wore the same sort of clothes as the other fathers and spoke as they did."[168] Tom Devine argues that the 1920s witnessed increased acceptance of Jewish immigrants, along with increased upward social mobility among Jews, an increase in Jewish participation in trade unions, and the decline of the Yiddish language.[169] The period also saw changing attitudes toward religious observance. Howard Denton recalls that once, during Yom Kippur in the 1920s, he was shocked to discover a large number of Jews in an Edinburgh café, "all eating and drinking. The café owner told us she always had lots of Jewish customers on fast days.... It was a fair indication of how the old ways were dying out as we all began to live like the Scots who surrounded us."[170]

Integration and increasing contact between Jews and Christians in the city led to a rise in instances of intermarriage. Ben Braber states that after the First World War "young Jews were increasingly able to choose a partner themselves," and that places in which Jews and non-Jews could socialize were proliferating.[171] Kenneth Collins argues that while there are no precise figures for intermarriage, "there is a clear impression that this was on the increase in the 1920s and 1930s. It was said to be commoner for Jewish men marrying non-Jewish women."[172] In a letter to the *Jewish Echo* in August 1928 the writer complained that the *Beth Din* was not rigorous enough in regulating intermarriage and proselytes. The author claimed:

> I know of a Glasgow case where a girl was admitted to the Jewish faith within two weeks after she married a Yiddish fellow. Surely that girl did not embrace Judaism out of conviction! No wonder there are so many Jewish boys marrying *Shikshes*, if they are encouraged by such a religious authority as the London *Beth Din*.[173]

The fact that the Jewish population in Edinburgh was smaller, coupled with the "traditional Jewish attitude towards marrying a Gentile," and the fact that conversion to Judaism was a "long and very demanding" process may have meant that cases of intermarriage were less numerous than in Glasgow. However, during a meeting of the Council of the Edinburgh Hebrew Congregation in April 1925 it was recorded that a request for a *Chuppah* had been made by a couple in which the bride was a Gentile, and that a "discussion took place concerning the caution that was necessary for granting applications in such cases."[174]

Integration was further developed by increasing social mobility, and a move out of the ghetto areas of Nicholson Street, Richmond Street, and the Pleasance. Some elements of the community were still plagued by chronic poverty. In March 1922, a report by the Edinburgh Jewish Board of Guardians noted "increasing poverty in the city," and complained about apathy from the city's Jewish community in terms of combating the problem. Following the Board's annual meeting in 1922 it was remarked that "out of a total of 2,000 Jews in the city, only eighteen were present at the meeting."[175] In October 1931, the Hebrew Benevolent Loan Society reported an increase of 30 subscribers, and had advanced £1,045 in loans during the previous 12 months.[176] During the same year's annual meeting of the Board of Guardians, the treasurer said that "claims on the Board's funds were increasing, and he appealed for additional support. The expenditure on relief during the year was over £500."[177]

However, a definite drift away from the slums occurred during the 1920s. The *Edinburgh Evening Dispatch* estimated in 1925 that "about half of the city's Jews were to be found in the southern suburbs."[178] The second generation tended to move away from commerce and toward professions, particularly medicine. In general, Edinburgh's Jewish community, after the First World War, was increasingly well educated, and Kenneth Collins states that by 1937 there were about 40 Jewish doctors in the city.[179] The *Jewish Echo* remarked during the same period that, "the old Ghetto, as it is today, gives the impression of a stronghold deserted by its own and now garrisoned by strangers.... Today only one or two shops bear the name of Hebrew occupants."[180] According to the article, some Jews in the city had risen from humble beginnings in the congested area around the Pleasance, to own "substantial businesses in other parts of the city."[181] In April 1924, it became clear that the premises at Graham Street were deteriorating, and it was decided by the leadership of the congregation to take the opportunity to select a site closer to the suburbs, where a new synagogue could be built. In March 1929 a site was found in Edinburgh's Newington district.[182] In June 1930 an appeal was made to the "Jews of Great Britain and the Empire" for funds necessary to meet the estimated £20,000 cost of the new synagogue.[183] Funds were forthcoming and the Beth Hamedrash of the new building was consecrated on 4 July 1930.[184] In September 1932 the Salisbury Road synagogue was consecrated by the Chief Rabbi Hertz, with the Lord Provost, magistrates, professors from Edinburgh University, Members of Parliament, and every member of Edinburgh Town Council present.[185] At the reception following the consecration of the synagogue, which was attended by over 1,400 people, Bailie Wilson Maclaren, the Chief Magistrate, paid tribute to the Jewish residents of Edinburgh stating that they were "law-abiding, and they loved their country."

Another manifestation of this integration was the desire of some Jews to become involved in the political and cultural life of the city, and the nation as a whole. In December 1920, Elias Fürst joined S.S. Stungo, and his brother Isaac Fürst, as a Justice of the Peace for the city and county of Edinburgh.[186] Elias, who was the oldest son of the Rev. Jacob Fürst, had a history of involvement in the political and cultural life of the city.

A former president of the Edinburgh Hebrew Congregation, Elias had been a member of the local National Insurance Committee, and a member of the local Prince of Wales Fund. He had also been a teenage supporter of Hearts Football Club, and went on to be one of the club's longest serving chairmen. His father had taken him to matches on the Sabbath, feeling that as it was done in striving for acceptance, this "did not imply betrayal of their past: it was merely good manners towards a generous host."[187] Aged just 17,

Elias became the "youngest ever paid-up member of Hearts," and went on to "bombard the committee with gratuitous financial advice, most of which went unheeded."[188] In 1902, however, Elias was appointed club auditor, and between 1902 and 1935, "he helped guide the club from crisis to financial security, oversaw the development of Tynecastle, steered the club through the traumatic years of the First World War, and helped usher in one of the club's most successful managers."[189] When Hearts won the Scottish Cup in 1906, Fürst was allowed to display the trophy in the window of his jewelers shop at 45 South Bridge, and in 1912, he was elected as chairman of the club aged 39. By 1920, Elias enjoyed "great popularity among the general population of the city," and he was frequently asked to referee important matches.[190] Jack Alexander argues that for all his success, "Fürst never quite managed to throw off his outsider status in the eyes of his fellow directors. Here this young Jewish kid comes along, so much more astute, and with so much more drive, than those around him."[191] Nonetheless, in 1930 Elias Fürst made history again as the first Hearts official, and Jew, to be elected as chairman of the Scottish Football League.[192]

In 1926, a young Jewish man named Michael Marcus became the youngest councilor in Scotland when he was elected to Edinburgh Town Council by a majority of 520. Marcus had been born in Knichen, near Bialystok, and had arrived in Scotland with his family aged two.[193] In 1918, Marcus got in contact with William Graham, who was then president of the Board of Trade, and Labour member of Edinburgh Town Council.[194] Under Graham's tutelage, Marcus joined the Labour movement and increasingly became involved in politics. Marcus graduated in Law from Edinburgh University in 1923, and after William Graham was elected to Parliament for Central Edinburgh, Marcus served as his election agent in late 1923.[195] He subsequently established a legal practice in the city, and sat on the Council of the Edinburgh Hebrew Congregation. In 1927, while working on behalf of Oscar Slater during the latter's appeal against a conviction for murder, Marcus announced his intention to stand for a seat in Parliament at the next General Election.[196] After some negotiation, Marcus was invited by the Dundee Trades and Labour Council to stand as the Labour candidate for Dundee, in an election which he subsequently won.[197] At the time of his election, at the age of 33, Marcus was the youngest MP in Parliament.

In an interview with the *Jewish Chronicle* in March 1930, Michael Marcus explained the importance of Edinburgh politics in forming his own political development, and also stressed that in he was "steeped in Jewish thought and learning, and animated with the spirit of Judaism."[198] Marcus further stated that "I naturally take up a definitely Jewish attitude in the House of Commons," and that the Commons was "not competent to pass judgement on such questions as *Schechita*." He declared that he was an ardent Zionist, in sympathy with the aims of Poale Zion, and further stated that it was his desire to advance the Zionist cause in Parliament, and that his speeches on the issue of Palestine were "pointedly nationalistic in the Jewish sense." Marcus also claimed to be working to increase Zionist support in the Labour Party, stating that "ninety-nine per cent of the Parliamentary Labour Party are pro–Zionists. The other one per cent is not anti–Zionist, but merely unaware of the facts."[199] In May 1931, Michael Marcus became the first Jew to be appointed to the Scottish Office.[200]

The ability of young, foreign-born Jews such as Elias Fürst and Michael Marcus to reach the heights of the Scottish Football League, the House of Commons, and the Scottish Office displays an ability to combine Jewish communal and religious affiliation with a desire to participate to the full in wider society. This younger generation which came of age in the 1920s was not hampered, as their parents may have been, by language barriers, or lack of education. Their ability to reach the political and cultural heights of Scottish society also betrays a vein of goodwill and tolerance which prevailed among a certain strata of Christian Scots, though it would be unwise to extrapolate from these examples more generalized conclusions about tolerance in Scottish society as a whole. The roots of this acceptance lay to some extent in the low rates of crime in the Jewish community, the successful way in which it looked after its poor, the fact that Jews rarely competed with Gentiles for employment, and the sacrifice of Edinburgh's Jews during the Great War. This cordial relationship also owed something to the legacy left by the Rev. Jacob Fürst, who advocated for Judaism and challenged prejudice, and this legacy was subsequently augmented by the activity of Rabbi Dr. Salis Daiches.

Edinburgh Jewry during the period 1918–1932 underwent dramatic change. For the first time since the middle of the 19th century, one could speak of a united Jewish community in the city. This unity was in large part due to the ambitions and ability of Rabbi Dr. Salis Daiches, who wished to improve the standing of the community both locally and nationally by doing away with the factionalism which had plagued it for more than three decades. Edinburgh Jewry under Daiches also became more assertive. Zionism was promoted to Gentile Scots and local politicians were lobbied in its name, with reasonable success. Daiches was also successful in advocating for Judaism in matters such as Scottish marriage law, and the slaughter of animals.

The extent to which Daiches was successful in turning public opinion against missionary activity is difficult to assess, though his impassioned pleas against ongoing proselytizing would have gone some way to drawing attention to the impact such organizations were having on their "targets," and Daiches was successful in exploding some of the more outrageous myths employed by evangelicals, such as those concerning the death of Judaism. Daiches was also successful in encouraging the *Beth Din* to act against the missions, lending his own local campaign national and even international significance.

It is also clear that many of the changes undergone by Edinburgh Jewry at this time were beyond the control of Rabbi Daiches. Trends of upward social mobility which had begun modestly before his arrival gained pace during the 1920s, and while there were still some elements of the community who struggled economically, educational opportunities and a culture of learning had contributed to an increasingly professional younger generation and a drift from the slum districts to the suburbs in the south of the city. The unity of the community and its move away from the grim locations of its past was symbolized in the movement of the spiritual home of Edinburgh Jewry to the new synagogue at Salisbury Road. The social mobility of Edinburgh Jewry and its physical movement from the city's "Jewish Quarter" was part of a wider process of integration which saw increased contact between Jew and Gentile in the city, and the development of an atmosphere conducive to good relations between the two communities. In this sense, while one could say that the Jewish community was united, one could also say that Edinburgh Jewry was increasingly united with the community of Edinburgh as a whole.

6

The Fight Against Fascism, 1933–1945

> "Would God that one far mightier be raised in this dear land, to tell the dupes of Hitler ... that foes of kinsfolk of King David's son are ours."—
> the Rev. Hugh Gordon Ross, Church of Scotland, Dundee 1934.[1]

For Edinburgh Jewry, the interwar period had been characterized by great strides toward communal unity, increased Jewish-Gentile interaction, the successful integration of the younger generations, and for some, an improvement in their socio-economic position. A new synagogue had been built to serve the city's united Jewish congregation, and by 1933, Rabbi Daiches had grown in influence and esteem, both within and without the Jewish community, to enable him to lay claim to the title of *de facto* "Chief Rabbi of Scotland."[2] The community was not without its problems however. There remained an element of Edinburgh Jewry which struggled with poverty. Worshippers at the new synagogue were regularly "subjected to inconvenience by constant requests for assistance" from the poor Jewish men who stood outside, and expenditures from the Board of Guardians and the Benevolent Loan Society remained high and would remain so for most of the decade.[3] The congregation was also shrinking. Entries in the minute books of the congregation reveal that the community was already aging rapidly, losing members through death, and failing to "gain proportionately new members," as younger Jews moved away geographically or perhaps even spiritually, from the Edinburgh Jewish community. It was estimated that by 1935 as little as 25 percent of Edinburgh Jewry was participating in organized religious life.[4]

The 1930s would prove a testing time for the community as Jews in Edinburgh were engulfed in domestic and international crises including the rise of Fascism in Britain and Continental Europe. This chapter commences with an exploration of the response of leading Edinburgh Jews to the rise of Fascism in Germany, and proceeds with an assessment of the manner in which the community was impacted by the arrival of Jewish refugees from Germany and Austria. The presence of Fascists and prominent anti-Semites in Edinburgh is analyzed, and the chapter examines the reaction of non-Jews in the city toward anti-Semitism at home and abroad. It is argued that the anti-Semitic policies of the Nazi Government in particular led to a radical transformation in relations between Edinburgh Jewry and the Church of Scotland, and the reasons for, and the manner of, this rapprochement is examined.

Edinburgh Jewry and the Boycott of German Goods

Edinburgh Jewry was rapid in its response to the rise of Hitler to power in Germany, and in the period shortly following the establishment of the Nazi regime this response manifested itself in three ways—the boycott of German goods, a series of public protests, and the lobbying of Christian organizations and civic leaders for intercession. These responses were commensurate with Jewish responses nationally and internationally.

The boycott movement had its origins in "a wave of terror" orchestrated by the SA during the first two weeks of March 1933. The desecration of synagogues and the boycott of Jewish businesses in Germany provoked a boycott of German goods by Polish Jews.[5] Within days the boycott movement spread to Jewish communities around the world. Just days after the signing of the Enabling Act, which legally cemented the German dictatorship, on 23 March 1933, several Jewish traders in Edinburgh began boycotting German goods.[6] Stating that he was acting against "the persecution of Jews in Germany," one Jewish trader explained to a reporter from *The Scotsman*: "It is the only thing a right-thinking Jew can do. We are horror-struck at the terrible state of affairs in Germany. If we could take stronger measures we would. As it is, we are cutting off all German trade."[7] In his first sermon following the wave of anti-Jewish violence, Rabbi Daiches protested against "the barbarous attitude adopted by Herr Hitler and his followers against a defenceless minority."[8] In addition, Daiches urged "the religious leaders of this country" to join in protest over Nazi treatment of Jews, and expressed his belief that the joint efforts of British Churches and politicians "would probably have a salutary effect on the new rulers of Germany, and would exercise a restraining influence on Hitler and his followers." The boycott of German goods and the outspoken nature of Scottish Jewish opposition to the Hitler regime did not go unchallenged in the Scottish press, and on one occasion it aroused the open hostility of a prominent German expatriate.[9]

In July 1933 Daiches ended a sermon condemning the reported desecration of a synagogue in Mannheim with an appeal to "representatives of public opinion in this country" to "protest emphatically against such outrages." It was, Daiches added, "high time that the Governments of all civilized nations made a real effort to stop the cruel persecution of Jews and Judaism in Germany."[10] By late 1933, Daiches had commenced lecturing at private members clubs, speaking to the Dunfermline Civic Club and the Union of Democratic Control on "Hitler's Policy" and advocating a show of "moral strength" against the Nazi regime. Daiches' diaries reveal that in 1938 he spoke to organizations and churches in Dundee, Dunfermline and across Edinburgh on "The Position of the Jew in the World Today."[11]

This relatively high-profile form of protest against the Hitler government was in contrast to the attitude of the British-Jewish elite. In particular, the Board of Deputies of British Jews, under President Neville Laski, was reluctant to lend support to the boycott movement. Geoffrey Alderman states that "the Board consistently rejected calls for an official Anglo-Jewish boycott of German goods."[12] Although the Board did not explicitly state as policy its opposition to the boycott movement until October 1933, as early as 26 March Laski had urged that "we must do nothing and say nothing which can be misinterpreted and utilized by the left wing of the Nazi movement to crush the advice and the execution of the advice which von Papen and the moderates in the Germany government have given their followers."[13] Laski's cautious approach, and his belief that the "excesses" of the new German government would be checked by moderating and sobering influences, also prevailed as the dominant stance of British public opinion during the early 1930s.[14]

It is clear however, that there were other considerations influencing the position of the Board and the British-Jewish leadership in general. Sharon Gewirtz argues that Laski's advocacy of a "low-profile" approach was a legacy of "earlier strategies of adaptation to immigrant life."[15] Gewirtz argues that the British-Jewish middle class believed that it was liberal tolerance which had enabled "the fulfilment of their social and economic aspirations" and that continued tolerance was required to protect this "newly acquired status." Crucially, it was believed that "Jews had to earn the tolerance of the gentile bourgeoisie, otherwise they might lose it." This desire of the Jewish middle class to "earn" the tolerance of gentile neighbours had in previous decades manifested itself in strategies to cope with the immigration of Eastern Jews, attempts to tackle crime associated with Jews such as the white slave trade, opposition to Zionism, and the many pains taken by community leaders to stress British patriotism and the Jewish contribution to the war effort. In the case of the boycott movement, it was felt that to boycott so visibly "as Jews" undermined the efforts of the British-Jewish elite to ensure that immigrant Jews "see themselves as English citizens first and Jews second."[16]

That these efforts had largely failed became quickly apparent to the Board of Deputies. The refusal of the Board to support the boycott became "the subject of bitter animosity within the community," and ordinary Jewish men and women increasingly viewed proclamations from the Board on the issue to be irrelevant.[17] Boycott activity remained sporadic until the establishment of the Jewish Representative Council for the Boycott of German Goods and Services (JRC) in September 1933. The JRC sought to coordinate all boycott initiatives in the belief that the use of this economic weapon was capable of "bringing down the Hitler government."[18]

In early October 1933, Laski issued a thinly veiled attack on the JRC, warning against the activities of those Jews who "by their own conduct fostered anti–Semitism."[19] Undeterred, the JRC proceeded to issue letters to every congregation in Britain, requesting those congregations to appoint a representative to attend a meeting in London in November for the "purpose of proclaiming in the name of British Jewry a boycott against German goods and services and to elect a permanent council to be known as the Jewish Representative Council."[20] The Council of the Edinburgh Hebrew Congregation received such a letter on 19 October. The minute books of the congregation record that at a meeting called to discuss the issue, it was "unanimously agreed that they could not support this movement. They stood behind the Board of Deputies and their policy as recently enunciated by Mr. Neville Laski."[21]

The reasons behind this decision were not explicitly stated in the minute books. The Council of the Edinburgh Hebrew Congregation may have been personally influenced by Laski himself—he had met with them in Edinburgh to discuss the "German situation" less than three weeks prior to the approach from the JRC.[22] It is also plausible that antagonism toward the boycott was the natural response of a Council which had shown reluctance in the past to involve itself in contentious issues "as Jews." In effect, the Council of the Edinburgh Hebrew Congregation adopted the policy of middle-class British-Jewry because they were representative of that group.

This reluctance to participate in the boycott did not reflect a uniform reluctance to participate in high-profile protest, or to react to anti–Jewish actions in Germany "as Jews." The Council had been approached by a Rev. Harry Miller in May 1933 with a request to attend a public meeting on Germany with representatives from the Christian Churches. The Council "on hearing this letter decided that the wisest course would be to leave the matter in abeyance at present."[23] However, the Council, over time, began to be more open in its willingness to consult with other religious bodies. On 14 September 1933, the Council participated in a public meeting with the Edinburgh Protestant Society "in connection with the German situation."[24] The meeting, at which over 800 were in attendance, was Chaired by Rabbi Daiches and presided over by the Earl of Cassillis. The meeting, which was also attended by several prominent MPs and members of the clergy, ended with a resolution to appeal to "the League of Nations to consider at the forthcoming Assembly of the League the position of the German Jews, and to take the appropriate steps to secure the restoration of their rights."[25] However, evidence suggests that, in relation to his approach to the Scottish Churches, Rabbi Daiches sought approval and close cooperation with Neville Laski and the Board of Deputies. In early May 1933 Daiches wrote to Laski stating that he was attempting to persuade the General Assembly of the Church of Scotland to make a direct protest against Nazi persecution of Jews. Laski replied on 9 May expressing his approval of the approach and added that "the importance of Edinburgh as a church centre, of course, cannot be over-estimated."[26]

By its willingness to cooperate with non–Jewish organizations and authorities, the leadership of Edinburgh Jewry was ahead of trends in the boycott movement. Sharon Gewirtz states that the leadership of the boycott movement only began to acknowledge the "powerlessness of Jews alone" to affect change in Germany at the end of 1934. Prior to this there was a belief that an economic boycott waged by world Jewry would weaken Germany sufficiently for either regime change or a departure from its anti–Semitic policies. Only in 1935 could one speak of a national and international shift in emphasis "towards the replacement of existing boycott organizations with non-sectarian organizations."[27] Rabbi Daiches' failure to speak in support of the boycott, and his calls for the intervention of gentile politicians and the Christian Churches in early 1933, perhaps reveal something of his own pessimistic assessment of the problem in Germany. While he had expressed the opinion in early 1933 that condemnation from spiritual and political leaders could have a restraining effect on the Nazi government, he made it clear that what was occurring was not a passing phase or temporary excess, but the threat of a "relapse into barbarism."[28]

Of course, it must be stated that the Council of the Edinburgh Hebrew Congregation did not speak for Edinburgh Jewry in its entirety. Like the official position of the Board of Deputies, the position of the Edinburgh Hebrew Congregation went unheeded by other sections of the community. In Scotland, the boycott movement found particular resonance with Jewish youth organizations. By August 1933, Captain Webber's Organization for Ending Hostilities to German Jews, a predecessor of the JRC, became affiliated to the Scottish Council of Jewish Youth Organizations.[29] Shortly thereafter, the branches of the youth organization in Edinburgh, Dundee, Aberdeen, Dunfermline and Greenock cooperated "in intensifying the boycott of German goods throughout Scotland."[30] In Dundee, support for the movement prevailed to such an extent that steps were taken to "exhibit the boycott certificate in all Jewish business premises."[31] That the boycott movement resonated in particular with Jewish youth may suggest that the Jewish identity expressed by their immigrant parents or grandparents imparted a "transmissible distinctiveness" which had been unaffected by the processes of integration, but which was not necessarily linked to the Jewish faith. Unlike first generation immigrants, this identity was not expressed in the independent *Shul* or the socialist circles, but in other ways which ran counter to the ambitions of the British-Jewish elite. This was most apparent in the boycott movement, and also the Zionist movement, which was increasingly seen as "the best hope for the victims of Nazi persecution."[32]

German-Jewish Refugees in Edinburgh

Another significant way in which Edinburgh Jewry was affected by the rise of Nazism was the influx into the city of Jewish refugees from Germany. From 1933 until 1937, the majority of refugees arriving in Britain were adult academics, doctors and dentists who had been expelled, or expected to be expelled from their positions in Germany. Marion Berghahn states that "the first group to leave Germany was in a fortunate position. It largely consisted of distinguished academics, well-connected businessmen, and famous artists."[33] These refugees had the ability to bring out some money and other possessions, and most tended to settle in the South-East of England.[34]

Edinburgh University proved to be a significant attraction for some, and in a number of instances, refugee scientists were actively sought by Edinburgh University officials. Bill Williams has stated that "the chances for refugees were at their best when a coincidence existed of refugee need and British advantage," and this is illustrated clearly in the story of Edinburgh University and German-Jewish refugee scientists.[35] From 1933 to 1938, a total of 2,600 German-Jewish academics were assisted in finding placements at British universities by the Academic Assistance Council [AAC] later the Society for the Protection of Science and Learning [SPSL].[36] By November 1938 the SPSL had been instrumental in placing seven scientists at Edinburgh University.[37] In April 1933, Professor Francis Crew, director of the Institute of Animal Genetics at Edinburgh University, wrote to Rabbi Daiches stating that he regretted the dismissal of Jewish scientists but that he also saw "a glorious chance for this country to recruit to itself first-class minds, for we have only got to take advantage of the stupidity of Germany to reinforce ourselves very considerably indeed."[38] In particular, Crew wished to recruit a Dr. Curt Stern. Stern had been employed at the Kaiser Wilhelm Institute for Biology at Berlin-Dahlem, but had left for a temporary fellowship in the United States just prior to Hitler becoming chancellor. Crew argued that "it will be impossible for Stern to return to Germany as a Jew." The reason for Crew's letter to Daiches was that as a foreign citizen, Edinburgh University could not pay Stern a salary, but that they could award him a fellowship if funding was made available. Stating that he would give his right hand to recruit Stern, but lamenting the fact that "my right hand has no market value," Crew asked the Edinburgh Hebrew Congregation to contribute £500 to a fellowship fund.[39] Less than two weeks later Crew wrote to the *Jewish Chronicle* stating that the Jewish community could "do no greater service to this country than to take steps to make it possible for [Jewish scientists] to come to this country here to find refuge." Crew added his desire to see the Jewish community of Great Britain raise the funds necessary for the requisite research fellowships.[40]

One notable scientist who did find a position at Edinburgh University was Professor Max Born, a leading authority on the atom. Professor Born had been working at Göttingen University when wholesale dismissals led to the displacement of 52 Jewish scientists.[41] Born and his wife became leading figures in Edinburgh's German-Jewish refugee community, and they later founded a Domestic Bureau which aimed to secure domestic employment for German-Jewish women.[42]

Marion Berghahn notes that while Jewish academics were well-received by senior university officials, "the foreign scholar was often faced with xenophobia or anti–Semitism.... The large influx of eminent scholars evoked jealousy and fear of competition, if not simply anti–German feelings on the part of native academics."[43] There is no evidence to suggest whether this was or was not the case at Edinburgh University.

One section of this first group of refugees did have particular difficulty in moving to Britain—Jewish physicians. Although Jews comprised less than one percent of the German population, 10 percent of German medical professionals were Jewish in 1933.[44] Effectively prohibited from continuing to practice medicine in Germany, the majority sought opportunities abroad. In 1933 the British government expressed its willingness to accept 500 doctors from Germany, but the British Medical Association [BMA] launched a major challenge to this initiative, resulting in the admission of less than 200, although the restriction was later relaxed further.[45] Added pressure from the BMA ensured that the German medical qualifications of refugee Jewish doctors were not recognized, with the result that a significant number of the medical refugees had to re-train or sit examinations. The coordination of the placement of refugees had largely fallen under the auspices of the Jewish Refugee Committee, based in London. In June 1933, Otto Schiff, chairman of the Jewish Refugee Committee, wrote to Rabbi Daiches stating that 25 Jewish doctors had been placed at medical schools in Edinburgh and expressed his thanks for "all that has been done in Scotland for German refugees."[46] According to the Medical Information Sub-Committee of the Jewish Medical and Dental Emergency Association, by September 1933 approximately 100 Jewish doctors in Britain were "attempting to obtain a British qualification, and of these thirty-five have been placed at Edinburgh."[47] Kenneth Collins stated that, as European refugees realized that regulations were more straightforward in Scotland, there was a clamor for places at the medical colleges in Glasgow and Edinburgh. By 1945, "several hundred refugee physicians from Central Europe obtained medical qualifications through the Scottish Triple Qualification Board."[48]

In November 1938, British visa restrictions were lifted for "transmigrants, trainees, domestics, and those whose maintenance in Britain was guaranteed."[49] This led to the arrival of a new wave of German-Jewish refugees in Edinburgh. This new wave was comprised primarily of young women, and children who had been evacuated under the *Kindertransport*. The result was the creation of a small and relatively close-knit refugee community. The linguistic and cultural differences between the new arrivals and Edinburgh's resident Jewish population did have the potential to bring about friction between the two. Kenneth Collins states that the bulk of Scottish Jewry was at that time "Lithuanian in origin and they had been traditionally regarded by German Jews as their cultural inferiors. In turn, the Eastern Europeans felt that the more assimilated German Jews had gone too far in their identification with German culture."[50] In Edinburgh, however, there is no evidence to suggest that relations were anything but cordial. The Edinburgh Hebrew Congregation cooperated with the Edinburgh University Jewish Students' Society to create a Refugee Social Club in February 1939. Reuben Cohen, president of the Edinburgh Hebrew Congregation, made a point of assuring those present at its opening "of the keen interest shown by the Jewish community in their welfare."[51]

One problem facing newly arrived refugees was that the majority of those young women who became domestic servants in Scottish households did so reluctantly, and this theme featured heavily in several reports on refugees written by Rabbi Daiches. Why these reports were written, or who they were intended to be read by is not clear. They were not published by the *Jewish Chronicle* and were not written in the form of correspondence. One report written in 1938 expresses Daiches' opinion on Jewish suicides in Germany and the downcast demeanor of many of the German-Jewish refugees who had been forced to take on domestic work.[52] Daiches wrote that, "the Jewish refugees in particular must understand clearly, and if they cannot see this for themselves it must be told them emphatically, in these days of wireless, aeroplanes, railways, motorcars, and telephones, middlemen are not needed and intellectual professions are overcrowded all over the world; so they must turn from trade and intellectual occupations, back to the land, to the earth."[53] Daiches' opinion on the future of Jewish refugees, and Jewry in general, was in keeping with his support for Zionism. Daiches believed strongly that the next generation of young Jews must prepare themselves for an agricultural life in Palestine, a belief that was shared by Neville Laski as well as the leadership of the Central British Fund for German Jewry.[54] Nowhere was this belief more apparent that in his work for Jewish children evacuated from Nazi Germany.

On 20 November 1938, Rabbi Daiches spoke to approximately 900 people who had gathered at the Salisbury Road synagogue. Among those present were "many Christian sympathizers including several ministers of Edinburgh churches."[55] The purpose of Daiches' address was to draw attention to the needs of Jewish refugees in Scotland, particularly the increasing number of child refugees, and to encourage contributions to "the various funds that have been created to render help to those who escape from the German furnace."[56] The sermon would have important repercussions. The following day Lord Traprain, nephew of the late Lord Balfour, wrote to Rabbi Daiches with a proposal which would transform the manner in which Jewish child refugees were received in Scotland. Until this point, Jewish children were housed in private Jewish homes in Glasgow and Edinburgh.[57] Traprain wrote that on reading the report of Daiches' sermon in *The Scotsman* it occurred to him that Whittingehame House "which is now vacant with the exception of a caretaker and his family, might be used for temporary accommodation for refugee children."[58] Daiches responded to the approach with great enthusiasm, and having seen the grounds of the estate, conceived of the idea of a "farm school," where refugee children could receive shelter as well as "training in agricultural work" to prepare them for a future life in Palestine.[59]

Significant numbers of Jewish child refugees began arriving in Edinburgh in December 1938. On the evening of 5 December 1938, Rabbi Daiches met a party of over a dozen Austrian and German Jewish children at Waverley Station and conveyed them to private Jewish homes in the city.[60] At this point, the funding arrangements for the farm school were still uncertain. The *Jewish Chronicle* reported that plans were underway for the homing of 200 children at Whittingehame, but that Jewish leaders in Edinburgh were still discussing arrangements with Jewish refugee authorities in London.[61] Ultimately, the majority of funding for the Whittingehame project did not come from Jewish sources, but from a "substantial grant" from the Scottish National Council for Refugees, an organization established by the Church of Scotland and under the supervision of Glasgow businessman Sir Cecil Weir.[62] On the evening of 26 December a further 18 Jewish youths arrived at Waverley, ranging in age from 8 to 16 years. Although these children too were placed with Jewish families in the city, Daiches was by now confident that his plans for Whittingehame would be fulfilled, and told reporters from *The Scotsman* that "the refugees will not remain permanently in Edinburgh. It is the intention to provide them with training to fit them for agricultural or other work in Palestine."[63]

Use of the estate for the purpose of housing German-Jewish children was dependent on approval from the German-Jewish Aid Committee in London, though by late January Rabbi Daiches was confident that "representatives of the Committee will travel to Scotland to inspect the house and make final arrangements."[64] Daiches had also been busy making his own arrangements for the refugees. By the end of January, he had become resolute in his ambition to send the children to Palestine on reaching the age of 18. Daiches had contacted Jewish authorities in Palestine who assured him that "5000 refugees could be accommodated immediately."[65] Although the equipping of the estate was costly, Daiches stated that funds were forthcoming from "various parts of Scotland, and it was interesting to note that many of the people who had written offering their help were not Jews."[66]

By mid-February consent had been given by the German-Jewish Aid Committee, and grants to equip the estate had been awarded by the Council for German Jewry and the Women's Appeal Committee for German and Austrian Women and Children. An advertisement for the "Farm School" in the *Jewish Chronicle* stated that the premises, which had been leased on "most generous terms," would be "run on orthodox lines," and that there were places for 200 children between the ages of 14 and 17.[67] On 23 February, 19 girls, comprising the first party of children to arrive at the school, were greeted at Whittingehame by Lord Traprain and a Miss Laquer, the matron of the school and the former headmistress of a domestic school in Frankfurt.[68]

The school was consecrated in mid-July 1939, after 160 boys and girls had been enrolled. The consecration was preceded by a minute's silence at the grave of Arthur Balfour, and was attended by Lord Traprain, who had since increased his involvement in the aid of refugees by becoming a member of the Scottish National Council for Refugees.[69] Lord Traprain's wife Jean took a great interest in the running of the school, and regularly corresponded with Rabbi Daiches on the progress of the children. In early June 1940 she wrote expressing her opinion on the nature of the Jewish education of the children. The Jewish education of the children was the responsibility of two "fully qualified" Hebrew masters. Apparently, Lady Traprain viewed the religious education to be overly rigorous, stating that, "I do not want to interfere with their religion, above all, not to let them feel that I am not in sympathy with it—I am: but I do feel that they are still children and growing so fast and needing sleep."[70] Greater concerns lay on the horizon.

In late June 1940 East Scotland was declared a protected area, and as a result, legislation similar to that affecting foreign Jews during the Great War was implemented, forcing almost 200 German-Jewish refugees to move west, with most making their way to Glasgow. The legislation primarily affected those individuals in Edinburgh who had been involved in domestic service and had been self-supporting.[71] The legislation does not seem to have affected the children resident at the Whittingehame Farm School, but the facility was not without problems. Rabbi Daiches recorded in 1943 that the school struggled to reach full enrolment capacity. Since each child placed at Whittingehame was backed with a £50 sponsorship, and the cost of establishing the facility had been great, it was financially essential to fill every available place in order for the school to be cost efficient. Daiches states that shortly following the opening of the school, he was "confronted by financial problems and material anxiety which it was beyond our powers to solve." By early 1942, the decision had been taken by an Edinburgh Committee to "save what could still be saved of the school by transferring it to smaller premises."[72]

The school was transferred to a small property in Midlothian called Polton House, and in November 1942 it was recorded that 50 boys and girls were enrolled there.[73] Although operating on a much smaller scale, the Farm School still operated departments such as gardening, poultry-keeping, shoemaking and domestic work.[74] Again, the school operated on grants from the Scottish National Council of Refugees. The Farm School closed in 1945 when the departure of pupils who had reached the age of 18, and the failure of authorities to find replacements, led to the return of financial difficulties.[75] The Farm School project was evidently a success in terms of homing and educating Jewish refugee children, though it is unclear whether or not the project bore fruit in the form of producing agricultural pioneers for Palestine. The number of children enrolled at the school remained low throughout its existence, never coming close to the 5,000 Daiches had discussed with officials in Palestine. In addition, Daiches recorded in 1943 that those who reached the age of 18 at Whittingehame secured employment not in Palestine, but "in different parts of Great Britain."[76] In 1945, Daiches reported that most of those males who reached the age of 18 at Polton House "volunteered for H.M. Forces."[77]

Of course, not all refugee children were homed at the two locations of the Farm School. Many were taken into private Jewish homes and some were taken into Christian homes. The latter situation proved troublesome for Jewish leaders in Edinburgh. The majority of those Jewish children who were received into Christian homes had been brought from the Continent by the Scottish Christian Council, which was operated by the Church of Scotland but remained distinct from the Scottish National Council for Refugees.[78] Problems relating to Jewish children in Christian homes appear to have begun in 1938. The "interests and religious welfare" of Jewish children in private homes was the concern of the Jewish Women's Committee, which had branches in Edinburgh and Glasgow. Religious classes were held regularly in convenient locations for refugee children, and efforts were made to obtain the consent of Christian foster-parents to allow those children under their care to attend. In some cases, this consent was obtained, along with consent to transfer the children to Whittingehame and later Polton House for High Festivals and Passover week.[79]

However, in the majority of cases where children had been brought to Scotland by Christian guarantors or the Scottish Christian Council, Daiches recorded that "relatives of the children, or even the parents themselves, have given their consent to the children being brought under Christian influence and even being reared as Christians."[80] Daiches was successful, in some instances, in utilizing the Jewish presence on the sub-committee of the Scottish National Council for Refugees to "detach unquestionably Jewish children from conversionist influences and Christian surroundings."[81] However, in those cases where "the attitude of the foster-parents has proved an insurmountable obstacle," and all efforts to bring the children under Jewish influence had been frustrated, Daiches and the Religious sub-Committee contemplated legal action to remove the children from their Christian homes.[82] Daiches recorded in 1943 that the presence of Jewish children in such homes was a particular source of personal anxiety because at that time the number of children at Polton House had dropped to 35, while "there are so many Jewish children in Christian homes and institutions for whom Jewish accommodation ought to be secured as soon as possible."[83]

While the response of Christian Scots toward the plight and arrival of German-Jewish refugees was generally characterized by warmth, generosity, and cooperation with Jewish organizations, by 1936 it was clear that there was antipathy toward foreign Jews from some sections in Edinburgh. In the majority of cases, this stemmed from anti-German attitudes and a failure to "recognize the special situation of the Jewish refugees from Germany."[84] Kenneth Collins stated that upon the outbreak of war, several Jews employed in domestic service lost their jobs and some even found themselves interned.[85]

In some cases, however, this antipathy carried a more anti-Jewish emphasis. The arrival of German Jewish refugees had come at a time when the number of foreign Jewish students studying at Edinburgh University began to peak. In November 1936 Lewis Spence, Scottish Nationalist leader, complained to the *Daily Mirror* that the number of Jews in Scotland's universities was proving detrimental to the interests of Scottish students. He stated that "an enormous number of foreign Jewish students are invading Edinburgh; the present figure is 18,000." Spence argued that some were from Germany, and that in general, Jewish students gained an advantage over native students by "working like slaves" and "applying for professional assistance."[86] The *Jewish Chronicle*, by way of response, argued that "it is doubted if there are sixty German students in Glasgow and Edinburgh combined," and stated that Scottish Nationalists had earlier drawn attention "to the fact that the great majority of the leading fifteen names of successful students in the examinations are Jewish-sounding." The *Jewish Chronicle* admitted that while there were a large number of Jewish students at Edinburgh University, the great majority were from the United States.[87]

These American Jewish students had taken the decision to study medicine at Edinburgh University because of quotas introduced by major American colleges and universities. These quotas had been introduced to cope with "the growing number of children of recent Jewish immigrants seeking admission," resulting in Jews taking a number of places vastly out of proportion to their representation in the general population. For example, at the turn of the century, Jews comprised 50 percent of those enrolled at Columbia University's College of Physicians and Surgeons, 40 percent of those enrolled at Cornell's School of Medicine, and 30 percent of those enrolled at Harvard's School of Medicine. By 1930, these figures had been reduced to seven percent, four percent, and four percent respectively.[88] The introduction of these quotas did little to inhibit Jewish demand for admission to medical faculties—many simply applied to other schools of medicine in the United States or traveled to study at foreign universities.

Regardless of national origin, Jewish demand for places at Scottish Universities, particularly those for the study of medicine, was indeed having a negative impact on the ability of Scottish students to secure their place on several courses. The *Jewish Chronicle*'s argument that foreign Jews were not having an adverse impact on University places became unsustainable when in January 1938 the level of Jewish applications had reached such proportions that Edinburgh University was forced to limit admission to those born within the British Commonwealth. Even then, noted the *Jewish Chronicle*, "the Americans continue to come," opting to study at the smaller medical colleges in Glasgow and Edinburgh.[89] Significantly, the issue had attracted the attention of the British Union of Fascists.[90]

Anti-Semitism and Fascism in Edinburgh, 1933–1945

The first organizations in Britain to lay claim to the title of "Fascist" were those who had been influenced by Mussolini's success in Italy. The first such groups were comprised of Scottish-Italians, and in 1924 there was a branch of blackshirted "Italian Fascismo" in Edinburgh and Leith. Thomas Linehan states that the group "evidently emerged in response to an attempt by the Mussolini regime to initiate Fascist formations in Scotland."[91]

The second group were the British Fascisti, or as they were later known, the British Fascists.[92] The British Fascists had been founded by an English woman, Rotha Lintorn-Orman, in 1923. Although the impact of the British Fascists on British society and political life was "marginal," the organization was significant for its focus on "a high degree of female activism and propaganda directed at women," and also for the fact that it initiated many future high-profile Fascists and anti-Semites.[93] By 1925, the British Fascists had a branch in Edinburgh, under the control of a Miss Blake, the self-styled "Area Commander for Edinburgh."[94] Blake introduced the idea of "children's clubs" to the organization, an idea "appropriated from the Church."[95] The Edinburgh branch also laid particular emphasis on aiding poor women in Edinburgh. In late 1925 a "Helping Hand" fund was set up for "our poorer Fascist sisters."[96] Overall the British Fascists in Scotland were under the leadership of the Earl of Glasgow.[97] Although support for the British Fascists in Scotland was minute, Tony Milligan argues that this did not necessarily reflect an absence of right-wing nationalism. Milligan argues that "the British Fascisti of the 1930s were a very-pale reflection of the much broader sympathy for Mussolini which existed among Scotland's upper and middle classes."[98] The British Fascists in Edinburgh, like their counterparts across Britain, would later decline with the rise of Fascism under Sir Oswald Mosley.

When Oswald Mosley left the Labour Party in 1931 and formed the New Party, ostensibly its prospects for success in Scotland looked promising. Scotland had established traditions of bigotry and, as has been shown in this book, there had been vociferous opposition to immigration and "the exploitative labour systems that these immigrants were subjected to."[99] Mosley made Scotland one of the New Party's "key centres of operation," and, although they performed poorly, five of its twenty-three candidates in the 1931 General Election stood in Scottish constituencies.[100]

In October 1932, Mosley launched the British Union of Fascists (BUF), with a separate launch in Scotland a year later. However, the BUF do not seem to have devoted significant time or effort to progress in Scotland until late in 1933.[101] In January 1934, *The Blackshirt* reported that "Fascism is making good progress in Edinburgh," that members in the city had "to contend with very little opposition so far," and that membership at the Edinburgh University branch was "growing rapidly." It was also reported that plans had been undertaken to alter BUF uniform policy to allow for a "grey kilt to be worn."[102] By February, the BUF had commenced canvassing in West Edinburgh. Women's groups were reported as being "well attended," and copies of "Fascist Week," were being sold on the streets of the city.[103]

Tony Milligan noted that after serious disturbances during a New Party meeting in Glasgow in 1931, Mosley never returned to the public platform in that city.[104] In addition, it became clear to the BUF leadership that "growth was notably larger in the East," and estimates suggest that BUF membership in Edinburgh was consistently higher than in Glasgow.[105] Mosley addressed a rally at Edinburgh's Usher Hall in June 1934, attracting over 2,500 people with the only opposition being a weak counter-demonstration outside attended by a small number of Scottish Nationalists and a large party of Communists.[106] Violence broke out after the rally as Blackshirts filed out of Usher Hall into waiting buses, with plainclothes detectives later testifying in court that Communists had attacked the buses with stones, resulting in the blinding of a 16-year-old Fascist. Five local laborers were later convicted of assaulting BUF members.[107]

The BUF evidently viewed Usher Hall as a success—the rally had been well attended, and the ensuing violence was easily blamed on Communist counter-demonstrators. By December 1934, the BUF were making plans for three separate branches in Edinburgh. Under the leadership of Richard A. Plathen, National Inspecting Officer for Scotland, and C. Bryham Oliver, Propaganda Officer for Scotland, the Edinburgh district of the BUF became "the only one anywhere in Scotland with an effective multi-branch structure."[108] Leading Fascist William Joyce toured Scotland in June 1935 and declared the country "Prepared for Fascism."[109] Shortly thereafter a leafleting campaign began in Edinburgh with over 42,000 pieces of Fascist literature being distributed by October. On 11 October 1936, Mosley returned to Usher Hall for what was described as "the biggest Blackshirt demonstration that Edinburgh has witnessed."[110] The *Jewish Chronicle* later reported that 150 stewards had been "imported into the city," and that "most disgraceful scenes were witnessed."[111]

It has been established that the BUF was active and enjoyed some small measure of success in Edinburgh. The question remains as to how this presence and these activities affected Edinburgh Jewry. Firstly, one must assess the presence of anti-Semitism among Edinburgh Fascists, and the extent to which their propaganda and leafleting targeted Jews. Henry Maitles argued that "from mid-1934 onwards anti-Semitism began to take a more prominent role in BUF pronouncements."[112] Regardless of BUF pronouncements, Rabbi Daiches seems to have held concerns about anti-Semitic propaganda in the city as early as 1933. In June 1933 Daiches wrote to Joseph Sacks, president of the Glasgow Jewish Representative Council, proposing the establishment of a "Scottish Council for the Defence of Jews and Judaism in Scotland."[113] This proposal may have arisen from a failure to differentiate between Mosley's Fascists and the National Socialism of Hitler. Geoffrey Alderman argues that this failure to differentiate was a major contributing factor to Jewish opposition to the BUF even prior to its official adoption of anti-Semitism.[114] Daiches' proposal "did not meet with general support" among the Glasgow Jewish leadership, who were most likely influenced by Neville Laski's call for British Jews to "adopt a deliberately low profile."[115] Although it was agreed by the committee in Glasgow that "such a project should not be entertained," anti-Semitic propaganda, and the presence of Fascists in the city, was an ongoing concern of Edinburgh Jewry.

Henry Maitles recorded that in 1934, "the Jewish Representative Committee commented on Nazi and anti-Semitic propaganda" circulating at Edinburgh University, and this appears to be the first instance of Fascist anti-Semitic material being distributed in the city.[116] It is not clear, however, whether this material emanated from the BUF. Other Fascist groups were operating in Edinburgh in the mid-1930s, the most virulently anti-Semitic being the Imperial Fascist League (IFL) under Arnold Leese. In March 1936 a report from Edinburgh in the *Jewish Chronicle* complained that IFL leaflets were being distributed in the city drawing attention to "the number of Jews concerned in crime, bankruptcy, fire-raising and other law-breaking pastimes."[117] Neville Laski had also written to Rabbi Daiches as early as 1933 discussing the presence of anti-Semitic pamphlets of German origin in Scotland.[118]

It must also be stressed that in the mid-1930s the Edinburgh BUF were under a local leadership opposed to anti-Semitism. Until October 1936, the Edinburgh BUF was largely organized by Propaganda Officer for Scotland, C. Bryham Oliver. Oliver left the BUF shortly after Mosley's second rally at Usher Hall, during which Mosley made several hostile references to Jews.[119] Oliver later stressed that he believed at that point that the principles that "there would be no discrimination against Jews," and that "Scottish affairs would be run by Scots" had been abandoned by the BUF. In his resignation statement Oliver asserted that "I shall continue to devote myself to the furtherance of the ideal of the Corporate State of Scotland, with no discrimination on account of race or creed."[120]

Tony Milligan argued that "from mid-1936 onwards, anti-Semitism became an increasingly important component of BUF identity in Scotland."[121] It is also clear that while the adoption of anti-Semitism was liable to alienate some members, it proved useful in attracting others. Alexander Young, who would later rise to prominence in the Edinburgh BUF, was a former member of the Edinburgh Protestant Society and Protestant Action. He joined the BUF in late 1936, and "the common ground which attracted Young to the BUF appears to have been anti-Semitism."[122] In September 1937, Oswald Mosley announced in Edinburgh that Blackshirt candidates would contest Labour seats at the city's municipal elections in November, stating that the decision had been taken in response to the refusal of Edinburgh's "Labour-controlled council" to grant facilities for Blackshirt open-air meetings. The BUF contested two wards, St. Giles and Canongate.[123] Alexander Young was selected as one of the BUF candidates, in an election which was to prove a disaster for the BUF, with the Blackshirt candidates polling just 51 votes in St. Giles and 41 votes in Canongate.[124]

It is difficult to assess a uniform response of Edinburgh Jewry to anti-Semitic propaganda and Fascism in the city. Physical confrontation between Edinburgh Jews and BUF members seems to have been minimal. In December 1934 *The Blackshirt* reported that a "Russian Jew" had persistently heckled an open-air meeting in the city, and in June 1937 the same publication claimed that during a Blackshirt march "at Simon Square Jewish opposition was encountered."¹²⁵ In general however, Edinburgh Jewry appears to have followed the philosophy of the Jewish Defence Committee which had been formed by the Board of Deputies in 1936: "to keep the community out of public view if at all possible and, in particular, to avoid street confrontations with the Fascists."

This low-profile approach was not always appreciated by other anti-Fascists in Edinburgh. In September 1936, E. McLeod Davis, joint secretary to the Edinburgh Peace Council, complained to the *Jewish Chronicle* about the nature of Jewish responses to Fascism in the city.¹²⁶ Davis argued that although several members of the Edinburgh Jewish community had "liberally responded to appeals for financial aid," this was done "as furtively and inconspicuously as possible." He ended his letter by stating, "I have yet to see a Jewish speaker on an anti-Fascist platform in Edinburgh. In my opinion this will not do; for it creates an utterly false impression of hole-and-corner cowardice.... Come with us into the open, let your voices be heard in our Councils and at our demonstrations."¹²⁷

This reluctance to demonstrate publicly against Fascism and anti-Semitism in Britain did not reflect a reluctance to challenge it by other means. Geoffrey Alderman has highlighted the counter-propaganda techniques of the Board of Deputies, whereby Jewish authorities supplied election literature to candidates in the major political parties, who would then distribute it as their own. Alderman states that "the technique was first used against the British Union of Fascists' candidates contesting the 1937 municipal elections," and this may go some way to explaining the devastating defeat that the BUF suffered nationally.¹²⁸ Evidence suggests that Edinburgh's Jewish leaders took the threat of anti-Semitic propaganda seriously and engaged in a counter-propaganda campaign locally. Rabbi Daiches was particularly keen to challenge allegations that Jews were "warmongering" against Germany. In a sermon delivered in February 1935 Daiches stated,

> It is utterly wrong to say that Jews in this country who come to the rescue of their brethren in other lands, or who protest against the persecution of the Jewish citizens of Germany in the best way they can, show by their attitude that they place the interests of Jewry about the interests of Britain.... It is only those who have ceased to be British in their outlook, and have absorbed alien ideas, who have lost the British spirit, and are copying foreign tyrants, it is only such detractors of British ideals that dare charge us with indifference to British interests because of our efforts to defend our oppressed and persecuted brethren, and to save them from utter destruction.¹²⁹

Local strategies for combating anti-Semitism were first discussed at a meeting of the Edinburgh B'nai B'rith at the North Station Hotel in April 1937, following a surge in anti-Semitic propaganda in the city.¹³⁰ Much of the material was German in origin and had been produced by the publishing firm U. Bodung-Verlag in Erfurt under the direction of prominent anti-Semitic publisher, Ulrich Fleischhauer. One of the most common pieces of international anti–Semitic propaganda produced by Fleischhauer was the "World-Service" newsletter, and in January there appears to have been a great increase in its distribution in Edinburgh. The front page of the January 1937 edition declared that the aim of the publication is to "enlighten ill-informed Gentiles" about "the machinations of the Jewish underworld." It contained the admonition that "Judah intends to plunge the Aryan people into a new world war."[131]

In late February Rabbi Daiches wrote to the Board of Deputies drawing attention to the increase in distribution of anti–Semitic literature in Edinburgh and requesting advice on countering it. A.G. Brotman, secretary of the Board of Deputies, replied on 17 February. Brotman was largely dismissive of *World-Service*, arguing that "it fails because of its over-exaggeration, and in a way we may consider ourselves not unlucky that the Germans seem to have no insight into the psychology of peoples other than their own."[132] Brotman added that even if the Board viewed it as dangerous, it would prove almost impossible to prevent its distribution as it "comes over in plain envelopes.... Further, the only sort of material that can be stopped in the post is that which comes under the technical definition of "obscene material," and I do not think even the worst emanations of the *Stürmer* would be regarded as obscene in the view of the Post Office."[133] Rabbi Daiches does not appear to have been wholly satisfied with the Brotman's response, and proceeded to send him more copies of *World-Service* along with copies of another anti–Semitic publication, *Aftermath*, which had been distributed in Edinburgh by the London-based Christian Aryan Syndicate.[134]

Brotman wrote to Daiches on 19 February stating that the Board was considering "taking up the matter of having questions put in the House of Commons on the subject," and wrote again on 30 March assuring Daiches that "we are taking steps with reference to the *World-Service* circulars, and hope to have a Question asked in the House as soon as it meets again."[135] Daiches, meanwhile, had undertaken an investigation into the source of some of the pamphlets and informed the Board that "there is now a printing service in London working for German propaganda."[136] Daiches also compiled a report in 1937 suggesting that anti–Semitic propaganda in Scotland was targeting "civil servants, clergymen, and teachers" and other people of influence, and that it was often sent to these people in plain envelopes via the British Post Office.[137]

In addition, in April 1940 Daiches sent a circular letter to Scotland's "League of Nations Unions," to counter allegations of a Jewish world conspiracy. Daiches wrote that "there were some Nazi sympathizers in this country who helped spread the allegation, and to instill this poisonous falsehood into the minds of simple people, who were ready to believe anything that was repeated often enough."[138]

It should be made clear that, in the sphere of Edinburgh Jewry, anti-Semitic propaganda and Fascist activity in Edinburgh was not solely a personal concern of Rabbi Daiches. At a meeting of the Board of Deputies of British Jews in April 1939, Reuben Cohen, president of the Edinburgh Hebrew Congregation, was the driving force behind an initiative to "handle the provincial propaganda campaign as efficiently and effectively as in London." Cohen had alerted the Board to the "need to defend the Jewish cause in those more remote districts where Jews do not reside and where sometimes unanswered anti-Jewish attacks went by default."[139] This may have been in response to a number of letters to the *Scotsman* in January 1939 alerting readers to the prevalence of anti-Jewish propaganda in the North-West Highlands.[140] In November 1939, at a meeting of the Edinburgh *B'nai B'rith*, Cohen stressed the "need for vigilance in regard to clandestine anti-Jewish and pro-Nazi activities."[141] In December, Cohen again reiterated the need for vigilance, and chaired a broader discussion on "Jewish Defence in Scotland."[142] In January 1940, at a meeting of the Edinburgh *B'nai B'rith*, Cohen informed members that he had been distributing literature from the Jewish Defence Committee of the Board of Deputies, "and that in some cases this distribution had had a very salutary effect."[143] In addition, members of the Edinburgh Jewish Ex-Servicemen's Association participated in the local branch of the Ex-Servicemen's Movement Against Fascism.[144] In February 1935 the Edinburgh Jewish Literary Society held a discussion on the idea that, "the Jewish people cannot survive the Fascist state."[145]

While the threat posed by anti-Semitic propaganda and Fascism in Edinburgh is debatable, and most likely negligible, it is clear that the leadership of Edinburgh Jewry took the threat seriously and participated in counter-propaganda activities of the kind utilized and advocated by the Board of Deputies in London. It is also evident that despite its great distance from London, the leadership of Edinburgh Jewry was keen to work with, and receive guidance from, the Board in its struggle to combat local anti-Jewish activity. However, another important aspect of the anti-Fascist struggle of Edinburgh Jewry was the persistence of Rabbi Daiches in his role as advocate for Jews and Judaism in Scotland. The rise of Fascism in Scotland, and the statements of prominent Fascists in the Scottish media did not go unchallenged by Rabbi Daiches. Through the large number of letters and articles he wrote for publication in Scottish newspapers, Daiches attained a higher national profile than at any time previously, and his productions represented a significant contribution to the countering of anti-Jewish propaganda in Scotland.

Henry Maitles has argued that "there are memoirs of Jews growing up in the 1930s in Glasgow and Edinburgh that make no mention of either the BUF or activity by anti-fascists," it is equally important to note that there are some which do.[146] Although Muriel Spark, who grew up in an assimilated Jewish family in Edinburgh, recorded that she never "had the sense of any racial discrimination," Martin Stannard stated that she later "recalled with distaste Blackshirts strutting around [Edinburgh] streets during the 1930s."[147] Stannard argued that "although she was largely untroubled by it, and never considered herself part of the tight-knit Jewish community, this nervousness was particularly felt by the city's Jews in a period of open anti-Semitism." In *Two Worlds*, David Daiches recalls that "Fascist rumblings" in Scotland "disturbed and angered my father."[148] Daiches further recalls that his father would "keep an eagle eye open for letters or articles in the Scottish press which showed any trace of sympathy with the Hitlerite position, and he would reply to each with a forceful and eloquent letter to the editor."[149]

The first such letter appeared in the *Scotsman* in May 1936. In an article titled "Rabbi's Reply to Sir Oswald Mosley," Rabbi Daiches challenged Mosley's recently uttered allegations that "the Jews were seeking to bring about a war between Britain and Germany."[150] Daiches' willingness to publicly challenge Fascist anti-Semitism brought about a period of prolonged confrontation in the pages of the *Scotsman*, during which Daiches alone defended the Jewish position against an increasing number of Fascist and anti-Semitic correspondents. In January 1938, one Margaret Collins, describing herself as "For the British Union of Fascists and National Socialists," specifically addressed Rabbi Daiches in a statement in which she described Jews as "a nation within a nation." The same issue contained another letter, from a J.A. MacDonald, who argued that "it is the intrinsic character of the Jew that is the cause of friction between himself and those among whom he dwells."[151]

In response to these letters Daiches wrote to the editor at the end of January 1938 stating that "the evil that is being wrought by the anti-Jewish agitation of the Fascists in this country becomes clearer every day." He pointed out that Scotland's Jews had "made the same sacrifices as other sections of the community in the Great War." Referring to some of the more extreme allegations made by Margaret Collins, Daiches asked "How is one to argue with such correspondents?"[152] Although exchanges were ongoing with Collins, MacDonald and many others until late 1941, by far the most vocal and influential opponent of Rabbi Daiches was a man believed by the Board of Deputies to be "the most prominent anti-Semite in the country"—Scottish Unionist MP for Peebles and Southern Midlothian from 1931 to 1945, founding member of the Right Club, and fanatical anti-Bolshevik, Captain Archibald Maule Ramsay.[153]

Captain Ramsay, a descendant of the Earls of Dalhousie, first emerged as a prominent figure on the British far-Right in the late 1930s. Described as a "deeply religious individual," Ramsay had been alarmed by the nature of the Bolshevik revolution. Developing "an aggressive and paranoid anti-Communist outlook," by 1937 Ramsay had subscribed to the belief that there was a Jewish world conspiracy.[154] In 1937 Ramsay joined the Nordic League, an organization which had a membership "confined to the upper-middle class" and had its origins in "a fanatical and occultist order, the White Knights of Britain, Britain's nearest equivalent to the American Ku Klux Klan."[155] Not content with membership of "the most fanatical and malevolent of the late 1930s pro-Nazi anti-war groups," Ramsay went on to found the Right Club in May 1939. The Right Club, which derived its membership from the same social class as the Nordic League, was a secretive organization which sought to unify Britain's disparate Fascist groups into a united anti-war movement.[156] By 1938, notes Geoffrey Alderman, Ramsay had "made a habit of asking anti-Semitic questions in the Commons."[157]

In January 1939 Ramsay wrote to the *Scotsman* asking Rabbi Daiches to admit to "the Jewish complexion" of the Third Communist International, and to accept that this represented "a group of Jews working for world revolution."[158] Daiches responded by raising doubts over the source of Ramsay's figures in relation to Jewish members of the Communist hierarchy. Ramsay wrote days later that Daiches was refusing to "dissociate himself from this godless revolutionary section of his race," and was instead attempting "to sidetrack the issue by warmongering references to Germany and Italy."[159] The duel between Daiches and Ramsay was fought with more than the written word—it also took the form of the spoken word. While Daiches toured the social clubs and societies of Edinburgh and its environs with his account of the current state of European Jewry, by January 1939 Captain Ramsay and his wife were touring in much the same venues, speaking instead on the theme of Jewish conspiracy. During one speech to the Arbroath Business Club, Ramsay's wife told the audience that "there was an international group of Jews who were behind world revolution in every single country at the present time," and that "Hitler must have his reasons for the way in which he is treating Jews."[160] On hearing reports of the speech, Daiches wrote to the *Scotsman* asking, "is it right to induce a Scottish audience to approve of Jewish persecution by such crude misrepresentation of facts?"[161]

Ramsay's outspoken manner and his transparent links to the British far-Right were ultimately his downfall. By the outbreak of war, the Nordic League was successfully infiltrated by MI5 personnel who concluded that Ramsay was not only "quite unbalanced," but that he was also working closely with Oswald Mosley and was a potential Fifth Columnist.[162] The Nordic League was also successfully infiltrated by the Board of Deputies. Neville Laski had employed a former Special Branch inspector, who successfully gained membership of the organization under an assumed identity. The infiltrator's investigations "revealed the degree to which the Nordic League sympathized with and had connections to the Nazi regime, as well as the extreme nature of its anti–Semitism, extending to advocacy of genocide."[163] When revelations about the organization seeped into the public sphere in 1940, it provoked "an angry local reaction towards the M.P.," although it is noteworthy that Ramsay's outspoken anti–Semitism had been tolerated by his constituency for some time.[164] Ramsay was arrested and interned under Defence Regulation 18B in May 1940. In August 1941 the General Purposes Committee of the Peebles and South Midlothian Unionist Association "decided to ask Captain Ramsay to resign his seat," a request he refused.[165]

In addition to the infiltration of Fascist groups and the initiation of Jewish counter-propaganda campaigns, the Board of Deputies pursued one other anti–Fascist strategy which was also adopted to a great extent by Edinburgh's Jewish leadership. Daniel Tilles states that the Board "endeavoured to cultivate links with a variety of non–Jewish groups in its fight against organized anti–Semitism. This, of course, generally involved politically neutral bodies, such as various Church institutions."[166] In Edinburgh, the level cooperation between the Jewish leadership and Church authorities would arguably eclipse that seen in any other part of Britain, and took place against a background of change in the Church of Scotland's attitudes toward Jews.

Changing Jewish-Christian Relations in Edinburgh, 1933–1945

As this book has shown, in the early 1930s relations between Edinburgh Jewry and the Presbyterian churches were tenuous and strained. Attempts at cooperation during the period of mass immigration had faltered in the persistence of Church attempts to proselytize among the Jews of the city and further afield, and the issuance of statements at official Church gatherings which served to offend Jewish sensibilities. There was mutual distrust, and even the putative Scottish "sense of reverence for the People of the Book" was felt by Jewish leaders to be misleading, since this attitude "was not of a kind that could make the Jew feel that he was regarded as an equal, and that his Christian neighbour desired his company and appreciated his value as a citizen."[167]

Although it has been argued that "a shift in religious consciousness became more apparent among many Scottish Christians with the rise of Nazism in Germany," it is clear that the transformation of relations between Jews and Christians in the country was gradual and took place over a number of years.[168] Of course, this book has shown that there were always a small number of ministers who made successive calls at General Assemblies for the cessation of missionary activity and a re-evaluation of the Church of Scotland's attitudes toward Jews, and that these voices were consistently drowned out by the clamor of the majority to convert the Jew around the globe. Rabbi Daiches wrote in 1930 that, "Scottish Christians are beginning to realize that they can do more good by helping the Jew to survive than by 'saving his soul' through conversion," but this optimism was not necessarily reflected in the attitudes of Church of Scotland missionary leaders.[169]

In June 1934, against the backdrop of public protest against Nazi Germany and the Jewish boycott of German goods, the Church of Scotland's Commission of Enquiry into Scottish Jews reported at the General Assembly that:

> the impact of the Jew on the life of Glasgow and, to a smaller extent, of Edinburgh, is stronger than ever it was and it keeps growing stronger.... The life of the Jew is permeating the life of the city in a host of subtle ways, far more ways than can be seen on the surface. The growing influence of the Jew on the Scottish folk is sufficient in itself to compel us to see a growingly serious Home Mission problem.[170]

By the end of 1934, actions in Nazi Germany were even being utilized by one Church of Scotland minister to vindicate an increase in missionary efforts. Failing to grasp the importance of racial theory underpinning Nazi anti-Semitism, the Rev. James Black of St. George's West Church, Edinburgh, and future Moderator of the Church of Scotland, informed his congregation in November 1934 that if "they took the Jews into the Christian Church they would settle all the problems that are troubling Europe.... If they made the Jews Christians they would do away with all the exclusions which were the main cause of the troubles in Europe at this time."[171] Evident in this statement is not only the belief that conversion would end Nazi persecution of Jews, but also that Jewish "exclusivity" was the root cause of anti-Semitism.

Church of Scotland attitudes to Nazi persecution changed slightly in 1935. In the report of the Jewish Missions at the 1935 General Assembly, distaste was expressed at the "thorough-going Prussian fashion" in which Germany "had dealt with the problem of the Jewish race among the peoples of the world."[172] Church attitudes also remained complex. The same report reacted with similar distaste to the increased immigration of Jews to Palestine. Most of these colonists, it was reported, were "men who did not even know the faith of their fathers and were frankly atheistical."[173]

The seminal point in the transformation of Jewish relations with the Church of Scotland came in late May 1936. At the General Assembly of the Church of Scotland a call was made to the Scottish people to "rid their minds of all narrow anti-Jew prejudice."[174] The Assembly expressed "profound regret that the past year has brought no alleviation of the sufferings caused to the Jewish people by the inhuman political, social and economic persecutions prevalent in Central and Eastern Europe," and protested against "the religious intolerance, the narrow nationalism, and race pride on which anti-Semitic hatreds are based."[175]

Of course, the Church of Scotland had protested against anti-Jewish persecutions before, mostly notably in relation to the Russian pogroms, but the reference to "religious intolerance" in the statement of 1936 was significant in indicating a move toward tolerance by the Church itself. Although not explicitly mentioned, the promulgation of the Nuremberg Laws in September 1935, and ensuing pessimism about the future of Jews under Hitler, may have played a significant role in bringing about a change in Church attitudes. In addition, the possible role played by the activity of Rabbi Daiches in speaking to various societies and clubs, and publicizing the situation of European Jewry cannot be discounted. Speaking on the issue of Jewish persecution, the Rev. Peter McGregor of Greenock stated that "we in this country knew very little of the suffering of the Jews on the Continent in recent years."[176] The change in attitude came about most likely as a combination of increased knowledge of the situation in Germany, distaste for Nazi anti–Semitism, and increased pessimism about the future of Jews in Central and Eastern Europe. The meeting ended with the Moderator of the Church of Scotland announcing that 27 September would be "a day of special intercession throughout the Church for the Divine blessing of the Jewish people."[177]

The focus on Jewish suffering and the seemingly untainted nature of the Assembly's sympathy with European Jewry moved Rabbi Daiches to contact the Rev. Professor Daniel Lamont, then Moderator of the Church of Scotland, to express his appreciation and gratitude. Daiches may also have seen the Church of Scotland as a significant potential ally in the fight against Fascism. Indeed, during the General Assembly the aforementioned Rev. Dr. James Black had warned that in Scotland "discrimination against Jews was subtly creeping in." Lamont replied on 9 June 1936 stating that "the Church of Scotland as a whole will rejoice to be assured that the attitude of its General Assembly to the shameful treatment meted out to the Jewish race in Germany and elsewhere has given satisfaction in Jewish circles."[178]

If the Church of Scotland's change in approach to Jews was motivated by the introduction of the Nuremberg laws and increased knowledge of the situation in Germany, its response differed significantly from that of the Church of England. Tom Lawson has stated that "in the main the Nuremberg laws passed without comment in the Anglican community."[179] In contrast to the Scottish Presbyterian focus on Jewish suffering, the Anglican community interpreted anti–Semitic policies and violence as part of a broader "totalitarian attack on Christian culture."[180] In addition, the Anglican tendency to see Nazism as entirely alien to Christian European traditions "ensured that the suggestion made by Rev. James Parkes, that the roots of anti–Semitism, and Nazi anti–Semitism at that, lay with Christianity was met with incredulity."[181] The Church of Scotland, on the other hand, seems to have viewed events in Europe first and foremost as cause for a re-examination of the

Church's relationship with Jews, and the recognition of the role of Christianity in fostering anti-Semitism. This recognition was most eloquently and forcefully expressed in the Church of Scotland's Report on the Jews in May 1939. The report stated that,

> Beyond all anticipation of what persecution in its recklessness might do, the worst of perils ever dreamed of has been surpassed, and such an avalanche of trouble has swept over the Jewish people that the Church's relationship to them can no longer be thought of as simply the relation of a Christian missionary Church to a non-Christian people, but as the relation of the Church to a great political, racial, and humanitarian problem. Never before has it been so sharply and startlingly forced on the mind of the Church that in the relation of Christendom to Jewry there has always been something utterly and shamefully wrong. A relationship always strained and discordant has starkly revealed unbelievable possibilities of terror.[182]

In 1938 Rabbi Daiches wrote to the *Jewish Chronicle* stating that at last the majority of representatives of the Scottish Churches were "ready to appreciate the Jew for what he is, rather than for what he might be if turned Christian."[183] Daiches' diaries reveal that in 1938 he was invited to several Presbyterian churches in Edinburgh to address congregations on the situation of Jews in Germany.[184] These invitations were part of a broader rapprochement between Scotland's Presbyterian Churches and Jewish leaders. In February 1938, the Rev. J.K. Cosgrove, Jewish minister in Glasgow, was invited to speak to students at the Scottish Congregational and United Free Church College, Edinburgh. Professor Allan Barr, who presided, stated that "he felt confident that this, their first visit from a member of the Jewish faith, was the beginning of a closer relationship and better understanding between Christians and their Jewish neighbours."[185]

The central theme of the 1938 General Assembly of the Church of Scotland was again the Jews. Several ministers devoted lengthy speeches to denouncing anti-Semitism in Europe and, in the words of the Rev. Dr. George Mackenzie, the "Heil Hitler set in London society."[186] There were calls for "some practical expression of sympathy with the persecuted Jews." Crucially, and in contrast to the Church response to Tsarist persecution, references to missions and proselytizing opportunities were entirely absent. The Assembly closed with the unanimous adoption of a resolution to renew Church protests "against the virulence and cruelty of the attacks still being directed against helpless Jewish minorities in Central and Eastern Europe," and an affirmation that "no Church can be truly Christian and anti-Semitic at one and the same time."[187]

In the aftermath of *Kristallnacht* in November, Rabbi Daiches received a letter from the Rev. Dr. James Black, now Moderator of the Church of Scotland. Black wrote that the Church "shall not cease to protest against the sorrows of your people. As you know, we regard you, in whatever country your people may live, as being fully entitled to every liberty and right that we claim for ourselves."[188] Daiches received similar sentiments from Robert Chisholm, general secretary of the National Bible Society of Scotland.[189]

By 1939, the Church of Scotland moved to solidify its ambition to offer "some practical expression of sympathy." This was manifested primarily in the aid of Jewish refugees. The 1939 General Assembly urged the British government to "spare no effort to come to the rescue of the refugees," and committed itself to the creation of a Scottish National Council for Refugees to coordinate the aid work of the already extant Scottish Christian Council.[190] During the Assembly, in presenting the report of the Committee of Jewish Missions, the Rev. Dr. George Mackenzie stated that "from familiarity they had grown callous to the fact that the black cloud of Jewish persecution had never lifted." The Rev. Dr. James Black, who had recently traveled to Central Europe to see the situation of the Jews at close quarters, delivered a speech laden with allusions to the complicity of Christianity in the development of anti–Semitism in Europe. Black stated that he had "squirmed with shame at the unspeakable persecutions that a nominal Christian Europe had meted out to [Jews] during the centuries," and that "I have had people look at me with the haunted eyes of trapped animals." In closing, Black asked those present to "make it impossible for the curse of anti–Semitism ... to blight their fair name in Britain," noting that there were "many political morons in their midst who would use the Jews for their own mean ends." Black also requested that those present "be ready to receive the stricken folk who had come to regard this free land as a final hope."[191]

Another significant aspect of the 1939 General Assembly was the expression of its new stance on Zionism. In contrast to earlier allusions to atheistic and materialistic settlers, the Convener of the Assembly declared that, with its recent White Paper on Palestine, the British Government had "scrapped the Balfour Declaration, with its guarantee of a Jewish national home." The Rev. Dr. George Mackenzie argued that the paper was the "death of Jewish trust in the integrity and sanctity of the British word," and that Arabs had "done nothing for the land except squat on it and impoverish it."[192] By contrast, argued Mackenzie, Jewish colonists "had put their capital, brains, labour, and love into it, with the result that they had restored to Palestine a little of its energy and fertility."

Rabbi Daiches was again impressed with the tone of the Assembly and publicly paid tribute in an article to the *Scotsman*. Daiches said that the sentiments of the Assembly "would find an echo in the hearts of Jews everywhere, and would be received with gratitude by the Jewish people as a whole." Daiches was particularly impressed with the sympathy shown by the Assembly for "that remnant of Israel that was seeking shelter and security, freedom and equality in its ancestral home."[193]

The practical element of Church sympathy also manifested itself in greater personal contact between representatives of the Church of Scotland and Edinburgh's Jews. In 1938, together with the Rev. Magnus Nicholson of Edinburgh's Fountainbridge Church, Rabbi Daiches founded the Edinburgh Society of Jews and Christians. The principal aim of the Society, as outlined in its Constitution, was "the creation and development of bonds of mutual understanding and respect between Jews and Christians."[194] Significantly given the backdrop of Fascism and anti–Semitic propaganda, another of the organization's chief aims was "the exposure and examination of the influences leading to and causing anti–Semitism, and consideration of appropriate means of dealing with them."[195] The Society drew its membership from representatives of the Jewish community, the Society of Friends, prominent Presbyterian ministers and a large number of laymen.[196]

The creation of bonds between Edinburgh Christians and Jews seems to have commenced in earnest in early 1939. Christian representatives were invited for a tour of the Salisbury Road synagogue and in return, Jewish representatives were invited for a tour of Greyfriars Church. Rabbi Daiches was unable to attend the tour, but his son Lionel participated in the discussion of the Old Testament which followed.[197] With the outbreak of war, the emphasis of the Society shifted toward the combat of anti–Semitism in Scotland, and the support of Zionism.[198] With the complete discrediting and collapse of British Fascism by 1941, the Society again switched focus to the fostering of inter-faith relations. In 1942 more than 850 Sunday school teachers visited the Edinburgh synagogue as part of a Society of Christians and Jews scheme to educate them about Jews and Jewish religious observances in order that they could "pass on their knowledge to those under their care."[199]

Philo-Semitism, pro–Zionism, and an aggressive campaign against anti–Semitism were hallmarks of the General Assemblies of the early 1940s, as well as the speeches of successive Moderators of the Church of Scotland. In May 1940 the General Assembly declared that "it is our duty as a Church to create such a strong public opinion that the hideous thing [anti–Semitism] will languish and die."[200] In July the Rev. Dr. Norman McLean, ex–Moderator of the Church of Scotland and then chaplain to the King, gave an account of his recent visit to Palestine while speaking at a luncheon organized by the National Labour Organization. He stated that he was "brought up in the faith that the Jews must return to Palestine before the Second Coming.... The Jew today is a first-rate fighting man. He had found his manhood and soul, working in the colonies of Palestine."[201] In December 1941, the Rev. Dr. J. Hutchison Cockburn, Moderator of the Church of Scotland, told a meeting of the Stirling and Dunblane Presbyterial Council to "remember what they owed to the Jews."[202]

At the 1942 General Assembly ministers discussed attitudes to Jews in

Scotland, and condemned the "unwelcome growing spirit of anti-Semitism in Glasgow." The Rev. T.B. Stewart-Thompson appealed to the Assembly to "see that Jews shall be treated in the same way as other men and judged by the same standard." He had been appalled to see "decent, church-going people" engage in the spread of anti-Semitic rumors. It was put by the Rev. W.W. Gould that anti-Jewish feelings were not a problem among the lower classes but was rather confined to "the upper strata of society."[203] This latter point was perhaps an allusion to the prominence of upper-class figures in the Fascist movements such as Captain Ramsay, and the fact that many of the complaints about Jewish refugees has arisen in the professions.

In February 1942 Edinburgh hosted the Conference of the Presbyterian Churches of Great Britain and Ireland. The aim of the conference was explicitly stated as "to consider the future of Jewry, particularly after the war."[204] A resolution was passed deploring the denial of human rights to Jews in Europe and urging all governments to restore the rights of European Jews. It was added that the representatives of the conference urged "His Majesty's Government, in conjunction with other Allied and friendly nations, to provide for some scheme of emigration for Jews who cannot find a home in Europe."[205]

The Edinburgh Society of Jews and Christians met shortly thereafter to discuss the resolution and, while it approved of the resolution generally, expressed the opinion that "its reference to emigration required further consideration and definition."[206] The implication, it could be surmised, was that the Society wished for more specific reference to Zionist claims on Palestine. The Society of Jews and Christians subsequently wrote to the Scottish Churches requesting a joint conference between Scottish Jewry and Scottish Churches "to explore the possibility of such action regarding the restoration and maintenance of the liberties, rights and post-war settlement or resettlement of the dispossessed Jews, and all other problems affecting the status of the Jew in the various nations of the world."[207] The Church of Scotland's official response was to "express their sympathy with the Jews in their suffering," and to refer the request to the Committee on General Administration.[208]

The proposal for a joint Christian-Jewish conference was later accepted, and in February 1943 the Church of Scotland hosted a conference of the Episcopal Church of Scotland, the Congregational Union, the Free Church, the Baptist Union, the United Free Church, the Methodist Synod, the Original Secessionist Church, and representatives from the Jewish communities of Scotland. The aim of the conference was to discuss "the position of the Jews in relation to the problem of post-war reconstruction."[209] The conference was remarkable not solely for the number of Churches it embraced in the name of discussing Jewry, but also for the fact that it included a significant number of Jewish representatives, and could be described as a genuinely cooperative effort. In the keynote address, Reuben Cohen, president of the Edinburgh

Hebrew Congregation outlined "the facts of Nazi persecution of the Jews and the consequent situation of Jewry." The conference unanimously agreed to a resolution stating that "the Christian Churches had a definite and urgent duty in combating anti–Semitism and educating public opinion."[210]

In assessing the impact of the change in the position of the Church of Scotland in relation to the Jews, it is important to appreciate the influence of the Church on the general public at this time. Although smaller congregations and a creeping atheism were growing problems for the Scottish Presbyterian Churches at this time, unlike the Church of England, the Church of Scotland could rely on its ongoing cultural and political involvement to remain "socially influential."[211] Church pronouncements concerning anti–Semitism, Zionism, and the treatment of Jews in Scotland are likely to have had some impact on the attitudes of the Scottish laity regarding these issues, a fact presumably not lost on Neville Laski when he pointed out to Rabbi Daiches as early as 1933 to bear in mind "the importance of Edinburgh as a church centre."[212]

However, if anti–Semitism failed to take root to any great extent in Scotland during the 1930s and early 1940s, one must be wary of attributing too much significance to the changing position of the Church of Scotland. Nominally, the Church of Scotland had always been opposed to prejudice against the Jewish race. This was clear during the era of Tsarist persecution, and concern about persecution permeated its many missionary reports. And yet in its persistence with missionary activity, its treatment of Jews as a "separate people," and its unwavering commitment to the idea of converting the Jewish people, a wall had been building between the Church of Scotland and the Jewish communities in its midst. Despite this wall between Scottish Jews and ecclesiastical officials, this book has shown that relations between Jew and Gentile in Edinburgh had improved consistently since the time of the Aliens Act, and that by the early 1930s, regardless of Church attitudes, Edinburgh's Jewish community enjoyed healthy, even esteemed, relations with local government, individual members of Protestant and Catholic clergy, the press, and prominent figures in the spheres of academia, business, and culture.

The level of sympathy shown by these elements of Scottish society to Jews in Edinburgh regarding the suffering of their co-religionists on the continent was at least commensurate with that of the Scottish Church. By the early 1930s Rabbi Daiches enjoyed a friendship with John McPhail, the editor of the *Edinburgh Evening News*, and McPhail frequently wrote editorials commending Edinburgh's Jewish community. For example, in June 1934 McPhail wrote that "the Jewish community in Edinburgh has made a valuable addition to our citizenship, and the Rabbi has added intellectual distinction to the city."[213] Referring to German persecution of Jews, McPhail asserted that "in exiling the intelligentsia of that country, so largely represented by Jews, the Germans are making a profound mistake."[214]

Articles on Scottish Jews appearing in the *Scotsman* were no less generous, with one article in 1938 ridiculing the exaggeration of Jewish influence. The article stated that "there was no Jew among the Scottish members of Parliament; in the municipal sphere there were two Jews in Glasgow Town Council; and among Scottish bank directors there was no Jew. It was notable too that Jews in Scotland seldom fell upon the rates and seldom appeared in the Police Courts."[215]

In relation to local government, in 1935 a Jew had been appointed Musical Adviser to the Edinburgh Education Authority, and the Authority continued to send requests to Rabbi Daiches for "a note of the days when children of the Jewish faith may be excused attendance at school on religious grounds."[216] In the aftermath of *Kristallnacht*, Edinburgh Town Council convened a special meeting and unanimously passed a resolution expressing "sympathy with our Jewish brothers and sisters in their present persecution."[217] Less than three weeks later Samuel Chapman, MP for Edinburgh South, presided over a public meeting in aid of German Jewry which generated over £4,500 in donations.[218]

Leading figures of Edinburgh Jewry also enjoyed close relations with William W. Darling, the Lord Provost, based largely on "the assistance he received from them during his term in office."[219] Darling, who was a member of the Scottish National Council for Refugees, condemned anti-Jewish prejudice in 1942, stressing his "acknowledgement of the Jewish community in Edinburgh." He added that "there are many unwise and unthinking and unreflecting people who try and break the unbroken links of the community."[220] Between 1942 and 1945 three Edinburgh Jews were appointed Justices of the Peace "on the recommendation of the Lord Provost," among them Rueben Cohen, president of the Edinburgh Hebrew Congregation.[221]

The involvement of lay people in refugee aid efforts such as the establishment of Whittingehame House must also be mentioned, and also the role of Freemasonry in establishing and furthering links between Edinburgh Jews and non-Jews. Lord Traprain, in offering the estate at Whittingehame and participating in the activities of the Scottish National Council for Refugees, shortly found himself appointed Grand Master of the predominantly Jewish Lodge Solomon.[222] In 1942 the Lodge gained widespread recognition for its donation of a mobile canteen for the use of Edinburgh's Civil Defence workers.[223] Cooperative relations were also witnessed at Edinburgh University, where in February 1939 the Students' Christian Movement and the Edinburgh Jewish Students Society joined cooperated in organizing a symposium on "the fight against anti-Semitism."[224]

It was this wide-ranging support and cooperation from so many sections of Edinburgh society which led Rabbi Daiches to declare in 1938 his appreciation for "the friendly and sympathetic attitude of the vast majority of the Scottish people towards Jews and Judaism, the fair and friendly attitude of the Scottish Press, and the sympathy of the Churches."²²⁵ Daiches himself attributed this benevolence to "the common reverence of all elements of the population for Israel's scared scriptures, the greatest force in shaping the character and growth of the Scottish people."²²⁶ Daiches omitted his own role, though it has been demonstrated in this book that this role was significant. In March 1944, the London-based Central Committee for Jewish Education pointed this out, congratulating Daiches on "the excellent work that you have been able to do in creating a feeling of friendship between Jews and non-Jews all over Scotland."²²⁷

It has been established that the fight against Fascism in Scotland, and the role of Edinburgh Jewry in that struggle, was complex but largely successful. It remains necessary to examine the impact of the war on Fascism in Europe on Edinburgh Jewry.

Edinburgh Jewry and the Second World War

Rabbi Daiches greeted the outbreak of war by telling the congregation at Salisbury Road to support the war effort to the full and that "no sacrifice can be too great to remove the Nazi terror from Europe." Now that war had been declared, Daiches was open in expressing his belief that such action should have come sooner, but that instead "this dreadful evil had been allowed to grow and expand for more than a decade."²²⁸

Along with the rest of the citizens of Edinburgh, the war made its first impact felt on Edinburgh Jewry with the daylight air raid carried out by the Luftwaffe on the Forth in October 1939. The intention of the attack, the first daylight raid on Britain, was to destroy three British battleships at Rosyth.²²⁹ Rabbi Daiches was contacted a few days after the raid by Rabbi Dayan M. Gollop, Senior Jewish Chaplain to H.M. Forces, who noted that "the air raid the other day did not seem to upset the civilians in Edinburgh very much, and I hope you are none the worse for your experience."²³⁰

Gollop rapidly became a frequent correspondent with Rabbi Daiches, as the pair coordinated provisions for the increasing number of Jewish soldiers who found themselves stationed in and around the city. In November 1939, Gollop urged Daiches to do his utmost to supply Jewish soldiers stationed near Edinburgh with kosher food. Gollop stated that negotiations had been ongoing with military officials to permit Jewish soldiers to receive pay instead of rations but that even "if a man does get it for a whole week, it will barely be enough to pay for his Jewish meat for one day."²³¹ Requests also came from individual soldiers, with one Gunner Joe Solomon asking for Daiches' intervention in relation to obtaining permission to attend synagogue on a Saturday morning, and for "some Jewish food which I miss very much here."²³²

In late November 1939, Daiches worked to ascertain the precise number of Jewish soldiers stationed in and around Edinburgh. He discovered that 35 Jewish soldiers were with the 57th (Glasgow) Searchlight Regiment at Colinton, that there were 5 Jewish soldiers with the 230th Battery in Edinburgh, 2 Jewish brothers with the 156th Field Ambulance at Polmont, 2 Jewish Sergeants with the 420th Battery in West Lothian, and a further 47 stationed with various other regiments, including the Black Watch.[233] By early 1940 Daiches was a regular visitor to these men, and was also a regular visitor to wounded Jewish servicemen at the Peebles Military Hospital where he distributed Jewish prayer books.[234] Jewish soldiers also became occasional worshippers at the Salisbury Road synagogue, particularly during High Holy days. During a service of "prayer and intercession" in September 1940, it was reported that the "large congregation included many members of H.M. Forces."[235] Rabbi Daiches also received correspondence from Edinburgh Jews stationed outside the city. He received a letter from one such soldier in 1943 who complained that "I dislike Glasgow intensely.... I'm sure it has something to do with the foul atmosphere and sordid surroundings."[236]

By 1943, a large number of Polish officers had come to be stationed in Edinburgh, where they were incorporated into the greater Allied Forces. Problems appear to have arisen in January 1943, when it was revealed that a number of Polish officers were engaged in the distribution of anti–Semitic material, and discrimination against Jewish soldiers under their command. The material was a propaganda sheet entitled "Walka" ("Battle") which contained "violent attacks on Russians, Czechs, and Jews."[237] It was discovered that the sheets were being printed in Edinburgh and were being issued "from hand to hand among Polish officers."[238] Later that month Jewish soldiers began complaining anonymously to the press. The *Jewish Chronicle* asserted that in Edinburgh "the lives of some of the Jewish soldiers were being made unbearable. Many of them complained that they were given a much larger proportion of duties to perform than non–Jews serving in the same units."[239] By February 1943, however, the problem seems to have been resolved as no further complaints were recorded.

Civilian Jews in Edinburgh also participated in the war effort. In 1939 a meeting of the Edinburgh Hebrew Congregation voted to form a Jewish War-Services Committee in the city to ensure support for Jewish servicemen in the area, and facilitate such things as hospitality for troops in private homes.[240] In addition to the contribution of a mobile canteen to civil defense workers by Lodge Solomon, it was reported in the *Jewish Chronicle* that almost all members of the Edinburgh Jewish Ex-Servicemen's branch were acting as Air Raid Precaution wardens or were performing other civil defense duties.[241] Rabbi Daiches also made regular visits to the West Lothian branch of the British Red Cross hospital, where he "did a great deal to make the old people, evacuated from London, feel that they were amongst friends of their own faith."[242]

The progress of the war, and the uncertain situation of European Jewry, appears to have aroused strong feelings in Rabbi Daiches, and during the 1940s he wrote a number of articles on the subject of "reprisals." In September 1940, Daiches wrote to the editor of the *Scotsman* advocating "persistent R.A.F. attacks on Berlin, Leipzig, Munich and Nuremberg." Daiches argued that "there was no need to associate such attacks with the killing of women and children," and stated that "if incidentally a million or two Berlin citizens will be compelled to spend their nights in shelters and be deprived of a few hours sleep, it might help to dampen their enthusiasm."[243] Daiches' outlook in 1940 was characterized by pessimism. In his message for Rosh Hoshanah in 1941, Daiches stated that "one of the darkest years in the history of Europe and of Israel has come to an end, and our eyes are turning anxiously to the future to see what signs there are of a new era coming in, in which good will triumph over evil."[244]

This pessimism regarding the course of the war and the future of European Jewry was influential in Daiches' moves to revive Zionism in Edinburgh. In January 1940, Daiches wrote to the *Jewish Chronicle* arguing that given the treatment of Jews in Europe "all unbiased people" should regard the establishment of a Jewish National Home as "an act of historical justice and the realisation of a noble ideal."[245] Later that year Daiches wrote that "to surround the terrorists [Palestinian Arabs] with a halo of patriotism and a fight for freedom is the height of folly. To deprive the Jews of their last hope to escape from Nazi and Fascist tyranny would be a crime against humanity."[246] As has been discussed, Daiches was instrumental during the war years in ensuring that Zionism was an element of Christian-Jewish cooperation, and in defending the Zionist position in the press. During this time Daiches and his wife also resurrected the Edinburgh Women's Zionist Society, and made numerous attempts to revive enthusiasm and fund-raising for Zionism among Edinburgh's Jews.[247]

By 1942, Daiches was asserting that "the evil" had been "fought and overcome," and wrote an article for the *Jewish Bulletin* in which he stated that "the horizon in the East will show signs of a new sunrise, which may yet illuminate the path that will lead Israel to a new life in its old-new land."[248] Daiches' pessimism seems to have lifted completely with the D-Day landings in June 1944, when he told the congregation at Salisbury Road that

> We have reached the turning point in the gigantic struggle in which the nations are engaged. The armies of the aggressor have been driven back, are being driven back, everywhere.... The first real breach was made this morning by the valiant sons of Britain and America in the walls of the "fortress of Europe," where wickedness, cruelty, inhumanity, hatred and fiendish persecution have become entrenched for years, and man's

sense of justice and fear of God have been constantly challenged, mocked, and derided.[249]

Rabbi Daiches lived to see the Third Reich crumble in its last days, but he did not see its final defeat. After suffering a fall and breaking his arm, Daiches was taken into a nursing home in Edinburgh, where he died on 2 May 1945, aged 65.[250] The many tributes paid to him reflected the success of his work for the development of Jewish-Christian relations in Edinburgh and Scotland generally. On 11 May 1945, before a Salisbury Road synagogue filled to capacity, Abel Phillips, honorary secretary of the Edinburgh Hebrew Congregation recalled that,

> In Edinburgh, centre of Scottish religion and intellectualism, he was respected and admired by the citizens as a Jewish scholar and religious leader of high attainment and deep sincerity. He brought to the non-Jewish population of this great city a close understanding of the Jew and his way of life.... He was a dominating figure in the spiritual and intellectual life of the Jewish community in this country.[251]

The rise of Fascism in Britain and Continental Europe brought with it many challenges, but also many opportunities to reveal the existing triumphs of Jewish-Christian relations in Edinburgh, and the accomplishments of the community. In relation to the boycott movement, sections of Edinburgh Jewry were able to participate to the full in the economic protest, and while Edinburgh's Jewish leaders favored a different response to the rise of Nazi Germany, it appears to have aroused little friction within the community. The response advocated by the Council of the Edinburgh Hebrew Congregation was to engage with local politicians, participate in public meetings, and work toward cooperation with religious bodies. While much of this was discreet in comparison with the more vocal proponents of the boycott, it was in keeping with the reaction of assimilated Anglo-Jewry. However, even the leaders of Edinburgh Jewry adopted high-profile opposition to Nazi treatment of Jews. Rabbi Daiches in particular sought to educate the Scottish public about the situation of German Jews through articles in the press, and lectures to societies and clubs.

Edinburgh Jewry was further challenged by the arrival of German-Jewish refugees. There were logistical issues as to how to shelter and provide work for the new arrivals, and Edinburgh Jewry responded with the establishment of refugee aid societies and employment bureaus. There was, seemingly, the potential for friction between Edinburgh's Jews and the refugees, arising primarily from cultural differences, but there is no evidence of significant problems in this respect. Indeed, the Council of the Edinburgh Hebrew Congregation and the Edinburgh University Jewish Students Society made great efforts to make refugees feel welcome, even establishing a Refugee Social Club. The provisions made for child refugees can be said to have been a triumph of Jewish-Christian relations. Substantial grants from Scottish Christian sources made possible to the opening of the farm school as Whittingehame, and later at Polton House. Edinburgh Jews took Jewish children into their private homes, and in many cases Jewish children were housed in non-Jewish homes without significant problems. Finances remained a burden of course, the community remained small and relatively poor, and Edinburgh's Jewish leadership continued to rely on funding from outside the community in order to achieve its ambitions for the farm school project.

The arrival of foreign Jews aroused hostility in some quarters. There were problems in particular with the number of Jewish students studying medicine in Edinburgh. More specifically anti-Semitic discourse began to affect Edinburgh Jewry with the dissemination of anti-Semitic and Fascist literature in the city from 1934. Although this was most commonly German in origin, it was felt by Jewish leaders that the presence of British Fascists in the city was also a growing problem. The Edinburgh branch of the British Union of Fascists, the strongest Fascist organization in Scotland at that time, was seemingly not anti-Semitic until after Mosley's second rally at Usher Hall in 1936. Until then, Fascist literature of British origin had been distributed in the city by a small number of members of the Imperial Fascist League and other small extremist groups. After 1936, as the problem of anti-Semitic propaganda grew, Edinburgh's Jewish leaders cooperated closely with the Board of Deputies to develop anti-Fascist strategies such as counter-propaganda, the discreet funding of non-Jewish anti-Fascist bodies, and the gathering of information on Fascist groups. Rabbi Daiches acted individually to counter Fascist allegations in the Press, and to further cooperation with neutral non-Jewish organizations, in particular with the Scottish Churches.

This period witnessed significant changes in the relationship between Jews and the ecclesiastical authorities of Scotland's Protestant churches. The nature of Nazi anti-Semitism and the ensuing pessimism about the future of European Jewry was a primary catalyst for this change, and the result was a revision of Church attitudes toward Jews and a move away from an exclusively missionary approach to the Jewish people. Along with this change came Church efforts to aid refugees, to support Zionism, and to move toward greater interfaith relations and mutual understanding.

Cooperation, sympathy and support for the Jews of Edinburgh also came from sections of Edinburgh society outside the Churches. Edinburgh's Jews were supported in the fight against Fascism and the aid of refugees by the local and national media, local government, individual politicians, and students. Much of this support and esteem was rooted in the immigrant experiences of Jews in the city, and bonds which had been forged by earlier generations.

These challenges and this support occurred against the backdrop of war.

6. The Fight Against Fascism, 1933–1945

There were significant contributions made by Edinburgh Jews to the war effort, not only in the actions of its men in the theatre of war, but also through the contribution of its civilians, who made substantial efforts to assist civil defense. The early course of the war led to efforts at a renewal of Zionist activity in the city, though it remains difficult to measure the success these efforts met with. During the war Rabbi Daiches made great individual efforts to bring about closer cooperation between Jews and Christian in the city. Daiches also involved himself personally in the assistance of Jewish soldiers and Jewish evacuees in and around the city. The esteem in which the Jewish community and he personally were held at the time of his death was a monument to his efforts to bring together two worlds.

7
Postscript, 1945–1950

"Edinburgh Jewry is not the largest community in Scotland, consisting as it does of some 350 families, or 1,500 people, but its importance is out of all proportion to its numbers, since it represents Jewry in the Scottish capital."—Jewish Chronicle, 1949.[1]

The immediate postwar period witnessed further change in Edinburgh's Jewish community. Christian-Jewish relations in the city would again undergo fundamental change, and the community would be affected by demographic changes, with the result that it grew noticeably older and smaller. Zionism became a staple of communal life to an extent perhaps not seen since the days of the immigrant culture in the early 1900s and, in contrast to the influence exerted by the community under the leadership of Rabbi Daiches, postwar Edinburgh Jewry, now smaller and without its much-respected leader, began to steadily lose its voice in communal and national affairs, bequeathing ever more aspects of its hitherto autonomous authority to the Glasgow Representative Council. This chapter will explore the reasons behind these changes, before embarking on a survey of the findings of this book.

Postwar Changes in Edinburgh Jewry

An active Zionist culture had been encouraged and maintained by Rabbi Daiches throughout the war years, and Palestine was often at the forefront of his writings and public pronouncements during the period. As previously discussed, Zionism formed an important element in Daiches' plans for Jewish refugee children in Scotland, and he further ensured that it was a prominent feature of the Society of Jews and Christians. These efforts, together with a pervading uncertainty about the future of European Jewry, contributed to new initiatives to reinvigorate Zionism in Edinburgh. These initiatives included fundraisers and the resurrection of the Edinburgh Women's Zionist Society under the leadership of Rabbi Daiches' wife.

The level of success these initiatives met with and the level of Edinburgh Jewish communal support shown for Zionism in the immediate postwar period appears to have been significant. The *Jewish Chronicle* reported in July 1945 that a major Zionist meeting had been held at the Regal Cinema in Edinburgh, during which several notable speakers, including Stella Isaacs, the Marchioness of Reading, urged Edinburgh Jews to support Jewish refugees in Europe, and argued that the present condition of the refugees "could only be ameliorated by the concerted action and united voice of world Jewry."[2] During the annual meeting of the Edinburgh Zionist Association in August 1945, it was remarked that although Zionism in Edinburgh had lost much through the death of Rabbi Daiches, it had been a "successful year."[3] During the last year of the war the EZA had raised substantial amounts of funding for the United Palestine Appeal (UPA), assisted the Sunderland Jewish community with Zionist educational and fund-raising efforts, and organized a "Palestine at War" exhibition in Edinburgh which had been visited by over 15,000 people.[4] The overall impression given by the annual report was that support for Zionism in the city was gaining in momentum. A second fundraising effort on behalf of the UPA in August 1946 raised a "considerable sum," and debates on the subject of Zionism were regularly held at the synagogue in Salisbury Road.[5] In January 1948, just months prior to the declaration of the Jewish state, Edinburgh Jewry contributed generously to the emergency appeal of the UPA. The support shown by Edinburgh Jewry for Zionism was very much in keeping with trends nationally. Richard Bolchover noted that:

> the period of the Second World War coincided with a shift in the demographic, economic, and managerial equilibrium that had previously characterized Anglo-Jewry.... The East European immigrants for whom the Zionist Caucus was the political anchor were now far more numerous than their opponents and it was only a matter of time before they managed to turn this fact to their political advantage.[6]

This shift in demographic, economic and managerial equilibrium is evident in Edinburgh. The origins of the Edinburgh community lay in more recent times compared with the origins of Jewish communities such as London. However, as this book has shown, those whose families had settled in the city during the period 1820–1870 evidently viewed themselves, and were viewed, as being distinct from the more recent immigrants from Eastern Europe. With the ageing and shrinking of the Jewish population in Edinburgh during and immediately after the war, the last vestiges of the original founding families were, if not already vanished in their entirety, certainly fewer in number and increasingly marginalized in political and managerial terms. Nationally, the war and the Holocaust had led to a large number of "converts" to Zionism, most notably in the case of Professor Harold Laski, brother to Neville, who announced in May 1945 that "he had always been an advocate of assimilation but was now firmly and utterly convinced of the need for the rebirth of the Jewish nation in Palestine."⁷ Increased Jewish support for Zionism had important repercussions not only for events in Palestine itself, but also for relations between Jews and Christians in Britain. Stephen Wendehorst noted that "the second half of the 1940s ... saw British Jews and the larger society drift apart more openly over such issues as the future of Palestine, Jewish Displaced Persons, and the memory of the *Shoah*."⁸ As Britain celebrated victory and peace, "Jews contemplated their great losses."⁹

In addition, with "pressures for national conformity relaxed after the victory over Germany, the separation of British Jews from the larger society in their attitude to rescue and Palestine policy came to stand out in stark relief."¹⁰ As the struggle against the British mandate was waged in Palestine, many British Jews abandoned Neville Laski's maxim to "be Englishmen first and Jews second," giving generously to aid in the purchase of arms for "Jewish underground armies fighting against British troops" and the "smuggling of refugees into the Holy Land."¹¹

With the bombing of the central offices of British mandate authority in Palestine, Jerusalem's King David hotel, in July 1946, a rift began to open between British Jews and the British government under Ernest Bevin and indeed, between British Jews and the British generally. When the Irgun hanged two British sergeants in a eucalyptus grove in July 1947, a wave of anti–Jewish violence swept through Britain. In the days following the hangings, no violence was reported in Edinburgh, but in Glasgow 17 Jewish-owned shops were attacked and badly damaged. During five days of anti–Jewish rioting in Liverpool, shops were destroyed and a synagogue was burned. In North Wales shops were attacked and daubed with such slogans as "Hitler was right," and in London a meeting of the Jewish Ex-Servicemen's Association had to be postponed when it was interrupted by a hostile crowd of 200 individuals. There were many similar scenes in towns and cities across Britain, and the level of anti–Jewish feeling was sufficiently high for Oswald Mosley to "attempt a come-back."¹²Edinburgh's Jews, like those across the country, feared a potential resurgence of Britain's Fascist and anti–Semitic elements. In December 1945 a decision had been reached to maintain the operation of the Edinburgh Jewish Defence Committee, and in 1947 the Committee was still active and declared itself to be "combating anti–Semitism in Edinburgh and surrounding areas."¹³ Locally, there were non–Jews who sympathized with the goal of banning Fascist groups permanently, but there is little evidence to suggest significant cooperation with Jews. In December 1947 the Edinburgh Trades Council passed a resolution "calling on the Government to take immediate steps to declare all forms of Fascist organizations, however named, and in no matter what guise, illegal in Great Britain," making specific reference to Oswald Mosley's "Union Movement."[14] This move, however, should be seen as part of traditional "red" opposition to Fascism rather than solidarity with Jews. Indeed, nationally a rift was forming between left-leaning Jews and the Labour party, largely owing to the reluctance of the latter to support the demands of Zionists. Also, while Trades Councils and the Labour Party were inclined to support legislation restricting British Fascists, "a proposal to outlaw anti-Semitism was rejected by the Labour Party conference in 1946: a similar proposal in the House of Commons in 1948 failed to get past its first reading."[15]

In the immediate aftermath of the war, disillusionment with Government actions in relation to the Mandate, and renewed anti-Jewish feeling in Britain provoked an inward-looking reaction from the leadership of Scottish Jewry. Although there was a substantial number of Christians present at Rabbi Daiches' memorial service in June 1945, relations between Jewish and Christian leaders in Scotland would struggle to reach their war-time heights. In January 1948, Rabbi Isaac Cohen was formally inducted as the successor of Rabbi Salis Daiches as spiritual head of the Edinburgh Hebrew Congregation.[16] Cohen had been born in Wales to Lithuanian immigrants and had very recently received his rabbinical diploma in London. He would remain in the post until 1959 when he was appointed Chief Rabbi of Ireland.[17] Cohen dedicated much of his inaugural address in Edinburgh to attacking "Britain and British officers" who "today associate themselves with Arab oppressions in the Holy Land, and appear to arrange themselves in opposition to the judgment of the United Nations Assembly, and to the centuries-old prayers, longings and stirring of the people of Israel."[18] The speech was well-received by a pro-Zionist audience of Christians and Jews, including ex-Moderator of the Church of Scotland, Dr. James Black. At a subsequent gathering, the Lord Provost, Sir Andrew Murray, trod the path of many of his successors in praising those present as "true and loyal citizens of the Scottish Capital."[19] However, it is clear that there was an underlying sense of dissatisfaction with the notion and nature of Christian-Jewish contact, at least on the part of Jewish representatives. The ability of Edinburgh Jewry to operate independently in terms of Christian-Jewish contact was impeded in April 1946, when the first moves were taken to incorporate the representation of Edinburgh, and the smaller Jewish communities of Scotland, into the Glasgow Jewish Representative Council, allowing the Council to speak on behalf of all Scottish Jews.[20]

By 1948, the Glasgow Jewish Representative Council had taken on much of this wider representative role and convened in December to discuss the future of Jewish-Christian meetings in Scotland. The consensus was overwhelmingly negative. Despite years of discussion and cooperation, and the gradual decline of the "Home Missions," there remained a lingering suspicion that the Church of Scotland's ultimate goal was to use joint meetings for the purpose of converting Jews. Christian support for Jewish refugees, and the cooperation of the Scottish Churches in the fight against Fascism and anti-Semitism was not acknowledged, and it was asserted that Christian representatives should "awaken their conscience over their responsibility in the matter of anti-Semitism," and that if there were to be future meetings they should be "on our terms." One representative stated that "the time had come to drop the association," and another argued that he "failed to see what could be the ultimate gain from such meetings."[21] The latter remark should be seen within the context of the goals of the Society of Christians and Jews, which had included support for Zionism and the combat of anti-Semitism. With a Jewish state established, and anti-Semitic organizations in Britain all but eradicated, the only remaining stated goal of the Society of Christians and Jews was "the creation and development of bonds of mutual understanding and respect between Jews and Christians." This appears, in itself, to have held little attraction. The Rev. Dr. I.K. Cosgrove, distinguished minister to the Garnethill congregation, and until recently interim minister to the Edinburgh congregation, argued that "these meetings, perhaps, should not have been started." After much discussion it was decided that "now that there is a State of Israel, we have to live in amicable relationships with our fellow citizens," and that "we cannot now afford to divorce ourselves from the association." Meetings between Jewish and Christian representatives did continue in the years ahead, though they appear to have been held more frequently in neutral surroundings, such as restaurants and public halls, than in Churches or synagogues. Such meetings seem to have ceased in Edinburgh.[22]

Edinburgh Jewry also changed substantially in terms of its composition and infrastructure. Between 1945 and 1948, more than 100 Jewish men who had served during the Second World War returned to Edinburgh, with most joining the Jewish branch of the British Legion.[23] A number of them returned blind or disabled.[24] During an official "Welcome Home" reception in June 1947, Reuben Cohen stated that 16 percent of the community had served in the war.[25] In late December 1945, the Edinburgh branch of the Trades Advisory Council, which had 85 members, held a discussion on assisting returning Jewish businessmen enter business. The Trades Advisory Council had been formally established in 1940 as an auxiliary arm of the Jewish Defence Committee. It was created for the purpose of advising the Committee on trade matters, and dealing generally with "the economic causes of anti-Semitism," and the "the defamers outside and the delinquents inside the trading community."[26] Presumably the Trades Advisory Council viewed the return of Jewish servicemen, and their incorporation into the local and national economy to be a potential source of friction in Jewish-Gentile relations.

War-time disruption and a declining population had a negative impact on the previously robust network of Jewish societies in Edinburgh. The Edinburgh Jewish Literary Society held no meetings between 26th March 1939 and 25th March 1945. The minutes of the Society for 1945–6 recorded "disappointing attendances," and in 1952 the few remaining members of the Society convened to discuss the reasons for its steep decline. The decline was attributed to the ageing of the community and a lack of younger members, increasing social attractions outside the Jewish community such as television and cinema, and a lack of strong leadership.[27] The last point suggests that the strong leadership of figures such as the Reverend Fürst and Rabbi Daiches, and their involvement in almost all aspects of communal life had been, or was at least seen as, a significant factor in steering the community and its societies through hard times in the past. Of course, the content of Literary Society discussions also began to change. Perhaps unsurprisingly, a dominant "talking-point" to emerge in 1948 was Israel, and events in the Jewish state and its position in the Cold War were the topic of much discussion in ensuing years. Another society impacted by war was the Edinburgh Maccabi—four members had been killed in action.[28]

There is also evidence that some Edinburgh Jews were attracted by organizations and societies which were not exclusively Jewish. One notable example was that of Simon Levi, a Jewish cabinet maker, native of the Ukrainian city of Kharkiv, and prominent member of the Edinburgh branch of the Scottish U.S.S.R. Society. In April 1946 Levi, with wood supplied by the St. Cuthbert's' Co-operative Association, produced a writing desk to be presented to Joseph Stalin.[29] It was formally handed over to the first secretary of the Soviet Embassy in London in October.[30] In November 1946, Edinburgh resident Bernard Chernack was chosen as "the first Jew to ever represent Scotland at table-tennis" at the European Table Tennis Cup.[31] It is also worth noting that the Edinburgh Festival was created in 1947 by Rudolf Bing, an Austrian Jew who had arrived in Britain in 1934.[32]

Numerically, by 1949 the community had declined to around 350 families or 1500 individuals.[33] This decrease in the population seems to have been due mainly to losing younger members to other British urban centers. The community remained united, comprising, according to Reuben Cohen, "Jews of all degrees, from Liberals to supporters of Machzikei Hadass."[34] The youth of the community were described as identifying themselves "ever more closely with Jewish life, although not in so marked a degree with synagogal life." Economically, there remained a poor element of Edinburgh Jewry, and there were very few who could be described as wealthy. However, the Edinburgh Hebrew Benevolent Loan Society remained in existence, as did the Board of Guardians, and Reuben Cohen stated in an interview in 1949 that the community "had a proud record in the field of charitable endeavour and in subscriptions to the Zionist cause."[35] By 1949, organized Edinburgh Jewry enjoyed relaxed, though not extensive formal relations with non–Jews. Anti-Semitism by this date was said to be "rare in Scotland, and unknown in Edinburgh."

The community was said to be "marked by no kind of strain or embarrassment."³⁶ Despite relinquishing much of its autonomous representative role to Jewish leaders in Glasgow, Edinburgh Jewry seems to have been content with the fact that its importance, as always, remained "out of all proportion to its numbers, since it represents Jewry in the Scottish capital."³⁷

Conclusion

In exploring and analyzing the history of Edinburgh Jewry, this book has sought to address a significant lacuna in both Scottish and Jewish history. Tony Kushner has pointed out that "local Jewish studies, especially in Britain, face a triple marginality."[1] The history of local Jewish communities has been largely marginalized by those working within the field of "mainstream" British history, a result of their "antipathy, patronisation or indifference" against minority studies.[2] Further, Kushner has argued that there are "hierarchies within the study of the Jewish diaspora itself in which certain countries and regions are seen to possess less significance than others. In this respect, British Jewish history has been regarded as being of minor importance, and its provincial experiences even more so."[3] Indeed, even within the field of British-Jewish studies, "the provinces have been especially sidelined."[4] To this it could be added that areas of Jewish settlement outside Manchester, Liverpool, Leeds and Glasgow have been even more neglected, and that prevailing historiographical opinion seems to hold that these communities were somehow less autonomous as well as less important.

This book has sought to make a contribution to Scottish historiography by shedding light on the history of a minority population in the Scottish capital—a history of great significance in understanding Scottish society, and in particular the city of Edinburgh, during this period. This study has provided grounds for re-examining the notion that Scotland was somehow less antagonistic toward its Jewish population than England. Indeed, assumptions to the effect that sectarianism acted as a buffer against anti-Semitism appear to have very little basis in fact, and this book has pointed to numerous instances where such reasoning is entirely refuted by the historical record. Further, this book has given significant attention for the first time to the Church of Scotland's attitudes toward the Jewish population in Scotland. These attitudes have been shown to be not only of great significance to the history of Jews in Scotland, but also to the broader history of the missionary endeavors of the Scottish Churches around the world. Despite some historiographical attention to the history of the Jewish population in Glasgow, and more recently to some of the smaller Jewish communities scattered across Scotland, no significant role has been attributed to the Church of Scotland. Arguably, in light of the findings of this study, this failure to recognize the significance of the role of the Church of Scotland in the Scottish-Jewish experience can be said to represent a serious omission.

In addition, this book has made a contribution to British-Jewish historiography. No assessment of the Scottish-Jewish experience would be valid without due attention being given to the experience of Jewish in the religious, cultural and political heart of Scotland. This book has sought to devote such attention, and to consider its broader implications, not only in terms of revisiting the received wisdoms of Scottish-Jewish historiography, but also the broader implications for British-Jewish historiography more generally. In this sense, the largely autonomous nature of Edinburgh, its distance both geographically and organizationally from London, the distinctive challenges it faced, and the importance of local leaders and personalities in steering Edinburgh Jewry through good times and bad, are sufficient grounds for asserting that the history of small "provincial" communities merit serious scholarly attention, that they need not be "anchored" explicitly to major metropolitan Jewry, and that no assumptions can be made about the "trends" of British-Jewish history without due consideration of Jewish life beyond the major metropoles. In addition, this book has provided a balanced, nuanced history of Jewish life during this period and, as stated at the outset of the study, has sought to acknowledge economic advancement as well as enduring poverty, settlement as well as transience, tolerance as well as antipathy, harmony as well as divisiveness, and success as well as failure. In this sense, this book could be described as a "post-revisionist" British-Jewish history.

One of the key findings of this study is that in many respects the experience of Edinburgh Jewry resembled that of the major British Jewish communities, and that Edinburgh's Jews were confronted by many of the changes and challenges that faced by their co-religionists across the country. In this sense, it is perhaps unsurprising that the book shares the focus of modern British-Jewish historiography on "Eastern European immigration, the Jewish poor, social class relations, anti–Semitism, and struggles for the control of the Jewish community."[5] Like many other British cities, Edinburgh had a small, mainly middle class, Jewish community prior to the period of "mass immigration" which occurred between 1881 and 1914. Unlike some Scottish towns, such as Aberdeen and Falkirk, Edinburgh did not witness the birth of a new community during this period, but it did witness the radical transformation of this existing Jewish community. In keeping with trends seen in large urban centers such as Glasgow, Manchester, Leeds, Birmingham, Liverpool and

Newcastle, Edinburgh's Jewish population was greatly enlarged by immigration. Nationally, the population of British Jews rose from 60,000 in 1880 to 300,000 in 1914.[6] Edinburgh's Jewish population did rise significantly during this period, though not at the same rate, or to the same extent, as Jewish communities in London, Glasgow, Manchester and Leeds.

Like other urban Jewish populations, Edinburgh Jewry was fundamentally changed in terms of its character. Edinburgh was faced with the common difficulty of dealing with a great and rapid increase in Jewish poverty, and the socio-economic gulf which separated established communities from their immigrant co-religionists. The relative homogeneity of Edinburgh Jewry was disrupted by the influx of immigrants with different religious and social cultures, and this disruption was typified in Edinburgh, as elsewhere, by the proliferation of separate immigrant congregations and communal institutions. Indeed, there were times when factionalism was so strong in Edinburgh that justification could be found in referring to Edinburgh's Jews as a collection of communities, rather than a single community. Although the efforts of leaders of the established Edinburgh Jewish community to maintain unity failed at that time, their response to the influx was in keeping with trends nationally. Jewish aid efforts in Edinburgh were informed by the desire to help their co-religionists, but also by broader British-Jewish concerns which necessitated the keeping of Jewish migrants off local poor rates, and the avoidance of circumstances which could encourage anti–Semitism. While established Edinburgh Jewry did not face a unique problem, as a relatively small and not very wealthy metropolitan community, evidence suggests that it had particular difficulty in coping with this problem, and Jewish poverty in the city appears to have been a singularly persistent issue.

Another way in which Edinburgh Jewry followed national trends was the economic profile of the immigrants. The majority were an impoverished mix of semi-skilled and unskilled labor. In common with immigrant populations in other major urban centers, these immigrants gravitated toward the clothing trade, cabinet-making, shoe-making and peddling. Edinburgh shared common problems such as sweating, though economic competition with the non–Jewish population does not appear to have been sufficient to cause intercommunal tension, and unlike some larger cities, Edinburgh did not become home to Jewish trade unions. The new immigrant population clustered socially and economically as well as residentially. Jewish residential clustering occurred in Edinburgh, as it did in Glasgow, London, Leeds, Manchester, and many smaller areas of Jewish immigrant settlement throughout Britain.

The history of Edinburgh Jewry also reflects broader British-Jewish trends in the increased social mobility and integration which characterized much of the interwar period. Across Britain, the ethnic cohesion of Eastern European Jewish immigrants was weakened by "economic mobility, occupational diversification and growing toleration."[7] This was exemplified in Edinburgh by the emergence of a new educated, professional and managerial class, along with an increasing number of shopkeepers and medium-sized business owners who participated to a greater extent in Scottish life. Edinburgh's Jews during the interwar period, like those across the country, began to move away from an inner-city existence and tended toward the adoption of the suburban "more comfortable middle class existence" which has come to typify contemporary British-Jewry.[8]

Like the majority of Jewish immigrant communities at this time, the early years of Edinburgh Jewry were typified by concerns relating to the maintenance of Jewish identity. The proliferation of Jewish societies, clubs, organizations and political movements which characterized Edinburgh Jewry before the Great War was part of a larger phenomenon in the Jewish Diaspora. Over time, a balance was struck between the maintenance of Jewish identity and the desire for socio-economic advancement. The coming of age of the first generation of British-born Jews of immigrant descent, combined with the pressures to assimilate which accompanied the Great War, contributed significantly to the period of increased integration which defined the interwar period.

What of the feelings this community evoked in non-Jews? This book has shown that Edinburgh Jewry's experience of anti-Semitism can also be said to have been in keeping with national trends. Edinburgh and Scotland were not immune to the anti-alien agitation which swept through much of England during the period of mass immigration, though this aspect of the Scottish-Jewish experience has been downplayed somewhat in both memoir and scholarship. At times this agitation took on a specifically anti-Semitic tone. In Edinburgh, too, we find the presence of anti-Semitic individuals and groups, though it is important to acknowledge that virulent anti-Semitism was, in the main, a marginal affair.

Less marginal perhaps was "middle class anti-Semitism." Edinburgh's Jewish community had certainly gained a large measure of acceptance and tolerance in the city by the interwar period. Middle-class Jews appear to have been well-received in the city's Masonic fraternities and business clubs. It could be argued, however, that the tolerance of Edinburgh's gentile bourgeoisie was in large part conditional. Much of the praise heaped on Edinburgh's Jews was related to conformity to Victorian middle-class values—for example, the way the community looked after "its" poor was widely praised. Sobriety, industry, charity, loyalty in the form of war sacrifice, low levels of criminality, frugality and piety were recurring themes in most public pronouncements on the city's Jewish population. The sympathy of local politicians and media outlets was also often couched in terms alluding to the "invisibility" of the community—in essence, arguing that the general Jewish population was acceptable as long as it remained inconspicuous and did little to draw attention to itself. There were occasions when this tolerance grew weak, and this was most apparent in issues which highlighted religious and cultural differences such as Sunday trading.

Edinburgh Jewry also seems to have followed trends seen in other provincial Jewish communities, with the exception of Manchester, Leeds and some towns on the south coast of England, in terms of its postwar demographic decline. As a result of declining religious observance, inter-marriage, emigration, and low birth rates Scotland's Jewish population has almost halved since 1950.[9]

The book has also pointed to certain aspects of the Edinburgh Jewish experience which could be regarded as unique or distinctive. Most notably, the interaction between the city's Jews and Scotland's Presbyterian churches appears to be without parallel. This is not to say that missionary activity was unheard of outside Edinburgh. Indeed, several British towns and cities, including London, Manchester, and Glasgow had at one time branches of the Society for the Propagation of the Gospel among the Jews and other similar organizations, and many of the tactics employed by conversionists in Edinburgh had echoes throughout Britain.[10] But no community of comparable size became the subject of such intensive conversionist efforts.

Part of this intense focus derived from a Scottish evangelical tradition which was subtly different from its Anglican counterpart. Unlike Anglican evangelism, in which the move to convert Jews was part of a broader mission to global "heathenism," the Church of Scotland "saw the conversion of others as an incidental bonus to the main purpose of their work—the conversion of Jews."[11] The Kirk's steadfast adherence to Paul's biblical injunction that salvation should come "to the Jew first" formed an unstable foundation for relations between Jews and ecclesiastical authorities in Edinburgh.[12] The response of Christian Edinburgh to the new Jewish population was informed by sympathy for Jewish suffering and poverty, but also by millenialist ambitions to hasten the conversion of Scottish, and world, Jewry. Leading clergy categorized immigrant Jews according to their compatibility with millenialist expectations—within this framework, a "bigoted" pious Jew was at least preferable to the "atheistic" Jew who was deemed not only a spiritual aberration and a traitor to "the faith of his fathers," but also an immediate danger to Scottish society. The same conception of Jews and Judaism informed Kirk attitudes to Zionism. Edinburgh's Jewish leaders displayed an acute awareness of this aspect of Christian motivations for inter-faith relations, which often formed a significant barrier to cooperation and dialogue.

It is also clear, however, that there was another side to the Church of Scotland's "interest" in Jews. The Kirk's exclusive missionary focus on Jews and its adherence to the belief that the divine covenant with "the People of the Book" remained extant, contributed to the Church of Scotland's adoption of the role of "defender" of Jews. Edinburgh's Jewish leaders were willing to avail themselves of this particular aspect of the Kirk, and against the backdrop of rising domestic and foreign Fascism, Christian-Jewish relations enjoyed an unprecedented level of success in the city. The same aspects of Kirk theology also evidently contributed to its ability to see Nazi anti–Semitism in a different light than the Anglican Church. Within the context of British bystanders to the Holocaust, the Kirk is notable for the clarity of its perception of Nazi anti–Semitism, its consistent and vocal opposition to Nazi policies, its support of European Jewish refugees, and for the manner in which it re-evaluated its own relationship with Jews in light of continental persecution. The collapse of continental and domestic Fascism and the establishment of the State of Israel, however, removed much of the impetus for Jewish engagement with inter-faith dialogue. As such, it could be argued that both Christians and Jews in Edinburgh held dual conceptions about the other. For the Kirk, the Scottish Jew could be objectified as the target of millenialist ambitions—a revered "Israelite"—or, he could be seen as an atheistic or pharisaic threat to Christian society. Edinburgh's Jews, on the other hand, could perceive of the Kirk's approaches as an existential threat to Jewish identity and tradition, or as being of potential usefulness in the fight against greater threats. Thus, the ebb and flow of Jewish-Christian cooperation in Edinburgh closely corresponded with the prevalence of threats to Jews at home and abroad, the two most intensive periods of inter-faith cooperation being the eras of Tsarist and Nazi persecution.

Another potentially unique aspect of the Edinburgh Jewish experience relates to identity. Did Edinburgh's Jews, at any point during this period, perceive themselves as being an important component of Scottish Jewry, or merely a distant, provincial branch of London-based British Jewry? Rabbi Dr. Salis Daiches for years protested against the name "Zionist Federation of England," asserting not only the separate identity of the constituent countries of the United Kingdom, but also that Jews in those countries partook, willingly or not, of something of that identity.[13] Daiches believed that Scottish Jews could and did differ in needs and tastes from English or Welsh Jews, and this book has pointed to numerous examples where local conditions such as Scottish religious cultures and legal practices presented unique problems for Scottish Jews which the London-based Jewish leadership was often unaware of. These experiences underpinned much of Daiches' efforts, unsuccessful in his lifetime, to create separate Scottish-Jewish organizations, and a district Rabbinate in which he would be formally recognized as Chief Rabbi of Scotland.

It should also be noted that Daiches was not alone in his belief that Scottish Jewry was distinct from English Jewry, or at least required different, more local organization and leadership. During the late 1920s the pages of Glasgow's *Jewish Echo* were liberally sprinkled with calls for a separation from the Chief Rabbi in London, and the creation of a Scottish *Beth Din* under Daiches. It was asserted that London-based leadership was a relic from a time when Britain's Jewish population was small and to a much greater degree geographically concentrated in and around the English capital. With tens of thousands of Jews now located even in the most remote parts of Britain, some provincial leaders saw no reason to concede authority to figures in London who did not or could not understand provincial concerns. Scottish Jewry appears to have been particularly eager to gain control over issues such as the provision of Jewish food and education. One accusation commonly made against the London *Beth Din* was its alleged complete inability to properly supervise interfaith marriages in Scotland. One correspondent in 1928 stated that since under the present regime "so many Jewish boys are marrying *shiksas* ... the future Scottish *Beth Din* should not have anything to do with its London predecessor."[14] The precise extent of this feeling, and whether or not it permeated much below the leadership ranks of Scottish Jewry is difficult to assess, though the debate did recur with some persistence throughout the 1920s. Thus, one of the central findings of this book is not only that there were social and class differences within Edinburgh Jewry, but that there was organizational and jurisdictional division within British Jewry as a whole. One of the major fault lines of this division was the English-Scottish border, and the focal point of the Scottish-Jewish push for autonomy was Edinburgh's rabbi.

The book has also offered glimpses which suggest that almost from the beginning, Edinburgh's immigrant population showed an interest in Scottish identity. Scottish history and aspects of Scottish culture were regularly discussed by the Literary Society, and anecdotal evidence points to the adoption of festivities such as Burns Night and Hogmanay. Kenneth Collins has pointed to use of tartans and thistles by Scottish Jewish organizations, and the existence of Scottish-Jewish pipe bands stating that, "Jews have been proud to adopt some Scottish imagery as their own."[15] Further, David Daiches has asserted that Edinburgh Jewry under his father achieved "a synthesis of the best of Jewish and Scottish thought and practice."[16] The book is permeated with contemporary allusions to a special relationship between Scots and Jews, a relationship supposedly based on a shared enthusiasm for the Old Testament and education, as well as the fact that the Scots, as well as any people, understood what it meant to "struggle to maintain distinctiveness in a sometimes unfriendly world."[17] Despite the hostility which accompanied the period of mass immigration, and hints of middle-class anti–Semitism, the bulk of interactions between Jews and non–Jews in the city seem to have been benign, and these allusions may go at least some way to explaining this. In their engagement with Scottish politics, education, culture, history, and sport, one can discern that by the interwar period, many Jews in the city conceived of themselves as Scottish as well as Jewish. This was generally matched by an acceptance not always afforded to the more traditional "others" in Scottish society, such as the Irish and the English. In this sense, Muriel Spark's comment that she was more embarrassed by her English mother than her Lithuanian-born Jewish father is quite telling. As Spark said, "foreigners were fairly treated but "the English" were something quite different."[18]

* * *

The Salisbury Road synagogue today is nestled among apartment blocks converted from Edwardian mansions, small shops, and restaurants. Obscured by trees and other buildings, it is invisible from Newington Road, one of Edinburgh's main thoroughfares. But behind the unassuming nature of this location, and the low-profile and small size of the community it serves, there lies the rich and complex history of a relatively small but important Jewish community and the city in which it came to dwell.

Chapter Notes

Introduction

1. *Statistical Account of Scotland 1791–99*, Vol. 10, p. 245: Cluny, County of Aberdeen.
2. *Ibid.*, Vol. 4, p. 86: Drainie, County of Elgin.
3. *Ibid.*, Vol. 10, p. 585: Kelso, County of Roxburgh.
4. *Statistical Account of Scotland 1791–99*, vol. 8, p. 107: Kilmartin, County of Argyle.
5. The early history of Edinburgh Jewry will be discussed later in the chapter.
6. Although one must acknowledge that language and accent may have distinguished them on the most local level.
7. Nathan Abrams and Harvey Kaplan, "Jews in Scotland: Myth and Reality," *History Scotland*, 6:4 (July/August 2006), p. 38.
8. Endelman, *The Jews of Britain*, p. 12.
9. *Ibid.*
10. David Daiches, *Was: A Pastime from Time Past* (London: Thames and Hudson, 1975), p. 54.
11. Todd Endelman, "English Jewish History," *Modern Judaism*, 11 (1991), 91–109, p. 91.
12. Tony Kushner, *Anglo-Jewry Since 1066: Place, Locality and Memory* (Manchester, Manchester University Press, 2009), p. 42.
13. Endelman, "English Jewish History," p. 92.
14. *Ibid.*, p. 92 & 97.

Chapter 1

1. Nathan Abrams and Harvey Kaplan, "Jews in Scotland: Myth and Reality," *History Scotland*, July/Aug. (2006), 38–43.
2. Daiches, "The Jew in Scotland," p. 196.
3. *Ibid.*
4. *Ibid.*, p. 197.

5. William Cunningham, "Differences of Economic Development in England and Scotland," *Scottish Historical Review*, 13 (1916), 168–88. Ben Braber counters this assertion, stating that "from time to time foreign traders, including Jews, were welcome in Scottish Royal burghs, but that local disabilities in other towns hampered their trade." Braber, *Jews in Glasgow*, p. 18.
6. *Ibid.*, p. 170.
7. *Ibid.*
8. Abrams and Kaplan, "Jews in Scotland," p. 38.
9. Levy, "Origins of Scottish Jewry," p. 128.
10. Herbert L. Willett, *The Jew Through the Centuries* (Chicago: Willett, Clark and Company, 1932), p. 304.
11. Levy, "Origins of Scottish Jewry," p. 129.
12. *Ibid.*
13. Quoted in Levy, "Origins of Scottish Jewry," p. 134.
14. For more on the readmission of Jews to England see David S. Katz, *Philo-Semitism and the Readmission of the Jews to England, 1603–1655* (Oxford: Oxford University Press, 1982).
15. Letter from the Rev. W.J. Couper to Rabbi Dr. Salis Daiches, 22 Jan. 1933. Papers of Rabbi Dr. Salis Daiches, National Library of Scotland, Acc. 12278 (hereafter PSD).
16. National Archives of Scotland Reference (hereafter NAS):CS164/69 Abraham Turing vs. Magistrates of Edinburgh.
17. Quoted in Daiches, "The Jew in Scotland," p. 198.
18. Daiches, "The Jew in Scotland," p. 199.
19. David Vital, *A People Apart: A Political History of the Jews in Europe, 1789–1939* (Oxford: Oxford University Press, 2001), p. 13. Vital added that the judge in this particular case made reference to the freedoms accorded wealthy Jewish merchant, Sir Solomon de Medina

(c.1650–1730), stating that if "a Jew trading in London" could receive such high honors, then "there was no evident reason why the witness or any other Jew should be thought of as incapable of bearing testimony."

20. Daiches, "The Jew in Scotland," p. 199.
21. Levy, "Origins of Scottish Jewry," p. 138. See also Stephen Massil," Joseph Hart Myers MD (1758–1823): First Jewish Graduate," *University of Edinburgh Journal*, 45:2 (2011).
22. Braber, *Jews in Glasgow*, p. 18
23. Karen Jillings, *Scotland's Black Death: The Foul Death of the English* (Stroud, Gloucestershire: Tempus, 2003), p. 134.
24. Anthony Julius, *Trials of the Diaspora: A History of Anti-Semitism in England* (Oxford: Oxford University Press, 2010), p. 76.
25. David Hume, *Essays and Treatises on Several Subjects* (London: Millar, 1758), p. 123.
26. Julius, *Trials of the Diaspora*, p. 114.
27. Ibid., p. 165.
28. Francis James Child (ed.) *The English and Scottish Ballads* (New York: Cooper Square, 1965), pp. 244–45.
29. Endelman, *The Jews of Britain*, p. 41.
30. Ibid., p. 42.
31. Ibid., p. 43.
32. Ibid., p. 50.
33. NAS: CC8/6/853: Process of Scandal: Rose Nathan vs. Francis Berlin alias Abraham Burnett.
34. Ibid.
35. Ibid.
36. NAS: CC8/6/853: Process of Scandal: Rose Nathan vs. Francis Berlin alias Abraham Burnett.
37. Ibid.
38. Ibid.
39. A letter from the Chief Rabbi to Rabbi Dr. Salis Daiches in 1925 drew the latter's attention to the fact that a Jew named David Fraenkel had also been resident in Edinburgh in 1790. See letter dated 2 Jan. 1925, PSD.
40. See David Edwin Keir (ed.) *The Third Statistical Account of Scotland: Edinburgh* (Edinburgh: William Collins & Son, 1966), pp. 30–32.
41. Ibid., p. 31.
42. Phillips, *A History of the Origins of the First Jewish Community in Scotland*, p. 5.
43. Ibid.
44. Cecil Roth, "Rise of Provincial Jewry," *Jewish Monthly*, 2 (1950), p. 86. However Abel Phillips states that the move took place in 1825. See Phillips, p. 10–11. The confusion seems to have arisen from the fact that North Richmond Street and Richmond Court were part of the same tenement building. Acknowledgment is due to Michael Tobias at Jewish Genealogy for providing the maps to clarify this issue.

45. Phillips, *A History of the Origins of the First Jewish Community in Scotland*, pp. 10–11.
46. Daiches, "The Jew in Scotland," p. 203.
47. Endelman, *The Jews of Britain*, p. 80.
48. Endelman, *The Jews of Britain*, p. 80.
49. Levy, "Origins of Scottish Jewry," p. 142.
50. *Extracts from First Report of the Commissioners of Religious Instruction*, Scotland, Edinburgh Presbytery, 1837, p. 18. Acknowledgment due to Michael Tobias at Jewish Genealogy for providing me with this source.
51. *Extracts from First Report of the Commissioners of Religious Instruction*, Scotland, Edinburgh Presbytery, 1837, p. 205.
52. National Library of Scotland Reference: Ry.III.a.2(66).
53. Collins, *Second City Jewry*, p. 19.
54. Levy, "The Origins of Scottish Jewry," p. 142.
55. Bazaar Souvenir Guide, 25 Oct. 1930, EHC New Building Fund, p. 3. PSD.
56. Daiches, "The Jew in Scotland," p. 204.
57. Daiches, "The Jew in Scotland," p. 204.
58. *The Evangelical Magazine and Missionary Chronicle*, 19 (London: Thomas Ward & Co., 1841), p. 531.
59. *The Evangelical Magazine and Missionary Chronicle*, 40 (London: Thomas Ward & Co., 1862), p. 367.
60. Endelman, *The Jews of Britain*, p. 82.
61. Ibid., p. 82.
62. NAS: JC26/1859/385: Trial Papers relating to Abraham Jacob, Hannah Jacob, for theft.
63. "The Monopoly of the London Retail Orange Trade by the Jews," *Blackwood's Edinburgh Magazine*, 22 (1827), p. 594. Endelman notes that by this date "the Irish had almost completely replaced the Jews" in the London street trade in oranges." This trade had once been dominated by working class Jews. See Endelman, *The Jews of Britain, 1656 to 2000*, p. 90.
64. "Judaism in the Legislature," *Blackwood's Edinburgh Magazine*, 62 (1847), p. 723.
65. Vital, *A People Apart*, p. 178.
66. "Judaism in the Legislature," *Blackwood's Edinburgh Magazine*, 62 (1847), p. 734.
67. "The Jew Bill," *Blackwood's Edinburgh Magazine*, 68 (1850), p. 73.
68. Ibid.
69. "The Jew Bill," *Blackwood's Edinburgh Magazine*, 68 (1850), p. 74.
70. Ibid., p. 75.
71. Ibid.
72. Polly Pinsker, "English Opinion and Jewish Emancipation," *Jewish Social Studies*, 14 (1952), 51–94 (p. 69). For an excellent example of the defense of Jewish civil liberties, see Baron Thomas Babington Macaulay's Jan. 1831 article entitled, "Statement of the Civil Disabil-

ities and Privations Affecting Jews in England," included in that months *Edinburgh Review.*
73. Levy, "Origins of Scottish Jewry," p. 145.
74. *Ibid.*, p. 146.
75. Endelman, *The Jews of Britain*, p. 128.
76. *Ibid.*, p. 129.
77. For a more in depth look at circumstances in Russia, see Harold Shukman, *War or Revolution: Russian Jews and Conscription in Britain, 1917* (London: Vallentine & Mitchell, 2006).

Chapter 2

1. *JC*, 18 Dec. 1891, p. 6.
2. *JC*, 3 Feb. 1882, p. 6.
3. *JC*, 17 Feb. 1882, p. 12.
4. *JC*, 17 Feb. 1882, p. 12.
5. See *JC*, 10 March 1882, p. 1, and *JC*, 21 July 1882, p. 3.
6. *JC*, 20 April 1883, p. 4.
7. Levy, "Origins of Scottish Jewry," p. 129.
8. Todd M. Endelman. "German Jews in Victorian England: A Study in Drift and Defection," in *Assimilation and Community: The Jews in Nineteenth-Century Europe*, ed. by Jonathan Frankel and Steven J. Zipperstein (Cambridge: Cambridge University Press, 1992), pp. 57–87 (p. 58).
9. This is not to say that there were no poor foreign Jews among the early settlers. A trial for theft in 1859 lists Abraham Jacob and Hannah Jacob as defendants. See NAS: JC26/1859/385. Presumably these were not wealthy traders.
10. Some of them do seem to have been very successful. For example, the furriers at Philip Levy & Co. Documents at the National Archives of Scotland show this company also had connections to the jewelry trade and household furniture as well as furs and skins. See NAS: CS96/3783. However, it is equally apparent that many struggled to make a living in the city. Henry Levy, a theatre proprietor is listed as applying for bankruptcy in 1878, in 1899 Alexander & Levitus & Co, dealers in jewels and hardware also filed for bankruptcy. Others were in the drapery and fruit trades. See for example NAS CS318/4/6 (Saul Solomon Asher), NAS CS318/59/114 (David W. Levy), and CS318/48/66 (G. Camberg).
11. Steven Singer, "Jewish Religious Thought in Early Victorian London," *AJS Review*, 10, 2 (1985), 181–210 (p. 183).
12. *Ibid.*, p. 181.
13. Eugene Harfield, *Commercial Directory of the Jews of the United Kingdom* (London: Hewlett & Pierce, 1894), p. 249.
14. Information on Jacob Michael's non-commercial life can be found in an obituary in the *JC*, 16 Oct. 1896, p. 7.
15. See Harfield, *Commercial Directory of the Jews*, p. 249, and also: http://www.familysearch.org/eng/search/frameset_search.asp PAGE=/eng/search/ancestorsearchresults.asp [accessed 20 July 2010 at 4:32 p.m.]. International Genealogical Index number: C116852, dates: 1863–1869, batch number: 6035516.
16. A PDF of Reis' birth certificate can be viewed at: http://www.manfamily.org/PDFs/Alphonse_Louis_Reis_Birth_Cert.pdf [accessed: 20/7/2010 at 4:08 p.m.].
17. Harfield, *Commercial Directory of the Jews*, p. 249.
18. *JC*, 16 June 1880, p. 10.
19. See *JC*, 29 April 1842, p. 125.
20. *JC*, 1 Sept. 1881, p. 9.
21. Obituary of Prof. Aaron Hart David in *JC*, 24 Nov. 1882, p. 5.
22. *JC*, 8 Sept. 1871, p. 3.
23. *JC*, 4 May 1883, p. 7.
24. *JC*, 15 April 1887, p. 11.
25. *JC*, 27 May 1887, p. 9.
26. *Ibid.*
27. Richard Shannon, *Gladstone: Volume One* (London: Hamish Hamilton, 1982), pp. 104–105.
28. *JC*, 31 Oct. 1890, p. 20.
29. *JC*, 24 July 1891, p. 14.
30. *JC*, 14 Aug. 1891, p. 5.
31. *Ibid.*
32. *JC*, 25 Sept. 1891, p. 7.
33. *JC*, 23 Oct. 1891, p. 16.
34. *JC*, 4 Sept. 1891, p. 11.
35. *JC*, 23 Oct. 1891, p. 16.
36. *JC*, 18 Dec. 1891, p. 6.
37. *JC*, 18 Dec. 1891, p. 6
38. Kenneth Collins, *Aspects of Scottish Jewry* (Glasgow: Glasgow Representative Council, 1987), p. 4.
39. *JC*, 1 July 1892, p. 6.
40. *Ibid.*
41. *JC*, 15 July 1892, p. 13.
42. *JC*, 8 March 1895, p. 10, *JC*, 16 July, 1897, p. 11 & *JC*, 17 March 1899, p. 24.
43. Heinz-Dietrich Lowe, *The Tsars and the Jews: Reform, Reaction and Anti-Semitism in Imperial Russia* (Reading: Harwood, 1993), p. 55.
44. Gainer, *The Alien Invasion*, p. 1.
45. Gainer, *The Alien Invasion*, p. 1.
46. *JC*, 10 May 1895, p. 9.
47. *Ibid.*
48. JC, 18 Sept. 1896, p. 14.
49. Gainer, *The Alien Invasion*, p. 156.
50. Gainer, *The Alien Invasion*, p. 7.
51. *JC*, 25 Sept. 1891, p. 7.
52. Gainer, *The Alien Invasion*, p. i.
53. Collins, *Aspects of Scottish Jewry*, p. 41.

54. See *JC*, 11 Nov. 1892, p. 20.
55. *JC*, 26 Feb. 1909, p. 31.
56. *JC*, 2 June 1893, p. 14.
57. *JC*, 2 June 1893, p. 14.
58. *JC*, 29 May, 1896, p. 18.
59. *JC*, 7 July, 1899, p. 27.
60. *JC*, 22 March 1895, p. 19.
61. *JC*, 30 April 1897, p. 23.
62. *JC*, 26 Dec. 1902, p. 23.
63. *Ibid.*
64. *JC*, 16 Jan. 1902, p. 28.
65. *JC*, 14 Sept. 1906, p. 27.
66. *JC*, 14 Sept. 1906, p. 27.
67. *JC*, 3 Feb. 1899, p. 26.
68. *JC*, 15 Nov. 1901, p. 27.
69. *JC*, 12 Feb. 1892, p. 20. See also Harfield's *1892 Commercial Directory of the Jews*, entry for Leith.
70. *JC*, 1 April 1892, p. 15.
71. *JC*, 18 Nov. 1904, p. 32.
72. *JC*, 19 Dec. 1902, p. 28.
73. *JC*, 31 Jan. 1902, p. 29. Mr. Michael and Mr. Isaacs often collaborated in philanthropic efforts, often directing their endeavors towards the children of the community. For example, during Chanukah 1904 they organized and funded entertainment and refreshments for 120 children at the Graham Street Synagogue.
74. *Scotsman*, 28 Dec. 1904, p. 7.
75. *Ibid.*
76. See Harfield, *Commercial Directory of the Jews*. The term "ghetto" is problematic, and its use and meaning here should be clarified. Traditionally, a ghetto was a compulsory residential area for Jews, usually walled and normally located in an impoverished quarter of a city with an already highly concentrated Jewish population. In Edinburgh, Jews were not compelled to live in a specific area, and there is no evidence that a single street ever became an area of purely Jewish residence. However, a greater proportion of Edinburgh's Jewish population did live within this network of streets, and the area was certainly viewed by some, notably Dean of Guild William Ormiston, as the "Jewish quarter." Significantly, memoirs also suggest that Jews tended to view this network of streets as being "Jewish," and part of an overall atmosphere of cultural and social segregation from the non-Jewish population. In this sense, the term "ghetto" is used here in the same manner as Todd Endelman's description of the Jewish East End in London. Endelman acknowledges that the East End was an area with a high but not exclusively Jewish population, but that more importantly the area became "for more than a few newcomers to London ... a social and cultural ghetto they rarely left." See Endelman, *The Jews of Britain, 1656 to 2000*, p. 145. Bill Williams has referred to residential clustering as leading to the creation of "a voluntary ghetto." See Bill Williams, *Jewish Manchester: An Illustrated History* (Derby: Breedon, 2008), p. 32.
77. *Scotsman*, 28 Dec. 1904, p. 7.
78. *Ibid.*
79. *Ibid.*
80. *Ibid.*
81. NAS: CH3/979: Minute Books of the Edinburgh Jewish Medical Mission, 19 Jan. 1905.
82. Account of the life and death of Lady Rosebery, in *JC*, 21 Nov. 1890, p. 8.
83. *JC*, 31 July 1885, p. 6. & *JC*, 5 Aug., p. 5.
84. *JC*, 28 Sept. 1888, p. 11.
85. *JC*, Oct. 19 1888, p. 14.
86. *JC*, 21 Nov. 1890, p. 8.
87. *Ibid.*
88. See *JC*, 11 Nov. 1892, p. 20, 4 June 1897, p. 9, & 12 Aug. 1898, p. 18.
89. Gainer, *Alien Invasion*, p. 157.
90. Quoted in *Ibid.*, p. 156.
91. *Ibid.*
92. See for example, Robert Rhodes James, *Rosebery* (London: Weidenfeld & Nicolson, 1963), and D.A. Hamer, *Liberal Politics in the Age of Gladstone and Rosebery* (Oxford: Clarendon Press, 1972).
93. Gainer, *Alien Invasion*, p. 156.
94. Gainer states that, "James Bryce at least was adamant that 'there is no present need for any legislation whatsoever.'" Gainer, *Alien Invasion*, p. 156.
95. *JC*, 4 May, 1894, p. 9.
96. *Ibid.*
97. *JC*, 5 June 1908, p. 22. Glasgow and Govan reported 65 Jewish families on Poor Law relief.
98. However, it must be stated that there were instances of individual immigrant Jews being involved in very severe crimes in Edinburgh, such as the rape of children and the running of large-scale brothels. See for example trial papers of Henry Solomon, NAS: JC/26/1873/161 and trial papers of Asher Barnard, NAS Reference: HH16/1.
99. *JC*, 16 March 1894, p. 19.
100. Collins, *Aspects of Scottish Jewry*, p. 42.
101. *JC*, 11 May 1906, p. 10.
102. *JC*, 3 Nov. 1893, p. 10.
103. *JC*, 17 July 1903, p. 18.
104. *JC*, 3 Nov. 1893, p. 9.
105. *Ibid.*
106. *Ibid.* This secession will be discussed in more detail in a later chapter.
107. *JC*, 10 Nov. 1893, pp. 7–8.
108. Allan Harman (ed.), *Mission of Discovery: The Beginning of Modern Jewish Evangelism* (Guernsey: Christian Focus, 1996), p. 5.
109. *Ibid.*

110. *JC*, 13 June 1862, p. 8.
111. *JC*, 4 June 1886, p. 12.
112. *JC*, 6 Aug. 1886, p. 6.
113. *JC*, 2 Jan. 1903, p. 30.
114. *JC*, 3 Feb. 1893, p. 19.
115. *JC*, 7 June 1895, p. 16.
116. *JC*, 4 Nov. 1898, p. 22.
117. *JC*, 11 July, 1902, p. 28.
118. Levison, *Christian and Jew*, p. 27.
119. NAS: CH3/979, Annual Report of the Edinburgh Jewish Medical Mission, 1902.
120. *Scotsman*, 21 March 1906.
121. The records of this organization span the period 1900–1932 and are held by the National Archives of Scotland.
122. NAS: CH3/979, Minute Books of the Edinburgh Jewish Medical Mission.
123. NAS: IRS21/1078, Tax Claim for the Edinburgh Jewish Medical Mission.
124. *Ibid.*
125. NAS: CH3/979 Annual Report of the Edinburgh Jewish Medical Mission, 1902.
126. NAS: CH3/979 Minute Books of the Edinburgh Jewish Medical Mission, 18 Dec. 1901.
127. NAS: CH3/979 Annual Report of the Edinburgh Jewish Medical Mission, 1902.
128. Levison, *Christian and Jew*, p. 28.
129. Kenneth Collins, *Scotland's Jews* (Glasgow: Scottish Council of Jewish Communities, 2008), p. 19.
130. Levison, *Christian and Jew*, pp. 27–8.
131. NAS: IRS21/1078 Edinburgh Jewish Medical Mission, Report for 1908.
132. Nahum Levison, Sir Leon Levison—The Lion-Hearted, available at http://www.hagefen.org.il/len/aalphabetic%20presentation/c13763/197091.php [accessed: 12/08/2010 at 3:09 p.m.].
133. Levison, *Christian and Jew*, p. 32.
134. *Ibid.*, p. 33.
135. Levison, *Christian and Jew*, p. 39.
136. NAS: IRS21/1078, Annual Report of the Edinburgh Jewish Medical Mission, 1907.
137. *Ibid.*
138. *Ibid.*
139. NAS: IRS21/1078 Edinburgh Jewish Medical Mission, Report for 1908.
140. NAS: IRS21/1078 Edinburgh Jewish Medical Mission, Report for 1908.
141. NAS: IRS21/1078, Annual Report of the Edinburgh Jewish Medical Mission, 1907.
142. Levison, *Christian and Jew*, p. 29.
143. *Ibid.*, p. 39.
144. NAS IRS21/1078, Annual Report of the Edinburgh Jewish Medical Mission, 1907.
145. *Ibid.*
146. *Ibid.*
147. *Ibid.*
148. *Ibid.*

149. NAS IRS21/1078, Annual Report of the Edinburgh Jewish Medical Mission, 1907.
150. Quoted in *JC*, 25 July, 1902, p. 28.
151. *Ibid.*
152. Quoted in *JC*, 1 Aug. 1902, p. 14.
153. *JC*, 15 June 1894, p. 17.
154. *JC*, 16 Dec. 1898, p. 26.
155. *JC*, 28 July 1899, p. 17.
156. *Ibid.*
157. *JC*, 4 Aug. 1899, p. 24.
158. *JC*, 18 Aug. 1899, p. 9.
159. *JC*, 26 July, 1901, p. 26.
160. *Scotsman* 21 June 1902, p. 9
161. *Scotsman*, 16 Jan. 1903, p. 6.
162. Jack Landa, *The Alien Problem and Its Remedy* (London, King & Son, 1911), p. 278.
163. David Daiches, *Edinburgh* (London: Hamish Hamilton, 1978), p. 222.
164. David Edwin Keir (ed.), *The Third Statistical Account of Scotland* (Edinburgh: William Collins, 1966), p. 100.
165. Tim Edensor (ed.), *Moving Worlds: Personal Recollections of 21 Immigrants to Edinburgh* (Edinburgh: Polygon, 1989), p. 1.
166. *Scotsman*, 17 Jan. 1911, p. 7.
167. Quoted in *JC*, 5 June 1903, p. 27.
168. *Ibid.*
169. *Scotsman*, 21 Feb. 1903, p. 12
170. *Ibid.*
171. *Scotsman*, 5 May 1903, p. 7.
172. *Ibid.*
173. *Scotsman*, 15 May 1903, p. 8.
174. *Ibid.*
175. *Ibid.*
176. Quoted in *JC*, 26 Feb. 1904, p. 9.
177. *Ibid.*
178. Scotsman, 19 May 1904, p. 4.
179. Henry Maitles, "Blackshirts Across the Border," p. 94.
180. *Scotsman*, 22 Dec. 1904, p. 6.
181. Helena Wray, "The Aliens Act 1905 and the Immigration Dilemma," *Journal of Law and Society*, 33 (2006), 302–323.
182. *Scotsman*, 3 Jan. 1906, p. 8.
183. *Scotsman*, 8 Feb. 1906, p. 6.
184. Wray, "The Aliens Act and the Immigration Dilemma," p. 303.
185. *Scotsman*, 24 April 1906, p. 7.
186. *Scotsman*, 24 April 1906, p. 7.
187. *Ibid.*
188. *Ibid.*
189. Reinecke, Christiane, "Governing Aliens in Times of Upheaval: Immigration Control and Modern State Practice in Early Twentieth-Century Britain, Compared with Prussia," *International Review of Social History*, 54 (2009), 39–65 (p. 41).
190. *JC*, 18 May 1906, p. 23.
191. *JC*, 6 March 1908, p. 19.
192. *JC*, 11 Sept. 1908, p. 18.

193. *Scotsman*, 20 April 1908, p. 8.
194. *Scotsman*, 18 July 1908, p. 11.
195. *Scotsman*, 18 July 1908, p. 11.
196. *Ibid.*
197. *Ibid.*
198. *Scotsman*, 27 Jan. 1909, p. 10.
199. *Ibid.*
200. *Scotsman*, 24 Sept. 1910, p. 12.
201. *Scotsman*, 20 Dec. 1910, p. 6.
202. Their identities would emerge early in the New Year, although speculation was rife that they were foreigners.
203. *Scotsman*, 20 Dec. 1910, p. 6.

Chapter 3

1. "Cosmopolitan Edinburgh: A Stir Among the Jews," clipping from *Jewish Echo*. PSD.
2. Rosalind Mitchison, *A History of Scotland* (London: Methuen, 1971), p. 399.
3. *Ibid.*
4. F.M.L. Thompson (ed.), *The Cambridge Social History of Britain 1750–1950 Volume 2, People and Their Environment* (Cambridge, Cambridge University Press, 1990), p. 9.
5. James McMillan, *Anatomy of Scotland* (London: Leslie Frewin, 1969), p. 9.
6. Ian H. Adams, *The Urban Scene, 1760–1980*, in Chalmers M. Clapperton (ed.), *Scotland: A New Study* (London: David & Charles, 1983), p. 159.
7. Mitchison, *A History of Scotland*, p. 400.
8. *Ibid.*, p. 16.
9. Richard Rodger, "Urbanisation in Twentieth Century Scotland," in T.M. Devine and R.J. Finlay (eds.), *Scotland in the 20th Century* (Edinburgh: Edinburgh University Press, 1996), p. 124.
10. Maitles, "Jewish Trade Unionists in Glasgow," p. 51.
11. *Ibid.*
12. Quoted in Suzanne Audrey, *Multiculturalism in Practice: Irish, Jewish, Italian and Pakistani Migration to Scotland* (Aldershot: Ashgate, 2000), p. 18.
13. Audrey, *Multiculturalism in Practice*, p. 18.
14. Adams, *The Urban Scene*, p. 161.
15. Mitchison, *A History of Scotland*, p. 381.
16. *Ibid.*
17. *Ibid.*, p. 402.
18. Sir John E. Gorst, *The Children of the Nation: How Their Health and Vigour Should Be Promoted by the State* (New York: E.P. Dutton and Company, 1907), p. 55.
19. Mitchison, *A History of Scotland*, p. 401.
20. *JC*, 28 July 1899, p. 17.
21. Collins, *Aspects of Scottish Jewry*, p. 11 & p. 44.
22. Henry Maitles, "Jewish Trade Unionists in Glasgow," p. 51.
23. David Daiches, *Was*, p. 137.
24. Linda Fleming, *Jewish Women in Glasgow*, p. 87.
25. Irena Kudenko and Deborah Phillips, "The Model of Integration? Social and Spatial Transformations in the Leeds Jewish Community," *Journal of Ethnic and Migration Studies*, 35 (2009), 1533–1549 (p. 1537).
26. *Ibid.*
27. Edensor (ed.), *Moving Worlds*, p. 6. It must be mentioned however that the Jewish Mission reports at the turn of the century commented on the "considerable" "diversity of nationality" among the Jews they encountered. See footnote p. 70. It is not clear whether this diversity of nationality was typical of the transmigrant community or the settled community.
28. Quoted in T.M. Devine, *The Scottish Nation 1700–2000* (London: Penguin, 2006), p. 520.
29. Daiches, *Two Worlds*, p. 97.
30. Fleming, *Jewish Women in Glasgow*, p. 98.
31. *Scotsman*, 17 Oct. 1901, p. 7.
32. Audrey, *Multiculturalism in practice*, p. 49.
33. *Scotsman*, 21 Feb. 1903, p. 12.
34. Gorst, *The Children of the Nation*, p. 10.
35. *Ibid.*, p. 69.
36. *Ibid.*, p. 70.
37. *Ibid.*, p. 21. Infant mortality among Jewish immigrants living in the slums of Edinburgh was, however, not unheard of. See for example the death of ten month old Hannah Stankie at her home in Nicolson Street in 1883. *JC*, 21 Sept. 1883, p. 1.
38. See Ó Gráda, *Jewish Ireland in the Age of Joyce*, p. 146.
39. *JC*, 2 Dec. 1910, p. 29.
40. Levison, *Christian and Jew*, p. 29.
41. *JC*, 14 March, 1902, p. 24.
42. *The Lancet*, "Report of *The Lancet*: Special Sanitary Commission on the Sweating System in Edinburgh," 23 (1888), p. 1261.
43. Cowan, p. 18.
44. *Ibid.*, p. 99.
45. Daiches, *Two Worlds*, p. 117.
46. *Otago Witness*, 10 July 1907, p. 15.
47. A report in the New Zealand-based *Ashburton Guardian* quotes a government source as ranking Edinburgh eleventh in Britain and Ireland in terms of its Jewish population in 1910. Edinburgh ranked behind smaller cities such as Dublin, Hull and Newcastle. Its Jewish

population did, however, exceed that of Bristol, Belfast, Swansea, Nottingham, Middlesbrough, and Portsmouth. See *Ashburton Guardian*, 21 Jan. 1910, p. 1.
48. Bill Williams, *Jewish Manchester: An Illustrated History* (Derby: Breedon, 2008), p. 43.
49. *Ibid.*, p. 32.
50. *Ibid.*
51. Williams, *Jewish Manchester*, p. 57.
52. Collins, *Aspects of Scottish Jewry*, p. 41.
53. *JC*, 18 July 1890, p. 15.
54. *JC*, 8 July 1892, p. 16.
55. *JC*, 3 Nov. 1893, p. 9.
56. Collins, *Aspects of Scottish Jewry*, p. 41.
57. Harfield, *Commercial Directory of the Jews*, p. 245.
58. *JC*, 31 March 1899, p. 24.
59. *JC*, 21 Feb. 1908, p. 24.
60. Collins, *Aspects of Scottish Jewry*, p. 41.
61. *Ibid.*
62. See Collins, *Aspects of Scottish Jewry*, p. 42.
63. See *JC*, 14 Feb. 1890, p. 11, and, 6 Oct. 1893, p. 17. An article printed on 29 Sept. 1893 (p. 15) states that, "The new synagogue in N. Richmond Street, which was recently purchased by the New Hebrew Congregation, was well filled during the New Year."
64. *JC*, 8 July 1892, p. 16.
65. *JC*, 10 Nov. 1893, p. 7.
66. *JC*, 17 Nov. 1893, p. 9.
67. See *JC*, 14 March 1890, p. 15, and *JC*, 22 Dec. 1893, p. 20.
68. For information on his unanimous election to Chair of the Rifle Lodge see *JC*, 6 Dec. 1889, p. 19.
69. See *JC*, 18 Nov. 1904, p. 32, and *JC*, 26 Oct. 1906, p. 33.
70. Home Office Reference: HO144/166/A42549.
71. Cesarani, *The Jewish Chronicle and Anglo-Jewry*, p. 77.
72. Louis Hyman, *The Jews of Ireland, From the Earliest Times to the Year 1910* (Shannon: Irish University Press, 1972), p. 165.
73. *Ibid.*
74. Ó Gráda, *Jewish Ireland in the Age of Joyce*, p. 95.
75. *Ibid.*
76. *JC*, 6 Dec. 1895, p. 16.
77. *JC*, 28 Aug. 1896, p. 7.
78. *JC*, 28 Aug. 1896, p. 7.
79. Copy of state of settlement of price for Graham Street Synagogue, and Correspondence and papers relating to sale of Church at Graham Street to the Edinburgh Hebrew Congregation. NAS: CH16/2/42, and NAS: CH16/2/36.
80. Collins, *Aspects of Scottish Jewry*, p. 6. For an analysis of the financial background to the building of the Garnethill Synagogue, see Collins, *Second City Jewry*, pp. 38–39. It must also be acknowledged that there were several, much more modest, Jewish places of worship in the city of Glasgow.
81. *JC*, 18 Dec. 1896, p. 2.
82. See *JC*, 19 Feb. 1897, p. 2.
83. *JC*, 4 June 1897, p. 9.
84. *JC*, 18 Feb. 1898, p. 24.
85. *JC*, 21 Jan. 1898, p. 28.
86. *JC*, 31 May 1907, p. 28.
87. *JC*, 29 Jan. 1904, p. 30.
88. Daiches, "The Jew in Scotland," p. 205.
89. *JC*, 29 Sept. 1893, p. 15.
90. *JC*, 26 Feb. 1904, p. 32.
91. *JC*, 4 March 1904, p. 11.
92. *JC*, 4 March 1904, p. 11.
93. *JC*, 21 Oct. 1892, p. 19.
94. *JC*, 2 Nov. 1894, p. 19.
95. Collins, *Aspects of Scottish Jewry*, p. 12.
96. *JC*, 8 Aug. 1890, p. 13.
97. Howard M. Sachar, *A History of Israel: From the Rise of Zionism to the Present* (New York: Alfred A. Knopf, 1982), p. 5.
98. *Ibid.*
99. *Ibid.*, p. 16.
100. Sachar, *A History of Israel*, p. 16.
101. *JC*, 14 Aug. 1891, p. 14.
102. *JC*, 18 Dec. 1891, p. 6.
103. Letter dated 26 July 1891, Papers of Edinburgh Chovevei Zion (hereafter PECZ) held at Scottish Jewish Archives Centre. Originals held at Central Zionist Archives, Jerusalem, File: A2/44.
104. Letter dated 26 Aug. 1891. PECZ
105. Letter dated 20 Aug. 1891. PECZ
106. Letters from M. Shapera and Marcus Levy to Dr. Hirsch, dated 30 Dec. 1891, PECZ
107. *JC*, 8 Jan. 1892, p. 8.
108. *JC*, 15 Jan. 1892, p. 16.
109. *JC*, 15 Jan. 1892, p. 16.
110. *Otago Witness*, 14 Jan. 1892, p. 26.
111. Letters dated 13 April 1892, and 14 Jan. 1893, PECZ
112. Letter dated 22 April 1893, PECZ
113. Sachar, *History of Israel*, p. 27.
114. Walter Laqueur, *A History of Zionism* (London: Tauris Parke, 2003), p. 80.
115. *JC*, 25 March 1892, p. 18.
116. The Rev. J. K. Goldbloom, "Reminiscences of Zionism in Great Britain," in Israel Cohen (ed.), *The Rebirth of Israel* (Connecticut: Hyperion, 1952), p. 61.
117. *JC*, 8 Sept. 1893, p. 16. This curious belief that Scots and Jews shared an affinity appears to have been quite prevalent in some circles. The Reverend Paterson bases his Zionist ambitions on it, and it certainly appears more prevalent among Christians than Jews. It possibly had its root in the zeal with which Scottish

churches carried out their missions to the Jews in and around Palestine, and also the sense that "Scottish Christianity" had a strong focus on the Old Testament. It was also the subject of jokes and stereotyping. Andrew Carnegie once pointed out that both Scots and Jews were "thrifty."
118. Ibid.
119. JC, 13 April 1894, p. 19.
120. JC, 10 May 1895, p. 20.
121. JC, 22 Sept. 1899, p. 26.
122. See Desmond Stewart, Theodor Herzl (London: Hamish Hamilton, 1974), p. 164.
123. Ibid.
124. Ibid., p. 137.
125. Quoted in Walid Khalidi (ed.), From Haven to Conquest: Readings in Zionism and the Palestine Problem Until 1948 (Washington: The Institute for Palestine Studies, 1987), p. 89.
126. JC, 24 Jan. 1896, p. 8.
127. JC, 6 Aug. 1897, p. 8.
128. Letter from B.L. Freeman to Dr. Hirsch 13 July 1896, PECZ.
129. Letter from Marcus Levy to Dr. Hirsch dated 27 Dec. 1897, PECZ.
130. Letter from Marcus Levy to Dr. Hirsch dated 8 Jan. 1898, PECZ.
131. Goldbloom, p. 62.
132. JC, 21 April 1899, p. 26.
133. JC, 16 March 1900, p. 28.
134. JC, 6 July 1900, p. 28.
135. Goldbloom, p. 63.
136. See JC, 16 June 1880, p. 10, and JC, 19 Nov. 1886, p. 3.
137. JC, 26 April 1895, p. 20.
138. JC, 26 April 1895, p. 20.
139. Collins, Second City Jewry, p. 76.
140. Daniel Elazar, The National-Cultural Movement in Hebrew Education in the Mississippi Valley, Jewish Community Studies, Jerusalem Centre for Public Affairs http://www.jcpa.org/dje/articles2/hebrew-mississippi.htm [accessed: 16/11/10 at 2:55 p.m.].
141. JC, 22 Sept. 1899, p. 29.
142. JC, 18 May 1900, p. 30.
143. JC, 4 Nov. 1904, p. 27.
144. JC, 31 May 1907, p. 28.
145. JC, 31 Aug. 1900, p. 20.
146. JC, 9 May 1902, p. 26.
147. Hyman, The Jews of Ireland, p. 193.
148. Levy, History of the Sunderland Jewish Community, p. 249.
149. Abrams, Caldonian Jews, p. 179.
150. Lacqueur, History of Zionism, p. 79.
151. JC, 16 Nov. 1900, p. 29.
152. JC, 11 Jan. 1901, p. 20. David Daiches described William Grant as "a somewhat eccentric gentleman, an Edinburgh Christadelphian, who professed himself a great friend of the Jews and an ardent Zionist. This gentleman … was a great bored, who liked the sound of his own voice and edited a strange magazine called Glad Tidings of the Coming Age." Mr. Hogg was described by Daiches as, "a more congenial pro-Semitic gentile … a kindly old man who would attend the Synagogue fairly frequently and was on friendly terms with many Jewish families." See Daiches, Two Worlds, pp. 36–7.
153. JC, 23 Nov., p. 23.
154. JC, 11 Jan. 1901, p. 20.
155. JC, 12 July 1901, p. 29.
156. JC, 25 July 1902, p. 28.
157. JC, 27 Feb. 1903, p. 27.
158. JC, 21 Feb. 1902, p. 28.
159. JC, 28 Feb. 1902, p. 27.
160. JC, 6 June 1902, p. 24.
161. JC, 14 March 1902, p. 28.
162. Jacob de Haas, Zionism: Jewish Needs and Jewish Ideals (London: Greenberg, 1901), p. 31.
163. New York Times, 19 Dec. 1902.
164. JC, 14 March 1902, p. 28.
165. JC, 14 Aug. 1903, p. 7.
166. Abrams, Caledonian Jews, p. 42.
167. Laqueur, A History of Zionism, p. 127.
168. JC, 9 Sept. 1904, p. 16.
169. Ibid.
170. Isaac Cohen, "Some Early Reminiscences and Impressions of Zionism in Sunderland," in Levy, History of the Sunderland Jewish Community, p. 262.
171. Laqueur, A History of Zionism, p. 157.
172. JC, 1 Dec. 1905, p. 29.
173. JC, 19 Jan 1906, p. 29.
174. JC, 16 March 1906, p. 38.
175. JC, 14 Sept. 1906, p. 20.
176. JC, 4 Feb. 1910, p. 14.
177. Devine, The Scottish Nation, p. 518.
178. Michael Fry, Edinburgh (MacMillan: London, 2009), p. 299.
179. It is clear that some Jews also engaged in gambling and betting operations, which occasionally attracted the attention of the authorities. See for example the trial of Morris Levinson and Max Jablonsky in 1911 for contravention of the Gambling and Betting Act, NAS: JC26/1911/15.
180. See Laurence Fontaine, History of Pedlars in Europe (Durham: Duke University Press, 1996), p. 119, and Audrey, Multiculturalism in Practice, p. 33.
181. Harvey Kaplan, The Jews of Edinburgh in 1901, Unpublished census analysis, Scottish Jewish Archives Centre.
182. Maitles, "Attitudes to Jewish Immigration in the West of Scotland to 1905," p. 48.
183. Maitles, "Attitudes to Jewish Immigration in the West of Scotland to 1905," p. 49.
184. Ibid.

185. Audrey, *Multiculturalism in Practice*, p. 105.
186. *JC*, 24 April 1903, p. 3.
187. Abrams, *Caledonian Jews*, p. 168.
188. Edensor (ed.), p. 6.
189. Pedlars Act 1871, Revised Statute from the UK Statute Law Database, http://www.opsi.gov.uk/RevisedStatutes/Acts/ukpga/1871/cukpga_18710096_en_1 [accessed: 24/04/2010, at 3.24 pm].
190. Hyman, *The Jews of Ireland*, p. 161.
191. Braber, *Jews in Glasgow*, p. 79.
192. Annual Report of the Edinburgh Jewish Medical Mission, 1913. NAS: IRS 21/1078.
193. Levison, *Christian and Jew*, p. 26.
194. *Ibid.*, p. 27.
195. Audrey, *Multiculturalism in Practice*, p. 104.
196. Kaplan, *The Gorbals Jewish Community in 1901*, p. 13. This figure is not as surprising as it may first appear. Kenneth Collins points out that "one of the reasons for the Jewish concentration in the cigarette trade was the presence in Glasgow of Jacob Kramrisch, the Austrian born Jewish manager of the Stephen Mitchell and Sons branch of the Imperial Tobacco Company in Glasgow from 1888 ... there was no indigenous British cigarette workforce and thus the industry was open to entry from the Jewish immigrants arriving in the country. Starting with only a few foreign employees Kramrisch was able to build up the Glasgow undertaking to employ over 600 workers with the Jews, numbering 160 males and 50 females, concentrated in the manufacture of the best quality cigarettes." See Collins, *Second City Jewry*, p. 61.
197. Harvey Kaplan, "A Snapshot of Edinburgh Jewry in 1881," *Edinburgh Star*, 36 (2000).
198. Devine, *The Scottish Nation*, p. 520.
199. Edensor (ed.), *Moving Worlds*, p. 8.
200. David Feldman, *Englishmen and Jews: Social Relations and Political Culture 1840–1914* (London: Yale University Press, 1994), p. 143.
201. Hugh Armstrong Clegg, *A History of British Trade Unions Since 1889: Volume 1* (London: Clarendon, 1964), p. 348.
202. Maitles, "Attitudes to Jewish Immigration in the West of Scotland to 1905," p. 49.
203. *JC*, 17 July 1903, p. 25.
204. Collins, *Aspects of Scottish Jewry*, p. 41. The group comprised what would become the Edinburgh Independent Hebrew Congregation.
205. *JC*, 24 July 1903, p. 26.
206. Feldman, *Englishmen and Jews*, p. 143.
207. David Feldman and Gareth Stedman Jones (eds.), *Metropolis London: Histories and Representations Since 1800* (London: Routledge, 1989), p. 58.

208. Maitles, "Attitudes to Jewish Immigration in the West of Scotland to 1905," p. 50.
209. *Ibid.*, p. 20.
210. *The Outlook*, 74 (1903), p. 933.
211. Audrey, *Multiculturalism in Practice*, p. 17.
212. *JC*, 31 May 1907, p. 28.
213. *The Lancet*, "Report of *The Lancet*: Special Sanitary Commission on the Sweating System in Edinburgh," 23 (1888), p. 1261.
214. *Ibid.*
215. Clegg, *A History of British Trade Unions Since 1889*, p. 348.
216. *JC*, 21 Aug. 1898, p. 23.
217. Braber, *Jews in Glasgow*, p. 87.
218. *Ibid.*
219. Cowan, *Spring Remembered*, p. 20.
220. *Ibid.*, p. 18.
221. *The Times* Online, "Abraham Goldberg: Distinguished Physician Who Was a World Authority on Porphyria" http://www.timesonline.co.uk/tol/comment/obituaries/article2672637.ece [accessed 1 Feb. 2010].
222. William Kenefick. "Comparing the Jewish and Irish Communities in Twentieth Century Scotland," *Jewish Culture and History*, 9 (2007), 60–78 (p. 72).
223. See Collins, *Go and Learn: The International Story of Jews and Medicine in Scotland*.
224. Obituary of the Rev. Dr. Abraham Harris, *JC*, 20 Feb 1891, p. 13.
225. Harvey Kaplan, "A Snapshot of Edinburgh Jewry in 1881," *Edinburgh Star*, 36 (2000), p. 11.
226. Harvey Kaplan, *The Jews of Edinburgh in 1901*, Unpublished census analysis, Scottish Jewish Archives Centre.
227. *Ibid.*
228. *Ibid.*
229. Berman and Trickett, "Cultural Transitions in First-Generation Immigrants," p. 458.
230. Abel Phillips, *History of the Edinburgh Jewish Literary Society, 1888–1963* (Glasgow: The Michael Press, 1963), p. 3.
231. Edensor (ed.), *Moving Worlds*, p. 7.
232. Endelman, "German Jews in Victorian England: a Study in Drift and Defection," p. 63.
233. This will be discussed later in the book.
234. Israel Finestein, "Jewish Emancipationists in Victorian England: Self-Imposed Limits to Assimilation," in *Assimilation and Community: The Jews in Nineteenth-Century Europe*, ed. by Jonathan Frankel and Steven J. Zipperstein (Cambridge: Cambridge University Press, 1992), pp. 38–56 (p. 38).
235. Collins, *Second City Jewry*, p. 188.
236. Fry, *Edinburgh*, p. 299.
237. Website of James Gillespie's School www.jamesgillespies.edin.sch.uk/ourschool.html [accessed: 25/11/2010 at 3:16 p.m.].

238. *JC*, 19 July 1889, p. 12.
239. Emily won a bursary entitling her to twelve months of free education at the school in July 1887, together with a certificate of merit. See *JC*, 5 Aug. 1887, p. 5. Both Louis and Maurice won several bursaries and prizes during the time at the school. See for example, *JC*, 17 Aug. 1900, p. 17. Other pupils who experienced a high level of success were Jack Alexander, and Flora Hyman. Jack, who lived in South Clerk Street won a bursary at James Gillespie's in 1906, which enabled him to have free education at Daniel Stewart's College for two years along with a grant of £3 per year. He also won first prizes in drawing and writing, a certificate of merit in Latin, and a second prize in English. See *JC*, 27 July 1906, p. 38.
240. *JC*, 31 May 1889, p. 15.
241. Website of George Watson's College www.gwc.org.uk/OurSchool/historyofGWC/index.html [accessed: 25/11/2010 at 3:13 p.m.].
242. *JC*, 18 Feb. 1898, p. 24. Also in attendance was Dr. Marshall, head of the Royal High School.
243. Records of George Watson's Boys College were kindly supplied to me by Mrs. Fiona Hooper, Head Librarian of the College.
244. *Ibid*.
245. Edinburgh and Leith Post Office Directory 1873–73, p. 320.
246. *JC*, 7 Jan. 1910, p. 11.
247. *Ibid*.
248. George Watson's Boys College, Prospectus, 1886–87. This prospectus is held in the Library of George Watson's College.
249. Records of George Watson's Boys College.
250. Based on information contained within the prospectus for George Watson's Boys College, 1902–1903.
251. Fry, *Edinburgh*, p. 299.
252. *JC*, 25 July 1902, p. 30.
253. *JC*, 16 Aug. 1895, p. 11.
254. *JC*, 7 Aug. 1903, p. 24.
255. *JC*, 17 Aug. 1900, p. 17.
256. *JC*, 8 Jan. 1909, p. 33.
257. See *JC*, 12 March 1909, p. 32.
258. *JC*, 18 Oct. 1907, p. 28.
259. *JC*, 4 Sept. 1908, p. 24.
260. *JC*, 24 April 1908, p. 28.
261. *JC*, 9 March 1900, p. 28.
262. See *JC*, 15 March 1889, p. 15, and *JC*, 22nd March 1889, p. 14.
263. Phillips, *History of the Edinburgh Jewish Literary Society*, p. 3.
264. *JC*, 18 Oct. 1895, p. 17.
265. Phillips, *History of the Edinburgh Jewish Literary Society*, p. 3.
266. Phillips, *History of the Edinburgh Jewish Literary Society*, p. 4.
267. According to Phillips, the ban was removed in 1906 on the urging of Lazarus Lipetz. *Ibid*., p. 5.
268. *Scotsman*, 12 Feb. 1988.
269. Phillips, *History of the Edinburgh Jewish Literary Society*, p. 4.
270. *JC*, 8 Nov. 1889, p. 14.
271. *JC*, 13 March 1896, p. 22.
272. *JC*, 4 July 1902, p. 12.
273. *Ibid*., p. 13.
274. *JC*, 4 July 1902, p. 13.
275. See *JC*, 6 March 1891, p. 16, 9 Dec. 1892, p. 19, 5 Jan. 1894, p. 20.
276. *JC*, 20 March 1896, p. 23.
277. *JC*, 16 Feb. 1906, p. 34.
278. *JC*, 10 July 1908, p. 32.
279. *JC*, 4 July 1902, p. 13.
280. *Ibid*.
281. *JC*, 14 Feb. 1890, p. 11. That is not to say that the two organizations were antagonistic towards each other. Young men from each Society gathered together in an evening of games and social activities in April 1908, in what could be construed as an effort to overcome the differences between the leadership of both congregations. The evening was reported as an overwhelming success. See *JC*, 10th April 1908, p. 38.
282. *JC*, 28th March 1890, p. 16.
283. *JC*, 10 Jan. 1910, p. 17.
284. Collins, *Aspects of Scottish Jewry*, p. 45. The Society had been informally hosting songs and comic plays and other theatrical occasions since at least 1892. See *JC*, 18 Nov. 1892, p. 20.
285. *JC*, 8 Jan. 1909, p. 33, and 21 May 1909, p. 16.
286. Collins, *Aspects of Scottish Jewry*, p. 45.
287. See for example, *JC*, 29 March 1901, p. 27, and 22 Jan. 1904, p. 31.
288. *JC*, 24 Nov. 1905, p. 40.
289. John Springhall, *Youth, Empire, and Society: British Youth Movements, 1883–1940* (Trowbridge: Redwood, 1977), p. 42.
290. *JC*, 8 July 1910, p. 29.
291. Springhall, *Youth, Empire, and Society*, p. 42.

Chapter 4

1. *JC*, 14 June 1911, p. 22.
2. Howard Denton, *The Happy Land* (Edinburgh: Ramsay Head Press, 1991), p. 1.
3. *Ibid*., p. 2.
4. Denton, *The Happy Land*, p. 1.
5. *Ibid*.
6. *Ibid*., p. 26.
7. See *JC*, 6 Jan. 1911, p. 13, 20 Jan. 1911, p. 13 & 10 Feb. 1911, p. 14.
8. *JC* 13 Jan. 1911, p. 15 & 26 May 1911, p. 35.

9. *JC*, 15 March 1912, p. 46.
10. See *JC* 7 Feb. 1913, p. 28, 18 July 1913, p. 22, 28 Nov. 1913, p. 29, 9 Jan. 1914, p. 14 & 27 Feb. 1914, p. 26.
11. *JC*, 2 June 1911, p. 14.
12. *JC*, 16 June 1911, p. 15.
13. *Lewis Rifkind* (Letchworth, Garden City Press, 1939). The book is held by the Scottish Jewish Archives Centre.
14. *JC*, 13 Jan. 1911, p. 15.
15. *JC*, 26 Jan 1912, p. 30.
16. Papers of the Edinburgh Jewish Literary Society, National Library of Scotland: ACC 10264.
17. *JC*, 13 Feb. 1913, p. 28.
18. *JC*, 10 Jan. 1912, 1913, p. 28.
19. *JC*, 9 Jan. 1914, p. 24.
20. Denton, *The Happy Land*, p. 10.
21. *JC*, 14 July, 1911, p. 28.
22. *Scotsman*, 17 July, 1911, p. 7.
23. Quoted in *JC*, 1 Sept. 1911, p. 10
24. Denton, *The Happy Land*, p. 10.
25. *Ibid*.
26. *Ibid.*, p. 30.
27. *Ibid*.
28. *JC*, 1 Sept. 1911, p. 15& p. 27.
29. *JC*, 14 July, 1911, p. 22.
30. *JC*, 3 Feb. 1911, p. 14.
31. *JC*, 10 Feb. 1911, p. 14.
32. *JC*, 27 Oct. 1911, p. 24.
33. *JC*, 14 Oct. 1910, p. 2.
34. Denton, *The Happy Land*, p. 29.
35. *Ibid.*, p. 36 & p. 39.
36. *JC*, 14 July, 1911, p. 28.
37. *JC*, 6 Oct. 1911, p. 17.
38. *JC*, 15 Nov. 1912, p. 29. This number should be compared with the fact that the North Richmond Street congregation had approximately 150 members during the same time period—see *JC*, 10 Feb. 1911, p. 16.
39. *JC*, 9 Aug. 1912, p. 21.
40. *JC*, 17 July, 1914, p. 24.
41. *JC*, 31 July, 1914, p. 22.
42. See Chapter 2, "The Jewish Charitable Effort in Edinburgh."
43. *JC*, 7 July, 1911, p. 16.
44. *JC*, 3 March, 1911, p. 14
45. Edinburgh Jewish Medical Mission Report for the Year 1913, NAS: IRS21/1078.
46. *Ibid*.
47. *JC*, 3 March, 1911, p. 14.
48. *JC*, 31 March, 1911, p. 21.
49. Collins, *Aspects of Scottish Jewry*, p. 42.
50. *JC*, 10 Jan, 1913, p. 28.
51. Maitles, "Jewish Trade Unionists in Glasgow," p. 59.
52. Denton, *The Happy Land*, p. 77.
53. *JC*, 3 July, 1914, p. 27.
54. Laqueur, *The History of Zionism*, p. 291.
55. Simon Dubnow, *Nationalism and History: Essays on Old and New Judaism* (Philadelphia, Meridian, 1961), p. 373.
56. Paul Keleman, "In the Name of Socialism: Zionism and European Social Democracy in the Inter-War Years," *International Review of Social History* 41 (1996), 331–350 (p. 333).
57. *JC*, 9 June, 1911, p. 17.
58. *JC*, 9 June, 1911, p. 17.
59. See *JC*, 9 June, 1911, p. 17. Rifkind is not named as an attendee.
60. *Lewis Rifkind Memorial Book*.
61. *JC*, 9 Jan. 1914, p. 24.
62. *JC*, 11 Feb. 1916, p. 13.
63. Fry, *Edinburgh*, p. 301.
64. *JC*, 22 Nov. 1912, p. 28.
65. *Ibid*.
66. Leigh Rayment's Historical List of MPs—Constituencies beginning with "E" (part 1) http://www.leighrayment.com/commons/Ecommons1.htm [accessed: 21/11/11 at 3:21 p.m.].
67. Quoted in the *JC*, 21 Aug. 1914, p. 13.
68. *JC*, 21 Aug. 1914, p. 13.
69. *Ibid*.
70. David Cesarani, "An Embattled Minority: The Jews in Britain During the First World War," in Tony Kushner and Kenneth Lunn (eds.), *The Politics of Marginality: Race, the Radical Right and Minorities in Twentieth Century Britain* (London: Frank Cass, 1990), p. 65.
71. Stefan Manz, "'Our sworn, subtle, savage, implacable, and perfidious foe!'—Germanophobia and Spy-Fever in Scotland, 1914–1918," in Joachim Fischer, Pól Ó Dochartaigh and Helen Kelly-Holmes (eds.). *Irish-German Studies*, 1 (2004), 28–37 (p. 28).
72. National Archives Reference HO 144/1432/295090. Naturalization records reveal that during the same period naturalization certificates were issued to twelve Germans, six Italians, two Swedes, two Dutchmen, two Swiss, two Danes, one Spaniard, one Romanian, and one Greek living in the city of Edinburgh. Based on surnames and country of origins, approx. 265 Jews, resident in Edinburgh, were issued with naturalization certificates between the years 1879 and 1934.
73. Louis Saipe, *A Century of Care: The History of the Leeds Jewish Welfare Board, 1878–1978* (Leeds: J. Jackman and Co., 1978), p. 24.
74. These trades also suffered most in Leeds. See *Ibid*.
75. *JC*, 4 Sept. 1914, p. 15.
76. *JC*, 4 Sept. 1914, p. 15.
77. *JC*, 13 Nov. 1914, p. 22.
78. *Ibid*.
79. *JC*, 5 Feb. 1915, p. 25.
80. See *JC*, 7 May 1915, p. 14, and 11 June 1915, p. 17. See also, Collins, *Aspects of Scottish Jewry*, p. 44.

81. Manz, "Germanophobia and Spy-Fever in Scotland," p. 35.
82. *Ibid.*, p. 16.
83. Charles Walker, *Wakefield: Its Times and Peoples* (Wakefield: New Millennium, 2000), p. 146.
84. Walker, *Wakefield: Its Times and Peoples*, p. 147.
85. *JC*, 23 July, 1915, p. 18.
86. *JC*, 6 Aug. 1915, p. 16.
87. *Ibid.*
88. *JC*, 23 July, 1915, p. 18.
89. *JC*, 13 Aug. 1915, p. 15.
90. Stefan Manz, "Civilian Internment in Scotland During the First World War," in Richard Dove (ed.) *Totally Un-English? Britain's Internment of "Enemy Aliens" During the Two World Wars* (The Yearbook of the Research Centre for German and Austrian Exile Studies), 7 (2005), 83–100 (p. 87).
91. *Ibid.*, p. 88. Depression and mental illness were also common among inmates.
92. *JC*, 5 Jan. 1900, p. 11.
93. *JC*, 17 Jan. 1902, p. 14. Christiaan De Wet, Boer General and future President of the Orange Free State.
94. *JC*, 20 June, 1902, p. 12.
95. *JC*, 11 Sept. 1914, p. 10.
96. The *JC* undertook to attempt to record every Jew serving with the armed forces during the Great War. See *JC*, 16 Oct, 1914, p. 13, & 13 Nov. 1914, p. 12–14. For an explanation of why the *JC* engaged in this effort, see Cesarani, *The Jewish Chronicle and Anglo-Jewry, 1841–1991*.
97. *Ibid.*
98. *JC*, 11 Sept. 1914, p. 14.
99. See, *JC*, 27 Nov. 1914, p. 26.
100. *JC*, 6 Aug. 1915, p. 16.
101. Quoted in *JC*, 29 Oct. 1915, p. 18.
102. *JC*, 15 June 1934, p. 40.
103. *JC*, 29 Jan. 1915, p. 8.
104. NAS: HH31/31/1: First World War Charities: Jewish Medical Mission.
105. *JC*, 4 Feb. 1916, p. 7.
106. *JC*, 4 Feb. 1916, p. 7.
107. *JC*, 11 Feb. 1916, p. 8.
108. *Ibid.*, p. 13.
109. *Ibid.*
110. *JC*, 25 Feb. 1916, p. 13.
111. Cesarani states that Greenberg's "devotion to Jewish nationalism was driven as much by the belief that it was vital to fight assimilation as by the need to create a Jewish state." See Cesarani, *The Jewish Chronicle and Anglo-Jewry*, p. 106.
112. NAS: HH31/31/1: First World War Charities: Jewish Medical Mission.
113. *Ibid.*, Secretary for Scotland's Decision.
114. Shukman, *War or Revolution: Russian Jews and Conscription in Britain 1917*, p. 3.
115. Shukman, *War or Revolution: Russian Jews and Conscription in Britain 1917*, p. 4.
116. *Ibid.*
117. *JC*, 14 Jan. 1916, p. 7.
118. Cissie Eppel (ed.), *Somewhere in France: Letters Home, Benjamin Eppel's 1914-18 War* (British Columbia: Cissie Eppel, 2010), entry: 5 April 1916. The patriotism and pride of serving Jews is prominent in Benjamin letters home. In a letter to his mother in late April, Benjamin referred to the Easter Rising in Ireland when he asked, "What do you think of the Dublin riots? Isn't it awful with us doing our bit for them? I hope they blow the city to bits." See entry: 29 April 1916.
119. *The Observer*, 7 April 1916, p. 2.
120. Eppel, *Somewhere in France*, entry: 26 June 1916.
121. See entries: 5 July, 1916, 27 Dec. 1916, and 24 April 1917.
122. See NAS: HH30/2/4/43 Jack Weinschel, HH30/2/4/38 Hyman Phillips, HH30/5/50 Berks Lyons, HH30/2/5/13 Louis Grant Gordon, HH30/2/4/49 Joseph Hyams, HH30/2/6/34 Louis Cohen, HH30/2/6/46 Bernard Goldstein, HH30/2/1/23 Samuel Goldstein, HH30/2/3/37 Myer Hyman Polivasky, HH30/1/4/8 David Holliday, HH30/2/6/42 Harry Brown, HH30/2/6/45 Morris Shulfine, HH30/2/6/49 David Hyman, HH30/2/7/14 Harris Simon, HH30/5/4/18 Jacob Napthali Wedeclefsky, HH30/5/1/12 David Walker Levy, HH30/5/4/17 Emanuel Hyams, HH30/4/8/25 Joseph Freedman, HH30/3/5/13 Harry Joel Eprile, HH30/3/4/23 Sydney Youde, HH30/3/3/21 Manuel Berman, HH30/3/3/9 Jacob Bernstein, HH30/3/3/8 Jacob Meyer Baker, HH30/3/1/19 Simon Harris, HH30/3/1/16 Hyman Levinson, HH30/2/6/28 Myer Goldberg, HH30/2/6/32 Jacob Lucas, HH30/2/5/47 George Pass, HH30/2/6/11 Joseph Levitt, HH30/2/2/35 Lewis Rifkind, HH30/2/1/31 Harry Ockrent, HH30/2/4/39 Bernard Factor, HH30/2/2/36 Abel Bernard Freeman, HH30/4/9/31 George Spark.
123. HH30/2/4/38 Hyman Phillips.
124. See for example, HH30/2/4/43 Jack Weinschel, HH30/2/6/34 Louis Cohen, HH30/2/6/46 Bernard Bernstein, HH30/2/3/37 Myer Hyman Poliwansky, HH30/2/7/14 Harris Simon, HH30/3/5/13 Harry Eprile, HH30/3/3/9 Jacob Bernstein.
125. See NAS: HH30/2/6/45 Morris Shulfine.
126. HH30/3/1/19 Simon Harris.
127. *Ibid.*
128. See NAS: HH30/2/5/47 George Pass, and HH30/2/6/42 Harry Brown. See also letter from the Ministry of Food to A. Phillips, President of the Edinburgh Hebrew Congregation, dated 16 Oct. 1918, attached to Minute Book of

the Edinburgh Hebrew Congregation 1918–1924.
129. HH30/2/2/35 Lewis Rifkind.
130. HH30/2/2/36 Abel Bernard Freeman. However, Harry Ockrent declared that his objection was his neutral stance on the conflict. He declared that, "This is my unalterable position and no power on earth can compell [sic] me to abandon my neutrality." HH30/2/1/31 Harry Ockrent
131. *JC*, 14 Jan. 1916, p. 7.
132. Cesarani, *The Jewish Chronicle and Anglo-Jewry*, p. 119.
133. NAS: HH30/2/2/36 Abel Bernard Freeman.
134. NAS: HH30/5/4/18 Jacob Napthali Wedeclefsky.
135. NAS: HH30/5/4/18 Jacob Napthali Wedeclefsky.
136. First World War: Conscientious Objectors and Exemptions from Service, Military Records Information 16, Website of the National Archives: http://www.nationalarchives.gov.uk/catalogue/rdleaflet.asp?sLeafletID=25 [accessed: 08/03/2010 at 3:23 p.m.].
137. *Ibid.*
138. NAS: JC26/1917/48 Trial Papers Relating to Joseph Levinson.
139. Shukman, *War or Revolution*, p. ix.
140. Edensor (ed.), *Moving Worlds*, p. 7.
141. Shukman, *War or Revolution*, p. 13.
142. Edensor (ed.), *Moving Worlds*, p. 6.
143. Shukman, *War or Revolution*, p. 13.
144. *Ibid.*, p. x.
145. See Minute Book of the Edinburgh Hebrew Congregation 1922.
146. NAS Reference: HH30/3/3/21 Manuel Berman.
147. NAS Reference: HH30/2/1/23 Samuel Goldstein.
148. Minute Book of the Edinburgh Hebrew Congregation, 1918. The worshippers at Roxburgh Place were largely foreign-born, resulting in the need for the rules of the new Council of the Edinburgh Hebrew Congregation to be printed in Yiddish as well as English. See MOEHC, 29 Sept. 1918.

Chapter 5

1. Letter from Asher Levinson to Rabbi Dr. Salis Daiches, 16 Feb 1944. PSD.
2. MOEHC, 8 Dec. 1918. See also letter from Edinburgh Hebrew Congregation to Rabbi Dr. Salis Daiches, 21 Oct. 1918 (Box Ten), PSD.
3. Michael T.R.B. Turnbull, "Daiches, Salis (1880–1945)," *Oxford Dictionary of National Biography* (Oxford: Oxford University Press, 2004). See also, BBC Memo, Control Room Edinburgh, Wednesday 2 May 1945, PSD. However, David Daiches states in *Two Worlds* that his father's birth certificate was dated 10th March 1881. See Daiches, *Two Worlds*, p. 82.
4. Michael T.R.B. Turnbull, "Daiches, Salis (1880–1945)," *Oxford Dictionary of National Biography* (Oxford: Oxford University Press, 2004).
5. *Ibid.*
6. Levy, *History of the Sunderland Jewish Community*, p. 225–6.
7. Pamphlet on "Service of Induction of Rabbi Dr. Salis Daiches." 9 Feb. 1919. PSD.
8. MOEHC, 8 Dec. 1918.
9. Daiches, *Two Worlds*, p. 97. Daiches adds that while Graham Street's congregation was growing at this time, the congregation at Roxburgh Place was dwindling.
10. *Ibid.*
11. Daiches, *Two Worlds*, p. 98.
12. Letter from Chief Rabbi Joseph Hertz to Rabbi Dr. Salis Daiches dated 12 Dec. 1918, in PSD (Box 10). Daiches also seems to have been unhappy with the original salary offer. On 21 Oct. 1918, he was offered £300 per annum; by 11 Dec. this had been revised to £350 per annum, plus a £25 removal expenses grant.
13. Levy, *History of the Sunderland Jewish Community*, p. 137. Ironically, while one of Salis Daiches' professed aims was to foster unity in Edinburgh, Levy states that "Within a few months of his leaving [Sunderland], trouble began to brew." See Levy, *History of the Sunderland Jewish Community*, p. 139.
14. Pamphlet on "Service of Induction of Rabbi Dr. Salis Daiches." 9 Feb. 1919. PSD. See also Daiches, *Two Worlds*, p. 74. Rabbi Daiches gave a separate inaugural address at Roxburgh Place for the Central *Shul* on 1 March 1919. See MOEHC, Leaflet 20 Feb. 1919.
15. *JC*, 14 July 1922, p. 16.
16. *Ibid.*
17. Daiches, *Two Worlds*, p. 100. David Daiches states that his father was eager to urge the community towards further integration with Scottish society, and to "make himself a real leader of his people and to build up a conception of the Jew in Scotland as the respected member of an important element in a pluralistic culture."
18. *Ibid.*, p. 98.
19. *JC*, 18 May 1917, p. 13.
20. Daiches, *Two Worlds*, p. 98.
21. *JC*, 12 Jan. 1924, p. 27.
22. First Division, March 18 1924, Alexander Levison v Salis Daiches, Closed Record, p. 8. Court Documents, PSD.
23. Daiches, *Two Worlds*, p. 97.

24. *Ibid.*
25. First Division, March 18 1924, Alexander Levison v Salis Daiches, Closed Record, p. 7. Court Documents, PSD.
26. Document recording meeting between the synagogues to discuss unification, Oct. 1919. PSD.
27. *Ibid.*
28. *JC*, 12 March 1920, p. 34.
29. First Division, March 18 1924, Alexander Levison v Salis Daiches, Closed Record, p. 7. Court Documents, PSD.
30. Letter from Abel Phillips to Rabbi Dr. Salis Daiches, dated 29 March 1920. PSD.
31. Letter from Isaac Hyman, Honourary Secretary of the Edinburgh Independent Hebrew Congregation, to Joseph Hertz, Chief Rabbi, dated 13 March 1922. PSD.
32. *JC*, 11 May 1917, p. 22.
33. *Ibid.*
34. Daiches, *Two Worlds*, p. 100. See also First Division, June 18 1924, Levison v. Daiches, Closed Record. PSD.
35. *Ibid.*
36. Letter from A. Feldman to the Rev. M. Rosenbaum (Office of the Chief Rabbi) regarding the opinion of Rabbi Rabinowitz's opinion on the founding of the IEHC. Dated 30 March 1922. PSD.
37. Letter from Rabbi Dr. Salis Daiches to Office of the Chief Rabbi, 8 March 1922. PSD.
38. Adler Report on Jewish Education, MOEHC, Book 1921–1925.
39. *Ibid.*
40. *JC*, 2 June 1922, p. 21. The article stated that the Rev. Nahum Levison had in the past acted as an agent in Edinburgh for a London-based missionary organization, and that, Alexander Levison was "holding his Hebrew class within two minutes walk of the place where is brother, Sir Leon Levison, was carrying on a Medical Mission to the Jews."
41. *Ibid.*
42. Daiches, *Two Worlds*, p. 101.
43. Letter from L.J. Greenberg to Rabbi Daiches, dated 2 May 1923. PSD.
44. First Division, March 18 1924, Alexander Levison v Salis Daiches, Closed Record, pp. 19–20. Court Documents, PSD.
45. Letter from the Chief Rabbi, J.H. Hertz to Rabbi Daiches, 1 Aug. 1923. PSD.
46. Letter from R. Theophilus to Messrs. Soames, Edwards and Jones, Solicitors to Rabbi Daiches. PSD.
47. Letter from L.J. Greenberg to Rabbi Daiches, 24 Jan. 1924. PSD.
48. First Division, 18 June 1924, Closed Record. Minute for Pursuer: Levison v JC. PSD.
49. Letter from L.J. Greenberg to Rabbi Daiches dated 3 Aug. 1923. PSD.
50. Daiches, *Two Worlds*, p. 100.
51. *Ibid.*, p. 101.
52. Letter from L.J. Greenberg to Rabbi Daiches, 11 Jan. 1924. PSD.
53. Letter from Thomas Connolly, J & F Solicitors to Rabbi Daiches. PSD.
54. Daiches, *Two Worlds*, p. 101.
55. *Ibid.*, p. 102.
56. *JC*, 7 Nov. 1924, p. 5. See also Daiches, *Two Worlds*, p. 103.
57. Collins, *Aspects of Scottish Jewry*, p. 44.
58. Sharon Gewirtz, "Anglo-Jewish Responses to Nazi Germany 1933–39: The Anti-Nazi Boycott and the Board of Deputies of British Jews," *Journal of Contemporary History*, 26 (1991), 255–276 (p. 257).
59. Daiches, *Two Worlds*, p. 103.
60. *JC*, 23 Feb. 1917, p. 11.
61. *Ibid.*
62. See *JC*, 15 March 1918, p. 21.
63. Quoted in *JC*, 27 May 1921, p. 36.
64. *JC*, 24 Jan. 1919, p. 21.
65. See for example, *JC*, 8 March 1918, p. 12.
66. Levison, *Christian and Jew*, p. 145.
67. There was also considerable pressure put on Daiches by the Jewish press, particularly the *JC*, to tackle missionary activity in Edinburgh. Even prior to his inauguration as Rabbi, the *JC* argued that Daiches would find "a veritable Aegean stable of chicanery and bribery with missionary activity animating it all." Abel Phillips wrote complaining to the editor that this was alarmist, and that "if there is an Aegean stable in Edinburgh...the stable will be found to contain the 3,000 oxen, not of missionary influence but of an alarming neglect of the Jewish education of the children, an indifference to matters Jewish—individually; and of deplorable disorganization burdened by a lack of recognition of public duty—communally." Thus, feeling in Edinburgh seems to have been that the *JC*, in exaggerating the threat of the missions, was contributing to a neglect of the community's more pressing problems. See *JC*, 13 Dec. 1918, p. 6 & 20 Dec. 1918, p. 26.
68. *JC*, 6 Aug. 1920, p. 6.
69. *JC*, 6 Aug. 1920, p. 6.
70. *The Scotsman*, 19 Nov. 1920, p. 9.
71. *Ibid.*
72. *Ibid.*
73. *Ibid.*
74. *Ibid.*
75. See for example, *The Scotsman*, 7 June 1921, p. 6.
76. *The Scotsman*, 19 Feb. 1920, p. 9.
77. Levison, *Christian and Jews*, p. 150.
78. *Ibid.*, p. 148.
79. *JC*, 27 May 1921, p. 36.

80. In 1921, John Hall, Convener of the Jewish Mission Committee, claimed that an appeal in 1920 for the relief of impoverished Jews in Vienna had raised £18,000 in Scotland alone. See *Scotsman*, 3 June 1921, p. 8.
81. *Scotsman*, 3 June 1921, p. 8.
82. *JC*, 21 Dec. 1923, p. 16.
83. *Ibid.*
84. *JC*, 4 Jan. 1924, p. 23.
85. *JC*, 12 Jan. 1924, p. 11.
86. Quoted in *JC*, 8 June 1923, p. 30.
87. *JC*, 25 Jan. 1924, p. 9.
88. *JC*, 7 March 1924, p. 9.
89. *JC*, 7 March 1924, p. 9.
90. Quoted in *JC*, 15 June 1928, p. 23.
91. *JC*, 27 July 1928, p. 9.
92. *JC*, 1 March 1929, p. 5.
93. *Ibid.*
94. *Scotsman*, 3 June 1921, p. 8.
95. *JC*, 9 June 1922, p. 24.
96. *JC*, 13 April 1923, p. 15.
97. *JC*, 18 May 1923, p. 29.
98. See for example, *JC*, 20 Feb. 1925, p. 38. It was alleged at that years General Assembly that the Jews' "whole scheme of belief and practice leads to unreality, and that in turn produces open neglect."
99. *JC*, 21 Aug. 1925, p. 23. Frederick Levison's description of Prof. Webster as, "a man who never minced words nor tried to mollify," appears to be something of an understatement in light of some of the comments, such as the above, attributed to the man.
100. *Ibid.*, p. 149.
101. See *JC*, 24 Dec. 1926, p. 26 & 22 July 1927, p. 30.
102. *JC*, 16 Dec. 1921, p. 18.
103. Quoted in *JC*, 28 Sept. 1923, p. 11.
104. *JC*, 15 Aug. 1924, p. 12.
105. *JC*, 30 May 1930, p. 33.
106. Letter from Edinburgh Hebrew Congregation to Rabbi Dr. Salis Daiches, 17 March 1936. PSD.
107. Daiches, *Two Worlds*, p. 94.
108. Quoted in *JC*, 12 Sept. 1924, p. 13, see also 19 Sept. 1924, p. 20.
109. Geoffrey Alderman, *Controversy and Crisis: Studies in the History of the Jews in Modern Britain* (Brighton: Academic Studies Press, 2008), p. 123.
110. Alderman, *Controversy and Crisis*, p. 123. See also, *JC*, 28 Oct. 1927, p. 24.
111. Alderman, *Controversy and Crisis*, p. 124.
112. Letter from the *Beth Din* contained in the Minutes Book of the Edinburgh Hebrew Congregation for 1930–1933.
113. Daiches, *Two Worlds*, p. 93.
114. *JC*, 25 Jan. 1929, p. 28.
115. The lobbyists were aided in their efforts by George Buchanan, Independent Labour M.P. for Glasgow. See *JC*, 15 Feb. 1929, p. 18.
116. Quoted in *JC*, 25 Nov. 1921, p. 27.
117. *JC*, 29 July 1921, p. 25.
118. Letter from the Colonial Office to the Edinburgh Zionist Association, 27 Feb. 1930. PSD.
119. Letter from the Colonial Office to the Edinburgh Zionist Association, 27 Feb. 1930. PSD.
120. *Ibid.*
121. *Ibid.* In Sept. 1930 Shiels sailed for his visit to Palestine. In an example of the pivotal role played by Edinburgh politicians in relation to Palestine during this period, Shiels was accompanied by George Mathers—M.P. for West Edinburgh. See *JC*, 26 Sept. 1930, p. 18.
122. Minutes Book of the Edinburgh Zionist Association (hereafter MEZA), 4 May 1930, Scottish Jewish Archives Centre. Daiches had been commenting on weak membership levels since at least 1921. However, poor support was apparently not some peculiar to Edinburgh, and it seems to have been declining among British Jews for some time during the 1920s. An article in the *JC* in Jan. 1922 quotes Daiches as saying "the small number of British delegates at the last Zionist Congress demonstrated the comparative lukewarmness of the bulk of the Jews of this country towards the Zionist ideal." See *JC*, 6 Jan. 1922, p. 36.
123. MEZA, 22 Oct. 1930.
124. MEZA, 4 May 1930.
125. MEZA, 29 Oct. 1930.
126. MEZA, 22 Oct. 1930.
127. *JC*, 27 Feb. 1924, p. 29, and 14 March 1930, p. 31.
128. *JC*, 30 Dec. 1921, p. 9.
129. See Levison, *Christian and Jew*, p. 149.
130. *JC*, 13 Jan. 1922, p. 24.
131. See *JC*, 10 Feb. 1922, p. 17.
132. Levison, *Christian and Jew*, p. 149.
133. Henry Rothfield vs. North British Railway Company (1918), NAS: CS252/1111.
134. *Ibid.* See also Michael Boella and Alan Pannett, *Principles of Hospitality Law* (London: Thomson, 1999), p. 154.
135. *JC*, 4 July 1919, p. 36. The award was revoked in 1920 when the proprietors of the hotel changed their statement to say that Rothfield had been excluded because he was soliciting business from other guests and had caused great disruption during his previous stays, annoying several British Army officers who had requested his exclusion. It was also revealed that Rothfield was a flamboyant character who had featured in numerous court cases in Scotland in relation to his business methods. See for example, Rothfield vs. James McCall (1919) NAS: CS253/2306 and Rothfield vs. Hyman

Cohen (1919) NAS: CS251/1513. See also Boella and Pannett, *Principles of Hospitality Law*, p. 154.
136. Collins, *Second City Jewry*, p. 167.
137. *JC*, 4 Nov. 1927, p. 18.
138. Ben Braber, "The Trial of Oscar Slater (1909) and Anti-Jewish Prejudices in Edwardian Glasgow," *History*, 88 (2003), p. 18 http://onlinelibrary.wiley.com/doi/10.1111/1468-229X.00262/pdf [accessed 11/11/11 at 9:59].
139. Cesarani, *The Jewish Chronicle and Anglo-Jewry*, p. 110.
140. Michael Fry, *Edinburgh*, p. 333.
141. *Ibid*.
142. Keir (ed.), *The Third Statistical Account of Scotland: Edinburgh*, p. 99.
143. *JC*, 15 Feb. 1924, p. 20.
144. *Ibid*.
145. Graham Walker, "Varieties of Scottish Protestant Identity," in T.M. Devine and Richard J. Finlay (eds.), *Scotland in the 20th Century* (Edinburgh: Edinburgh University Press: 1996), p. 260.
146. Tom Gallagher, *Glasgow: The Uneasy Peace—Religious Tension in Modern Scotland* (Manchester: Manchester University Press, 1987), p. 150. However, Ratcliffe later adopted Fascism following a visit to Nazi Germany, and by 1940 was a rabid and notorious anti-Semite.
147. Gallagher, *Glasgow: The Uneasy Peace*, p. 165.
148. *Jewish Echo*, 2 March 1928, p. 11.
149. Egal Feldman, *Catholics and Jews in 20th Century America* (Illinois: University of Illinois Press, 2001), p. 47.
150. Robert Miles and Anne Dunlop, "Racism in Britain: The Scottish Dimension," in Peter Jackson (ed.) *Race and Racism: Essays in Social Geography* (London: Allen and Unwin, 2005), p. 107. As a benchmark of popular support for Cormack, it is worth noting that he was elected to Edinburgh Town Council in 1934, and held the seat until 1962. See Fry, *Edinburgh*, p. 347.
151. "Why Scotland Has Never Hated Jews … We Were Too Busy Hating Each Other," *Sunday Herald*, 17 Oct. 2004.
152. *Edinburgh Evening Dispatch*, 8 Dec. 1924.
153. *Ibid*.
154. *JC*, 30 Jan. 1920, p. 32.
155. Quoted in *JC*, 2 Nov. 1922, p. 33.
156. Quoted in *JC*, 26 Oct. 1923, p. 24.
157. *JC*, 14 July 1922, p. 18.
158. *JC*, 14 July 1922, p. 18. In an interesting note on Masonic relations in Edinburgh, Howard Denton recalls that "The only time I got to mix with Scottish children was when Father, a staunch Freemason of the Solomon Lodge in Duncan Street, took us to the annual party." See Denton, *The Happy Land*, p. 26.

159. *Ibid*.
160. *JC*, 11 Nov. 1927, p. 13. However, it is clear from numerous autobiographical accounts that instances of epithets being leveled at Jews were not unheard of. Evelyn Cohen recalls that in Glasgow children would ask one another if they were "a Billy, a Dan, or an old tin can. A Billy was a Protestant, a Dan was a Catholic. And an old tin can was a Jew…. Vaguely, we always knew of someone who got beaten up by the gangs." See Evelyn Cohen, *Spring Remembered*, p. 101.
161. Rabbi Salis Daiches, "The Fellowship of Jews and Christians Movement in Scotland," *Bulletin of the Society of Jews and Christians*, Dec. 1942. PSD.
162. Quoted in *JC*, 1 June 1923, p. 15.
163. *JC*, 12 Sept. 1919, p. 15.
164. *JC*, 4 March 1921, p. 12.
165. *JC*, 23 Dec. 1921, p. 32.
166. *JC*, 17 March 1922, p. 32.
167. *JC*, 11 Nov. 1927, p. 30.
168. Spark, *Curriculum Vitae*, p. 21.
169. Devine, *The Scottish Nation*, p. 521.
170. Denton, *The Happy Land*, p. 30.
171. Ben Braber, *Jews in Glasgow*, p. 67.
172. Collins, *Aspects of Scottish Jewry*, p. 27.
173. *Jewish Echo*, 17 Aug. 1928, p. 6.
174. MOEHC, 29 April 1925.
175. *JC*, 24 March 1922, p. 32.
176. *JC*, 26 June 1931, p. 26.
177. *JC*, 16 Oct. 1931, p. 26.
178. Quoted in Collins, *Aspects of Scottish Jewry*, p. 45.
179. *Ibid*., p. 48.
180. *Jewish Echo*, Clipping of unknown date, PSD.
181. *Ibid*.
182. *JC*, 22 March 1929, p. 21.
183. *JC*, 13 June 1930, p. 21.
184. *JC*, 4 July 1930, p. 26.
185. *JC*, 16 Sept. 1932, p. 24.
186. *JC*, 10 Dec. 1920, p. 28.
187. *Scotsman*, 19 Aug. 2006.
188. Jack Alexander, *McCraes Battalion: The Story of the 16th Royal Scots* (Edinburgh: Mainstream Publishing, 2003), p. 60.
189. *Ibid*.
190. *JC*, 10 Dec.1920, p. 28.
191. *Scotsman*, 19 Aug. 2006.
192. *Ibid*.
193. *JC*, 14 March 1930, p. 25.
194. *Ibid*.
195. *JC*, 12 Nov. 1926, p. 31.
196. *JC*, 30 Sept. 1927, p. 28.
197. *JC*, 30 Nov. 1928, p. 6. See also *JC*, 21 June 1929, p. 30.
198. *JC*, 14 March 1930, p. 25.
199. *Ibid*.
200. *JC*, 15 May 1931, p. 6.

Chapter 6

1. Letter from the Rev. Hugh Gordon Ross, Victoria Street Church, Dundee, to Rabbi Dr. Salis Daiches, 21 Sept. 1934. PSD.
2. *JC*, 17 Feb. 1933, p. 8. It should be stated that Rabbi Daiches had, for several years, been urging the Chief Rabbi in London to create "District Rabbinates" throughout Britain and the Empire, a move which would see him formally acknowledged as Chief Rabbi of Scotland. As early as July 1919, a movement had begun in Glasgow to support the creation of a District Rabbinate for Scotland. See for example, PSD, letter from Mr. D. Kissenisky to Chief Rabbi, Dr. J.H. Hertz, 11 July 1919. Hertz believed that the Jewish community was not "ripe for it," and that any move in that direction would be slow, requiring at least "a Rabbinate Conference and 18 months of intensive differences of opinion." See letter from Chief Rabbi J.H. Hertz to Rabbi Daiches dated 21 July1919, PSD. Enthusiasm for the idea, as featured in the *JC*, remained high for a few years before fading into obscurity.
3. See for example, MOEHC, 3 Sept. 1933. See also, *JC*, 20 Oct. 1933, p. 36, *JC*, 3 Nov. 1933, p. 31, *JC*, 28 Dec. 1934, p. 22.
4. MOEHC, 24 Feb. 1935.
5. Sharon Gewirtz, "Anglo-Jewish Responses to Nazi Germany 1933–39," p. 258.
6. *Scotsman*, 27 March 1933, p. 9.
7. *Ibid.*
8. *Ibid.*
9. See for example, *Scotsman*, 21 April 1933, p. 11. One Otto Schlapp, a native of Germany and the first Professor of German at Edinburgh University, responded to Rabbi Daiches' protests in the pages of *Scotsman* in April 1933. Schlapp argued that "many peasant proprietors and aristocratic landowners" in German provinces, specifically Alsace and Hesse, had been "ruined by Jewish usurers." Schlapp continued to argue that the immigration of large numbers of Eastern Jews had "brought to a head the problem of Jews in Germany." Although he held dubious opinions about Jews, Schlapp stated that he was not a supporter of the Nazi regime.
10. *Scotsman*, 31 July 1933, p. 7.
11. *Scotsman*, 27 Oct. 1933, p. 6. See also diary of Rabbi Dr. Salis Daiches (1938). PSD.
12. Alderman, *The Jewish Community in British Politics*, p. 121.
13. Gewirtz, "Anglo-Jewish Responses to Nazi Germany 1933–39," p. 259 Here Laski expressed the belief that the "excesses" of the new government were the result of left-wing elements, more specifically, the SA. This belief was not entirely without foundation. Thomas Grant states that "The agenda of the SA was not well-defined, but, as time wore on, it became apparent that the SA did possess an agenda of its own, distinct from that of the Nazi movement as a whole. Insofar as the SA concerned itself with influencing the composition of Nazi ideology, the SA political program aimed to radicalize the NSDAP. Correspondingly, the politics of the SA was more left wing than that of the party Proper. This was noted by contemporaries and has been documented since." See Thomas D. Grant, *Stormtroopers and Crisis in the Nazi Movement: Activism, Ideology and Dissolution* (London: Routledge, 2004), p. 89.
14. *Ibid.*, p. 263.
15. *Ibid.*, p. 256.
16. Gewirtz, "Anglo-Jewish Responses to Nazi Germany 1933–39," p. 258.
17. Alderman, *The Jewish Community in British Politics*, p. 121. See also Gewirtz, "Anglo-Jewish Responses to Nazi Germany 1933–39," p. 259–60.
18. Gewirtz, "Anglo-Jewish Responses to Nazi Germany 1933–39," p. 260–61.
19. Alderman, *The Jewish Community in British Politics*, p. 121. Laski's personal views on this subject, and how these views impacted on Laski's own local Jewish community in Manchester, are thoroughly explored in Williams, *Jews and Other Foreigners*, p. 12.
20. MOEHC, 19 Oct. 1933.
21. *Ibid.*
22. *JC*, 29 Feb. 1933, p. 16.
23. MOEHC, 25 May 1933.
24. MOEHC, 25 May 1933. See also poster for the event in the papers of Rabbi Dr. Salis Daiches, PSD. The poster states "To Protest against the Persecution of the Jews under the Dictatorship of Hitler in Germany. Come and hear the man who knows—Dr Salis Daiches—He knows all about it—You don't."
25. *JC*, 29 Sept. 1933, p. 15.
26. Letter from Neville Laski to Rabbi Dr. Salis Daiches, dated 9 May 1933. PSD.
27. Gewirtz, "Anglo-Jewish Responses to Nazi Germany 1933–39," p. 262.
28. *Scotsman*, 27 March 1933, p. 9.
29. *Glasgow Herald*, 5 Aug. 1933, p. 7.
30. *Ibid.*
31. *JC*, 10 Nov. 1933, p. 31.
32. Collins, *Aspects of Scottish Jewry*, p. 50.
33. Marion Berghahn, *Continental Britons: German-Jewish Refugees from Nazi Germany* (Oxford: Berghahn Books, 2007), p. 78.
34. *Ibid.*
35. Williams, *Jews and Other Foreigners*, p. 36.
36. *Ibid.*, p. 50.
37. Williams, *Jews and Other Foreigners*, p. 57, footnote 105. This figure compares with 37

at Oxford, 25 at Cambridge, 11 at the LSE, 9 at Manchester, and 8 at Birmingham.
38. Letter from Francis Crew to Rabbi Daiches, 10 April 1933. PSD.
39. Letter from Francis Crew to Rabbi Daiches, 10 April 1933. PSD. There is no evidence available to confirm that this money was raised or that Stern was recruited by Edinburgh University. However, the records of the Institute of Animals Genetics at Edinburgh University state that Crew was successful in bringing in "many scientists," among them notable German-Jewish scientists Hermann Muller (1890–1967), and Charlotte Auerbach (1899–1994). See Records of the Institute of Animal Genetics, Edinburgh University Library Special Collections Division, Ref. Code: GB 0237 Da 57 IAG. Bill Williams has stated that across Britain "offers of Fellowships were often conditional on support being received from other [non-university] sources." See Williams, *Jews and Other Foreigners*, p. 42.
40. *JC*, 21 April 1933, p. 26.
41. *JC*, 30 April 1937, p. 26.
42. Collins, *Aspects of Scottish Jewry*, p. 50.
43. Berghahn, *Continental Britons*, p. 81. Berghahn acknowledges the role played by the BMA but states that only fifty doctors were admitted. However, a report from the Medical Information Sub-Committee of the Jewish Medical and Dental Emergency Association states that the number of doctors admitted to Great Britain was around 180. See *JC*, 15 Sept. 1933, p. 23.
44. Kenneth Collins, "European Refugee Physicians in Scotland, 1933–1945," in *Social History of Medicine*, Nov. 2009, 1–18 (p. 1).
45. Berghahn, *Continental Britons*, p. 83.
46. Letter from Otto Schiff to Rabbi Dr. Salis Daiches, PSD.
47. *JC*, 15 Sept. 1933, p. 23.
48. Collins, "European Refugee Physicians in Scotland, 1933–1945," p. 1.
49. Berghahn, *Continental Britons*, p. 110.
50. Collins, *Aspects of Scottish Jewry*, p. 51.
51. *JC*, 24 Feb. 1939, p. 38.
52. Daiches' diaries reveal that in 1938 he also began distributing money from the EHC German Jews Fund to individual Rabbis and religious figures in Vienna, Leipzig, Berlin and Czechoslovakia. See Diary of Rabbi Daiches, 1938. PSD.
53. Report on Suicides in Germany and Jewish Refugees in Scotland, 1938. PSD.
54. See Williams, *Jews and Other Foreigners*, p. 14.
55. *Scotsman*, 21 Nov. 1938, p. 10.
56. *Ibid.*
57. Report on Jewish Refugee Children in Scotland, 24 Sept. 1943. PSD.
58. Letter from Lord Traprain to Rabbi Dr. Salis Daiches, 21 Nov. 1938. PSD.
59. Report on Jewish Refugee Children in Scotland, 24 Sept. 1943. PSD.
60. *Scotsman*, 6 Dec. 1938, p. 7.
61. *JC*, 9 Dec. 1938, p. 17.
62. Report on Jewish Refugee Children in Scotland, 24 Sept. 1943. PSD. See also *JC*, 2 June 1939, p. 33. Sir Cecil Weir was noted for his organizational abilities, having organized the 1938 Empire Exhibition. He was later honorary secretary of the Scottish Liberal Federation and Civil Defense Commissioner for the West of Scotland. See obituary in *Glasgow Herald*, 31 Oct. 1960, p. 8.
63. *Scotsman*, 27 Dec.1938, p. 6.
64. *Scotsman*, 21 Jan. 1939, p. 15.
65. *Ibid.*
66. *Ibid.*
67. *JC*, 17 Feb. 1939, p. 31.
68. *JC*, 24 Feb. 1939, p. 38.
69. See *JC*, 14 July 1939, p. 29 & *JC*, 11 Aug. 1939, p. 20.
70. Letter from Lady Traprain to Rabbi Daiches, 4 June 1940. PSD.
71. *JC*, 28 June 1940, p. 13.
72. Report on Jewish Refugee Children in Scotland, 24 Sept. 1943. PSD.
73. *JC*, 20 Nov. 1942, p. 4.
74. *JC*, 19 Jan. 1945, p. 13.
75. *JC*, 9 Feb. 1945, p. 5.
76. Report on Jewish Refugee Children in Scotland, 24 Sept. 1943. PSD.
77. *JC*, 9 Feb. 1945, p. 5.
78. Report on Jewish Refugee Children in Scotland, 24 Sept. 1943. PSD. See also *JC*, 2 June 1939, p. 33. Significantly, the sub-committee of the Scottish National Council for Refugees, unlike the Scottish Christian Council, consisted of Christians and Jews.
79. Report on Jewish Refugee Children in Scotland, 24 Sept. 1943. Papers of Rabbi Dr. Salis Daiches, NLS Acc. 12278.
80. *Ibid.*
81. *Ibid.*
82. *Ibid.*
83. *Ibid.* The Children's Sub-Committee of the Scottish National Council for Refugees revealed that by 1944 "they had 556 children on their list." See *JC*, 7 April 1944, p. 11.
84. Collins, *Aspects of Scottish Jewry*, p. 68.
85. *Ibid.*, p. 69. The British government later reversed its policy of interning German-Jewish refugees, and many went on to join the military forces or do other forms of war service.
86. Quoted in *JC*, 20 Nov.1936, p. 44.
87. *JC*, 20 Nov. 1936, p. 44.
88. Benjamin Ginsberg, "Identity and Politics: Dilemmas of Jewish Leadership in America," in L. Sandy Maisel and Ira N. Forman

(eds.), *Jews in American Politics* (Oxford: Rowman and Littlefield, 2001), p. 6.
89. *JC*, 21 Jan. 1938, p. 11.
90. Alderman, *The Jewish Community in British Politics*, p. 120.
91. Thomas Linehan, *British Fascism 1918–1939: Parties, Ideology and Culture* (Manchester: Manchester University Press, 2000), p. 133.
92. Matthew Hendley, "Women and the Nation: The Right and Projections of Feminised Political Images in Great Britain, 1900–1918," in Julie V. Gottlieb and Thomas Linehan (eds.), *The Culture of Fascism: Visions of the Far Right in Britain* (London: Tauris, 2004), p. 16.
93. *Ibid.*
94. Julie Gottlieb, *Feminine Fascism: Women in Britain's Fascist Movement* (London: Tauris, 2003), p. 285.
95. *Ibid.*
96. *Ibid.*, p. 29 & p. 40.
97. Maitles, *Blackshirts Across the Border: The British Union of Fascists in Scotland*, p. 92.
98. Tony Milligan, "The British Union of Fascists' Policy in Relation to Scotland," *Scottish Economic and Social History*, xix (1999), 1–17 (p. 2).
99. See Milligan, *The British Union of Fascists' Policy in Relation to Scotland*, p. 1 and Maitles, "Blackshirts Across the Border," p. 93.
100. Milligan, *The British Union of Fascists' Policy in Relation to Scotland*, p. 2.
101. *Ibid.*, p. 4.
102. *The Blackshirt*, 12 Jan. 1934, p. 3.
103. *The Blackshirt*, 23 Feb. 1934, p. 3.
104. Milligan, *The British Union of Fascists' Policy in Relation to Scotland*, p. 7.
105. See, Milligan, *The British Union of Fascists' Policy in Relation to Scotland*, p. 7, and Maitles, "Blackshirts Across the Border," p. 96.
106. Milligan, *The British Union of Fascists' Policy in Relation to Scotland*, p. 9. See also *The Blackshirt*, 5 June 1934, p. 7.
107. *The Blackshirt*, 5 June 1934, p. 7 & 8 June 1934, p. 24.
108. See *JC*, 10 July 1936, p. 17 & Milligan, *The British Union of Fascists' Policy in Relation to Scotland*, p. 9.
109. *The Blackshirt*, 22 Feb. 1935 & 18 Oct. 1935.
110. *The Blackshirt*, 17 Oct. 1936, p. 3.
111. *JC*, 11 Dec. 1936, p. 15.
112. Maitles, "Blackshirts Across the Border," p. 94.
113. Letter from Joseph Sacks to Rabbi Daiches 15 June 1933. PSD.
114. Alderman, *The Jewish Community in British Politics*, p. 116.
115. Letter from Joseph Sacks to Rabbi Daiches 15 June 1933, PSD. See also Alderman, *The Jewish Community in British Politics*, p. 121.

116. Maitles, "Blackshirts Across the Border," p. 98.
117. *JC*, 13 March 1936, p. 31.
118. Letter from Neville Laski to Rabbi Daiches, 9 May 1933. PSD.
119. Milligan, *The British Union of Fascists' Policy in Relation to Scotland*, p. 14.
120. Quoted in *Ibid.*, p. 9.
121. *Ibid.*, p. 13.
122. Milligan, *The British Union of Fascists' Policy in Relation to Scotland*, p. 13.
123. *JC*, 24 Sept. 1937, p. 13.
124. *JC*, 5 Nov. 1937, p. 24.
125. See *The Blackshirt*, 21 Dec. 1934, p. 12 & Milligan, *The British Union of Fascists' Policy in Relation to Scotland*, p. 14.
126. *JC*, 11 Sept. 1936, p. 17.
127. *Ibid.*
128. Alderman, *The Jewish Community in British Politics*, p. 122.
129. "The Unity of Israel Sermon," 16 Feb. 1935. PSD.
130. *JC*, 23 April 1937, p. 43. See also letter from Edinburgh B'nai B'rith to Lionel Daiches, 7 May 1937 commenting on ongoing meetings to discuss anti-Semitic propaganda in Scotland. PSD.
131. *World-Service*, Jan. 1937. PSD.
132. Letter from A.G. Brotman to Rabbi Dr. Salis Daiches, 17 Feb. 1937. PSD.
133. Letter from A.G. Brotman to Rabbi Dr. Salis Daiches, 17 Feb. 1937. PSD.
134. Letter from A.G. Brotman to Rabbi Dr. Salis Daiches, 20 April 1937. PSD.
135. Letter from A.G. Brotman to Rabbi Dr. Salis Daiches, 19 Feb. 1937 & 30 March 1937. PSD.
136. Letter from A.G. Brotman to Rabbi Dr. Salis Daiches, 30 March 1937. PSD.
137. Report on the Menace of Nazi Propaganda, 1937. PSD.
138. "Address to League of Nations Union Society," *St. Paul's Parish Monthly*, Leith, 26 April 1940. PSD.
139. *JC*, 28 April 1939, p. 14.
140. See for example, *Scotsman*, 14 Jan. 1939, p. 15. One correspondent related a case where he attempted to buy a brand of cake in a shop, but was told by the shopkeeper "You shouldn't be buying that rubbish. Do you not know that they are made by Jews?"
141. *JC*, 17 Nov. 1939, p. 20.
142. *JC*, 1 Dec. 1939, p. 21.
143. *JC*, 12 Jan. 1940, p. 18.
144. *JC*, 31 July 1936, p. 24. The Ex-Servicemen's Movement Against Fascism was arguably another means by which the British-Jewish leadership combated Fascism without doing so explicitly as Jews. While the organization nominally embraced all races and

creeds, in 1936 more than 70 percent of its members were Jewish and it was noted by the *JC* that it was "in constant communication" with the Board of Deputies.

145. Syllabus 1934-35, Edinburgh Jewish Literary Society. Papers of Edinburgh Jewish Literary Society, NLS Acc.9647.

146. Maitles, "Blackshirts Across the Border," p. 94. Maitles specifically mentions David Daiches' *Two Worlds*, which does in fact contain references to the author's father's response to BUF activities.

147. See Spark, *Curriculum Vitae*, p. 107 & Martin Stannard, *Muriel Spark: The Biography* (London: Weidenfeld and Nicolson, 2009), pp. 25 & p. 34.

148. Daiches, *Two Worlds*, p. 93.
149. Daiches, *Two Worlds*, p. 93
150. *Scotsman*, 18 May 1936, p. 8.
151. *Scotsman*, 14 Jan. 1938, p. 11.
152. *Scotsman*, 22 Jan. 1938, p. 15.
153. Alderman, *The Jewish Community in British Politics*, p. 120.
154. Linehan, *British Fascism 1918-39*, p. 142.
155. See *Ibid.*, p. 143 & Nicholas Atkin, "Withstanding Extremes: Britain and France, 1918-1940," in Nicholas Atkin and Michael Biddiss (eds.), *Themes in Modern European History, 1890-1945* (London: Routledge, 2009), p. 259.
156. Linehan, *British Fascism 1918-39*, p. 142. See also Richard Thurlow, *Fascism in Britain: From Oswald Mosley's Blackshirts to the National Front* (London: Tauris, 2006), p. 164.
157. Alderman, *The Jewish Community in British Politics*, p. 120.
158. *Scotsman*, 14 Jan. 1939, p. 15.
159. *Scotsman*, 18 Jan. 1939, p. 13.
160. *JC*, 27 Jan. 1939, p. 20.
161. *Ibid.*
162. See Martin Pugh, *Hurrah for the Blackshirts: Fascists and Fascism in Britain Between the Wars* (London: Jonathan Cape, 2005), p. 231 and Thurlow, *Fascism in Britain*, p. 164.
163. Daniel Tilles, "Some Lesser Known Aspects: The Anti-Fascist Campaign of the Board of Deputies of British Jews, 1936-40," in Geoffrey Alderman (ed.), *New Directions in Anglo-Jewish History* (Massachusetts: Academic Studies Press, 2010), p. 97.
164. Daniel Tilles, "Some Lesser Known Aspects," p. 97.
165. *JC*, 8 Aug. 1941, p. 19. Ramsay would hold his seat until the 1945 General Election, when he refused to contest his constituency.
166. Daniel Tilles, "Some Lesser Known Aspects," p. 97.
167. Salis Daiches, "Fellowship of Jews and Christians Movement in Scotland," in *Bulletin of the Society of Jews and Christians*, Dec. 1942. PSD.
168. Elizabeth E. Imber, *Saving Jews*, p. 79.
169. Quoted in *Ibid.*
170. Quoted in *JC*, 8 June 1934, p. 41.
171. Quoted in *JC*, 23 Nov. 1934, p. 31.
172. Quoted in *JC*, 31 May 1935, p. 36.
173. *Ibid.*
174. Quoted in *JC*, 29 May 1935, p. 34.
175. *Ibid.*
176. *Ibid.*
177. *Ibid.*
178. Letter from the Rev. Professor Daniel Lamont to Rabbi Daiches, 9 June 1936. PSD.
179. Tom Lawson, *The Church of England and the Holocaust: Christianity, Memory and Nazism* (Woodbridge: The Boydell Press, 2006), p. 5.
180. *Ibid.*
181. *Ibid.*, p. 107.
182. Quoted in *JC*, 19 May 1939, p. 17.
183. *JC*, 6 May 1938, p. 34.
184. Diary of Rabbi Daiches, 1938. See for example, entries for 15 Nov. and 1 Dec., PSD.
185. *JC*, 11 Feb. 1938, p. 36.
186. Quoted in *JC*, 3 June 1938, p. 40.
187. *Ibid.*
188. Quoted in *JC*, 25 Nov. 1938, p. 26.
189. Letter from Robert Chisholm to Rabbi Daiches, 15 Nov. 1938. PSD.
190. *JC*, 2 June 1939, p. 33.
191. *JC*, 2 June 1939, p. 33.
192. *Ibid.*
193. *Scotsman*, 26 May 1939, p. 6.
194. Salis Daiches, "Fellowship of Jews and Christians Movement in Scotland," in *Bulletin of the Society of Jews and Christians*, Dec. 1942. PSD.
195. *Ibid.*
196. *JC*, 24 Feb. 1939, p. 38.
197. *JC*, 7 April 1939, p. 24.
198. *JC*, 8 Dec. 1939, p. 18, 5 June 1942, p. 15.
199. *JC*, 29 May 1942, p. 10 and 27 Nov. 1942, p. 10.
200. *JC*, 31 May 1940, p. 15.
201. *JC*, 11 July 1940, p. 4.
202. *JC*, 5 Dec. 1941, p. 23.
203. *JC*, 29 May 1942, p. 1.
204. *JC*, 13 Feb. 1942, p. 24.
205. *Ibid.*
206. *JC*, 5 June 1942, p. 15.
207. Salis Daiches, "Fellowship of Jews and Christians Movement in Scotland," in *Bulletin of the Society of Jews and Christians*, Dec. 1942. PSD.
208. *JC*, 5 June 1942, p. 15.
209. *JC*, 12 Feb. 1943, p. 10.
210. *Ibid.*
211. See Emma Macleod, "A Unique and Glorious Mission: Women and Presbyterian-

ism in Scotland, 1830–1930," *Victorian Studies*, 5 (2003), 749–951, and Callum Brown, *Religion and Society in Twentieth-Century Britain* (London: Longman, 2006), pp. 19 & p. 47.
212. Letter from Neville Laski to Rabbi Dr. Salis Daiches, dated 9 May 1933, PSD.
213. See Daiches, *Two Worlds*, p. 99 & *JC*, 15 June 1934, p. 40.
214. *Ibid*.
215. *Scotsman*, 9 Nov. 1938, p. 9. Although of course, this statement begs the question: to what was the author implying that a Jewish M.P. or a Jewish bank director would present Scotland with a "Jewish Question."
216. See *JC*, 22 Feb. 1935, p. 41 & Letter from Edinburgh Education Authority to Rabbi Daiches, 27 Oct. 1937. PSD.
217. *JC*, 9 Dec. 1938, p. 17.
218. *JC*, 30 Dec. 1938, p. 33.
219. *JC*, 6 Oct. 1944, p. 13.
220. See *JC*, 2 Oct. 1942, p. 7 & 6 Nov. 1942, p. 10.
221. See *JC*, 11 Dec. 1942, p. 11, 3 Dec. 1943, p. 11, & 9 Feb. 1945, p. 15.
222. *JC*, 6 Nov.1942, p. 10.
223. *Ibid*.
224. *JC*, 24 Feb.1939, p. 38.
225. *JC*, 6 May 1938, p. 34.
226. *Ibid*.
227. Letter from Central Committee for Jewish Education to Rabbi Daiches, 1 March 1944. PSD.
228. *JC*, 15 Sept. 1939, p. 23.
229. Letter from Private Ashbrook to Rabbi Daiches, 24 Sept. 1941 & letter from Rabbi Dayan M. Gollop to Rabbi Daiches, 18 Oct 1939. PSD.
230. Letter from Rabbi Dayan M. Gollop to Rabbi Daiches, 18 Oct. 1939. PSD.
231. Letter from Rabbi Dayan M. Gollop to Rabbi Daiches, 7 Nov. 1939. PSD.
232. Letter from Gunner Joe Solomon to Rabbi Daiches, 9 Nov. 1939, PSD.
233. Letters from Rabbi Dayan M. Gollop to Rabbi Daiches, 9 Nov. 1939, 13 Nov. 1939, 29 Nov. 1939, and 9 Feb. 1940. PSD.
234. Letter from Rabbi Dayan M. Gollop to Rabbi Daiches, 9 Feb. 1940. PSD.
235. *JC*, 13 Sept. 1940, p13.
236. Letter from Jewish soldier stationed in Glasgow to Rabbi Daiches, 10 Aug. 1943. PSD.
237. *JC*, 8 Jan. 1943, p. 7.
238. *Ibid*.
239. *JC*, 15 Jan. 1943, p. 10.
240. *JC*, 15 Dec. 1939, p. 21.
241. *JC*, 14 Feb. 1941, p. 13.
242. Letter from British Red Cross to Flora Daiches, 3 May 1945. PSD.
243. Letter to editor of Scotsman, 24 Sept. 1940. PSD.

244. Message for Rosh Hoshanah 5701. PSD.
245. *JC*, 12 Jan. 1940, p. 10.
246. Article on Palestine, Sept. 1940. PSD.
247. See Invitation to Women's Zionist Society, 21 Oct. 1940. PSD.
248. Salis Daiches, "Darkness and Dawn," *Jewish Bulletin*, 13 (1942), p. 2. PSD.
249. National Day of Prayer—Service in Edinburgh Synagogue 6 June 1944. PSD.
250. BBC Memo, Control Room, Edinburgh, 2 May 1945. PSD.
251. *JC*, 11 May 1945, p. 11.

Chapter 7

1. *JC*, 5 Aug. 1949, p. 5.
2. *JC*, 6 July 1945, p. 13.
3. *JC*, 3 Aug. 1945, p. 12.
4. *Ibid*.
5. See *JC*, 16 Aug. 1946, p. 12 & *JC*, 31 Jan. 1947, p. 13.
6. Richard Bolchover, *British Jewry and the Holocaust* (Newcastle: Athenaeum Press, 1994), p. 37.
7. Alderman, *The Jewish Community in British Politics*, p. 125.
8. Stephen Wendehorst, *British Jewry, Zionism, and the Jewish State, 1936–1956* (Oxford: Oxford University Press, 2012), p. 38.
9. *Ibid*.
10. *Ibid*.
11. Alderman, *The Jewish Community in British Politics*, p. 125.
12. See *Ibid*., p. 130, *JC*, 8 Aug. 1947, p. 14, & *Scotsman*, 4 Aug. 1947, p. 5.
13. See *JC*, 14 Dec. 1945, p. 13 & *JC*, 3 Jan. 1947, p. 15.
14. *JC*, 26 Dec. 1947, p. 12.
15. Alderman, *The Jewish Community in British Politics*, p. 130.
16. *JC*, 11 June 1948, p. 12.
17. *JC*, Obituaries, 25 Jan. 2008, p. 32.
18. *JC*, 11 June 1948, p. 12.
19. *Ibid*.
20. *JC*, 5 April 1946, p. 13.
21. *JC*, 5 April 1946, p. 13.
22. The early 1950s brought new strains, particularly when Scottish missionaries began to find it very difficult to get visas permitting them entry to Israel. In 1950 rumors began circulating in Edinburgh that the Israeli government "was trying to expel the Mission from Israel." See *JC*, 25 March 1950, p. 12.
23. *JC*, 5 March 1948, p. 12.
24. *JC*, 20 Dec. 1946, p. 15.
25. *JC*, 13 June 1947, p. 14.
26. Bolchover, *British Jewry and the Holocaust*, p. 47.

27. Abel Phillips and Lionel Kochan, *The History of the Edinburgh Jewish Literary Society, 1888–1963* (Glasgow: The Michael Press, 1963), p. 10.
28. *JC*, 22 March 1946, p. 13.
29. *JC*, 26 April 1946, p. 12.
30. *JC*, 25 Oct. 1946, p. 15.
31. *JC*, 22 Nov. 1946, p. 19.
32. *JC*, 5 Sept. 1947, p. 6.
33. Based on a survey undertaken by Reuben Cohen. See *JC*, 5 Aug. 1949, p. 5.
34. *Ibid*.
35. *JC*, 5 Aug. 1949, p. 5.
36. *Ibid*.
37. *Ibid*.

Conclusion

1. Kushner, *Anglo-Jewry Since 1066*, p. 42.
2. *Ibid*.
3. *Ibid*., p. 258.
4. *Ibid*., p. 42.
5. Lloyd p. Gartner, "Review of Geoffrey Alderman's *Modern British Jewry* (1992)," in Peter Y. Medding (ed.), *Values, Interests and Identity: Jews and Politics in a Changing World* (Oxford: Oxford University Press, 1995) p. 250.
6. Marlena Schmool, "The Ethnic Question on the British Census: A Jewish Perspective," *Patterns of Prejudice*, 32 (1998), 65–71 (p. 66).
7. Todd Endelman, *The Jews of Britain, 1656 to 2000*, p. 240.
8. Geoffrey Alderman, "The Political Conservatism of Jews in Britain," in Peter Y. Medding (ed.), *Values, Interests and Identity: Jews and Politics in a Changing World* (Oxford: Oxford University Press, 1995), p. 250.
9. *JC*, "Special Report: The Decline of Scotland's Jews," 18 March 2010. See also, Avrum Erlich, *Encyclopedia of the Jewish Diaspora: Origins, Experiences, and Culture, Volume Three* (Santa-Barbara: ABC-CLIO, 2009), p. 916.
10. See for example Williams, *The Making of Manchester Jewry, 1740–1875*, p. 166, and Max Eisen, "Christian Missions to the Jews in North American and Great Britain," *Jewish Social Studies*, 10 (1948), 31–66.
11. Michael Marten, "Anglican and Presbyterian Presence and Theology in the Holy Land," *International Journal for the Study of the Christian Church*, 5 (2005), 182–199 (p. 183).
12. Robert Carroll & Stephen Prickett (eds.), *The Bible: Authorised King James Version with Apocrypha*, Romans 1:16 (Oxford: Oxford University Press, 1998) p. 190.
13. Daiches, *Was*, p. 54.
14. See for example, *Jewish Echo*, 29 June 1928, p. 2, 27 July 1928, p. 3, 3 Aug. 1928, p. 4, 10 Aug. 1928, p. 4 & 17 Aug. 1928, p. 6.
15. Kenneth Collins & Ephraim Borowski, "Scotland's Jews: The Community and Political Challenges," *Jerusalem Centre for Public Affairs*, 55 (March 2010) http:www.jcpa.org/article/scotlands-jews-community-and-political-challenges-2 [accessed 14 May 2012 at 11:13 a.m.].
16. David Daiches, "Jewish Identity in Scotland," in Kenneth Collins and Ephraim Borowski (eds.) *Scotland's Jews: A Guide to the History and Community of the Jews in Scotland* (Glasgow: Scottish Council of Jewish Communities, 2008), p. 7.
17. Collins, *Scotland's Jews*, p. 8.
18. Spark, *Curriculum Vitae*, p. 13.

Bibliography

Primary Sources and Archival Documents

National Archives of Scotland

CC8/6/853: Process of Scandal: Rose Nathan vs. Francis Berlin alias Abraham Burnett.
CH16/2/36: Correspondence and papers relating to sale of Church at Graham Street to the Edinburgh Hebrew Congregation.
CH16/2/42: Copy of state of settlement of price for Graham Street Synagogue.
CH3/979: Annual Report of the Edinburgh Jewish Medical Mission, 1902.
CH3/979: Minute Books of the Edinburgh Jewish Medical Mission.
CS164/69: Abraham Turing vs. Magistrates of Edinburgh.
CS251/1513: Rothfield vs. Hyman Cohen (1919).
CS252/1111: Henry Rothfield vs. North British Railway Company (1918).
CS253/2306: Rothfield vs. James McCall (1919).
CS318/4/6: Bankruptcy/Saul Solomon Asher.
CS318/48/66: Bankruptcy/G. Camberg.
CS318/59/114: Bankruptcy/David W. Levy.
HH16/1: Papers relating to the trial Asher Barnard and the Cosmo Club Immorality Case.
HH30: Records of the Lothian and Peebles Military Appeals Tribunal:
    HH30/2/4/43 Jack Weinschel
    HH30/2/4/38 Hyman Phillips
    HH30/2/5/50 Berks Lyons
    HH30/2/5/13 Louis Grant Gordon
    HH30/2/4/49 Joseph Hyams
    HH30/2/6/34 Louis Cohen
    HH30/2/6/46 Bernard Goldstein
    HH30/2/1/23 Samuel Goldstein
    HH30/2/3/37 Myer Hyman Polivasky
    HH30/1/4/8 David Holliday
    HH30/2/6/42 Harry Brown
    HH30/2/6/45 Morris Shulfine
    HH30/2/6/49 David Hyman
    HH30/2/7/14 Harris Simon
    HH30/5/4/18 Jacob Napthali Wedeclefsky
    HH30/5/1/12 David Walker Levy
    HH30/5/4/17 Emanuel Hyams
    HH30/4/8/25 Joseph Freedman
    HH30/3/5/13 Harry Joel Eprile
    HH30/3/4/23 Sydney Youde

HH30/3/3/21 Manuel Berman
HH30/3/3/9 Jacob Bernstein
HH30/3/3/8 Jacob Meyer Baker
HH30/3/1/19 Simon Harris
HH30/3/1/16 Hyman Levinson
HH30/2/6/28 Myer Goldberg
HH30/2/6/32 Jacob Lucas
HH30/2/5/47 George Pass
HH30/2/6/11 Joseph Levitt
HH30/2/2/35 Lewis Rifkind
HH30/2/1/31 Harry Ockrent
HH30/2/4/39 Bernard Factor
HH30/2/2/36 Abel Bernard Freeman
HH30/4/9/31 George Spark
HH31/31/1: First World War Charities: Jewish Medical Mission.
IRS21/1078, Tax Claims and Annual Reports of the Edinburgh Jewish Medical Mission.
JC/26/1873/161: Trial papers of Henry Solomon.
JC26/1859/385: Trial Papers relating to Abraham Jacob, Hannah Jacob, for theft.
JC26/1911/15: Papers relating to the trial of Morris Levinson and Max Jablonsky (1911) for contravention of the Gambling and Betting Act.
JC26/1917/48 Trial Papers Relating to Joseph Levinson.

SCOTTISH JEWISH ARCHIVE CENTRE

A2/44: Papers of the Edinburgh Chovevei Zion:
    Letter from B.L. Freeman to Dr. Hirsch, 13 July 1896.
    Letter from M. Shapera to Dr. Hirsch, dated 30 Dec. 1891.
    Letter from Marcus Levy to Dr. Hirsch, dated 27 Dec. 1897.
    Letter from Marcus Levy to Dr. Hirsch, dated 8 Jan. 1898.
    Letter from Marcus Levy to Dr. Hirsch, dated 30 Dec. 1891.
    Letter from William Paterson to Dr. Hirsch, 20 Aug. 1891.
    Letter from William Paterson to Dr. Hirsch, dated 13 April 1892.
    Letter from William Paterson to Dr. Hirsch, dated 14 Jan. 1893.
    Letter from William Paterson to Dr. Hirsch, dated 22 April 1893.
    Letter from William Paterson to Dr. Hirsch, dated 26 Aug. 1891.
Minutes Book of the Edinburgh Zionist Association, 1930. (Uncatalogued).

NATIONAL LIBRARY OF SCOTLAND

Acc. 10264: Papers of the Edinburgh Jewish Literary Society:
    Syllabus 1934–35, Edinburgh Jewish Literary Society.
Acc. 12278: Papers of Rabbi Dr. Salis Daiches:
    "Address to League of Nations Union Society," St. Paul's Parish Monthly, Leith, 26 April 1940.
    Article on Palestine, Sept. 1940.
    Bazaar Souvenir Guide, 25 Oct. 1930, EHC New Building Fund.
    BBC Memo, Control Room Edinburgh, Wednesday 2 May 1945.
    Court Documents, First Division, 18 June 1924, Closed Record. Minute for Pursuer: Levison v JC.
    Court Documents, First Division, March 18 1924, Alexander Levison v Salis Daiches.
    Diary of Rabbi Dr. Salis Daiches (1938).
    Document recording meeting between the synagogues to discuss unification, Oct. 1919.
    Invitation to Women's Zionist Society, 21 Oct. 1940.
    Letter from A. Feldman to the Rev. M. Rosenbaum, 30 March 1922.
    Letter from A.G. Brotman to Rabbi Dr. Salis Daiches, 17 Feb. 1937.
    Letter from A.G. Brotman to Rabbi Dr. Salis Daiches, 19 Feb. 1937.
    Letter from A.G. Brotman to Rabbi Dr. Salis Daiches, 20 April 1937.

Letter from A.G. Brotman to Rabbi Dr. Salis Daiches, 30 March 1937.
Letter from Abel Phillips to Rabbi Dr. Salis Daiches, 29 March 1920.
Letter from Asher Levinson to Rabbi Dr. Salis Daiches, 16 Feb 1944.
Letter from British Red Cross to Flora Daiches, 3 May 1945.
Letter from Central Committee for Jewish Education to Rabbi Daiches, 1 March 1944.
Letter from Chief Rabbi J.H. Hertz to Rabbi Daiches, 21 July 1919.
Letter from Chief Rabbi Joseph Hertz to Rabbi Dr. Salis Daiches, 12 Dec. 1918.
Letter from D. Kissenisky to Chief Rabbi, Dr. J.H. Hertz, 11 July 1919.
Letter from Edinburgh B'nai B'rith to Lionel Daiches, 7 May 1937.
Letter from Edinburgh Education Authority to Rabbi Daiches, 27 Oct. 1937.
Letter from Edinburgh Hebrew Congregation to Rabbi Dr. Salis Daiches, 21 Oct. 1918.
Letter from Edinburgh Hebrew Congregation to Rabbi Dr. Salis Daiches, 17 March 1936.
Letter from Francis Crew to Rabbi Daiches, 10 April 1933.
Letter from Gunner Joe Solomon to Rabbi Daiches, 9 Nov. 1939.
Letter from Isaac Hyman to Joseph Hertz, Chief Rabbi, 13 March 1922.
Letter from Jewish soldier stationed in Glasgow to Rabbi Daiches, 10 Aug. 1943.
Letter from Joseph Sacks to Rabbi Daiches 15 June 1933.
Letter from L.J. Greenberg to Rabbi Daiches, 3 Aug. 1923.
Letter from L.J. Greenberg to Rabbi Daiches, 11 Jan. 1924.
Letter from L.J. Greenberg to Rabbi Daiches, 2 May 1923.
Letter from L.J. Greenberg to Rabbi Daiches, 24 Jan. 1924.
Letter from Lady Traprain to Rabbi Daiches, 4 June 1940.
Letter from Lord Traprain to Rabbi Dr. Salis Daiches, 21 Nov. 1938.
Letter from Neville Laski to Rabbi Daiches, 9 May 1933.
Letter from Neville Laski to Rabbi Dr. Salis Daiches, 9 May 1933.
Letter from Otto Schiff to Rabbi Dr. Salis Daiches, June 1933.
Letter from Private Ashbrook to Rabbi Daiches, 24 Sept. 1941.
Letter from R. Theophilus to Soames, Edwards and Jones, Solicitors to Rabbi Daiches, unknown date.
Letter from Rabbi Daiches to editor of Scotsman, 24 Sept. 1940.
Letter from Rabbi Dayan M. Gollop to Rabbi Daiches, 13 Nov. 1939.
Letter from Rabbi Dayan M. Gollop to Rabbi Daiches, 18 Oct 1939.
Letter from Rabbi Dayan M. Gollop to Rabbi Daiches, 29 Nov. 1939.
Letter from Rabbi Dayan M. Gollop to Rabbi Daiches, 7 Nov. 1939.
Letter from Rabbi Dayan M. Gollop to Rabbi Daiches, 9 Feb. 1940.
Letter from Rabbi Dayan M. Gollop to Rabbi Daiches, 9 Nov. 1939. 9 Feb. 1940. PSD.
Letter from Rabbi Dr. Salis Daiches to Office of the Chief Rabbi, 8 March 1922.
Letter from the Rev. Hugh Gordon Ross, Victoria Street Church, Dundee, to Rabbi Dr. Salis Daiches, 21 Sept. 1934.
Letter from the Rev. Professor Daniel Lamont to Rabbi Dr. Salis Daiches, 9 June 1936.
Letter from the Rev. W.J. Couper to Rabbi Dr. Salis Daiches, 22 Jan. 1933.
Letter from Robert Chisholm to Rabbi Daiches, 15 Nov. 1938.
Letter from the Chief Rabbi to Rabbi Dr. Salis Daiches, 2 Jan. 1925.
Letter from the Chief Rabbi, J.H. Hertz to Rabbi Daiches, 1 Aug. 1923.
Letter from the Colonial Office to the Edinburgh Zionist Association, 27 Feb. 1930.
Letter from Thomas Connolly, J & F Solicitors to Rabbi Daiches, unknown date.
Message for Rosh Hoshanah, 5701.
National Day of Prayer—Service in Edinburgh Synagogue 6 June 1944.
Pamphlet on "Service of Induction of Rabbi Dr. Salis Daiches." 9 Feb. 1919.
Rabbi Salis Daiches, "The Fellowship of Jews and Christians Movement in Scotland," *Bulletin of the Society of Jews and Christians*, Dec. 1942.
Report on Jewish Refugee Children in Scotland, 24 Sept. 1943.
Report on Suicides in Germany and Jewish Refugees in Scotland, 1938.
Report on the Menace of Nazi Propaganda, 1937.
Salis Daiches, "Darkness and Dawn," *Jewish Bulletin*, 13 (1942).
"The Unity of Israel Sermon," 16 Feb. 1935.
World-Service, Jan. 1937.
Ry.III.a.2(66). An account of the trial and sentence of Charles and Margaret M'Mahon accused of the murder and robbery of a Jew on the Easter road to Leith."

Edinburgh Hebrew Congregation Archive

Leaflet on Rabbi Daiches' Inaugural address at Roxburgh Place, 20 Feb. 1919.
Letter from the *Beth Din* contained in the Minutes Book of the Edinburgh Hebrew Congregation, 1930–1935.
Letter from the Ministry of Food to A. Phillips, President of the Edinburgh Hebrew Congregation, 16 Oct. 1918.
Minutes Book of the Edinburgh Hebrew Congregation, 1918–1921.
Minutes Book of the Edinburgh Hebrew Congregation, 1921–1924.
Minutes Book of the Edinburgh Hebrew Congregation, 1930–1935.
Report on Jewish Education, contained in Minutes Book, 1921–1924.

The National Archives

HO144/166/A42549: Naturalization Certificate of Bernard Turiansky.
HO 144/1432/295090: Naturalization Records for those resident in Edinburgh, 1879–1934.

George Watson's Boys College Archives

Admissions Book for George Watson's Boys College, 1871.
Admissions Book for George Watson's Boys College, 1877.
Admissions Book for George Watson's Boys College, 1878.
Admissions Book for George Watson's Boys College, 1881.
George Watson's Boys College, Prospectus, 1886–1887.
George Watson's Boys College, Prospectus, 1902–1903.

Newspapers, Magazines and Yearbooks

Ashburton Guardian
Blackshirt
Edinburgh Evening Dispatch
Edinburgh Evening News
Edinburgh Review
Edinburgh Star (1989–current).
Glasgow Herald
Jewish Chronicle (1841–current).
Jewish Echo (1924–1994) back issues available for consultation at Scottish Jewish Archives Centre and the Mitchell Library, Glasgow.
New York Times
Observer
Otago Witness
The Scotsman
Sunday Herald

Other Published Contemporary Sources

de Haas, Jacob, *Zionism: Jewish Needs and Jewish Ideals* (London: Greenberg, 1901).
Edinburgh and Leith Post Office Directory, 1873–1873.
The Evangelical Magazine and Missionary Chronicle, 19 (London: Thomas Ward & Co., 1841).
The Evangelical Magazine and Missionary Chronicle, 40 (London: Thomas Ward & Co., 1862).
Extracts from First Report of the Commissioners of Religious Instruction, Scotland, Edinburgh Presbytery, 1837.
Gorst, John E., *The Children of the Nation: How Their Health and Vigour Should Be Promoted by the State* (New York: E.P. Dutton and Company, 1907).

Harfield, Eugene, *Commercial Directory of the Jews of the United Kingdom* (London: Hewlett & Pierce, 1894).
"The Jew Bill," *Blackwood's Edinburgh Magazine*, 68 (1850).
"Judaism in the Legislature," *Blackwood's Edinburgh Magazine*, 62 (1847).
Lancet, "Report of *The Lancet*: Special Sanitary Commission on the Sweating System in Edinburgh," 23 (1888).
Landa, Jack, *The Alien Problem and Its Remedy* (London, King & Son, 1911).
Lewis Rifkind (Letchworth, Garden City Press, 1939).
"The Monopoly of the London Retail Orange Trade by the Jews," *Blackwood's Edinburgh Magazine*, 22 (1827).
Statistical Account of Scotland 1791–1799, vol. 4.
Statistical Account of Scotland 1791–1799, vol. 8.
Statistical Account of Scotland 1791–1799, vol. 10.
White, Arnold, *The Destitute Alien in Great Britain: A Series of Papers Dealing with the Subject of Foreign Immigration* (London: S. Sonnenschein & Co., 1892).
_____. *The Hidden Hand* (London: Grant Richards, 1917).

Memoir/Autobiography

Bermant, Chaim, *Coming Home* (London: Allen & Unwin, 1976).
Cohen, Israel (ed.), *The Rebirth of Israel* (Connecticut: Hyperion, 1952).
Cowan, Evelyn, *Spring Remembered—A Scottish Jewish Childhood* (Edinburgh: Corgi, 1974).
Daiches, David, "My Father and His Father," *Commentary*, 20 (1995), 522–533.
Daiches, David, *Two Worlds: An Edinburgh Jewish Childhood* (London: Sussex University Press, 1974).
Daiches, David, *Was: A Pastime from Time Past* (London: Thames and Hudson, 1975).
Denton, Howard, *The Happy Land* (Edinburgh: Ramsay Head Press, 1991).
Edensor, Tim (ed.), *Moving Worlds: Personal Recollections of 21 Immigrants to Edinburgh* (Edinburgh: Polygon, 1989).
Eppel, Cissie (ed.), *Somewhere in France: Letters Home, Benjamin Eppel's 1914–18 War* (British Columbia: Cissie Eppel, 2010).
Glasser, Ralph, *Growing Up in the Gorbals* (London: Thirsk, 2001).
Levison, F., *Christian and Jew: Leon Levison, 1881–1936* (London: Pentland Press, 1989).
Spark, Muriel, *Curriculum Vitae* (London: Constable, 1992).

Unpublished Theses and Conference Papers

Fleming, Linda, "Jewish Women in Glasgow c1880–1950: Gender, Ethnicity and the Immigrant Experience" (Unpublished Ph.D. thesis, University of Glasgow, 2005).
Imber, Elizabeth E., "Saving Jews: The History of Jewish-Christian Relations in Scotland, 1880–1948" (Unpublished Master's Thesis, Department of Judaic and Near Eastern Studies, Brandeis University, 2010).
Kaplan, Harvey, "The Jews of Edinburgh in 1901" (Unpublished census analysis, Scottish Jewish Archives Centre).
Maitles, Henry, "Anti-Semitism and Responses to It in the West of Scotland" (Unpublished MPhil thesis, University of Strathclyde, 1990).

Secondary Sources

Abrams, Nathan, *Caledonian Jews: A Study of Seven Small Communities in Scotland* (Jefferson, NC: McFarland, 2009).
Abrams, Nathan, and Kaplan, Harvey, "Jews in Scotland: Myth and Reality," *History Scotland* 6:4 (2006), 38–43.

Alderman, Geoffrey, *Controversy and Crisis: Studies in the History of the Jews in Modern Britain* (Brighton: Academic Studies Press, 2008).
Alderman, Geoffrey, *The Jewish Community in British Politics* (London: Clarendon Press, 1983).
Alderman, Geoffrey (ed.), *New Directions in Anglo-Jewish History* (Massachusetts: Academic Studies Press, 2010).
Alexander, Jack, *McCraes Battalion: The Story of the 16th Royal Scots* (Edinburgh: Mainstream Publishing, 2003).
Atkin, Nicholas, and Biddiss, Michael (eds.), *Themes in Modern European History, 1890–1945* (London: Routledge, 2009).
Audrey, Suzanne, *Multiculturalism in Practice: Irish, Jewish, Italian and Pakistani Migration to Scotland* (Aldershot: Ashgate, 2000).
Berghahn, Marion, *Continental Britons: German-Jewish Refugees from Nazi Germany* (Oxford: Berghahn Books, 2007).
Berman, Dina, and Trickett, Edison J., "Cultural Transitions in First-Generation Immigrants: Acculturation of Soviet Jewish Refugee Adolescents and Parents," *Journal of Cross-Cultural Psychology* 32 (2001), 456–477.
Boella, Michael, and Pannett, Alan, *Principles of Hospitality Law* (London: Thomson, 1999).
Bolchover, Richard, *British Jewry and the Holocaust* (Newcastle: Athenaeum Press, 1994).
Braber, Ben, *Jews in Glasgow, 1879–1939* (London: Vallentine Mitchell, 2007).
Braber, Ben, "The Trial of Oscar Slater (1909) and Anti-Jewish Prejudices in Edwardian Glasgow." *History* 88 (2003), 262–279.
Bristow, Edward J., *Prostitution and Prejudice: The Jewish Fight Against White Slavery 1870–1939* (New York: Schocken, 1983).
Brown, Callum, *Religion and Society in Twentieth-Century Britain* (London: Longman, 2006).
Campbell, Donald, *Edinburgh: A Cultural and Literary History* (Northampton: Interlink, 2003).
Carroll, Robert and Prickett, Stephen (eds.), *The Bible: Authorized King James Version with Apocrypha* (Oxford: Oxford University Press, 1998).
Cesarani, David, *The Jewish Chronicle and Anglo-Jewry, 1841–1991* (Cambridge: Cambridge University Press, 1994).
Cesarani, David (ed.), *Jews and Port Cities: 1590–1990: Commerce, Community and Cosmopolitanism* (London: Vallentine Mitchell, 2006).
Child, Francis James (ed.), *The English and Scottish Ballads* (New York: Cooper Square, 1965).
Clapperton, Chalmers (ed.), *Scotland: A New Study* (London: David & Charles, 1983).
Clegg, Hugh Armstrong, *A History of British Trade Unions Since 1889: Volume 1* (London: Clarendon, 1964).
Collins, Kenneth, *Aspects of Scottish Jewry* (Glasgow: Glasgow Representative Council, 1987).
Collins, Kenneth, *Be Well! Jewish Immigrant Health and Welfare in Glasgow, 1860–1914* (East Linton: Tuckwell, 2001).
Collins, Kenneth, "European Refugee Physicians in Scotland, 1933–1945." *Social History of Medicine* 22 (2010), 513–530.
Collins, Kenneth, *Go and Learn: The International Story of Jews and Medicine in Scotland* (Aberdeen: Aberdeen University Press, 1988).
Collins, Kenneth, *Second City Jewry: The Jews of Glasgow in the Age of Expansion, 1790–1919* (Glasgow: Scottish Jewish Archives, 1990).
Collins, Kenneth, and Borowski, Ephraim, "Scotland's Jews: The Community and Political Challenges." *Jersusalem Centre for Public Affairs* 55 (2010).
Collins, Kenneth, and Borowski, Ephraim (eds.), *Scotland's Jews: A Guide to the History and Community of the Jews in Scotland* (Glasgow: Scottish Council of Jewish Communities, 2008).
Cunningham, William, "Differences of Economic Development in England and Scotland," *Scottish Historical Review* 13 (1916), 168–188.
Daiches, Salis, *Edinburgh* (London: Hamish Hamilton, 1978).
Daiches, Salis, "The Jew in Scotland." *Records of the Scottish Church Society* 3 (1929), 196–209.

Devine, T.M., *The Scottish Nation 1700-2000* (London: Penguin, 2006).
Devine, T.M., and Finlay R.J. (eds.), *Scotland in the 20th Century* (Edinburgh: Edinburgh University Press, 1996).
Dubnow, Simon, *Nationalism and History: Essays on Old and New Judaism* (Philadelphia, Meridian, 1961).
Eisen, Max, "Christian Missions to the Jews in North America and Great Britain," *Jewish Social Studies* 10 (1948), 31-66.
Englander, David (ed.), *A Documentary History of Jewish Immigrants in Britain* (London: Leicester University Press, 1994).
Erlich, Avrum, *Encyclopedia of the Jewish Diaspora: Origins, Experiences, and Culture, Volume Three* (Santa-Barbara: ABC-CLIO, 2009).
Evans, Richard J., *In Defence of History* (London: Granta, 1997).
Feldman, David, *Englishmen and Jews: Social Relations and Political Culture 1840-1914* (London: Yale University Press, 1994).
Feldman, David, and Stedman Jones, Gareth (eds.), *Metropolis London: Histories and Representations Since 1800* (London: Routledge, 1989).
Feldman, Egal, *Catholics and Jews in 20th Century America* (Illinois: University of Illinois Press, 2001).
Fontaine, Laurence, *History of Pedlars in Europe* (Durham: Duke University Press, 1996).
Frankel, Jonathan, and Zipperstein, Steven J. (eds.), *Assimilation and Community: The Jews in Nineteenth-Century Europe* (Cambridge: Cambridge University Press, 1992).
Fry, Michael, *Edinburgh* (MacMillan: London, 2009).
Gainer, Bernard, *The Alien Invasion: The Origins of the Aliens Act 1905* (London: Heinemann, 1972).
Gallagher, Tom, *Glasgow: The Uneasy Peace—Religious Tension in Modern Scotland* (Manchester: Manchester University Press, 1987).
Gartner, L.P., "Anglo-Jewry and the Jewish International Traffic in Prostitution, 1885-1914," *Association for Jewish Studies Review* 7 (1982), 129-178.
Gartner, L.P., *The Jewish Immigrant in England 1870-1914* (London: Simon, 1973).
Gewirtz, Sharon, 1991. "Anglo-Jewish Responses to Nazi Germany 1933-39: The Anti-Nazi Boycott and the Board of Deputies of British Jews." *Journal of Contemporary History* 26 (1991), 255-276.
Gottlieb, Julie V., and Linehan, Thomas (eds.), *The Culture of Fascism: Visions of the Far Right in Britain* (London: Tauris, 2004).
Grant, Thomas D., *Stormtroopers and Crisis in the Nazi Movement: Activism, Ideology and Dissolution* (London: Routledge, 2004).
Hamer, D.A., *Liberal Politics in the Age of Gladstone and Rosebery* (Oxford: Clarendon Press, 1972).
Harman, Allan (ed.), *Mission of Discovery: The Beginning of Modern Jewish Evangelism* (Guernsey: Christian Focus, 1996).
Holmes, Colin, *Anti-Semitism in British Society 1876-1939* (London: Edward Arnold, 1979).
Holmes, Colin, *"John Bull's Island": Immigration and British Society 1871-1971* (London: Macmillan, 1988).
Holmes, Colin, *A Tolerant Country? Immigrants, Refugees, and Minorities in Britain* (London: Faber & Faber, 1991).
Hume, David, *Essays and Treatises on Several Subjects* (London: Millar, 1758).
Hyman, Louis, *The Jews of Ireland, from the Earliest Times to the Year 1910* (Shannon: Irish University Press, 1972).
Jackson, Peter (ed.), *Race and Racism: Essays in Social Geography* (London: Allen and Unwin, 2005).
James, Robert, *Rosebery* (London: Weidenfeld & Nicolson, 1963).
Jillings, Karen, *Scotland's Black Death: The Foul Death of the English* (Stroud, Gloucestershire: Tempus, 2003).
Jordanova, Ludmilla, *History in Practice* (London: Arnold, 2000).

Julius, Anthony, *Trials of the Diaspora: A History of Anti-Semitism in England* (Oxford: Oxford University Press, 2010).
Kaplan, Harvey, *A Scottish Shtetl—Jewish Life in the Gorbals, 1880-1974* (Glasgow: Glasgow Jewish Representative Council, 1984).
Kaplan, Harvey, "A Snapshot of Edinburgh Jewry in 1881." *Edinburgh Star* 36 (2000).
Katz, David S., *Philo-Semitism and the Readmission of the Jews to England, 1603-1655* (Oxford: Oxford University Press, 1982).
Keir, David Edwin (ed.), *The Third Statistical Account of Scotland: Edinburgh* (Edinburgh: William Collins & Son, 1966).
Kenefick, William, "Comparing the Jewish and Irish Communities in Twentieth Century Scotland." *Jewish Culture and History*, 9 (2007), 60-78.
Keogh, Dermot, *Jews in 20th Century Ireland* (Cork: Cork University Press, 1998).
Khalidi, Walid (ed.), *From Haven to Conquest: Readings in Zionism and the Palestine Problem Until 1948* (Washington: The Institute for Palestine Studies, 1987).
Kudenko, Irena, and Phillips, Deborah, "The Model of Integration? Social and Spatial Transformations in the Leeds Jewish Community." *Journal of Ethnic and Migration Studies* 35 (2009), 1533-1549.
Kushner, Tony, *Anglo-Jewry Since 1066: Place, Locality and Memory* (Manchester, Manchester University Press, 2009).
Kushner, Tony, and Lunn, Kenneth (eds.), *The Politics of Marginality: Race, the Radical Right and Minorities in Twentieth Century Britain* (London: Frank Cass, 1990).
Laqueur, Walter, *A History of Zionism* (London: Tauris Parke, 2003).
Lawson, Tom, *The Church of England and the Holocaust: Christianity, Memory and Nazism* (Woodbridge: The Boydell Press, 2006).
Lebzelter, Gisela, *Political Anti-Semitism in Britain, 1918-1939* (New York: Holmes & Meier, 1978).
Levy, Abraham, "The Origins of Scottish Jewry," *Transactions of the Jewish Historical Society of England*, 1958.
Levy, Arnold, *History of the Sunderland Jewish Community* (London: Macdonald, 1956).
Linehan, Thomas, *British Fascism 1918-1939: Parties, Ideology and Culture* (Manchester: Manchester University Press, 2000).
Lowe, Heinz-Dietrich, *The Tsars and the Jews: Reform, Reaction and Anti-Semitism in Imperial Russia* (Reading: Harwood, 1993).
Macleod, Emma, "Review of a Unique and Glorious Mission: Women and Presbyterianism in Scotland, 1830-1930," *Victorian Studies* 45 (2003), 749-751.
Maise, L. Sandy, and Forman, Ira N. (eds.), *Jews in American Politics* (Oxford: Rowman and Littlefield, 2001).
Maitles, Henry, "Attitudes to Jewish Immigration in the West of Scotland to 1905." *Scottish Economic & Social History* 15 (1995), 44-65.
Maitles, Henry, "Blackshirts Across the Border: The British Union of Fascists in Scotland," *Scottish Historical Review* 82 (2003), 92-99.
Maitles, Henry, "Jewish Responses to Fascism in the West of Scotland," *Local Historian* 2 (1997), 106-117.
Manz, Stefan, "Civilian Internment in Scotland During the First World War," in Richard Dove (ed.), *Totally Un-English? Britain's Internment of "Enemy Aliens" During the Two World Wars* (The Yearbook of the Research Centre for German and Austrian Exile Studies), 7 (2005), 83-100.
Manz, Stefan, "'Our Sworn, Subtle, Savage, Implacable, and Perfidious Foe!'—Germanophobia and Spy-Fever in Scotland, 1914-1918," in Fischer, Joachim, Ó Dochartaigh, Pól, and Kelly-Holmes, Helen (eds.). *Irish-German Studies* 1 (2004), 28-37.
Marten, Michael, "Anglican and Presbyterian Presence and Theology in the Holy Land." *International Journal for the Study of the Christian Church* 5 (2005), 182-199.
Massil, Stephen, "Joseph Hart Myers MD (1758-1823): First Jewish Graduate," *Edinburgh University Journal* 42:2 (2011).
McMillan, James, *Anatomy of Scotland* (London: Leslie Frewin, 1969).

Medding, Peter Y. (ed.), *Values, Interests and Identity: Jews and Politics in a Changing World* (Oxford: Oxford University Press, 1995).
Milligan, Tony, "The British Union of Fascists' Policy in Relation to Scotland," *Scottish Economic and Social* History 19 (1999), 1–17.
Mitchison, Rosalind, *A History of Scotland* (London: Methuen, 1971).
Ó Gráda, Cormac, *Jewish Ireland in the Age of Joyce* (Princeton: Princeton University Press, 2006).
Phillips, Abel, *A History of the Origins of the First Jewish Community in Scotland* (Edinburgh: John Donald, 1979).
Phillips, Abel, and Kochan, Lionel, *The History of the Edinburgh Jewish Literary Society, 1888–1963* (Glasgow: The Michael Press, 1963).
Pinsker, Polly, "English Opinion and Jewish Emancipation (1830–1860)," *Jewish Social Studies* 14 (1952), 51–94.
Pugh, Martin, *Hurrah for the Blackshirts: Fascists and Fascism in Britain Between the Wars* (London: Jonathan Cape, 2005).
Reinecke, Christiane, "Governing Aliens in Times of Upheaval: Immigration Control and Modern State Practice in Early Twentieth-Century Britain, Compared with Prussia," *International Review of Social History* 54 (2009) 39–65.
Roth, Cecil, *History of the Jews in England* (Oxford: Oxford University Press, 1941).
Sachar, Howard M. *A History of Israel: From the Rise of Zionism to the Present* (New York: Alfred A. Knopf, 1982).
Saipe, Louis, *A Century of Care: The History of the Leeds Jewish Welfare Board, 1878–1978* (Leeds: J. Jackman and Co., 1978).
Schmool, Marlena, "The Ethnic Question on the British Census: A Jewish Perspective," *Patterns of Prejudice* (1998), 65–71.
Shannon, Richard, *Gladstone: Volume One* (London: Hamish Hamilton, 1982).
Shukman, Harold, *War or Revolution: Russian Jews and Conscription in Britain, 1917* (London: Vallentine & Mitchell, 2006).
Singer, Steven, "Jewish Religious Thought in Early Victorian London," *AJS Review* 10 (1985), 181–210.
Sokolovsky, Joan, "The Making of National Health Insurance in Britain and Canada: Institutional Analysis and Its Limits," *Journal of Historical Sociology* 11 (1998), 247–280.
Springhall, John, *Youth, Empire, and Society: British Youth Movements, 1883–1940* (Trowbridge: Redwood, 1977).
Stannard, Martin, *Muriel Spark: The Biography* (London: Weidenfeld and Nicolson, 2009).
Stewart, Desmond, *Theodor Herzl* (London: Hamish Hamilton, 1974).
Thompson, F.M.L. (ed.), *The Cambridge Social History of Britain 1750–1950 Volume 2, People and Their Environment* (Cambridge, Cambridge University Press, 1990).
Thurlow, Richard, *Fascism in Britain: From Oswald Mosley's Blackshirts to the National Front* (London: Tauris, 2006).
Turnbull, Michael T.R.B., "Daiches, Salis (1880–1945)," *Oxford Dictionary of National Biography* (Oxford: Oxford University Press, 2004).
Vital, David, *A People Apart: A Political History of the Jews in Europe, 1789–1939* (Oxford: Oxford University Press, 2001).
Walker, Charles, *Wakefield: Its Times and Peoples* (Wakefield: New Millennium, 2000).
Wendehorst, Stephen, *British Jewry, Zionism, and the Jewish State, 1936–1956* (Oxford: Oxford University Press, 2012).
Willett, Herbert L., *The Jew Through the Centuries* (Chicago: Willett, Clark and Company, 1932).
Williams, Bill, *Jewish Manchester: An Illustrated History* (Derby: Breedon, 2008).
Williams, Bill, *"Jews and Other Foreigners": Manchester and the Rescue of the Victims of European Fascism, 1933–1940* (Manchester: Manchester University Press, 2011).
Williams, Bill, *The Making of Manchester Jewry, 1740–1875* (Manchester: Manchester University Press, 1985).
Wray, Helena, "The Aliens Act 1905 and the Immigration Dilemma," *Journal of Law and Society* 33 (2006), 302–323.

Index

Aberdeen 5, 59, 79, 132, 162, 202
Academic Assistance Council 163
academic refugees 163–4
Adler, Rabbi Dr. Hermann 39, 67
Aliens Act (1905) 44, 48, 49, 51, 52–6
Aliens Act (1911) 44, 56, 58
Aliens Bill (1894) 36
Aliens Restriction Act (1914) 115
Anglo-Jewish Association 22, 71, 146
anti-Semitism 2, 7, 9, 10, 14, 18–22, 26, 28, 42, 45, 47, 53, 57, 61, 72, 76, 80, 98, 116, 118, 128, 139, 143, 146–50, 159, 161, 162, 164, 170, 172–199, 201–4, 206, 207
Ashenheim family 18, 21
assimilation 7, 9, 24, 25, 81, 94, 100, 101, 105, 196
Austria 150, 159, 166, 199, 217

Balfour, Arthur 145–5, 166, 167
Balfour, Francis 166–7, 187
Balfour Declaration 144, 183
Beth Din 23, 143, 153, 157, 207
Bevin, Ernest 196
Bing, Rudolf 199
Black, the Rev. James 180–3, 197
Black Death 14
Black Watch 117, 118, 189; *see also* military service
Blackwood's Edinburgh Magazine 19–20
Board of Deputies of British Jews 2, 23, 25, 71, 142, 146, 160, 161, 162, 174–9, 192
Board of Guardians (London) 26; *see also* Edinburgh Jewish Board of Guardians
Board of Trade 26, 29, 30, 31, 32, 36, 50, 51, 155
Born, Max 164
Bower, Walter 14
boycott of German goods 159–63
British Medical Association 164
British Union of Fascists 170–6
Brown, David 13, 14

cabinet making 26, 88, 89, 115, 199
Caledonian Rubber Company 62, 65, 66, 98
Canongate 16, 17, 19, 173
Catholics 5, 19, 20, 55, 87, 140, 141, 142, 144, 149, 150, 186
Central British Fund for German Jewry 166
Central Hebrew Congregation 35, 108–10, 120, 126, 127–130
Chapman, Samuel 145, 187
Chernack, Bernard 199
children (Jewish) in Edinburgh 7, 34, 35, 36, 40, 43, 45, 46, 48, 63, 80, 81, 92–7, 100, 102, 104, 106, 110, 131–3, 141, 144, 146, 165–9, 170, 187, 192, 194, 212, 222
Chovevei Zion 71–7, 79, 80, 215; *see also* Zionism
Christian Aryan Syndicate 175
Christian Zionism 72–4, 80, 145, 146, 151, 183–4, 192
Church of Scotland 2, 5, 10, 19, 27, 29, 38, 72, 73, 96, 128, 139, 140, 151, 159, 162, 166, 168, 179–86, 188, 197, 201, 202, 205, 206
class consciousness 110–3; *see also* socialism
Cohen, Reuben 165, 176, 185, 198, 199
Cohen, Rabbi Isaac 197
Communism 151, 172, 177, 178, 199
conscription 27, 103, 121–3, 125; *see also* military service
Cormack, John 149–50
Cosgrove, the Rev. J.K. 182, 198
Crew, Francis 163–4
crime 19, 37, 48, 52–7, 62, 89, 108, 148, 151, 156, 160, 204

D-Day landings 190
Daiches, David 8, 61, 64, 129, 131, 134, 135, 142, 143, 177, 207
Daiches, Rabbi Israel 127
Daiches, Lionel 184
Daiches, Rabbi Dr. Salis 1, 2, 7, 8, 11, 14, 15, 16, 17, 18, 70, 102, 127–148, 150–2, 156, 156–

241

169, 172–178, 180–184, 186–195, 197, 199, 206–7
Daiches, Samuel 127
Dalry 38, 62, 64, 66, 70, 71, 95, 97
Daniel, Moses 17
Darling, William 187
Daughters of Zion 104, 105; see also Zionism
De Haas, Jacob 81–2
Denton, Howard 104, 106, 107, 108, 112, 153
deportations 51, 52, 55, 103, 116, 117
Dresner, Phillip 33, 87
Dreyfus, Alfred 75, 76
Dundee 59, 79, 147, 155, 158, 160, 162
Dunfermline 118, 160

East Africa Scheme 82
economic activity 6, 7, 8, 10, 11, 17, 20, 21, 22, 26, 29, 32, 37, 50, 53, 58–65, 83–92, 111, 195, 199, 202, 204
Edinburgh Evening News 107, 114, 116, 143, 151, 186
Edinburgh Festival 199
Edinburgh Hebrew Congregation 7, 23, 24, 27, 31, 33, 35, 37, 38, 65, 67–71, 78, 81, 95–7, 100, 108–110, 117, 120, 126–137, 152–155, 161, 162, 164, 165, 176, 186, 187, 189, 191
Edinburgh Hebrew Philanthropic Society 23, 30; see also Jewish charitable work
Edinburgh Independent Hebrew Congregation 67, 131, 132, 133, 135
Edinburgh Jewish Board of Guardians 29, 31, 32, 33, 34, 35, 36, 97, 110, 115, 136, 137, 152, 153, 158, 199; see also Jewish charitable work
Edinburgh Jewish Cricket Club 105
Edinburgh Jewish Debating Club 105
Edinburgh Jewish Girl's Social Club 105
Edinburgh Jewish Literary Society 98–102, 104, 105, 113, 150, 152, 176, 198, 199, 207
Edinburgh Jewish Medical Mission 2, 6, 35, 40, 41, 42, 43, 63, 86, 97, 111, 135–140; see also missionaries
Edinburgh Jewish Rambling Club 105
Edinburgh Jewish Representative Council 103, 115, 116, 117, 120, 121, 126
Edinburgh Jewish Students Society 97, 105, 112, 165, 187, 191
Edinburgh New Hebrew Congregation 67, 70, 71, 78, 95, 100, 109, 130, 131
Edinburgh Peace Council 174
Edinburgh Review 20
Edinburgh Society of Jews and Christians 184, 185, 197–8
Edinburgh Trades Council 196
Edinburgh Zionist Association 77, 79, 80, 82, 83, 97, 145, 146, 195; see also Zionism
education 6, 23, 43, 78, 79, 86, 92, 93–6, 99, 106, 107, 110, 131, 132, 141, 144, 151, 156, 157, 167, 187, 188, 208
English language classes 41, 42, 94, 108

Eprile family 31, 100
Evans-Gordon, William 48, 49, 51

Falkirk 79, 202
fascism 7, 158–193, 197, 198, 206
France 17, 75, 98, 118, 119, 122, 126
Free Church of Scotland 2, 28, 38, 42, 138, 139, 140, 141, 185
Freemasonry 68, 133, 141, 150, 151, 187, 189, 204, 215, 224
Fürst, Elias 154, 155, 156
Fürst, Isaac 97, 98, 100, 108, 109, 110, 111, 114, 116, 120, 154
Fürst, the Rev. Jacob 18, 24, 26, 28, 32, 35, 37, 39, 40, 43, 45, 50, 66, 69, 70, 72, 75, 78, 79, 95, 97, 99, 101, 108, 109, 117, 121, 127, 136, 138, 156, 199

gambling 216
George Watson's College 95–6
German-Jewish Aid Committee 166–7
Germanophobia 113–5
Germans in Edinburgh 7, 17, 47, 50, 52, 90, 97, 113, 114, 116, 117, 147, 163–9
Germany 2, 7, 17, 98, 116, 126, 127, 143, 150, 159, 160–6, 169, 174, 177–82, 196
Gladstone, William 23, 26
Glasgow 1, 2, 7, 18, 26, 27, 28, 31, 32, 36, 37, 46–8, 53, 59, 61, 64, 69, 71, 78, 82, 83, 84, 87–9, 91, 92, 94, 105, 109, 111, 113, 115–6, 139, 144, 148, 149, 153, 165–172, 176, 180, 182, 185, 187, 189, 194, 196, 197, 200–3, 205, 207
Glasstone, Samuel 27–8
Goldberg, Abraham 92
Goldsmid, Albert 72, 75, 101
Goldston family 24, 84, 96, 98, 99
Gollop, Rabbi Dayan 188
Graham, William (M.P.) 145, 155
Graham Street synagogue 37, 42, 69, 78, 96, 117, 130, 151, 152, 154
Grant, William (banker and Zionist) 80
Greenberg, Leopold 2, 80, 120, 121, 133–5, 148

Hardie, Keir 50
Harrison, George 23
health 60, 63–4
Heart of Midlothian F.C. 154–5
Hebrew (language) 12, 19, 24, 35, 41, 77, 78, 79, 81, 92, 94, 97, 98, 99, 105, 106, 108, 110, 115, 131–3
Hebrew Benevolent Loan Society 31, 57, 86, 110, 136, 137, 153, 158, 199
Heriot Watt College 97, 98, 123
Herzl, Theodor 75, 76, 80, 82
housing (for immigrants) 34, 47–8, 60–4, 104
Housing of the Working Classes Act (1885) 63–4
Hume, David 14, 127
Hutchison, Thomas 152

Hyamson, Rabbi Dr. Moses 109
Hyman, Isaac 131

Imperial Fascist League 173, 192
intermarriage 46, 81, 205, 207
internees 103, 115–7, 126
Ireland 8, 36, 68, 82, 99
Irgun 196
Irish immigrants 5, 19, 20, 47, 59, 63, 90, 149, 208
Isaacs, Maurice 33, 38, 67, 68, 71, 108, 111
Isaacs, Stella 195
Israel 7, 72, 74, 75, 183, 198, 199, 206; *see also* Palestine
Italian immigrants 47, 53, 84, 85, 86, 107, 149, 170

James Gillespie's School 95
Jewish charitable work 24, 30–8, 70, 111, 204
Jewish Chronicle 2, 23, 25, 26, 28, 29, 30, 31, 32, 36, 38, 40, 66, 67, 69, 71, 72, 76, 78, 81, 82, 85, 95, 105, 164, 172–4, 182, 189, 190
Jewish Colonial Trust 77, 79, 81
Jewish Ex-Servicemen's Association 176, 189, 196
Jewish Lads' Brigade 101
Jewish Medical and Dental Emergency Association 164
Jewish Refugee Committee 164
Jewish Representative Council for the Boycott of German Goods and Services 161; *see also* boycott of German goods
Jewish Territorial Organization (ITO) 83
Joel, Moses 17–8

Kaplan, Harvey 84, 93
Kindertransport 7, 165–9, 192, 194
King David Hotel bombing 196
Kook, Rabbi Abraham Isaac 133–4
Kristallnacht 182, 187
Ku Klux Klan 149–50, 17

Labour Party 50, 100, 113, 145, 155, 156, 171, 173, 197
Lamont, the Rev. Daniel 181
Lancet 64, 90, 91
Laski, Harold 195
Laski, Neville 2, 160, 161, 162, 165, 172, 173, 178, 186, 195, 196
Law Society of Scotland 97
Leeds 29, 51, 61, 63, 68, 93, 111, 113, 115, 116, 127, 201
Leith 16, 18, 21–9, 32, 33, 36, 47, 51, 52, 87, 93, 96, 108, 119, 145, 170
Leven riot 114, 123
Levine, the Rev. Isaac 70, 72, 100
Levison, Alexander 132, 133, 134, 135
Levison, Leon 41, 42, 44, 86, 119, 120, 132, 135, 136, 137, 140
Levison, Nahum 132

Lisenheim, Moses Henry 18
Lithuania 56, 61, 92, 94, 105, 125, 127, 150, 165, 197, 208
Liverman, Louis 110, 120
Liverpool 24, 70, 196, 201, 202
Local Government Bill, Scotland (1929) 144
London 5, 15, 16, 17, 19, 21, 23, 24, 26, 28, 30, 32, 35, 37, 44, 46–50, 52, 56, 57, 61, 63, 64, 65, 66, 69, 72, 73, 77, 80, 83, 88, 89, 93, 99, 101, 111, 113, 117, 119, 120, 121, 127, 132, 140, 148, 152, 161, 164, 166, 175, 176, 182, 188, 190, 195, 196, 197, 199, 202, 203, 205, 206, 207
Lyon, Herman 15–7

Maclean, the Rev. Dr. Norman 140, 184
Marcus, Michael 129, 131, 155–6
marriage laws 142
May Laws 29
McPhail, John 186
Merchant Company of Edinburgh 68, 108
Military Appeals Tribunals 2, 6, 104, 123–7, 136
military service 25, 117–9, 122–6, 152, 188, 189, 193
missionaries 2, 19, 35, 38–44, 57, 64, 86, 92, 96, 98, 103, 111, 119–20, 128, 132, 133, 135–140, 141, 142, 156, 157, 179, 180, 182, 183, 186, 192, 197, 201, 205; *see also* Edinburgh Jewish Medical Mission
Mosias, Moses 13
Mosley, Oswald 171, 172, 173, 177, 178, 192, 196
Munro, Robert 121
Myers, Joseph Hart 14

National Bible Society of Scotland 183
National Registration Bill (1915) 121
National Social Purity Crusade 108
National Socialist German Workers Party 159–63, 166, 172, 175, 176, 178–81, 186, 188, 190–2, 206; *see also* Germany
Nordic League 178
Nuremberg Laws 181

Oliver, C. Bryham 172, 173
Ormiston, William 45, 60
Otto, Julius Conradus 12

Palestine 38, 41, 71–83, 118, 133, 134, 136, 141, 144, 145, 146, 151, 156, 165–8, 180, 183, 184, 185, 194, 195, 196; *see also* Israel
Park Place synagogue 21, 22, 24, 25, 26, 35, 37, 39, 65, 66, 67, 69, 70, 72, 78, 98
Paterson, the Rev. William 22, 27, 28, 30, 72, 73, 74
Phillips, Abel 17, 94, 98, 130, 191
Plathen, Richard 172
Pleasance (area in Edinburgh) 58, 60, 142, 151, 153, 154
Poale Zion 112–3, 120, 156; *see also* Zionism
Poland 21, 26, 29, 31, 36, 46, 49, 50, 56, 59, 70, 86, 97, 104, 134, 147, 149, 150, 159

Polish officers in Edinburgh 189
political preferences 100, 113
Polton House 168-9, 192
poverty 9, 10, 19, 31, 32, 35, 37, 38, 40, 43, 44, 48, 57, 63, 70, 86, 92, 103, 109-111, 126, 136, 138, 150, 153, 158, 202, 203, 205
Protestant Action 149, 150, 173

Queen, Isaac 13-4

Rabin, Paulus Scialitti 12
Rabinowitz, Jacob Rabbi 70, 71, 77, 79, 82, 131, 222
Ramsay, Archibald Maule 7, 177-9, 185
Ratcliffe, Alexander 149-50
Reform Judaism 23
Reis family 24, 68, 99, 111, 118
Richmond Court synagogue 17, 18, 19, 21
Rifkind, Lewis 105-6, 113, 123, 124, 131
Rosebery, 5th Earl of 23, 29, 35, 36, 69
Rosenbloom, Sydney 97
Roth, Cecil 9, 18
Rothfield, Henry 147
Rothschild, Hannah (Lady Roseberry) 35
Royal Commission on Alien Immigration 48-50
Royal High School 97
Royal Infirmary, Edinburgh 137, 152
Royal Society for the Prevention of Cruelty to Animals 143
Russia 6, 7, 21, 22, 23, 25-31, 36, 40, 41, 42, 46, 47, 51, 52, 56, 68, 71, 72, 75, 81, 90, 93, 96, 98, 104, 107, 112, 115, 119, 121, 125, 126, 135, 149, 181
Russian Refugees Relief Society 27, 29, 30, 72
Russo-Jewish Committee 27, 29, 32

Sacks, Joseph 172
Salisbury Road synagogue 154, 157, 166
Sarolea, Charles 150-1
Schiff, Otto 164
Scotsman 2, 7, 27, 34, 35, 39, 46-56, 62, 137, 140, 143, 144, 145, 146, 150, 159, 166, 176, 177, 178, 183, 187, 190
Scottish Christian Council 168-9, 183
Scottish Council of Jewish Youth Organizations 162
Scottish diaspora 51, 59, 65, 148, 149
Scottish Miner's Union 49-51
Scottish National Council for Refugees 166-9, 187
Scottish National Operative Tailors 88
Scottish National Party 169, 171
Scottish Premier League 2, 155, 156
Scottish Protestant League 149
sectarianism 20, 149-50, 201
shechita 123, 133, 143, 155
Shiels, Drummond 145
Slater, Oscar 148, 155
socialism 100, 110-3, 163, 199

Society for the Protection of Science and Learning 163
Spark, Muriel 152, 177, 208
Spence, Lewis 169
sport 101, 105, 154, 155, 156, 208
Stalin, Joseph 199
Stern, Curt 163-4
Stevenson, Alexander 152
students 25, 93, 97, 105, 112, 123, 169-70, 187, 191, 192; *see also* University of Edinburgh
Stungo family 81, 82, 97, 100, 119, 154
suburbanization 154
Sunday trading 53, 60, 205
Sunderland 29, 79, 127, 128, 195
sweating system 89-91, 203

tailoring 26, 51, 62, 66, 67, 68, 83, 86-92, 111, 112, 115, 123
Talmud Torah 78
Teitelman, the Rev. Jacob 109
Trades Advisory Council 198
Trades Union Congress 29
transmigrants 27, 30, 50, 55, 74, 138, 165
Tredegar riots 107; *see also* Wales
tuberculosis 60, 63
Turiansky, Bernard 67, 68, 71, 95, 97, 234
Turing, Abraham 12-3

United Palestine Appeal 195
United States of America 7, 27, 28, 29, 46, 50, 63, 65, 93, 135, 163, 169, 170
University of Edinburgh 12, 14, 19, 25, 27, 38, 41, 65, 72, 93, 96, 97, 106, 112, 115, 118, 124, 128, 146, 150, 154, 155, 163, 164, 165, 169, 170, 172, 187, 191
Usher Hall 171-2, 173, 192

Wakefield internment camp 116; *see also* internees
Wales 8, 107, 135, 141, 196
Weir, Cecil 166
White, Arnold 30
Whittingehame House 166-8, 187, 192
Wilhelm, Kaiser Friedrich 2, 93
women (Jewish) in Edinburgh 43, 79, 80, 81, 84, 164, 165, 167, 168, 190, 195
World War I 6, 42, 58, 103, 104, 113-126
World War II 7, 188-193

Yiddish 41, 42, 46, 70, 77, 78, 128, 129, 153, 221
Young, Alexander 173
Young Men's Zionist 83, 104, 105, 112
Young People's Guild 146

Zangwill, Israel 83, 120
Zionism 2, 6, 8, 71-83, 97-9, 101, 104, 105, 112, 113, 120, 136, 140, 141, 144-6, 149, 150, 151, 155, 156, 160, 163, 165, 183-6, 190, 192-9, 205, 206

www.ingramcontent.com/pod-product-compliance
Lightning Source LLC
Chambersburg PA
CBHW051217300426
44116CB00006B/613